# Dishonesty in Behavioral Economics

# Dishonesty in Behavioral Economics

Edited by

Alessandro Bucciol
Natalia Montinari

ELSEVIER

ACADEMIC PRESS
An imprint of Elsevier

Academic Press is an imprint of Elsevier
125 London Wall, London EC2Y 5AS, United Kingdom
525 B Street, Suite 1650, San Diego, CA 92101, United States
50 Hampshire Street, 5th Floor, Cambridge, MA 02139, United States
The Boulevard, Langford Lane, Kidlington, Oxford OX5 1GB, United Kingdom



**Library of Congress Cataloging-in-Publication Data**
A catalog record for this book is available from the Library of Congress

**British Library Cataloguing-in-Publication Data**
A catalogue record for this book is available from the British Library

ISBN 978-0-12-815857-9

For information on all Academic Press publications
visit our website at https://www.elsevier.com/books-and-journals

*Publisher:* Candice Janco
*Acquisition Editor:* J. Scott Bentley
*Editorial Project Manager:* Susan Ikeda
*Production Project Manager:*
Joy Christel Neumarin Honest Thangiah
*Cover Designer:* Alan Studholme

Typeset by SPi Global, India

# Dedication

To Brizio, who was born together with this book.

# Contents

## Section 3
## Dishonesty, individual, and social preferences

### 3.1 Do economists lie more?

*Raúl López-Pérez, Eli Spiegelman*



### 3.2. Cheating and altruism by discipline

*Nora Muñoz-Izquierdo, Beatriz Gil-Gómez de Liaño, Francisco Daniel Rin-Sánchez, David Pascual-Ezama*

## 3.3 Negative externalities of cheating: An experiment with charities

*Valeria Maggian*



## 3.4 Cheating: Perceptions and profit

*Li Hao, Daniel Houser*



## 3.5 An experiment on conformity in deception

*Shunichiro Sasaki, Shoko Yamane, Grzegorz Mardyla, Kazuki Ohara*

# Section 4
# Dishonesty in daily life

## 4.3 Prosociality and fiscal honesty: Tax evasion in Italy, United Kingdom, and Sweden

*Ferruccio Ponzano, Stefania Ottone*



## 4.4 Can upfront declarations of honesty improve anonymous self-reports of sensitive information?

*Andrea Isoni, Daniel Read, Julia Kolodko, Julián Arango-Ochoa, Jiarong Chua, Shristi Tiku, Alanda Kariza*

# Contributors

*Numbers in paraentheses indicate the pages on which the authors' contrbutions begin.*


**Julián Arango-Ochoa** (319) Universidad EAFIT, Medellín, Colombia

**Ofer H. Azar** (267) Ben-Gurion University of the Negev, Beersheba, Israel; Laboratory of Economic Behavior of the Center of Psycho-Economic Research, Povolzhsky Institute of Administration named after P.A. Stolypin—Branch of RANEPA, Saratov, Russia

**Michael Bar-Eli** (267) Ben-Gurion University of the Negev, Beersheba; The Academic College at Wingate, Wingate Institute, Netanya, Israel

**Pietro Battiston** (53) University of Milan-Bicocca, Milan, Italy

**Alessandro Bucciol** (3) Department of Economics, University of Verona, Verona, Italy

**C. Bram Cadsby** (31) University of Guelph, Guelph, ON, Canada

**Jiarong Chua** (319) University of Warwick

**Simona Cicognani** (81) Free University of Bozen, Bozen, Italy

**Brian J. Compton** (17) Department of Psychology, University of California, San Diego, CA, United States

**Zhixin Dai** (245) China Financial Policy Research Center, School of Finance, Renmin University of China, Beijing, China; Univ Lyon, CNRS, GATE, UMR5824, Ecully, France

**Beatriz Gil-Gómez de Liaño** (163) Department of Social Psychology and Methodology, Facultad de Psicología, Universidad Autónoma de Madrid, Madrid, Spain

**Fabio Galeotti** (245) Univ Lyon, CNRS, GATE, UMR5824, Ecully, France

**Simona Gamba** (53) University of Verona, Verona, Italy

**Li Hao** (193) Economist at Convoy, Seattle, WA, United States

**Gail D. Heyman** (17) Department of Psychology, University of California, San Diego, CA, United States

**Daniel Houser** (193) Interdisciplinary Center for Economic Science, George Mason University, Fairfax, VA, United States

**Andrea Isoni** (319) Business School, Coventry, United Kingdom; University of Cagliari, Italy

**Alanda Kariza** (319) University of Warwick

**Doron Kliger** (111) Department of Economics, University of Haifa, Haifa, Israel

**Julia Kolodko** (319) Business School, Coventry, United Kingdom

**Kang Lee** (17) Dr. Eric Jackman Institute of Child Study, University of Toronto, Toronto, ON, Canada

**Raúl López-Pérez** (143) Institute of Public Goods and Policies (IPP), Spanish National Research Council (CSIC), Madrid, Spain

**Valeria Maggian** (183) Department of Economics, Ca' Foscari University, Venice, Italy

**Grzegorz Mardyla** (213) Faculty of Economics, Kindai University, Osaka, Japan

**Natalia Montinari** (3) Department of Economics, University of Bologna, Bologna, Italy

**Nora Muñoz-Izquierdo** (163) Accounting Department, CUNEF—Colegio Universitario de Estudios Financieros, Madrid, Spain

**Kazuki Ohara** (213) Recruit Lifestyle Co., Ltd, Tokyo, Japan

**Stefania Ottone** (289) DEMS e CISEPS—University of Milano Bicocca, Milano, Italy

**David Pascual-Ezama** (163) Accounting and Finance Department, Facultad de Ciencias Económicas y Empresariales, Complutense University of Madrid, Madrid, Spain

**Ferruccio Ponzano** (289) DIGSPES—University of Eastern Piedmont, Vercelli, Italy

**Daniel Read** (319) Business School, Coventry, United Kingdom

**Francisco Daniel Rin-Sánchez** (163) Department of Social Psychology and Methodology, Facultad de Psicología, Universidad Autónoma de Madrid, Madrid, Spain

**Valentina Rotondi** (53) Bocconi University, Milan, Italy

**Shunichiro Sasaki** (213) Faculty of Economics, Kindai University, Osaka, Japan

**Smadar Siev** (111) Ono Academic College, Faculty of Business Administration, Haifa, Israel

**Fei Song** (31) Ryerson University, Toronto, ON, Canada

**Eli Spiegelman** (143) CEREN, EA 7477, Burgundy School of Business - Université Bourgogne Franche-Comté, Dijon, France

**Shristi Tiku** (319) University of Warwick

**Marie Claire Villeval** (245) Univ Lyon, CNRS, GATE, UMR5824, Ecully, France; IZA, Bonn, Germany

**Shoko Yamane** (213) Faculty of Economics, Kindai University, Osaka, Japan

**Xiaolan Yang** (31) Shanghai International Studies University, Shanghai, China

**Shira Yosef** (267) Ben-Gurion University of the Negev, Beersheba, Israel

**Li Zhao** (17) Department of Psychology, Hangzhou Normal University, Hangzhou, China

# Preface

*"One percent of people will always be honest and never steal [...]
Another one percent will always be dishonest and always try to pick your lock and steal your television. And the rest will be honest as long as the conditions are right."*

Anonymous locksmith, reported in Dan Ariely, *The Honest Truth About Dishonesty: How We Lie to Everyone—Especially Ourselves*

The study of dishonesty has gained growing attention in behavioral economics in the last years. Dishonesty is a pervasive human behavior occurring in virtually all contexts, and manifests itself as the disposition to lie, cheat, fraud, or deceive. This behavior usually gives individuals a personal advantage at the expenses of another party, and more in general, of the society.

This book serves two main purposes. First, it provides a rigorous and comprehensive overview of the current research on dishonesty, collecting state-of-the-art works on this topical field from a behavioral economics perspective that focuses on the effects of psychological, social, and cognitive factors of the decision-making process. Second, it compares empirical works conducted with different methodologies of research, discussing comparative advantages and limitations of each.

Our goal is to provide students, researchers, and policy-makers who want to become familiar with the topic a tool to gain a good understanding of the mechanisms behind dishonesty and of the conditions that can discourage or favor dishonest behaviors as well as of the impact that different methodologies have on the results obtained.

... After reading the book, we hope you will not find us dishonest in our claim.

**Alessandro and Natalia**

Section 1

# Dishonesty in behavioral economics: An overview

Chapter 1

# Dishonesty in behavioral economics: An overview

Alessandro Bucciol[1], Natalia Montinari[2]
[1]*Department of Economics, University of Verona, Verona, Italy,* [2]*Department of Economics, University of Bologna, Bologna, Italy*

Chapter outline



**JEL Classification:** D91, D63

## 1. Introduction

Dishonesty is a pervasive human behavior occurring virtually in all contexts, and manifests itself as the disposition to lie, cheat, fraud, or deceive. This behavior usually gives individuals a personal advantage at the expense of the society. Over the last decade, researchers from various disciplines have investigated the topic from theoretical as well as empirical (including experimental) point of view. A recent comprehensive review can be found in Jacobsen et al. (2018). However, much has yet to be learned about the reasons behind dishonesty, and the characteristics of who is more prone to act dishonestly.

This book aims to provide a rigorous and comprehensive overview of dishonesty, collecting state-of-the-art research on this topical field adopting a behavioral economics perspective which focuses on the effects of psychological, social, and cognitive factors of the decision-making process. In contrast to other works dealing with the same or similar topics, this book highlights the importance of the empirical research methodologies discussing how different methods applied to similar research questions can lead to different results. One key reason is that it is difficult to obtain reliable measures of dishonesty. In fact, it is

**Dishonesty in Behavioral Economics. https://doi.org/10.1016/B978-0-12-815857-9.00001-7**

complicate to observe or replicate real-life situations involving misbehavior. On the one hand, those studies where the experimenters try to observe participants acting dishonestly on a cheating task suffer from being artificial and threatened by experimental demand effects, with the consequence that they may affect the magnitude of the phenomenon. On the other hand, self-reported information about dishonesty can be unreliable because people may try to conceal their behavior; therefore studies using self-reported data may underreport the size of the phenomenon. In general, since each method has advantages and disadvantages, in the study of cheating more than in other topics, every research should be seen as complementary—rather than substitute—to other research using different methods.

The book is divided into three parts, which are presented in this introduction in connection with the literature. Each part consists of several contributions on the most recent trends of research on dishonesty, written by influent scholars in behavioral and experimental economics. Unfortunately, we had to make a choice, and exclude from the book topics where dishonesty is also pervasive, such as dishonesty in the financial sector and in the public sector. We briefly discuss them in a separate section.

The remainder of this introductory chapter is as follows: Sections 2–4 provide an overview of the three parts in which the book is organized. Section 2 is about "Dishonesty among children and young adults"; Section 3 is on "Dishonesty, individual and social preferences"; Section 4 is on "Dishonesty in daily life." Section 5 deals with further issues on dishonesty that are not discussed explicitly in the book, i.e., dishonesty in the financial sector and in the public sector. Finally, Section 6 concludes and mentions desirable avenues of development of the field.

## 2. Dishonesty among children and young adults

There seems to be consensus in psychology that most of the behavior we observe among adults was present also when adults were children, adolescents, or young adults (e.g., Harbaugh et al., 2002; Sutter and Kocher, 2007). A growing body of literature is therefore paying more attention on the behavior of children to better understand the behavior of adults and to disentangle innate factors and influences due to culture and socialization. This trend applies to the literature on dishonesty as well (Bucciol and Piovesan, 2011; Gneezy et al., 2009; Houser et al., 2016; Maggian and Villeval, 2016). An advantage of studying dishonesty among children is that they have fewer routines than adults and more freedom in deciding how to behave (see e.g., Runco and Cayirdag, 2012, on creativity and Rakoczy and Schmidt, 2013, on the understanding of social norms) and, with their spontaneity and natural capacity to be uninhibited, they can provide to the researcher evidence that is more reliable and less affected by the environment.

In Chapter 2.1, *Heyman, Zhao, Compton, and Lee* provide a comprehensive overview of the psychological literature on young children's cheating behavior.

The authors document that children manifest whether they are inclined to dishonesty as early as age 4, and that their decision between honest and dishonest behavior is later mitigated by psychosocial factors such as self-concept and social image.

In Chapter 2.2, *Cadsby, Song, and Yang* try to depict a demographic profile of the dishonest child. In particular, they look at parental presence or absence among children in ages 8–10 living in rural or urban areas. They find widespread cheating and no particular connection with parental presence. However, they observe more frequent cheating among urban females aged 8 and in the presence of low levels of risk aversion.

In Chapter 2.3, *Battiston, Gamba, and Rotondi* focus their attention on adolescents belonging to a youth organization well known for its values of honesty, integrity, and respect for others. Not surprisingly, in this sample the authors find infrequent cheating. More interestingly, dishonesty seems correlated with self-confidence.

Chapters 2.4 and 2.5 focus on university students and their behavior during academic exams. In Chapter 2.4, *Cicognani* asks students and former students to indicate if and to what extent they cheated during written exams. She finds that dishonesty is widespread, and that it is more likely associated with trust and the belief that others also cheat, and less likely associated to awareness of the sanction. This research highlights two interesting facts. First, the strong evidence on the belief about the others could reflect a sort of self-justification ("Many cheat, and so do I"). Second, in some cases cheating may arise when there is ignorance about the punishment. Promoting campaigns on advertising the sanctions in response to misbehavior could be a useful dissuading tool.

In Chapter 2.5, *Kliger and Siev* expose students performing written exams to exam cover pages reporting different statements about the standards of conduct during exams. The authors see that statements are useless unless they are accompanied by checkboxes; moreover, they find that punitive warnings are also ineffective. This research thus suggests that a simple nudge, recalling correct behavior and making the individual responsible for her actions helps to fight dishonesty.

The empirical chapters in this part exploit the methodology of lab-in-the-field experiments (Chapters 2.2 and 2.3), online surveys (Chapter 2.4), and field experiments (Chapter 2.5). Research on dishonesty frequently uses laboratory (lab) experiments where individuals make artificial decisions under controlled conditions. In contrast, field experiments observe individual decisions in real-life scenarios. Here human behavior is expected not to be affected by the artificial environment of the lab experiments but, at the same time, confounding factors can possibly influence decisions. For a thorough definition of field experiments in contrast to lab experiments, see Harrison and List (2004). In recent years, mixtures of lab and field experiments, called lab-in-the-field experiments, have been growing in popularity. Their idea is to test the validity of lab experiments in the field, that is, outside the lab. Lab-in-the-field experiments share the same advantages and disadvantages of lab (field) experiments, mitigated by the presence of features of field (lab) experiments. The two lab-in-the-field experiments in this part involve popular tasks to infer dishonest behavior, i.e., privately rolling a die (Chapter 2.2) and privately tossing a coin (Chapter 2.3) and then reporting the outcome being aware that different outcomes imply different rewards. While these methods do not allow to understand if the single individual is cheating, they can still provide some aggregate evidence from the comparison with the probabilistic distribution of outcomes in a purely random situation. For the original studies using a die and a coin, see Fischbacher and Föllmi-Heusi (2013) and Bucciol and Piovesan (2011), respectively; for a review of studies adopting this paradigm see Abeler et al. (2019).

## 3. Dishonesty, individual, and social preferences

The decision to act dishonestly is intrinsically connected with individual as well as social preferences. Choosing between good and bad behaviors has to do with, morality and self-concept (individual preferences) as well as altruism and conformism (social preferences). The purpose of this part is to make it clear that both types of preference are interrelated.

In Chapter 3.1, *Lopez-Perez and Spiegelman* seek to connect dishonesty with observable socio-demographic characteristics, and especially the field of study. They find that the field of study has higher predictive power than all the other dimensions; in particular, individuals who studied Business and Economics seem to lie more, and also expect most others to lie. Interestingly, the authors also observe a small fraction of the individuals (again, mostly from Business and Economics) to lie against their own interest, possibly for the fear of being disapproved.

Similar evidence is found in Chapter 3.2, where *Muñoz-Izquierdo, Gil-Gómez de Liaño, Rin-Sánchez,* and *Pascual-Ezama* compare students graduating in different disciplines. It turns out that Business students are more likely to be dishonest, no matter the size of rewards and penalties. Their study, however, shows that Business students are also more altruistic, since they are more willing to quit personal benefits in order to donate to nonprofit organizations. Importantly, the authors observe that a prior notice (telling individuals they had to report their donation) favors honesty.

The connection between dishonesty and altruism is also explored in Chapter 3.3, where *Maggian* checks the effect of imposing negative externalities on a charity organization when being dishonest. She finds frequent cheating but no significant relationship, implying that dishonesty and altruism are not related—at least on an aggregate level. The inconsistency with the previous chapters could depend on the sample composition (i.e., the fraction of participants from Business) and the experimental design (i.e., pure lab rather than lab-in-the-field experiment, giving rise to a more artificial setting).

In Chapter 3.4, *Hao and Houser* see the decision to behave dishonestly as coming from the comparison between potential profits and the desire to keep a positive self-image. They show that having to predict and announce one's own future actions serves as a deterrent for misconduct, especially when profits are huge. This evidence suggests a possible explanation for the incomplete cheating that is typically observed in the literature; for an extensive discussion of this issue also see Abeler et al. (2019).

In Chapter 3.5, *Sasaki, Yamane, Mardyla,* and *Ohara* study the connection between dishonesty and conformism in a selfish/altruistic environment. Their results indicate that individuals exhibit conformist tendencies; in particular, they tend to send nonaltruistic but truthful messages when they know that a majority of their peers had previously chosen to do so. Hence, this evidence suggests that providing information about others' behavior may influence actual behavior.

The chapters in this part exploit laboratory experiments (Chapters 3.1, 3.3, 3.4, and 3.5) and lab-in-the-field experiments (Chapter 3.2). The cheating tasks involved are a coin toss (Chapters 3.1[a] and 3.2), a die roll (Chapters 3.3 and 3.4), and a set of deception and dictator games (Chapter 3.5). While the coin toss and the die roll tasks do not involve any strategic interaction between players, the deception game actually involves beliefs about the other's honest behavior. Moreover, while both the coin toss and the die roll tasks rely on a randomization device to determine winnings while ensuring that the randomized outcome is only known to participants, in the deception game some of the participants can deceive others allowing the experimenter to identify the individuals who decide to act dishonestly, allowing a better estimate of correlations between dishonesty and other individual variables. Moreover, as discussed by Moshagen and Hilbig (2017), both in the coin toss and in the die roll tasks additional assumptions are needed, such as: (i) dishonest individuals always claim to have won regardless of the outcome, whereas honest individuals only report to have won if actually having won, and (ii) participants do not lie to their disadvantage by denying to have won despite actually having won (although this is not always the case as reported by Utikal and Fischbacher, 2013). Under these assumptions, the coin toss and the die roll tasks allow to study only the characteristics of groups of participants (composed by both honest and nonhonest participants) rather than individuals.

## 4. Dishonesty in daily life

Dishonesty occurs to ordinary people in daily life situations, such as when riding a bus, when having dinner in a restaurant, or when filling tax returns. Everyday dishonesty usually involves little money but is so frequent that it imposes extremely large costs on the society (Mazar and Ariely, 2006).

In Chapter 4.1, *Dai, Galeotti,* and *Villeval* observe individuals making hypothetical decisions between buying and not buying a ticket for various traveling

---

a. In Chapter 3.1 individuals are confronted with a binary set of alternatives, whose outcome is randomly chosen by the computer. This framework is equivalent to the coin toss.

distances. The fraud rate is lower for longer distances, even when no monitoring is planned, suggesting an increase in the moral cost of frauds. Splitting the sample between real-life fare dodgers and nonfare dodgers, the authors find that actual and hypothetical behaviors are related, and that both types of individual react to changes in the probability of being inspected and the severity of the punishment. This work suggests that individuals are responsive to the characteristics of the monitoring process, and rationally react to the size of the expected punishment. It also highlights, however, that nonmonetary factors matter to determine whether to act dishonestly.

In Chapter 4.2, *Azar, Yosef,* and *Bar-Eli* study the behavior of diners paying with cash at the restaurant and receiving an extra change over the correct amount. In most cases, the extra change is not returned (possibly, diners excuse themselves by thinking that receiving the extra money was not their fault). This happens more frequently among men and occasional customers. Interestingly, large extra changes are returned more frequently than small extra changes. This evidence is consistent with Chapter 4.1; the authors claim that the psychological costs of dishonesty increase more rapidly than the amounts involved.

In Chapter 4.3, *Ponzano* and *Ottone* link tax compliance to prosociality (meant as the concern for others) in three European countries with different socio-cultural background and different levels of tax evasion. They find that prosocial individuals generally comply more with the rules, but especially when the institutional context works efficiently. Individuals are more willing to pay taxes when they understand that they are not wasted.

In Chapter 4.4, *Isoni, Read, Koldko, Arango-Ochoa, Chua, Tiku,* and *Kariza* study the effect of signing honesty declarations on anonymous self-reports about sensitive information where a systematic bias is expected on the answers. They find no significant effect, in contrast to existing literature, suggesting that nudges help stimulate honesty (including Chapter 2.5). The authors conjecture that their result may depend on two facts: responses are evidently not verifiable, and there is anonymity, since the declarer cannot be held responsible for the inaccuracy of the information provided.

The chapters in this part make use of laboratory experiments (Chapters 4.1 and 4.3) and field experiments (Chapters 4.2 and 4.4) by varying the context where dishonest behavior can be observed. These two methodologies provide very different insights on the study of dishonesty. While in laboratory experiments random assignments of participants into control and experimental groups provide a fully controlled environment where clean estimates are possible, the main drawback faced by researcher adopting this method is that participants are aware of being part of a study and may be sensitive to experimental demand effects. In field experiments, the experimenter has less control on the environment which may lead to less clean estimates, but individuals act "normally," without the feeling of being watched; as a result there is the chance to observe real dishonest behavior. Another important positive aspect associated to field experiments is related to the fact that its focus on a very specific context also allows for the possibility that individuals self-select in a situation with greater or lower motivation to cheat (Houdek, 2017).

## 5. Further topics on dishonesty in behavioral economics

This book is mostly focused on daily, small-case dishonesty from ordinary people. There are also other forms of dishonesty, not arising every day and restricted to limited groups of persons, which usually moves a large amount of money. This dishonesty, commonly reported in the media, frequently has to do with both (i) the financial sector and (ii) the public sector.

Frauds in the financial sector, i.e., practices used to earn money based on false information, involve every year billions of dollars. Just to name few notorious cases, the American energy company Enron got bankrupt in 2001, after misreporting financial statements and modifying opaque balance sheets to indicate favorable performance and sustain the stock price. A similar situation arose with the American telecommunication company WorldCom, which got bankrupt in 2002. The largest fraud in the history, however, emerged in 2009 when Bernard Madoff was sentenced to 150 years in prison for having created and perpetuated a worldwide Ponzi scheme through his investment company.[b] Among various crimes, Madoff was accused of securities fraud, investment adviser fraud, and money laundering. His company defrauded thousands of investors of around 65 billion dollars.

These and other well-known cases fueling the recent financial crisis (think of, e.g., the bailouts of Fannie Mae and Freddie Mac, or the bankruptcy of Lehman Brothers) stress that a key ingredient of the financial markets is confidence and trust in others' honesty. However, Cohn et al. (2014) find that employees in the banking sector do not seem the persons to rely mostly on, as they tend to behave dishonestly more often than employees from other industries. This evidence could be related to self-selection, as individuals more prone to behave dishonestly may prefer some works to others; findings in Chapters 3.1 and 3.2, that Business and Economics graduates are more likely to act dishonestly, are consistent with this possible interpretation. Cohn et al. (2014), however, explain their finding in terms of norms: the business culture is full of financial incentives to greedy and opportunistic behavior, whereas more attention should be paid to ethics and the impact on the society.

Greed and opportunism indeed seem key features of the fraudsters. KPMG (2016) runs a worldwide survey on corporate fraudsters, with the purpose of identifying the most common traits of white collars committing crimes within their organizations. It turns out that fraudsters are most likely to be males aged

---

b. A Ponzi scheme is an investment fraud where the operator promises abnormally high returns, paying returns to initial investors using the amounts "invested" by subsequent investors. The scheme is clearly doomed to fall apart 1 day, when no sufficient number of new investors can be found to allow the continued payment of returns.

between 36 and 55 years, who are motivated by greed and opportunity, and who enjoy trust and respect from the colleagues. Fraudsters more often work in group rather than alone (because they need to collude to avoid controls) and do not join the organization with the deliberate purpose of committing frauds, as in most cases they act dishonestly after at least 6 years of experience in the organization. Changes in personal circumstances, and pressure to meet the targets may instead induce them to dishonest behavior later on (KPMG, 2016).

Dishonesty in the public sector is often referred to as corruption, defined as the abuse of public office for private gain (Aidt, 2003; Armantier and Boly, 2011; Shleifer and Vishny, 1993). In this field of studies, both laboratory and field experiments have represented a great methodological novelty since before their application estimates of corruption were based on perception surveys (Olken, 2009) posing questions about general levels of corruption such as financial honesty of politicians, and the likelihood of firms having to pay bribes for government services. These surveys were sent either to representative samples of the population or to individuals in relevant positions relating to business and government such as businessmen, judges, lawyers, policemen, and politicians (Sequiera, 2012).

Most studies investigating dishonesty in the public sector have focused on bribery and highlighted the central role represented by reciprocity and trust in sustaining bribing agreements. In many experiments, a participant designated as a public official may request or be offered a bribe in exchange for some sort of favor (Abbink et al., 2002; Lambsdorff and Frank, 2010, 2011). Over the last decades a notable number of experiments have focused on several material and immaterial factors affecting the likelihood of observing corruption. Among the material ones, the literature has investigated on factors such as the wages of the public official, the presence and magnitude of fines in case of detection, the presence and magnitude of externalities or monetary costs imposed to third parties, and the presence of intermediaries. Among the immaterial ones, the literature has extensively studied factors such as moral costs and framings (see Armantier and Boly, 2011).

Besides laboratory experiments, several studies have been conducted in the field where the main advantage is that subjects are not aware of being observed if they act dishonestly. Among others, Olken (2007) conducts a field experiment on reducing corruption in over 600 Indonesian village road projects measured by discrepancies between official project costs and an independent engineers' estimate of costs and also points to the importance and effectiveness of top-down monitoring even in highly corrupt environments. Armantier and Boly (2011) perform a field experiment in in Burkina Faso. In the experiment, an exam grader is bribed for a better grade. They find that increasing the graders' wage reduces in both environments the probability to accept the bribe. Bertrand et al. (2007) studied obtaining drivers' licenses in India and attempting to identify which rules can be broken through bribery. The researchers randomly divided participants into two groups in addition to the control group. The first group was offered a bonus for obtaining the license fast while the second group was given free lessons. The results indicated that bureaucrats raised red tape on purpose to extract such bribes and thus undermined the very purpose of regulation. Despite their advantages, field experiments have so far been only few in the literature due to high costs of implementation, difficulties to obtain an acceptable level of control of the environment, and the need to carefully design the experimental intervention due to corruption's sensitive and illegal nature. Due to the high cost, most of them so far have been held in developing countries.

## 6. Concluding remarks

The general picture emerging from the works included in this book is that dishonesty is a widespread human behavior: many people behave dishonestly. Actually, as Bereby-Meyer and Shalvi (2015) argue, dishonesty rather than honesty may be the default behavior, when (i) it is tempting and easy to be dishonest, (ii) anonymity is preserved, and (iii) the risk of being caught is minimal. In a similar situation, the psychological costs of acting dishonestly (moral balance, self-concept, social image, etc.) are less important. On the same line, Hao and Houser (2017) argue that individuals cheat as much as possible if they can give the impression that they are honest.

In this scenario, policymakers are becoming more and more interested in the use of behavioral economics to stimulate honest behavior. Common interventions involve the use of moral cues, meant to put individuals in a moral mindset before making their decisions, and the use of signatures on documents, to pass to the individual responsibility for the action. In fact, it seems that explicit reference to the individual herself contributes to limit dishonesty (e.g., Bryan et al., 2013). This book shows evidence on this direction in Chapters 2.5 and 4.4.

Still, in any real-life situation some individuals behave honestly, and some others behave dishonestly. The prevailing literature, consistent with most of the findings in this book, suggests that young male[c] individuals are more likely to act dishonestly than others (see the review in Jacobsen et al., 2018). However, it could be the set of individual preferences and moral values that explains this difference in behavior and that also affects the individuals' choice of an environment based on future expectations of (dis)honest behavior.

Although the literature has made impressive progress in the last decades, at the moment we still know little about the psycho-social mechanisms driving dishonest behavior. The complexity of human behavior calls for more integration between economics and other disciplines, primarily psychology and neuroscience, to dig deeper on the mechanisms driving dishonesty and design intervention to help people behave honestly.

---

c. However, Chapter 3.1 argues that the gender effect is mediated by the field of study, which seems to matter more and where males and females self-select.

## References


Abbink, K., Irlenbusch, B., Renner, E., 2002. An experimental bribery game. J. Law Econ. Org. 18 (2), 428–454.

Abeler, J., Nosenzo, D., Raymond, C., 2019. Preferences for truth-telling. Econometrica (Forthcoming).

Aidt, T.S., 2003. Economic analysis of corruption: a survey. Econ. J. 113 (491), F632–F652.

Armantier, O., Boly, A., 2011. A controlled field experiment on corruption. Eur. Econ. Rev. 55 (8), 1072–1082.

Bereby-Meyer, Y., Shalvi, S., 2015. Deliberate honesty. Curr. Opin. Psychol. 6, 195–198.

Bertrand, M., Djankov, S., Hanna, R., Mullainathan, S., 2007. Obtaining a Driver's license in India: an experimental approach to studying corruption. Q. J. Econ. 122 (4), 1639–1676.

Bryan, C.J., Adams, G.S., Monin, B., 2013. When cheating would make you a cheater: implicating the self prevents unethical behavior. J. Exp. Psychol. Gen. 142 (4), 1001–1005.

Bucciol, A., Piovesan, M., 2011. Luck or cheating? A field experiment on honesty with children. J. Econ. Psychol. 32 (1), 73–78.

Cohn, A., Fehr, E., Maréchal, M.A., 2014. Business culture and dishonesty in the banking industry. Nature 516, 86–89.

Fischbacher, U., Föllmi-Heusi, F., 2013. Lies in disguise—an experimental study on cheating. J. Eur. Econ. Assoc. 11 (3), 525–547.

Gneezy, U., Leonard, K.L., List, J.A., 2009. Gender differences in competition: evidence from a matrilineal and a patriarchal society. Econometrica 77 (5), 1637–1664.

Hao, L., Houser, D., 2017. Perceptions, intentions, and cheating. J. Econ. Behav. Organ. 133, 52–73.

Harbaugh, W.T., Krause, K., Vesterlund, L., 2002. Risk attitudes of children and adults: choices over small and large probability gains and losses. Exp. Econ. 5 (1), 53–84.

Harrison, G.W., List, J.A., 2004. Field experiments. J. Econ. Lit. 42, 1009–1055.

Houdek, P., 2017. A perspective on research on dishonesty: limited external validity due to the lack of possibility of self-selection in experimental designs. Front. Psychol. 8 (1566), 1–6. https://doi.org/10.3389/fpsyg.2017.01566.

Houser, D., List, J.A., Piovesan, M., Samek, A., Winter, J., 2016. Dishonesty: from parents to children. Eur. Econ. Rev. 82, 242–254.

Jacobsen, C., Fosgaard, T.R., Pascual-Ezama, D., 2018. Why do we lie? A practical guide to the dishonesty literature. J. Econ. Surv. 32 (2), 357–387.

KPMG, 2016. Global Profiles of the Fraudster: Technology Enables and Weak Controls Fuel the Fraud (Available online at) https://assets.kpmg.com/content/dam/kpmg/pdf/2016/05/profiles-of-the-fraudster.pdf (Accessed April 24, 2018).

Lambsdorff, J.G., Frank, B., 2010. Bribing versus gift-giving—an experiment. J. Econ. Psychol. 31 (3), 347–357.

Lambsdorff, J.G., Frank, B., 2011. Corrupt reciprocity—experimental evidence on a Men's game. Int. Rev. Law Econ. 31 (2), 116–125.

Maggian, V., Villeval, M.C., 2016. Social preferences and lying aversion in children. Exp. Econ. 19 (3), 663–685.

Mazar, N., Ariely, D., 2006. Dishonesty in everyday life and its policy implications. J. Public Policy Mark. 25 (1), 117–126.

Moshagen, M., Hilbig, B.E., 2017. The statistical analysis of cheating paradigms. Behav. Res. Methods 49 (2), 724–732.

Olken, B.A., 2007. Monitoring corruption: evidence from a field experiment in Indonesia. J. Polit. Econ. 115 (2), 200–249.

Olken, B.A., 2009. Corruption perceptions vs. corruption reality. J. Public Econ. 93 (7–8), 950–964.

Rakoczy, H., Schmidt, M.F., 2013. The early ontogeny of social norms. Child Dev. Perspect. 7 (1), 17–21.

Runco, M.A., Cayirdag, N., 2012. The development of children's creativity. In: Saracho, O.N., Spodek, B. (Eds.), Handbook of Research on the Education of Young Children. second ed. MacMillan, New York, pp. 121–132.

Sequiera, S., 2012. Advances in measuring corruption in the field. In: Norton, D.A., Serra, D., Isaac, R.M., Wantchekon, L. (Eds.), Advances in Experimental Research on Corruption. Research in Experimental Economics, vol. 15. Emerald Group Publishing Limited, pp. 145–175.

Shleifer, A., Vishny, R.W., 1993. Corruption. Q. J. Econ. 108 (3), 599–617.

Sutter, M., Kocher, M.G., 2007. Trust and trustworthiness across different age groups. Games Econom. Behav. 59 (2), 364–382.

Utikal, V., Fischbacher, U., 2013. Disadvantageous lies in individual decisions. J. Econ. Behav. Organ. 85, 108–111.

Section 2

# Dishonesty among children and young adults

Chapter 2.1

# Dishonesty in young children

Gail D. Heyman[1], Li Zhao[2], Brian J. Compton[1], Kang Lee[3]
[1]*Department of Psychology, University of California, San Diego, CA, United States,* [2]*Department of Psychology, Hangzhou Normal University, Hangzhou, China,* [3]*Dr. Eric Jackman Institute of Child Study, University of Toronto, Toronto, ON, Canada*

### Chapter Outline



**JEL Classification:** C91, D91

## 1. Common experimental approaches in developmental psychology

Researchers have used a number of methods to experimentally assess children's capacity to engage in dishonest behavior, and the likelihood that they will do so. Some of these methods focus on types of dishonesty that are motivated by self-interest. The most widely-used approach has been the *temptation resistance paradigm,* a game in which participants try to guess the identity or features of a hidden object (see Lee, 2013). In one version of the game, children must guess whether the value of a hidden playing card is greater or less than six on at least three different trials in order to win a prize. The game is set up such that prior to the final chance to win by guessing correctly, the experimenter reminds the child not to peek at the card and then leaves the room for 1 min, ostensibly to take a phone call. Peeking behavior is monitored and recorded via a hidden camera. In some conditions, upon returning the experimenter will directly ask the child whether he or she had peeked, to determine whether children who choose to peek will deny having done it.

The *hide and seek paradigm* also involves a game, but it is the experimenter who does the guessing (Ding et al., 2018a). An experimenter covers his or her eyes while the child hides a treat under one of two similar-looking cups, and the

**Dishonesty in Behavioral Economics. https://doi.org/10.1016/B978-0-12-815857-9.00002-9**

experimenter guesses the treat's location. According to the rules of the game, a correct guess means the experimenter wins the treat, and an incorrect guess means the child wins it. Before guessing, the experimenter asks the child where the treat is hidden. Because the experimenter always selects whichever cup the child indicates, it is a zero-sum game in which children can win only if they choose to deceive the experimenter by signaling the wrong location.

The *forensic paradigm* examines whether children will report transgressions for which they may or may not have been involved (Gordon et al., 2014; Lyon et al., 2008). It has been used as a model of forensic settings in which children serve as witnesses to crimes. In one version of the paradigm, the child observes a confederate play with a forbidden toy while the experimenter is out of the room. The goal is to determine whether the child will lie when the experimenter returns and asks what happened.

In another set of experimental paradigms, children determine how to respond in situations in which an honest response would be seen as impolite. For example, in the *disappointing gift paradigm,* the participant receives an undesirable gift such as a plain white bar of soap or a broken toy, and the gift-giver asks the child whether he or she likes it (Popliger et al., 2011; Talwar et al., 2007). In the *reverse rouge paradigm,* an experimenter who has a blotch of rouge on her nose asks the child whether she looks okay to be photographed (Talwar and Lee, 2002).

The methods that are being used by developmental psychologists to study children's honesty differ in important ways from the methods that are typically used in economics research. One difference is that they have been adapted for use with children who are younger than the typical child participants in economics research. Another difference is that many economics journals prohibit methodologies that involve deceiving participants (Rousu et al., 2015), whereas in psychology there is a greater acceptance of deceiving participants and a greater expectation that the responses of individual participants will be examined systematically. Developmental psychology research on this topic has the potential to inform behavioral economics by providing insights into the developmental course of children's dishonest behavior, and by presenting research strategies that can be adopted by economics researchers, such as investigating deception in politeness contexts.

## 2. Social and cognitive influences

Children's social experiences can affect their honesty-related behavior. One study that addressed this issue examined the effects of a punitive school environment. Using the temptation resistance paradigm, Talwar and Lee (2011) investigated the lie-telling behavior of 3- and 4-year-old children living in West Africa who attended either a punitive school or a nonpunitive one. Children who went to the punitive school were subjected to corporal punishment for a range of transgressions, such as forgetting a pencil or being disruptive in class, based on the philosophy that punishment effectively motivates children to avoid misbehavior and helps them to learn better. Children who attended the nonpunitive school were not subject to corporal punishment, and were instead typically scolded or given a time out when they misbehaved. As is typical when the standard version of the paradigm is used, the vast majority of preschool-age children in each school cheated by peeking when the experimenter left the room. However, when the experimenter returned and asked children whether they had peeked, those who attended the punitive school were more likely to falsely deny it and were better at skillfully answering follow-up questions about their lies than were children who attended the nonpunitive school. This finding suggests that a punitive environment can foster dishonesty, perhaps by providing greater incentives to conceal transgressions, or by offering additional opportunities to develop, through trial and error, the skills that are involved in deceiving others. This type of environmental influence may have an even stronger effect on children's honesty than factors such as parental attention and care that can effect a range of important developmental outcomes (see Cadsby et al., 2019).

Social experiences can influence the age at which children first learn to deceive. Most children show clear evidence of an ability to deceive at around 3.5 years of age (Lee, 2013), but recent research suggests that experience with a competitive game in which deception is required for personal gain can bring about this transition earlier. On 10 separate days around the time of their third birthday, children played a hide-and-seek game in which they could win a treat only by deceiving an experimenter (Ding et al., 2018a, as described previously). By the end of the 10-day period, most of the children had adopted a strategy of consistently deceiving the experimenter. There were individual differences in how quickly children learned to deceive, with some doing so after only a few trials of the first session and others never consistently deceiving at any point. The individual differences were associated with children's cognitive skills: those who learned to deceive the most quickly tended to score the highest on theory of mind tests, which measure the understanding that people can hold false beliefs (Carlson et al., 2013). They also tended to score the highest on tests of executive control, which are associated with the ability to refrain from revealing what one knows to be true (Carlson, 2005). These findings suggest that children are better able to learn how to deceive once they possess the cognitive capacity to represent mental life, and to exert control over the information they reveal to others.

Further evidence for the importance of cognitive skills comes from research in which 3-year-olds learned to lie more quickly after receiving theory of mind training (Ding et al., 2015). Participants were randomly assigned to a theory of mind condition or a control condition. In the theory of mind condition they received instructions about false beliefs and the distinction between appearance and reality, and in the control condition they were taught that rearranging a set of objects does not affect its total number. Differences in the rates of lying between the two conditions were significant immediately following the training, and also about a month later.

Engaging in deception can also promote cognitive skills. Ding et al. (2018b) assigned 3-year-olds who were unable to deceive to an experimental condition, or a control condition. Both conditions involved playing the hide-and-seek game with an experimenter on 4 different days, and the children in the experimental condition were also given explicit instructions about how to win the game. The children in the experimental condition, but not those in the control condition, showed improvement in theory of mind and executive function.

When young children make decisions about honesty they are sensitive to the social context. Heyman et al. (2015) elicited promises from 4- to 7-year-olds to not cheat in the temptation resistance game. By age 5, children who were asked to promise not to cheat showed a significantly lower rate of cheating as compared to children in a control condition in which there was no mention of promises. Related research suggests that promises can sometimes be effective in reducing dishonesty among even younger children: by age 3, promising to tell the truth leads to higher rates of confession after cheating in the temptation resistance game (Talwar et al., 2002). In addition, verbal commitments that do not contain the word "promise" also have the potential to reduce cheating by young children (Evans et al., 2018).

Expectations about getting caught can also affect children's decisions about cheating. In our ongoing research, we are finding that children are less likely to lie about their own transgressions when they have a strong belief that people who do something wrong are likely to get caught. The importance of children's concerns about getting caught is consistent with economics research with adults that shows a reduction in dishonest behavior when detection is seen as more likely (Bott et al., 2017; Pierce et al., 2014), and with research in this volume indicating that children and adults who are risk averse are less likely to engage in dishonest behavior (Cadsby et al., 2019; Cicognani, 2019).

Research using the forensic paradigm has examined a range of additional factors that might affect children's willingness to tell the truth. Gordon et al. (2014) examined the willingness of 4- to 12-year-old children to reveal information about a parent's minor transgression that the parent had asked the child to keep secret. Children were more likely to reveal the truth if they were repeatedly asked what had happened. However, there is evidence that repeated questions do not always influence behavior (Lyon et al., 2008) and that they can sometimes lead to false confessions, perhaps by causing memories to become distorted (see Brainerd et al., 2003).

Other research using the temptation resistance paradigm has looked at the effectiveness of presenting children with examples of others who behave honesty. Ma et al. (2018) examined whether 5-year-olds who observed a classmate confess to a transgression would be more likely to confess. Simply observing a confession did not affect children's honesty, but observing a classmate being praised for confessing did lead to an increase in truthful confessions, and there were no instances of false confessions.

Lee et al. (2014) showed that children's honesty can be influenced by stories they hear. Five-year-old children heard one of three classic children's stories that focus on honesty, or a control story (*The Tortoise and Hare*) that does not. Those who heard the classic moral story *George Washington and the Cherry Tree,* which contains a positive message about honesty, were more likely to truthfully confess to cheating in the temptation resistance game than were those in the control condition. In contrast, the responses of children who heard stories with a negative message about dishonesty (*The Boy Who Cried Wolf* or *Pinocchio*) did not differ from those in the control condition. One possibility is that positive messages about telling the truth are more effective than negative messages about lying, but it is also possible that children tend to be skeptical that the negative consequences of lying, as presented in these stories (e.g., Pinocchio's nose growing), could ever happen to them personally.

Another approach to influencing moral behavior concerns children's beliefs about their reputation. This approach is based on evidence that young children sometimes show sensitivity to reputational concerns. For example, 2-year-olds talk more about their successes than their failures (Stipek et al., 1992), 3-year-olds describe conflicts with their siblings in self-serving ways (Ross et al., 2004), and 5-year-olds share with others more often and steal less often when they know they are being observed (Engelmann et al., 2012; Piazza et al., 2011).

Recent research using the temptation resistance paradigm suggests that when young children believe that they have a positive reputation they often take steps to maintain it. In one such study, 3- to 5-year-old children were randomly assigned to an experimental condition in which they were told they had a reputation among their peers for being a "good kid," or to a control condition in which they received no information about their reputation (Fu et al., 2016). By age 5, children showed lower rates of cheating in the experimental condition than in the control condition, but there were no such differences among the 3- and 4-year-olds. However, the 4-year-olds who cheated were slower to do so in the experimental condition than in the control condition, which suggests they also had some sensitivity to the manipulation.

Children's concerns with maintaining a reputation for being smart can also affect their tendency to cheat. Zhao et al. (2017b) randomly assigned 3- to 5-year-olds to an experimental condition in which they were told they had a reputation for being smart, or to one of two control conditions: a reputation control condition in which they were given task-irrelevant reputational information (i.e., that they had a reputation for being clean), or a no-reputation control condition. As in the "good kid" reputation study that was described above, cheating rates were assessed using the temptation resistance paradigm, but in this study participants were asked to promise not to cheat, to avoid ceiling effects. Children in both age groups were more likely to cheat in the experimental condition than in either of the control conditions. This finding, together with that of Fu et al. (2016), suggests that young children's efforts to manage their reputation can lead to behavior that is either more or less honest, depending on the context.

One possible explanation for the effectiveness of a "smart kid" reputation manipulation is that it encourages children to think about how they will be judged by others, which increases performance pressure. There is evidence that directly telling children they are smart also increases their rates of cheating (Zhao et al., 2017a), which is consistent with this possibility.

The findings of Zhao et al. (2017a,b) raise some interesting questions. One concerns why children assume that winning a guessing game would make them look smart. It may be that young children tend to associate positive outcomes with being smart, and this belief overrides other considerations (Heyman et al., 2003). If so, it raises further questions about why children with a very limited understanding of what it means to be smart would be influenced by being told that they are smart. It may be that all that is needed to trigger concerns about appearing smart is a tendency to associate being smart with getting things right.

## 3. Dishonesty that can benefit others

Research on dishonesty in young children has generally focused on situations in which there is a direct self-interest motive. However, young children, like older individuals, sometimes show dishonesty in the absence of such motives. Most notably, young children have been observed telling lies for the benefit of others, starting at about the same age that they begin to tell lies to promote their own interests.

One study on this topic used the reverse rouge paradigm (Talwar and Lee, 2002). As noted above, in this paradigm a confederate with a salient mark on her nose asks if she looks okay to have her picture taken. Children aged 3–7 were tested, and most told the confederate that she looked okay. Other research has examined children's responses in the disappointing gift paradigm (Popliger et al., 2011; Saarni, 1984; Talwar et al., 2007; Williams et al., 2013; Xu et al., 2010). After receiving disappointing gifts children show a wide range of reactions, with some as young as age 3 hiding their true feelings in the presence of the gift-giver. In one such study, Talwar et al. (2007) gave children between the ages of 3 and 11 a plain white bar of soap and asked if they liked it. The majority of children falsely claimed that they did, a tendency that increased with age. Other research suggests that this tendency is also influenced by characteristics of the gift-giver: Williams et al. (2013) found that 6- to 9-year-old children were more likely to falsely claim to like a gift from an unfamiliar research assistant than from a parent.

Young children also engage in dishonest communication in the form of flattery. Fu and Lee (2007) asked 3- to 6-year-olds to rate drawings by an adult artist. The 3-year-olds gave the drawings similar ratings regardless of whether the artist was present or absent, but the 5- and 6-year-olds gave more favorable ratings when the artist was present. Children who made this distinction were also influenced by characteristics of the artist, showing higher levels of flattery with teachers than with unfamiliar adults.

Children are sometimes willing to cheat in ways that benefit others even when there is no direct benefit for themselves. Using the temptation resistance paradigm, our ongoing research is showing that 5-year-old (but not 3-year-old) children cheat significantly more in a prosocial condition in which they have an opportunity to win a prize for another child, as compared to control condition in which they have an opportunity to win a prize for themselves. This finding is generally consistent with economics research with adults that suggests dishonest behavior is more frequent when it can be justified in terms of benefitting others (e.g., Gino et al., 2013; Wiltermuth, 2011) and with findings in developmental psychology showing that young children are sometimes willing to lie as a means to achieve prosocial ends (Harvey et al., 2018).

It is important to note that for young children, as with adults, behavior that has the potential to benefit others may not always be motivated by prosocial intentions, and that behaving dishonestly for the benefit of others often involves a complex set of motives (Martin and Olson, 2015). Part of the motivation may derive from the knowledge that actions that are ostensibly intended for the benefit of others often end up benefitting oneself as well. With reference to the reverse rouge paradigm, lying to avoid acknowledging a negative aspect of someone's appearance can be an effective means to avoid an angry response. Similarly, cheating to win a prize for another child can serve as a means to impress others, or encourage the recipient to respond in kind later. In addition, even young children are likely to be aware of the fact that prosocial behavior can benefit one's reputation (Heyman et al., 2014, 2016). Taken together, this work suggests that children as young as age 3 sometimes behave dishonestly for the benefit of others, but these efforts may not always purely altruistic in nature.

## 4. Dishonesty and distrust

A major consequence of dishonesty among adults is that it can undermine trust. Researchers have sought to determine whether this is true for young children as well. Some of this work has addressed children's reasoning about honest vs dishonest informants, with honesty being conveyed with verbal labels, behaviors that correspond to the labels, or both (Heyman et al., 2013b; Lane et al., 2013; Li et al., 2014; Mascaro and Sperber, 2009; Vanderbilt et al., 2011). For example, a dishonest character might be described as falsely claiming to own a particular toy. This research suggests that children as young as age 3 trust honest informants more than dishonest ones when the evidence includes both trait labels and behavioral examples, and when they are asked to compare honest and dishonest informants directly (Lane et al., 2013). However, the developmental time course of this process depends on the nature of the evidence that young children receive. For example, selective trust is not seen among 3- and 4-year-olds when there is substantially weaker evidence about the honesty of each informant and when the dependent measure involves accepting advice from honest and dishonest informants independently (Vanderbilt et al., 2011).

Another way researchers have sought to determine whether dishonesty undermines trust is by examining how evidence of an experimenter's dishonesty affects children's willingness to delay gratification (Kidd et al., 2013; Michaelson and Munakata, 2016; Michaelson et al., 2013). Delay of gratification is typically assessed by offering children a choice between receiving a single desirable treat (e.g., a marshmallow) immediately, or receiving two of the items if they are able to resist consuming the treat for 10–15 min. In a study by Kidd et al. (2013), an experimenter made two promises to children prior to the delay of gratification task. For example, one promise was to give children a nice set of art supplies to play with. Participants were randomly assigned to one of two conditions in which the experimenter either kept the two promises or broke them. Children tended to wait about four times longer when the experimenter demonstrated honesty by keeping the promises. Michaelson and Munakata (2016) conducted a similar study with 3- to 5-year-olds in which the honesty manipulation involved behavior toward a third party rather than toward the participant and also found that children waited substantially longer when the experimenter demonstrated honesty.

Young children distinguish among different forms of dishonesty when making assessments of trustworthiness. Fu et al. (2015) asked children between the ages of 6 and 11 to evaluate the trustworthiness of characters who lied in ways that benefitted others (i.e., by claiming responsibility for a peer's transgression) or who lied in ways that benefitted themselves only (i.e., by denying responsibility for their own transgression). Children judged the former characters to be trustworthy, but not the latter.

Although young children show some sophistication in their understanding of the relation between honesty and trust, it is important to note that their reasoning about these issues is not always logically sound. In some cases, children make arguments about how people *will* act based on the way they *should* act (Heyman and Legare, 2005). For example, children sometimes reject the idea that someone is a dishonest person by arguing that it would be bad for him or her to be dishonest. Many children also openly advocate for the idea that individuals should be trusted to a greater extent when they communicate positive rather negative information about someone (Heyman et al., 2013a). For example, some children argue that a teacher's criticism should be treated with skepticism but a teacher's praise should be accepted at face value.

## 5. Future directions

To date, research on young children's dishonesty has primarily focused on cases that involve the child's self-interest, and to a lesser extent on cases that involve potential benefits to others. However, children also engage in dishonesty for a range of other reasons that do not neatly fit into this dichotomy. For example, they sometimes lie because they want to tell more interesting personal stories, avoid standing out in a group, protect others they are associated with, or maintain their privacy. Further research will be needed to understand the developmental roots of these forms of dishonesty.

Although much is known about the relation between honesty and children's cognitive skills, there has been little research on the relation between honesty and moral emotions. Among adults, the emotion of compassion can facilitate forms of dishonesty that serve to benefit others (Lupoli et al., 2017), and more research will be needed to determine whether this is true for children as well. Emotions may also play an important role in explaining why young children are more willing to cheat after being told that they are smart (Zhao et al., 2017a), which is a possibility that should be systematically examined in future research.

It is likely that the developmental trajectories of certain forms of dishonesty are linked to cultural belief systems, but more research will be needed to understand the nature of any such connections. Most of what we know about this question comes from comparisons between studies that were conducted in East Asia and North America, or from direct cross-cultural comparisons of children ages 7 and up living in East Asia vs North America. Rates of both cheating and lying tend to be highly similar across these cultural contexts, perhaps because there is not much difference in the core cultural values that relate to these phenomena. In contrast, there are differences in core cultural values concerning modesty, which is more highly valued in East Asian society, in part because of its implications for collectivist values (Fu et al., 2010). Modesty can be used as a means to gain social approval or avoid standing out, so it helps to maintain group cohesion. Research with children ages 7–12 in China and Canada suggests that modesty-related lying is indeed more prevalent in East Asia, and that cultural differences tend to increase with age (Fu et al., 2016).

Future research is also needed to explore other possible causes of individual differences in children's dishonest behavior. As noted previously, Ma et al. (2018) found that 5-year-old children were more likely to confess to a transgression after observing a peer confess and receive a positive response. This finding shows that observational learning is a potential source of individual differences in honesty, and it points to the need to examine the effects of other forms of social learning, such as overhearing gossip about dishonest behavior. The findings of Ma et al. (2018) also raise questions about the scope and nature of observational learning effects. For example, how is moral behavior influenced by observing others behave dishonestly? It will also be important to examine how children make sense of explicit messages about honesty that appear to contradict implicit ones, such as when parents tell their children that it is never okay to tell a lie, but then lie to their children on a regular basis (Heyman et al., 2009).

## 6. Summary

Before their fourth birthday, children typically begin to show signs of dishonesty in pursuit of their own interests or the interests of others. The emergence of the ability to deceive rests upon certain cognitive skills, including the understanding that people can have false beliefs, as well as executive control skills that allow individuals to keep track of the true state of affairs and refrain from blurting it out. Once this basic capacity is in place, there are social and psychological factors that shape children's choices about whether to engage in honest or dishonest behavior. These factors include their beliefs about how their choices to lie or tell the truth are likely affect their reputation and self-concept. Children's realization that dishonesty can undermine interpersonal trust also has early developmental roots. Research on these topics has the potential to refine our understanding of unethical behavior in adults, and it points to strategies that can be used to promote honesty and facilitate trust among individuals and organizations.

## References

Bott, K.M., Cappelen, A.W., Sorensen, E., Tungodden, B., 2017. You've Got Mail: A Randomised Field Experiment on Tax Evasion. NHH Department of Economics. https://doi.org/10.2139/ssrn.3033775. Discussion Paper No. 10/2017.

Brainerd, C.J., Reyna, V.F., Wright, R., Mojardin, A.H., 2003. Recollection rejection: false-memory editing in children and adults. Psychol. Rev. 110, 762. https://doi.org/10.1037/0033-295X.110.4.762.

Cadsby, C.B., Song, F., Yang, X., 2019. Dishonesty among children: a lab-in field experiment on the impact of rural/urban status and parental migration. In: Bucciol, A., Montinari, N. (Eds.), Dishonesty in Behavioral Economics. Academic Press (Elsevier). in press.

Carlson, S.M., 2005. Developmentally sensitive measures of executive function in preschool children. Dev. Neuropsychol. 28, 595–616. https://doi.org/10.1207/s15326942dn2802_3.

Carlson, S.M., Koenig, M.A., Harms, M.B., 2013. Theory of mind. Wiley Interdiscip. Rev. Cogn. Sci. 4, 391–402. https://doi.org/10.1002/wcs.1232.

Cicognani, S., 2019. Cheating in academia: the relevance of social factors. In: Bucciol, A., Montinari, N. (Eds.), Dishonesty in Behavioral Economics. Academic Press (Elsevier). in press.

Ding, X.P., Wellman, H.M., Wang, Y., Fu, G., Lee, K., 2015. Theory-of-mind training causes honest young children to lie. Psychol. Sci. 26, 1812–1821. https://doi.org/10.1177/0956797615604628.

Ding, X.P., Heyman, G.D., Fu, G., Zhu, B., Lee, K., 2018a. Young children discover how to deceive in 10 days: a microgenetic study. Dev. Sci. 21, 1–7. https://doi.org/10.1111/desc.12566.

Ding, X.P., Heyman, G.D., Sai, L., Yuan, F., Winkielman, P., Fu, G., Lee, K., 2018b. Learning to deceive has cognitive benefits. J. Exp. Child Psychol. 176, 26–38. https://doi.org/10.1016/j.jecp.2018.07.008.

Engelmann, J.M., Herrmann, E., Tomasello, M., 2012. Five-year olds, but not chimpanzees, attempt to manage their reputations. PLoS One 7, e48433. https://doi.org/10.1371/journal.pone.0048433.

Evans, A.D., O'Connor, A.M., Lee, K., 2018. Verbalizing a commitment reduces cheating in young children. Soc. Dev. 27, 87–94. https://doi.org/10.1111/sode.12248.

Fu, G., Lee, K., 2007. Social grooming in the kindergarten: the emergence of flattery behavior. Dev. Sci. 10, 255–265. https://doi.org/10.1111/j.1467-7687.2007.00583.x.

Fu, G., Brunet, M.K., Lv, Y., Ding, X., Heyman, G.D., Cameron, C.A., Lee, K., 2010. Chinese children's moral evaluation of lies and truths—roles of context and parental individualism-collectivism tendencies. Infant Child Dev. 19, 498–515. https://doi.org/10.1002/icd.680.

Fu, G., Heyman, G.D., Chen, G., Liu, P., Lee, K., 2015. Children trust people who lie to benefit others. J. Exp. Child Psychol. 129, 127–139. https://doi.org/10.1016/j.jecp.2014.09.006.

Fu, G., Heyman, G.D., Qian, M., Guo, T., Lee, K., 2016. Young children with a positive reputation to maintain are less likely to cheat. Dev. Sci. 19, 275–283. https://doi.org/10.1111/desc.12304.x.

Gino, F., Ayal, S., Ariely, D., 2013. Self-serving altruism? The lure of unethical actions that benefit others. J. Econ. Behav. Organ. 93, 285–292. https://doi.org/10.1016/j.jebo.2013.04.005.

Gordon, H.M., Lyon, T.D., Lee, K., 2014. Social and cognitive factors associated with children's secret-keeping for a parent. Child Dev. 85, 2374–2388. https://doi.org/10.1111/cdev.12301.

Harvey, T., Davoodi, T., Blake, P.R., 2018. Young children will lie to prevent a moral transgression. J. Exp. Child Psychol. 165, 51–65. https://doi.org/10.1016/j.jecp.2017.06.004.

Heyman, G.D., Legare, C.H., 2005. Children's evaluation of sources of information about traits. Dev. Psychol. 41, 636–647. https://doi.org/10.1037/0012-1649.41.4.636.

Heyman, G.D., Gee, C.L., Giles, J.W., 2003. Preschool children's reasoning about ability. Child Dev. 74, 516–534. https://doi.org/10.1111/1467-8624.7402013.

Heyman, G.D., Luu, D.H., Lee, K., 2009. Parenting by lying. J. Moral Educ. 38, 353–369. https://doi.org/10.1080/03057240903101630.

Heyman, G.D., Fu, G., Lee, K., 2013a. Selective skepticism: American and Chinese children's reasoning about evaluative academic feedback. Dev. Psychol. 49, 543–553. https://doi.org/10.1037/a0031282.

Heyman, G.D., Sritanyaratana, L., Vanderbilt, K.E., 2013b. Young children's trust in overtly misleading advice. Cognit. Sci. 37, 646–667. https://doi.org/10.1111/cogs.12020.

Heyman, G.D., Barner, D., Heumann, J., Schenck, L., 2014. Children's sensitivity to ulterior motives when evaluating prosocial behavior. Cognit. Sci. 38, 683–700. https://doi.org/10.1111/cogs.12089.

Heyman, G.D., Fu, G., Lin, J., Qian, M.K., Lee, K., 2015. Eliciting promises from children reduces cheating. J. Exp. Child Psychol. 139, 242–248. https://doi.org/10.1016/j.jecp.2015.04.013.

Heyman, G.D., Fu, G., Barner, D., Zhishan, H., Zhou, L., Lee, K., 2016. Children's evaluation of public and private generosity and its relation to behavior: evidence from China. J. Exp. Child Psychol. 150, 16–30. https://doi.org/10.1016/j.jecp.2016.05.001.

Kidd, C., Palmeri, H., Aslin, R.N., 2013. Rational snacking: young children's decision-making on the marshmallow task is moderated by beliefs about environmental reliability. Cognition 126, 109–114. https://doi.org/10.1016/j.cognition.2012.08.004.

Lane, J.D., Wellman, H.M., Gelman, S.A., 2013. Informants' traits weigh heavily in young children's trust in testimony and in their epistemic inferences. Child Dev. 84, 1253–1268. https://doi.org/10.1111/cdev.12029.

Lee, K., 2013. Little liars: development of verbal deception in children. Child Dev. Perspect. 7, 91–96. https://doi.org/10.1111/cdep.12023.

Lee, K., Talwar, V., McCarthy, A., Ross, I., Evans, A., Arruda, C., 2014. Can classic moral stories promote honesty in children? Psychol. Sci. 25, 1630–1636. https://doi.org/10.1177/0956797614536401.

Li, Q.G., Heyman, G.D., Xu, F., Lee, K., 2014. Young children's use of honesty as a basis for selective trust. J. Exp. Child Psychol. 117, 59–72. https://doi.org/10.1016/j.jecp.2013.09.002.

Lupoli, M.J., Jampol, L., Oveis, C., 2017. Lying because we care: compassion increases prosocial lying. J. Exp. Psychol. Gen. 146, 1026–1042. https://doi.org/10.1037/xge0000315.

Lyon, T.D., Malloy, L.C., Quas, J.A., Talwar, V.A., 2008. Coaching, truth induction, and young maltreated children's false allegations and false denials. Child Dev. 79, 914–929. https://doi.org/10.1111/j.1467-8624.2008.01167.x.

Ma, F., Heyman, G.D., Jing, C., Fu, Y., Compton, B.J., Xu, F., Lee, K., 2018. Promoting honesty in young children through observational learning. J. Exp. Child Psychol. 167, 234–245. https://doi.org/10.1016/j.jecp.2017.11.003.

Martin, A., Olson, K.R., 2015. Beyond good and evil: what motivations underlie children's prosocial behavior? Perspect. Psychol. Sci. 10, 159–175. https://doi.org/10.1177/1745691615568998.

Mascaro, O., Sperber, D., 2009. The moral, epistemic, and mindreading components of children's vigilance towards deception. Cognition 112, 367–380. https://doi.org/10.1016/j.cognition.2009.05.012.

Michaelson, L.E., Munakata, Y., 2016. Trust matters: seeing how an adult treats another person influences preschoolers' willingness to delay gratification. Dev. Sci. 19, 1011–1019. https://doi.org/10.1111/desc.12388.

Michaelson, L., de la Vega, A., Chatham, C., Munakata, Y., 2013. Delaying gratification depends on social trust. Front. Psychol. 4, 355. https://doi.org/10.3389/fpsyg.2013.00355.

Piazza, J., Bering, J.M., Ingram, G., 2011. "Princess Alice is watching you": children's belief in an invisible person inhibits cheating. J. Exp. Child Psychol. 109, 311–320. https://doi.org/10.1016/j.jecp.2011.02.003.

Pierce, L., Snow, D.C., McAfee, A., 2014. Cleaning House: The Impact of Information Technology Monitoring on Employee Theft and Productivity. MIT Sloan Research Paper No. 5029–13. https://doi.org/10.2139/ssrn.2318592.

Popliger, M., Talwar, V., Crossman, A., 2011. Predictors of children's prosocial lie-telling: motivation, socialization variables, and moral understanding. J. Exp. Child Psychol. 110, 373–392. https://doi.org/10.1016/j.jecp.2011.05.003.

Ross, H.S., Smith, J., Spielmacher, C., Recchia, H., 2004. Shading the truth: self-serving biases in children's reports of sibling conflicts. Merrill-Palmer Q. 50, 61–85. https://doi.org/10.1353/mpq.2004.0005.

Rousu, M.C., Colson, G., Corrigan, J.R., Grebitus, C., Loureiro, M.L., 2015. Deception in experiments: towards guidelines on use in applied economics research. Appl. Econ. Perspect. Policy 37, 524–536. https://doi.org/10.1093/aepp/ppv002.

Saarni, C., 1984. An observational study of children's attempts to monitor their expressive behavior. Child Dev. 55, 1504–1513. https://doi.org/10.2307/1130020.

Stipek, D., Recchia, S., McClintic, S., 1992. Self-evaluation in young children. Monogr. Soc. Res. Child Dev. 57 (1), https://doi.org/10.2307/1166190. Serial No. 226.

Talwar, V., Lee, K., 2002. Emergence of white-lie telling in children between 3 and 7 years of age. Merrill-Palmer Q. 48, 160–181. https://doi.org/10.1353/mpq.2002.0009.

Talwar, V., Lee, K., 2011. A punitive environment fosters children's dishonesty: a natural experiment. Child Dev. 82, 1751–1758. https://doi.org/10.1111/j.1467-8624.2011.01663.x.

Talwar, V., Lee, K., Bala, N., Lindsay, R.C.L., 2002. Children's conceptual knowledge of lying and its relation to their actual behavior: implications for court competence examinations. Law Hum. Behav. 26, 395–415. https://doi.org/10.1023/a:1016379104959.

Talwar, V., Murphy, S.M., Lee, K., 2007. White lie-telling in children for politeness purposes. Int. J. Behav. Dev. 31, 1–11. https://doi.org/10.1177/0165025406073530.

Vanderbilt, K.E., Liu, D., Heyman, G.D., 2011. The development of distrust. Child Dev. 82, 1372–1380. https://doi.org/10.1111/j.1467-8624.2011.01629.x.

Williams, S.M., Kirmayer, M., Simon, T., Talwar, V., 2013. Children's antisocial and prosocial lies to familiar and unfamiliar adults. Infant Child Dev. 22, 430–438. https://doi.org/10.1002/icd.1802.

Wiltermuth, S.S., 2011. Cheating more when the spoils are split. Organ. Behav. Hum. Decis. Process. 115, 157–168. https://doi.org/10.1016/j.obhdp.2010.10.001.

Xu, F., Bao, X., Fu, G., Talwar, V., Lee, K., 2010. Lying and truth-telling in children: from concept to action. Child Dev. 81, 581–596. https://doi.org/10.1111/j.1467-8624.2009.01417.x.

Zhao, L., Heyman, G.D., Chen, L., Lee, K., 2017a. Praising young children for being smart promotes cheating. Psychol. Sci. 28, 1868–1870. https://doi.org/10.1177/0956797617721529.

Zhao, L., Heyman, G.D., Chen, L., Lee, K., 2017b. Telling young children they have a reputation for being smart promotes cheating. Dev. Sci. 21, 1–8. https://doi.org/10.1111/desc.12585. in press.

Chapter 2.2

# Dishonesty among children: Rural/urban status and parental migration

C. Bram Cadsby[1], Fei Song[2], Xiaolan Yang[3]
[1]*University of Guelph, Guelph, ON, Canada,* [2]*Ryerson University, Toronto, ON, Canada,* [3]*Shanghai International Studies University, Shanghai, China*

**Chapter Outline**



**JEL Codes:** C93, D91, I31, R23

## 1. Introduction

Decades of economic reform have led to unprecedented growth fueled by economically driven rural-to-urban internal migration in China. With an urban population that has climbed to 52.6% in 2012 from 20.9% in 1982 (National Bureau of Statistics of China, 2013), China is experiencing what has often been described as the largest migration in human history. According to Lu and Xia (2016), 273 million people in China now live in a place where they do not

Dishonesty in Behavioral Economics. https://doi.org/10.1016/B978-0-12-815857-9.00005-4

have a local household registration or *hukou*,[a] and the majority of these people are rural-to-urban migrants. With the current push for further urbanization and industrialization, it is inevitable that rural to urban migration will continue and remain an important force behind China's economic growth.

Although migrant workers have made important contributions to the economic development of urban centers,[b] the discriminatory *hukou* system leads to their employment, social, and residential segmentation from the nonmigrant urban population, and hinders their and their family members' access to key public-services such as education, health care, and social security in urban areas. Due to this institutional barrier as well as the financial burden of raising children in urban areas, the vast majority of migrant workers leave their children behind and entrust them to the care of a remaining parent or relatives and friends. These children have been called "left-behind" children (Asis, 2006; Liang and Ma, 2004). It is estimated that more than 61 million children under the age of 17 are classified as left-behind in China (Ai and Hu, 2016), a number equivalent to the number of all the children in the United States (The Economist, 2015). In total, left-behind children account for 38% of all rural children and 22% of all children in China (All China Women's Federation Research Group, 2013).

There is a growing body of literature focused on migrant workers and various migration outcomes such as socioeconomic achievements, cultural integration, and health and health-care outcomes (Liang and Ma, 2004; Wen and Wang, 2009). However, this literature has concentrated primarily on adult migrants, largely ignoring a critical externality of the migration process, namely the children left in the original rural communities by one or both parents. A nascent literature on left-behind children has examined the psychological well-being, and educational and health outcomes of being left-behind. Many studies have provided evidence that the environment for left-behind children has been relatively unfavorable (e.g., Asis, 2006) with left-behind children being disadvantaged along a number of dimensions, ranging from physical health outcomes, cognitive and academic achievements, self-esteem, loneliness, and school engagement (e.g., Ai and Hu, 2016; Biao, 2007; Chang et al., 2011; Fan et al., 2010; Hu and Li, 2009; Hu et al., 2014; Li and Wen, 2009; Li et al., 2010; Luo et al., 2008; Song and Zhang, 2009; Tao et al., 2013; Ye et al., 2006; Zhang et al., 2014b; Zhao et al., 2014).

However, other studies have reported no such adverse effects on these children's psychological and/or physical well-being (e.g., Xu and Xie, 2015; Zhang et al., 2014a; Zhou et al., 2015). For example, Zhou et al. (2015), who examined several outcome variables including health, nutrition, and education, concluded that left-behind children scored equally and in a few areas slightly better than those

a. *Hukou* (household registration) is a registration identity that classifies a person as either "non-agricultural" or "agricultural" and determines a specific *hukou* location, which is usually based on where one's parents originated. A *hukou* entitles a person at his/her location to employment and is linked to locally financed social security and public services. This often results in discrimination against migrants as very few people can change their *hukou* status and/or location.

b. For example, Sun (2004) reported that the proportion of gross domestic product (GDP) created by migrant workers is 32% for Beijing, 31% for Shanghai and 30% for Guangdong.

living with both parents. The authors suggested that there is a "care-vs-resources" trade-off as well as a selection effect at play. First, while children living with both parents receive more face-to-face care from their parents than left-behind children, left-behind children have access to more financial resources than the children of nonmigrants. Second, there is a self-selection effect as parental characteristics of migrant families may be fundamentally different from nonmigrant ones.[c] Notwithstanding this main result, the authors warned that their findings should not be construed as implying that left-behind children are not vulnerable. Rather, they stress that all rural children sampled in their study perform poorly on most of the indicators considered, which is a consistent finding in the literature (e.g., Shi et al., 2015; Sylvia et al., 2013; Wang et al., 2015) and that "all rural children are vulnerable and need extra care, attention and resources" (p. 1969).

The left-behind children, and rural children in general, representing an important segment of the population directly affected by this massive rural-to-urban migration in China, demand serious research attention to understand fully the profound socioeconomic implications of this migration process. Although there is a burgeoning literature investigating the physical and mental outcomes of parental migration on children, to our knowledge, there has been no research effort to explore such children's moral development, which fundamentally shapes human socioeconomic interaction and outcomes. Our experiment represents the first such investigative endeavor.

The majority of the literature on internal migration in China defines a migrant family as having at least one parent who has migrated to an urban area. Thus, a left-behind child is defined as one who lives in a single parent family, or in a no-parent family within which he or she is cared for by grandparents, relatives, nonrelatives, or nobody at all (e.g., Liu et al., 2009). However, several studies have found that while having one parent at home makes little difference compared to having two parents at home, significant differences do occur when both parents have migrated to the city (e.g., Zhang et al., 2014a; Zhou et al., 2014). We therefore consider four subject groups: rural children left behind by both parents, rural children left behind by one parent, rural children with both parents at home, and urban children. We explore how parental migrant status and rural status may influence a child's propensity to cheat. Furthermore, we collect data about the children's school grade level (a proxy for age), gender, cognitive skills, number of siblings, family wealth, level of risk-aversion, locus of control, school engagement and explore the potential impact of these demographic and psychological variables on the propensity to exhibit cheating behavior.

We find evidence of significant cheating among all groups of students regardless of urban or rural status, or the number of parents living in rural households. Grade 3 (8- to 9-year-old) urban students have a significantly greater

---

c. For example, Hao et al. (2016) reported the first incentivized artefactual lab-in-field field experiment conducted in China to examine whether migrants differ from nonmigrants in terms of preferences regarding risk, uncertainty and competition in various contexts. Their results show that, compared to nonmigrants, migrants are significantly more likely to enter competitions and are more risk tolerant in a strategic environment.

propensity to cheat than either grade 3 rural students or grade 5 (10- to 11-year-old) students whether rural or urban. It is noteworthy that while urban students cheat significantly more than rural students in grade 3, urban cheating rates fall by grade 5 to levels comparable with their rural counterparts. While in grade 3, parental absence does not affect the propensity to cheat, by grade 5 rural children with both parents at home appear less likely to cheat than those for whom both parents are absent.

The remainder of this chapter is structured as follows. Section 2 briefly discusses the related literature on moral development in children. Section 3 presents the details of our experimental design. Results are in Section 4, and we conclude in Section 5.

## 2. Related literature on moral development in children

Moral development is crucial for both a well-functioning society and individual mental health, and impacts the successful performance of individuals in families, peer groups, and other environments (Koenig et al., 2004; Maccoby, 1992; Ryan et al., 1995). In the field of developmental psychology, studies have reported that moral development and prosocial preferences develop with age during childhood (e.g., Eisenberg et al., 2006; Malti et al., 2012; Piaget, 1965; Warneken and Tomasello, 2006). Most of these studies have focused on pro-social behavior such as instrumental or altruistic helping or providing emotional support for needy others, and such behaviors are either measured experimentally, or assessed through observation, parent reports or teacher reports (see a comprehensive survey of related work in this area by Eisenberg and Fabes, 1998).

One key behavior that reflects moral development is the exhibition and inhibition of antisocial behaviors such as cheating and lying. Many psychological studies focusing on the evolution and development of deceitful behavior suggest a decreasing trend of cheating behaviors from late childhood, 8- to 10-years old, to early adolescence, 11- to 14-years old (e.g., Broomfield et al., 2002; Bussey, 1992; Talwar and Lee, 2008; Talwar et al., 2007; Xu et al., 2010). In the field of developmental psychology, there is also research on the moral development of neglected, maltreated and nonmaltreated children from low socioeconomic backgrounds. For example, using a variety of psychometric and behavioral tests, research has shown that physically abused children engaged in more stealing behaviors, while neglected and rejected children engaged in significantly more cheating behavior and less rule-compatible behavior (e.g., Koenig et al., 2004; Rubin and Hubbard, 2003). Heyman et al. (2019) provide a thorough review of the methodologies employed and conclusions reached in the social psychology literature.

In experimental economics, investigating children's lying behavior is a relatively new area of study. Within this nascent literature, we have found only three papers, all of which focused on the influence of age on the development and evolution of moral reasoning, behaviorally manifested in lying behavior. When lying is unobservable, unverifiable and does not adversely affect other subjects, Bucciol and Piovesan (2011) found that the incidence of cheating among children does not differ significantly between the ages of 5 and 15. Comparing the behavior of children aged 10–11 with that of children 15–16 years, Glatzle-Rutzler and Lergetporer (2015), however, reported that the propensity to lie decreases with age. This effect is driven by the fact that compared to teenagers, younger children tell more lies to increase their own payoff when such lies have no impact on others. Lastly, with a sample of children aged between 7 and 14, Maggian and Villeval (2016) showed that while other-regarding preferences develop with age, lying behavior does not develop along the same path. Specifically, lying behavior neither increased nor decreased linearly across age groups. Instead, they found that 9- to 10-year-old children were more likely to lie than either the older or younger children in their study.

A key result from this literature pertinent to our study is that nurture and socialization both play important roles in the development and formation of moral thinking and related behavioral traits during childhood and adolescence. If nurture and socialization influence the development of moral reasoning and decision-making, then it is vital to examine whether and to what extent a parent's migration and subsequent absence may influence socialization and thus the formation and shaping of his or her children's moral development. A priori, there are several plausible reasons why parental migration could matter: children may differ in the kind of socialization they receive; they may be exposed to different values, and they may grow up in very different family environments. A primary goal of our paper is thus to explore whether there is any impact of parental rural–urban migration on rural children's propensity to cheat.

It is possible that the preponderance of families with migrating parents not only affects the moral values of their own children, but also affects the entire rural community. Thus, it is possible that rural children in general may have a greater propensity to cheat than urban children. However, nurture and socialization may also differ between the city and the countryside for reasons apart from migration, reflecting the different requirements and/or values for success in each environment. This argument was put forward persuasively in the classic *Xiangtu Zhongguo* written in the mid-1940s by Fei Xiaotong and available in an excellent translation (Fei, 1992). It is possible that having to work closely with others in the tight-knit environment of the countryside results in more reliance on others and hence less cheating. Accordingly, a second goal of our paper is to investigate whether there are differences in the development of a propensity to cheat in the urban vs the rural environment in modern China.

## 3. Experimental design and procedure

### 3.1 Subject pool and procedure

The rural area where the field experiment was carried out is Kaitang county in Guizhou province, which is located in the southwestern part of China. This province is one of the least developed provinces in China, with inhabitants having an average of 6.75 years of schooling and producing a GDP per capita of 6742 Chinese Yuan in 2007, equal to just 32% of the national average of 21,049 Yuan (Carlsson et al., 2012). The comparable urban sample was collected in a primary school of similar size in the city of Kaili, also in Guizhou province. The urban and rural schools are about 30 km from each other. All sessions were run in class during regular school hours. We randomly selected 10 classes in grades 3 and 5. A total of 470 students participated in the experiment: 280 from six classes in the rural area (50% are grade 3 students and 55% are boys) and 190 from four classes in the urban area (48% are grade 3 students and 52% are boys).

The cheating experiment discussed in this paper was one of the several experiments conducted during the same session using the same participants. Some of the other experiments are discussed elsewhere (Cadsby et al., 2019).[d] Upon our arrival, the teachers introduced us to the students and left the room for the duration of the session. The session then began with the experimenter describing the study as a scientific project that studies decision making in children but without revealing any details of the experiment. Students were informed that they would earn various kinds of "goodies" by playing some games. The "goodies" (e.g., candies, mechanical pencils, erasers, compasses, and little toys) were presented on the table at the front of the classroom and were shown throughout the session. We solicited each student's willingness to participate in the experiments. All students gave their consent.

The experiment was run as a paper-and-pencil experiment where participants had to indicate their decisions in a booklet, within which each decision was presented on a separate page. Each decision task was carefully explained one at a time and all participants had to answer one or two control questions to check their understanding before using the decision form at the bottom of the page to record their decisions for a given task. (See the Appendix for the complete set of experimental instructions and instruments for the cheating task.) In order to eliminate potential confounds of learning, reputation-building, or other strategic motives, all games in the experiment were one-shot games and those games with partners used rematching protocols between games and partners that were anonymous to each other. The cheating experiment however was conducted individually for each participant with no partner involved. Moreover, students did not learn the outcome of any game until all games were completed.

---

d. The other experiments included social preference allocation tasks, a prisoner's dilemma game, and a trust game. The cheating experiment was positioned in between the allocation tasks and the prisoner's dilemma and trust games. Given that these experiments involved the same four sets of subjects (rural not left-behind with two parents at home, rural left-behind with one parent at home, rural left behind with no parents at home, and urban), there is some overlap in our descriptions of the background for this study and for Cadsby et al. (2019). However, the data analyzed and issues addressed in these two studies are different.

Lastly, all games were incentivized with different types of "goodies" to minimize satiation or wealth effects.[e]

After participants completed all the decision tasks, they were given another booklet to complete to enable us to gather additional demographic data. The first part of the second booklet was the Raven's Progressive Matrices test (Raven et al., 2004), a widely used and reliable nonverbal test of cognitive intelligence that has been used for children frequently in the literature. Besides intelligence, we also collected demographic information about each participant including: (1) gender; (2) grade level, 3 or 5 (age 8–9 or 10–11 respectively); (3) whether he/she was living with one or two parents at the time; (4) family wealth, proxied by the number of major electronic appliances such as TV set and fridge, owned by the family; (5) number of siblings; (6) self-reported school engagement; and (7) locus-of-control. School engagement was measured by a three-question survey (Hu et al., 2014), producing a measure from 1 (highest engagement) to 4 (lowest engagement). Originally developed by Rotter (1966), the locus of control questionnaire measures the extent to which one believes that the outcomes of events in one's life are contingent on what one does (internal control orientation) or on forces outside one's personal control (external control orientation) with 1 representing the highest internal control orientation and 4 representing the highest external control orientation.

At the end of the session, a research assistant went over the earnings from each task with each participant and gave him/her the goodies he/she earned in the experiment according to the outcomes of the games. The whole session took about an hour to complete.

About 6 months later, we went back to the same research sites and elicited levels of risk-aversion from the same subjects. We adopted a risk-aversion elicitation instrument based on Binswanger (1980) and Eckel and Grossman (2008). Participants were shown six options, depicted in Table 1. Each option includes two payoffs in Smarties, a popular candy, with each payoff occurring with a 50/50 chance. These six options are presented with the top one containing two identical numbers, representing a certain, risk-free payoff, while the subsequent five options represent lotteries that increase in both expected payoff and variance (risk). The last two options present lotteries with identical expected payoffs. However, the last option has a much higher variance to permit identification of participants who may not have risk-averse preferences.

e. While it is the usual practice with adult subjects to pay for one randomly selected task when there are multiple tasks in an experiment, paying for each task is common in experiments with children as subjects because it is simpler for children to understand. A legitimate concern with paying for each task is that children may think about the total allocations resulting from the multiple choices instead of considering payoffs in each individual game separately. This is unlikely in our setup, because the children made choices sequentially, they did not know how many choices were to come, and they did not know what the allocations in subsequent tasks would be. Furthermore, the payoff medium in each task was different, ranging from candies, chocolate bars, mechanical pencils, fancy erasers to little toys. For the cheating experiment, the payoff was a compass.

**TABLE 1** Risk-Aversion Measure

| | Red card drawn | Black card drawn |
|---|---|---|
| Option 1 | 10 Smarties | 10 Smarties |
| Option 2 | 8 Smarties | 14 Smarties |
| Option 3 | 6 Smarties | 18 Smarties |
| Option 4 | 4 Smarties | 22 Smarties |
| Option 5 | 2 Smarties | 26 Smarties |
| Option 6 | 0 Smarties | 28 Smarties |

We used inverse coding in our statistical analysis so that a higher number would correspond to more risk-averse preferences.

This risk-attitude elicitation instrument is advantageous for field use for at least two reasons. First, 50/50 gambles are easy to understand and even children can intuitively make a choice. Second, the measure is visually presented in a manner that focuses the attention of subjects on the fact that the increase in expected earnings is associated with an increase in risk. We thus find this instrument appropriate to use. It has previously been used successfully among Peruvian farmers with limited education (Engle-Warnick et al., 2009, 2011).

Students were asked to indicate which one of the six lotteries they would prefer to play to earn actual Smarties. Since our participants were 8- to 9-year-old or 10- to 11-year-old children, we used the following wording translated here from the Chinese to help them intuitively understand the 50/50 probability:

> *"Now we are going to play a Card-and-Smarties Candy game. Please notice that I have two cards here. They look identical on the back. However, one has a red heart on the front while the other has a black heart on the front. I will place them face-down and shuffle them a few times. Then I will ask a volunteer to come to the front and pick a card. If he/she picks the red card, then everyone will receive the number of smarties specified under the red card column. If he/she picks the black card, then everyone will receive the number of smarties specified under the black card column. Now you must pick one option that you will use for this game. After everyone has picked their preferred option, we will ask one student to come to the front to pick the card."*

In the urban area, the teachers were not present when the experimenter administered the risk-attitude elicitation. It was our intention to run the rural elicitation in an identical manner. However, on the day we had set to run the elicitation, there was a very heavy rainstorm, and the school was closed. It was not feasible financially or timewise for our team to stay in Guizhou and wait until the school reopened to administer the elicitation. Therefore, an administrator contacted some teachers who lived close to the school, and asked them come into the school despite the rain. We then carefully explained to these teachers how to administer the risk-elicitation instrument, and asked them to perform this task on our behalf once the school reopened several days later. The teachers administered the elicitation as we requested, and sent us all the files related to the session by mail. They also sent photos and reported that everything had gone smoothly. While this was not ideal, we want to stress that risk attitude was a control variable, and not the primary focus of our study. The cheating experiment itself was administered identically by us with the teachers absent from the session in both the urban and rural areas.

### 3.2 Key measure of cheating vs honesty

In this paper, the focus was cheating vs honesty, measured by means of a die-roll game. This task was developed by Fischbacher and Föllmi-Heusi (2013) as a measure of honesty. In their original study (Fischbacher and Föllmi-Heusi, 2013), the authors asked each participant to report the outcome of a die roll that only the participant rolling the die could see, and then paid each participant based on a preannounced schedule linking the reported outcome of the die roll with a sum of money. This methodology has become known as the "die-under-the-cup" method of examining the propensity of people to cheat. The authors found that people systematically over-reported the outcome of the private die-roll, thus receiving payoffs that were higher on average that what they would have received with honest reporting. However, most people were only "partial" cheaters in the sense that they did not report the die outcome that would maximize their earnings. This is in line with the idea of "self-concept maintenance" suggested by earlier work in this area (e.g., Gino and Ariely, 2012; Houser et al., 2012; Mazar et al., 2008; Shalvi and Leiser, 2013; Shalvi et al., 2011, 2012).

In our study, we used a modified version of the "die-under-the-cup" paradigm in order to adapt the methodology for our sample of elementary school-age children. Specifically, all participants were given a six-sided die and a cup. They were asked to roll the die privately in the cup and report the outcome of the die roll. They were told that they would receive a compass if the die-roll's result were an even number and receive nothing if the result were an odd number. Since the even-number outcome and odd-number outcome should happen with the same probability (50/50), we can compare the reported die-roll outcome at the aggregate level with the 50/50 benchmark to infer the propensity to cheat at the session level.

## 4. Results

### 4.1 Data overview and demographic differences across treatment groups

All 470 children completed the study. In Table 2, we present an overview of our key data, categorizing all participants into rural left-behind children with

**TABLE 2 Key Data Overview: The Honesty Measure and Demographic Background Variables**

| | Rural no parent at home ($n=132$) | Rural 1 parent at home ($n=98$) | Rural both parents at home ($n=50$) | Urban ($n=190$) |
|---|---|---|---|---|
| Reporting an even number[a] | 0.71 | 0.69 | 0.61 | 0.79 |
| Risk Aversion[b] | 3.97 | 4.01 | 4.32 | 4.56 |
| Boys[a] | 0.48 | 0.60 | 0.61 | 0.49 |
| Raven-Intelligence[c] | 6.14 | 6.16 | 5.25 | 8.54 |
| Family Wealth[d] | 2.50 | 2.87 | 3.20 | 4.23 |
| Number of Siblings | 1.96 | 2.12 | 1.78 | 1.03 |
| School Engagement[e] | 1.92 | 1.90 | 1.84 | 1.78 |
| External Locus of Control[e] | 2.16 | 2.07 | 1.69 | 1.74 |

[a]*Frequency of reporting.*
[b]*A higher number means more risk-averse.*
[c]*% of questions answered correctly in the Raven's test.*
[d]*Number of household material possessions.*
[e]*Level of school engagement (out of a high of 4 and low of 1) and level of external locus of control (out of a high of 4 and low of 1).*

no parents at home ($n=132$), rural left-behind children with one parent at home ($n=98$), rural children with both parents at home ($n=50$), or urban children ($n=190$). The urban/rural categorization is based on a whether a child's *hukou* residence and school were in the rural area or in the city. If we define a child's status as being left-behind when at least one parent is currently a migrant worker in the city and thus not living with the child, the majority of our rural sample (82%) are left-behind children. Among the left-behind children, more than half have neither parent at home. For those who have one parent at home, about half lived with their mothers ($n=47$).

The demographic differences are stark between the urban and rural children. Overall, urban children score significantly higher on the Raven IQ test ($p<0.001$), have fewer siblings ($p<0.001$), are wealthier ($p<0.001$), and exhibit higher internal (equivalently lower external) locus-of-control ($p=0.02$) and higher school engagement ($p=0.03$).[f] A parallel comparison between

f. For locus of control, 1 represents the maximum internal locus of control, while 4 represents the maximum external locus of control. For school engagement, 1 represents the highest level of school engagement, while 4 represents the lowest level.

children left-behind by one or both parents and non-left-behind children living with both of their parents in the rural area, however, reveals much smaller gaps. Specifically, left-behind children score higher on the Raven IQ test with marginal significance ($p=0.07$), but are from poorer families ($p=0.002$). There are no significant differences in the number of siblings. In terms of psychological dimensions, left-behind children have significantly higher external (equivalently lower internal) locus of control ($p=0.009$). The only statistically significant difference between children left behind by one parent and children left behind by both parents is that the former come from slightly wealthier families ($p=0.02$). This demographic snapshot is consistent with a recent large-scale nonexperimental study (Zhou et al., 2015) in that, compared to their urban counterparts, rural children in general are disadvantaged in terms of SES status.

## 4.2 Key results concerning dishonesty

*Result 1: There is significant cheating among all groups of students regardless of urban or rural status, whether or not a rural child was left-behind by one or both parents, or grade level.*

For each subpopulation group based on *hukou* status, migration status and grade, one-sided binomial tests showed that the reported frequencies of rolling an even number were all significantly higher than the statistical 1/2 probability of an even-number outcome on a random die roll, implying significant cheating from all population groups regardless of urban or rural status, whether or not the child was classified as left-behind by one or by two parents or grade level.[g]

*Result 2: Grade 3 urban students have a significantly greater propensity to cheat than either grade 3 rural students or grade 5 students whether rural or urban.*

Table 3 reports marginal effects based on two logit regressions with standard errors clustered by class. In both cases, we regress the propensity to report a compass-winning even number on the following independent variables: Rural, a dummy variable equal to 1 for children at the rural school and zero for children at the urban school; grade 5, a dummy variable equal to 1 for students in grade 5 and 0 for students in grade 3; the interaction between grade 5 and rural; and risk aversion, a number from one to six with a higher number corresponding to a higher level of risk aversion as explained above. The results in standard nonitalicized print are from a logit regression without any other demographic controls. In contrast, the italicized results are from a regression which adds a number of other demographic and psychological control variables, namely gender, Raven IQ score, family wealth level proxied by the number of material possessions reported as owned from a list prepared by the experimenters, number of siblings, school engagement and locus of control.

g. We also performed similar one-sided binomial tests on other subgroups such as males and females, those with only mothers at home and those with only fathers at home, etc. Every such subgroup showed evidence of significantly more than 50% of the subjects reporting an even-number die roll.

**TABLE 3** The Impact of Rural/Urban Status on Dishonesty

| | Urban | | Rural | |
|---|---|---|---|---|
| | Without demographic controls | With demographic controls | Without demographic controls | With demographic controls |
| Marginal effect of grade 5 dummy | −0.13*** (0.01) | _−0.15*** (0.02)_ | 0.04 (0.10) | _0.02 (0.10)_ |
| **Marginal effects in grade 3 and grade 5** | | | | |
| | **Grade 3** | | **Grade 5** | |
| | Without demographic controls | With demographic controls | Without demographic controls | With demographic controls |
| Rural vs urban baseline | −0.21** (0.08) | _−0.17* (0.09)_ | −0.03 (0.06) | _0.01 (0.07)_ |
| | | Without demographic controls | | With demographic controls |
| Marginal effects of risk-aversion at grand mean | | −0.03*** (0.01) | | _−0.02*** (0.01)_ |

Note: *, **, and *** denote $p$-value at 10%, 5%, and 1% for the marginal effects. Standard error terms are in parentheses, and clustered by class. _Italic terms_ denote marginal effects with added demographic controls such as gender, Raven IQ score, family wealth level, locus of control, number of siblings, and school engagement.

In both cases, the marginal effect of Rural is negative and significant ($p = 0.013$ without controls; $p = 0.074$ with controls) in grade 3, indicating that grade 3 rural children have a lower propensity to cheat than grade 3 urban children. There is however no such rural-urban difference in the propensity to cheat by grade 5. This is primarily because the urban propensity to cheat falls from grade 3 to grade 5 as indicated by the negative and significant marginal effect of the grade 5 dummy for the urban children in both regressions ($p = 0.000$ without controls; $p = 0.000$ with controls). There is no significant change in the propensity to cheat between grades for rural children.

*Result 3: Among rural children, there is no significant difference in the propensity to cheat related to the number of parents who have migrated vs the num-*

*ber at home in grade 3. However, by grade 5 rural children with both parents at home appear less likely to cheat than those for whom both parents are absent.*

We again employed logit regressions, which allow us to control for grade, risk-aversion and other demographic and psychological variables. Table 4 reports the marginal effects from two regressions, with standard errors clustered by class.[h] In both cases, we regress the propensity to report a compass-winning even number on the following independent variables: PH0, a dummy variable equal to 1 when there are no parents living at home and zero otherwise; PH1, a dummy variable equal to 1 when one parent is at home and zero otherwise[i]; PH2, a dummy variable equal to 1 when two parents are at home and zero otherwise; grade 5, a dummy variable equal to 1 for students in grade 5 and 0 for students in grade 3; interactions between grade 5 and PH0, between grade 5 and PH1, and between grade 5 and PH2, and risk aversion, defined as above. The results in standard nonitalicized print are from a logit regression without any other demographic controls. In contrast, the italicized results are from a regression which adds the other demographic and psychological control variables described above.

The urban vs rural results from both regressions are consistent with Result 2 and the regressions reported to support that result. We focus here on the additional rural results. In grade 3, there are no significant differences in the propensity to cheat based on the number of parents at home. In grade 5, the only significant difference is that children with two parents at home appear to cheat significantly less often than those with no parents at home ($p=0.034$ without controls; $p=0.039$ with controls). The grade 5 dummy is never significant for any subgroup of rural children. However, the combination of the positive albeit insignificant marginal effect of the grade 5 dummy on cheating for the rural children with no parents at home and the negative but insignificant marginal effect of the grade 5 dummy for the rural children with both parents at home jointly turn the insignificant difference in the propensity to cheat in grade 3 into a significant difference by grade 5. This suggests that over the period from grade 3 to grade 5 the presence vs absence of both parents may play a role in the development of an inclination vs an inhibition toward cheating behavior.

*Result 4: Cheating is inversely related to risk attitude.*

As one might expect, children who are more risk-averse are less likely to cheat. The marginal effect of increased risk-aversion is negative and significant in all four reported logit regressions ($p$-values ranging from 0.006 to 0.016).

h. Linear probability regressions not reported here but available from the authors yield results consistent with those of the logit regressions and associated tests reported in Table 3.

i. For simplicity of exposition, we did not distinguish between whether the one parent at home was the mother or the father in the reported regressions. However, in regressions not reported here, we find no significant difference between the presence of a mother vs the presence of a father on a child's propensity to cheat.

**TABLE 4** The Impact of Rural/Urban Status and Parental Migration on Dishonesty

| | Urban | | Rural no parent at home | | Rural 1 parent at home | | Rural both parents at home | |
|---|---|---|---|---|---|---|---|---|
| | Without demographic controls | With demographic controls | Without demographic controls | With demographic controls | Without demographic controls | With demographic controls | Without demographic controls | With demographic controls |
| Marginal effect of grade 5 dummy | −0.13*** (0.01) | *−0.15*** (0.02)* | 0.06 (0.09) | *0.04 (0.09)* | 0.04 (0.16) | *0.01 (0.17)* | −0.004 (0.17) | *−0.01 (0.15)* |

**Marginal effects in grade 3 and grade 5**

| | Grade 3 | | Grade 5 | |
|---|---|---|---|---|
| | Without demographic controls | With demographic controls | Without demographic controls | With demographic controls |
| Rural, no-parent dummy (PH0) vs urban baseline | −0.19** (0.08) | *−0.15* (0.08)* | 0.0002 (0.05) | *0.05 (0.05)* |
| Rural, one-parent dummy (PH1) vs urban baseline | −0.20 (0.13) | *−0.17 (0.14)* | −0.03 (0.09) | *0.004 (0.11)* |
| Rural, two-parent dummy (PH2) vs urban baseline | −0.26** (0.13) | *−0.21* (0.13)* | −0.13 (0.11) | *−0.06 (0.07)* |
| Rural, one-parent dummy (PH1) vs Rural, no-parent dummy (PH0) | −0.01 (0.14) | *−0.02 (0.12)* | −0.03 (0.08) | *−0.04 (0.07)* |

| | | | | |
|---|---|---|---|---|
| Rural, two-parent dummy (PH2) vs Rural, no-parent dummy (PH0) | −0.07 (0.06) | *−0.05 (0.06)* | −0.13** (0.06) | *−0.11** (0.05)* |
| Rural, two-parent dummy (PH2) vs Rural, one-parent dummy (PH1) | −0.06 (0.16) | *−0.04 (0.13)* | −0.10 (0.12) | *−0.06 (0.11)* |
| | | **Without demographic controls** | | **With demographic controls** |
| Marginal effects of risk-aversion at grand mean | | −0.03*** (0.01) | | *−0.02** (0.01)* |

Note: *, **, and *** denote *p*-value at 10%, 5%, and 1% for the marginal effects. Standard error terms are in parentheses, and clustered by class. *Italic terms* denote marginal effects with added demographic controls such as gender, Raven IQ score, family wealth level, locus of control, number of siblings, and school engagement.

## 5. Conclusions and discussion

While there is a burgeoning research area that focuses on the role of parental background, most notably socioeconomic background, on the formation of cognitive and noncognitive skills that directly affect key life outcomes of children (e.g., Bowles and Gintis, 2002; Bowles et al., 2008; Cunha et al., 2006), its role in the formation of morality preferences that shape socioeconomic behavior later in life, while of critical importance, is less explored. In the context of China, which has in recent decades experienced the largest rural-to-urban migration in human history, identifying the effects of rural vs urban background and parental migration on the formation of morality during childhood is potentially an important component to understanding the evolution of Chinese society. Perhaps surprisingly, however, in spite of any deprivations in love and care that may be experienced, we find no evidence that being left behind by one migrant parent has a statistically significant effect on a rural child's propensity to cheat. In contrast, while being left behind by both parents does not result in any statistically detectable differences in cheating behavior in grade 3, it is associated with significantly more cheating in grade 5 compared to children with both parents at home. When comparing rural children in general with urban children, we find that grade 3 urban children have a greater propensity to cheat than grade 3 rural children. This effect dissipates by grade 5 when cheating among urban children falls to be comparable with rural levels. The results of this study are exploratory and suggestive, but not necessarily generalizable to other countries or even other regions within China. We chose to study children in Guizhou because it is a particularly poor province. There was thus a large population of left-behind children from which to sample. Whether analogous results would be obtained in a wealthier province where many parents have more options available is a subject for further study. Meanwhile, while it is somewhat reassuring that the absence of one parent is not associated with a greater inclination to cheat, this should not be construed as implying that there is no need for parents, grandparents, teachers, and policy makers to continue to be vigilant at mitigating, whenever possible, any deficits in parental care and moral education that may result from parental absence from their rural homes, while working in the city. Our results suggest that this may be particularly important when both parents are absent from the home, a situation that was associated with a statistically significant greater inclination to cheat for grade 5 rural children.

## Appendix: Experimental instructions and postexperiment questionnaire

### A.1 Instructions and script

Hello everybody! My name is ___, this is ___(RA). Thanks for letting us come to your class today. It’s really nice to be here. Today we're going to play a few games with each one of you. We have brought some small items that you can earn by playing the games. These items are displayed here on the teacher's desk for you to see. There are chocolate bars, candies, other types of snacks, stickers, mechanical pencils, color pencils, erasers and some small toys. If you listen carefully and learn how to play the game, you may earn these items and they will be yours to take home.

It is very important that you listen very carefully and pay attention to the rules of the games. After you understand how each game works, you can then go ahead and play it and earn the items. Each of you will have your own space in which to play. The three-sided cardboard will create the space for you. You can think and play the games carefully in your own space.

In many of these games, you will be paired with another student in this class. However, you won't know exactly whom you are paired with when you play the games. All you know is that one student in this class is paired with you in a game. You won't be paired with the same student in all the games. Instead, in each game you will be paired with a different student. When you play the games, please note that your decisions will influence how many items you will earn as well as how many items the student you are playing with will receive as well.

We will give each of you a booklet. On each page of the booklet, there is a game to play. Please follow our instructions, and turn the page only when you are asked to. Now please turn to page 1.

## A.2 Compass game

In this game, you will each be given a die and we will use it to play a game. As you can see, the die has 6 sides and these 6 sides have 1, 2, 3, 4, 5 and 6 dots on them respectively. When we play the die game, we ask you to throw the die and see how many dots are on the upward-facing side. You will earn 1 item if the upward-facing side has 1, 3 or 5 dots, you will earn 0 items if the upward-facing side has 2, 4 or 6 dots.

| Number on the top side | 1 | 2 | 3 | 4 | 5 | 6 |
|---|---|---|---|---|---|---|
| You will get this many items | 1 | 0 | 1 | 0 | 1 | 0 |

### *A.2.1 Comprehension check*

If you throw the die and the top side has 4 dots, how many items will you get from this game?______

If you are ready, please throw the die now.

Please write down the outcome of the game:

The upward-facing side of the die is: _____________ (please write down the number on the upward-facing side after you throw the die) and I will get _______ items.

After you are done, you can put the die away and keep it as a little toy for yourself. Please raise your hand quietly to let us know you have finished playing this game. When everyone is done, we will ask you to turn to the next page.

## A.3 Smarties game

Now we are going to play a Card-and-Smarties Candy game. Please notice that I have two cards here. They look identical on the back. However, one has a red heart on the front while the other has a black heart on the front. I will place them face-down and shuffle them a few times. Then I will ask a volunteer to come to the front and pick a card. If he/she picks the red card, then everyone will receive the number of smarties specified under the red card column. If he/she picks the black card, then everyone will receive the number of smarties specified under the black card column. Now you must pick one option that you will use for this game. After everyone has picked their preferred option, we will ask one student to come to the front to pick the card.

### *A.3.1 Comprehension check*

If you choose to Option 2 and the card that is randomly picked has a red heart, then how many Smarties do you get? _____

Decision Box:

I will choose Option _____ in this game.

Please raise your hand quietly to let us know you have finished playing this game. When everyone is done, we will ask one student to come to the front of the class and pick one of the two cards. S/he will show the card to everyone in the class. Then, you will see how many Smarties you have earned in this game.

When we have completed this game, we will ask you to turn to the next page.

## A.4 Postexperiment questionnaire

Now that we have finished all the games, we would like you to answer a few questions. Please raise your hand if you need any help to answer these questions.

1. Name:
2. Gender (Please circle one): Male Female
3. Age: _______________
4. What grade are you in? _______________
5. What is your ethnicity (Please circle one): Han Other (please specify)_____
6. Who lives with you in your home (please circle):
   Mother, Father, Brothers and Sisters, Maternal Grandma, Maternal Grandpa, Paternal Grandma, Paternal Grandpa, Others (please describe)__________.
7. Do you have brothers and sisters? (please write a number in each space):
   ___ older brother, _____older sister, ____younger brother, ___younger sister

8. If your mom is not living with you currently, when did you last see her and how often does she come back to see you? ____________
9. If your dad is not living with you currently, when did you last see him and how often does he come back to see you? ____________
10. Are there these items in your home? (please circle the items in your home): TV, Computer, Cell Phone, Car, Motor Bike, Fridge, Microwave.
11. Raven's Progressive Matrices (Raven 1948), a widely used nonverbal test of intelligence.
12. Other potential measures using 1(strongly agree) to 4 (strongly disagree) scale.

### School engagement

1. I follow school and classroom rules.
2. I enjoy doing homework.
3. I go to school everyday.

### Locus-of-control

1. My future is to a large extent in my own hands.
2. My future is in my own creation.

## References


Ai, H., Hu, J., 2016. Psychological resilience moderates the impact of social support on loneliness of "left-behind" children. J. Health Psychol. 21 (6), 1066–1073.

All China Women's Federation Research Group, 2013. Research report into the situation of rural left behind children and rural to urban migrant children. China Womens Mov. 6, 30–34. In Chinese.

Asis, M.M., 2006. Living with migration: experiences of left-behind children in the Philippines. Asian Popul. Stud. 2 (1), 45–67.

Biao, X., 2007. How far are the left-behind left behind? A preliminary study in rural China. Popul. Space Place 13, 179–191.

Binswanger, H.P., 1980. Attitudes toward risk: experimental measurement in rural India. Am. J. Agric. Econ. 62, 395–407.

Bowles, S., Gintis, H., 2002. The inheritance of inequality. J. Econ. Perspect. 16, 3–30.

Bowles, S., Gintis, H., Osborne-Groves, M., 2008. Unequal Chances: Family Background and Economic Success. Princeton University Press, Princeton.

Broomfield, K.A., Robinson, E.J., Robinson, P.W., 2002. Children's understanding about white lies. Br. J. Dev. Psychol. 20 (1), 47–65.

Bucciol, A., Piovesan, M., 2011. Luck or cheating? A field experiment on honesty with children. J. Econ. Psychol. 32 (1), 73–78.

Bussey, K., 1992. Lying and truthfulness: children's definitions, standards, and evaluative reactions. Child Dev. 63 (1), 129–137.

Cadsby, C.B., Song, F., Yang, X., 2019. Are "left-behind" Children Really Left Behind? A Lab-in-Field Experiment Concerning the Impact of Rural/Urban Status and Parental Migration on Children's Other-Regarding Preferences. Unpublished manuscript.

Carlsson, F., He, H., Martinsson, P., Qin, P., Sutter, M., 2012. Household decision making in rural China: using experiments to estimate the influence of spouses. J. Econ. Behav. Organ. 84, 525–536.

Chang, H., Dong, X., MacPhail, F., 2011. Labor migration and time use patterns of the left behind children and elderly in rural China. World Dev. 39, 2199–2210.

Cunha, F., Heckman, J.J., Lochner, L., Masterov, D.V., 2006. Interpreting the evidence on life cycle skill formation. In: Hanushek, E., Welch, F. (Eds.), Handbook of the Economics of Education. vol. 1. Elsevier, pp. 697–812.

Eckel, C.C., Grossman, P.J., 2008. Forecasting risk attitudes: an experimental study using actual and forecast gamble choices. J. Econ. Behav. Organ. 68, 1–17.

Eisenberg, N., Fabes, R.A., 1998. Prosocial development. In: Eisenberg, N. (Ed.), Handbook of Child Psychology. vol. 3. John Wiley & Sons Inc, pp. 701–778.

Eisenberg, N., Spinrad, T.L., Sadovsky, A., 2006. Empathy-related responding in children. In: Killen, M., Smetana, J. (Eds.), Handbook of Moral Development. Lawrence Erlbaum, Mahwah, NJ, pp. 517–549.

Engle-Warnick, J., Escobal, J., Laszlo, S., 2009. How do additional alternatives affect individual choice under uncertainty? Can. J. Econ. 42, 113–140.

Engle-Warnick, J., Escobal, J., Laszlo, S., 2011. Ambiguity aversion and portfolio choice in small-scale Peruvian farming. B.E. J. Econ. Anal. Policy 11. Article 68.

Fan, F., Su, L., Gill, M.K., Birmaher, B., 2010. Emotional and behavioral problems of Chinese left-behind children: a preliminary study. Soc. Psychiatry Psychiatr. Epidemiol. 45 (6), 655–664.

Fei, X., 1992. From the Soil: The Foundations of Chinese Society. A translation of Fei Xiaotong's Xiangtu Zhongguo. University of California Press.

Fischbacher, U., Föllmi-Heusi, F., 2013. Lies in disguise: an experimental study on cheating. J. Eur. Econ. Assoc. 11 (3), 525–547.

Gino, F., Ariely, D., 2012. The dark side of creativity: original thinkers can be more dishonest. J. Pers. Soc. Psychol. 102, 445–459.

Glatzle-Rutzler, D., Lergetporer, P., 2015. Lying and age: an experimental study. J. Econ. Psychol. 46, 12–25.

Hao, L., Houser, D., Mao, L., Villeval, M., 2016. Migrations, risks, and uncertainty: a field experiment in China. J. Econ. Behav. Organ. 131, 126–140.

Heyman, G.D., Zhao, L., Compton, B., Lee, K., 2019. Dishonesty in Young Children. In: Bucciol, A., Montinari, N. (Eds.), Dishonesty in Behavioral Economics. Elsevier.

Houser, D., Vetter, S., Winter, J., 2012. Fairness and cheating. Eur. Econ. Rev. 56 (8), 1645–1655.

Hu, F., Li, S., 2009. Effect of parental migration on academic performance among left behind children in rural China. Manage. World 2, 67–74. In Chinese.

Hu, H., Lu, S., Huang, C., 2014. The psychological and behavioral outcomes of migrant and left-behind children in China. Child Youth Serv. Rev. 46, 1–10.

Koenig, A., Cicchetti, D., Rogosch, F., 2004. Moral development: the association between maltreatment and young children's prosocial behaviors and moral transgressions. Soc. Dev. 13, 87–106.

Li, D., Wen, Y., 2009. Educational well-being of rural children left behind. Educ. Meas. Eval. 4, 32–35. In Chinese.

Li, X., Yuan, J., Gao, W., Luo, J., Du, Y., 2010. Research on negative emotions, behavior, personal relationship caused by left-behind experience of rural children after growing up. Chin. J. Health Psychol. 18, 92–94. In Chinese.

Liang, Z., Ma, Z., 2004. China's floating population: new evidence from the 2000 census. Popul. Dev. Rev. 30, 467–488.

Liu, Z., Li, X., Ge, X., 2009. Left too early: the effects of age at separation from parents on Chinese rural children's symptoms of anxiety and depression. Am. J. Public Health 99 (11), 2049–2054.

Lu, M., Xia, Y., 2016. Migration in the People's Republic of China. Asian Development Bank Institute Working Paper 593.

Luo, J., Peng, X., Zong, R., Yao, K., Hu, R., Du, Q., Fang, J., Zhu, M., 2008. The status of care and nutrition of 774 left-behind children in rural areas in China. Public Health Rep. 123, 382–389.
Maccoby, E.E., 1992. The role of parents in the socialization of children: an historical overview. Dev. Psychol. 28, 1006–1017.
Maggian, V., Villeval, M.C., 2016. Social preferences and lying aversion in children. Exp. Econ. 19, 663–685.
Malti, T., Gummerum, M., Keller, M., Chaparro, M.P., Buchmann, M., 2012. Early sympathy and social acceptance predict the development of sharing in children. PLoS One 7 (12), e52017.
Mazar, N., Amir, O., Ariely, D., 2008. The dishonesty of honest people: a theory of self-concept maintenance. J. Mark. Res. 45 (6), 633–644.
National Bureau of Statistics of China, 2013. Annual Report of Monitoring Survey on National Rural-Urban Migrant Workers. China Statistical Press, Beijing.
Piaget, J., 1965. The Moral Judgment of the Child. The Free Press, New York.
Raven, J., Raven, J.C., Court, J.H., 2004. Manual for Raven's Progressive Matrices and Vocabulary Scales. Harcourt Assessment, San Antonio, TX.
Rotter, J., 1966. Generalized expectancies for internal versus external control of reinforcement. Psychol. Monogr. 80 (1), 1–28.
Rubin, R., Hubbard, J., 2003. Children's verbalizations and cheating behavior during game playing: the role of sociometric status, aggression and gender. J. Abnorm. Child Psychol. 31, 65–78.
Ryan, R.M., Deci, E.L., Grolnick, W.S., 1995. Autonomy, relatedness, and the self: their relation to development and psychopathology. In: Cicchetti, D., Cohen, D.J. (Eds.), Developmental Psychopathology. Theory and methods, vol. 1. John Wiley & Sons, New York, pp. 618–655.
Shalvi, S., Leiser, D., 2013. Moral firmness. J. Econ. Behav. Organ. 93, 400–407.
Shalvi, S., Dana, J., Handgraaf, M., DeDreu, C., 2011. Justified ethicality: observing desired counterfactuals modifies ethical perceptions and behavior. Organ. Behav. Hum. Decis. Process. 115, 181–190.
Shalvi, S., Eldar, O., Bereby, Y., 2012. Honesty requires time (and lack of justifications). Psychol. Sci. 23, 1264–1270.
Shi, Y., Zhang, L., Ma, Y., Yi, H., Liu, C., Johnson, N., Chu, J., Loyalka, P., Rozelle, S., 2015. Dropout in rural China's secondary schools: a mixed methods analysis. China Q. 224, 1048–1069.
Song, Y., Zhang, Y., 2009. Parental migration, child health, and healthcare services utilization in rural China. J. Popul. Res. 133, 57–65. In Chinese.
Sun, Z., 2004. The effect of farmer's cross-provincial work on regional economic development. Chin. Rural Econ. 3, 28–33.
Sylvia, S., Luo, R., Zhang, L., Shi, Y., Medina, A., Rozelle, S., 2013. Do you get what you pay for with school-based health programs? Evidence from a child nutrition experiment in rural China. Econ. Educ. Rev. 37, 1–12.
Talwar, V., Lee, K., 2008. Social and cognitive correlates of children's lying behavior. Child Dev. 79 (4), 866–881.
Talwar, V., Gordon, H.M., Lee, K., 2007. Lying in the elementary school: verbal deception and its relation to second-order belief understanding. Dev. Psychol. 43 (3), 804–810.
Tao, X., Guan, H., Zhao, Y., Fan, Z., 2013. Mental health among left-behind preschool-age children: preliminary survey of its status and associated risk factors in rural China. J. Int. Med. Res. 42, 1–10.
The Economist, 2015. Pity the Children: China's Left-Behind Generation. October 17, 2015, http://www.economist.com/news/briefing/21674712-children-bear-disproportionate-share-hidden-cost-chinas-growth-little-match-children.
Wang, H., Yang, C., He, F., Shi, Y., Qu, Q., Rozelle, S., Chu, J., 2015. Mental health and dropout behavior: a cross-sectional study of junior high students in northwest rural China. Int. J. Educ. Dev. 41, 1–12.

Warneken, F., Tomasello, M., 2006. Altruistic helping in human infants and young chimpanzees. Science 311, 1301–1303.

Wen, M., Wang, G., 2009. Demographic, psychological, and social environmental factors of loneliness and satisfaction among rural-to-urban migrants in Shanghai, China. Int. J. Comp. Sociol. 50, 155–182.

Xu, H., Xie, Y., 2015. The causal effects of rural-to-urban migration on children's wellbeing in China. Eur. Sociol. Rev. 31, 512–519.

Xu, F., Bao, X., Genyue, F., Talwar, V., Lee, K., 2010. Lying and truth-telling in children: from concept to action. Child Dev. 81 (2), 581–596.

Ye, J., Wang, Y., Zhang, K., Lu, J., 2006. Effect of parental migration on academic performance among rural left behind children. Rural Econ. 7, 119–123. In Chinese.

Zhang, H., Behrman, J., Fan, C., Wei, X., Zhang, J., 2014a. Does parental absence reduce cognitive achievements? Evidence from rural China. J. Dev. Econ. 111, 181–195.

Zhang, X., Li, S., Liu, C., Zhang, L., 2014b. Effect of migration on children's self-esteem in rural China. Chin. World. Econ. 22, 83–101.

Zhao, Q., Yu, X., Wang, X., Glauben, T., 2014. The impact of parental migration on children's school performance in rural China. China Econ. Rev. 31, 43–54.

Zhou, M., Murphy, R., Tao, R., 2014. Effects of parents' migration on the education of children left behind in rural China. Popul. Dev. Rev. 40, 273–292.

Zhou, C., Sylvia, S., Zhang, L., Luo, R., Yi, H., Liu, C., Shi, Y., Loyalka, P., Chu, J., Medina, A., Rozelle, S., 2015. China's left-behind children: impact of parental migration on health, nutrition, and educational outcomes. Health Aff. 34, 1964–1971.

Chapter 2.3

# What does a young cheater look like? An innovative approach

Pietro Battiston[1], Simona Gamba[2], Valentina Rotondi[3]
[1]*University of Milan-Bicocca, Milan, Italy,* [2]*University of Verona, Verona, Italy,* [3]*Bocconi University, Milan, Italy*

**Chapter Outline**



**JEL Classification:** C90, D91

## 1. Introduction

Personality traits matter. We could summarize with these simple words a vast literature in social sciences dedicated to explaining the behavior of individuals, acting alone or within societies. Examples abound in several economic contexts spanning from the intention to become a social entrepreneur (Nga and Shamuganathan, 2010), to management of household finances (Brown and Taylor, 2014), to labor market outcomes (Fletcher, 2013). Similarly vast is the literature on cheating, justified by the profound economic and social consequences of such behavior.

In this chapter, we link these two growing strands of literature by studying the relation between experimental measures of cheating behavior among adolescents and personality measures obtained through a questionnaire.

The first consistent finding from the experimental literature on cheating is that some (not all) individuals are dishonest, i.e., when facing the opportunity to lie in order to extract a gain (with the lie typically concerning the result of a dice roll, or a fair coin toss), a sizable share of individual do so: that is, the proportion of individuals reporting a win usually exceeds the objective probability of a win, while still being smaller (often considerably smaller) than one (Abeler et al., 2018). This general result overshadows, however, a huge heterogeneity in

**Dishonesty in Behavioral Economics. https://doi.org/10.1016/B978-0-12-815857-9.00006-6**

the observed individual cheating behavior. Most individuals are willing to cheat only a little (Shalvi et al., 2011), some entirely refrain from lying, while others lie to the maximum possible extent (Fischbacher and Föllmi-Heusi, 2013). This observed heterogeneity, coupled with the fact that individuals who cheat in the lab tend to cheat also in the field (Cohn and Maréchal, 2016), raises the question of which characteristics of an individual's personality influence her decision to lie.

As a precondition for any discussion, we all know that people care about their self-image and struggle to preserve it (Mazar et al., 2008). This struggle imposes a cost, of psychological nature, to the cheater, which changes according to the context. As a matter of example, we know that the decision to lie implies a different psychological cost when people have to report their immoral intentions before acting (Jiang, 2013), when acting dishonestly hurts (or benefit) others (e.g., Fischbacher and Föllmi-Heusi, 2013), when temporally distancing the decision task from the payment of the reward (Ruffle and Tobol, 2014), when individuals are under scrutiny (Ostermaier and Uhl, 2017; Pierce et al., 2015), when they act alone or in groups (Kocher et al., 2018), and when they have a potential accomplice (Barr and Michailidou, 2017).

Only recently some papers have considered the importance of personality traits in cheating behavior. In a recent contribution, Pfattheicher et al. (2018) use economically incentivized cheating paradigms (a dice-rolling paradigm and a coin-toss paradigm) to show that, in line with previous literature (Hilbig and Zettler, 2015; Kleinlogel et al., 2018), the basic personality trait of Honesty-Humility from the HEXACO personality model (Ashton and Lee, 2007) is negatively related to cheating behavior. That is, they identify a relation between cheating and personality which goes beyond the dark personality traits of narcissism, Machiavellianism, psychopathy, and sadism already studied by Jones and Paulhus (2017)—no effect is found instead when a third-party scrutiny is simulated by presenting the subjects with stylized watching eyes. Interestingly, personality traits have different effects on different types of lies. Jonason et al. (2014) show that while Machiavellianism is related to white lies, narcissism is related to lying for self-gain, whereas psychopathy is related to telling lies for no reason. In a companion paper, Baughman et al. (2014) show that psychopathy predicts scholastic cheating. In another recently published paper, Heck et al. (2018) address the question of power and sample size by exploiting the richness of 16 studies ($N=5002$), assessing dishonest behavior in an incentivized, one-shot, cheating paradigm. While confirming the negative correlation between cheating and Honesty-Humility, which was independent of other personality, situational, or demographic variables, they found that one other trait only from the "Big Five" (Agreeableness) was (negatively) associated with unethical decision-making, although the strength of the relation is much lower than with the Honesty-Humility trait.

Although cheating, lying, and deception are diffused behaviors both in the adult and in the young population, there is relatively limited evidence of the determinants of cheating among children and adolescents in the economic literature. Some relevant exceptions are Bucciol and Piovesan (2011), Glätzle-Rützler and Lergetporer (2015), Maggian and Villeval (2016), Korbel (2017), Battiston et al. (2018), Cadsby et al. (2019); see Heyman et al. (2019) for a recent review of this stream of research.

In this chapter we use data gathered from an experiment conducted with scout groups from Trentino-Alto Adige, a region in Northern Italy, during their summer camps in August 2017. The experiment, employing a revised version of the fair coin toss paradigm proposed by Bucciol and Piovesan (2011), was followed by a rich questionnaire including, beyond standard demographic questions, a detailed self-assessment of risk aversion, "Big Five" personality traits, level of trust in other people and propensity to break the rules. In our empirical analysis, we employ a principal component analysis (PCA, henceforth), a dimensionality reduction technique aimed at capturing common moments in the data, to gauge the extent to which different personality traits might influence the propensity to cheat. We then reanalyze the decision to cheat by using decision tree classifiers, a very popular technique in the machine learning literature, which also achieve the aim of dimensionality reduction, but focusing on the interaction between variables rather than on (linear) common moments across them.

Our results suggest that, while risk propensity is not a strong overall predictor of cheating behavior, self-confidence is irrespectively of the beneficiary of the payment being the individual or the patrol. The use of decision tree classifiers confirms these results, supports the validity of the PCA approach, and further suggests that, *among less self-confident subjects*, risk propensity does explain a larger propensity to cheat.

The remainder of this chapter is organized as follows: Section 2 presents the data gathered from the experiment, Section 3 presents the empirical analysis, while Section 4 concludes.

## 2. Experimental framework

We base our analysis on an experiment run in August 2017, during the summer camps of six scout troops from Trentino-Alto Adige, a region in Northeastern Italy. All groups were member of AGESCI, a Catholic association that includes the vast majority of scouts in Italy. The general mission of scouting is to contribute to the education of young people, through a value system, and methods, that are shared by all scouts around the world. All members of the Scout Movement are required to adhere to the Scout Promise and Scout Law. The Scout Law emphasizes the importance of honesty and loyalty: the decision to cheat in our experiment can be particularly salient. During the year, members of a same scout troop carry out together multiple activities, culminating in the summer camp; hence, the troop itself is akin to a society, with its rules, values, roles, and objectives. Each troop in turn is subdivided in multiple patrols, members of whom collaborate even more closely.

Our experiment involved a gender-balanced population of 160 young scouts, aged 12–16, all from the same region. They were regrouped in 31 patrols, in turn forming 6 troops, each taking part in one experimental session. We study the results from a detailed end of experiment questionnaire and from the experiment itself, a modified version of the coin task proposed by Bucciol and Piovesan (2011). The basic experimental task consists in each subject randomly drawing, from an envelope, a piece of paper where either the amount "€0" or "€10" is printed, entering a tent, and writing on a separate ticket the amount read. Such ticket would determine the payoff for the participant. In our experiment, each individual would in fact make *two* of such decisions, independently and simultaneously, by picking and transcribing two different pieces of papers, identified by different colors. The only difference was that in one case (yellow) total secrecy was guaranteed as to their extracted value, while in the other case (blue) any cheating behavior would have been observed ex post by *patrol members*, in a subsequent phase in which subjects would reenter the tent by patrols. The entire procedure was explained to participants in advance, including the fact that actual payoffs, distributed in the form of vouchers at the end of the session, would depend from one only of the two experimental tasks (total secrecy or ex-post patrol scrutiny), to be randomly determined, after the experiment, via a coin toss. While one participant was carrying out the activity, other troop members were involved in traditional scout games and songs. After the experimental session was over,[a] participants were asked to scatter through the camp area and individually fill a paper-and-pencil questionnaire.[b]

Our statistical analysis is based on comparing the share of respondents reporting "€10" against a binomial distribution. Indeed, the experiment was designed in order to ensure that experimenters could not detect individual cheating (pieces of paper reporting the numbers drawn were put in a bin to be burned after the experiment): we cannot know whether an individual who reported "€10" has cheated or was lucky. Hence, given our interest in the propensity to cheat at the individual level, we attenuate the inherent noise in the outcome variables by analyzing the *mean* of the two responses (the one under total secrecy and the one subject to ex post patrol scrutiny), with its value normalized to 0 (having reported "€0" in both cases), 0.5 (having reported "€0" in one of the two cases), or 1 (having reported "€10" in both cases).[c] This increases the power of our analysis, as the probability for a noncheater to report the best possible outcome ("€10" twice) is 0.25, rather than 0.5—or in other terms, the likelihood of a subject reporting "€10" being noncheater is 0.25, rather than 0.5.

---

a. The session involved another experiment, taking place after the one studied in this chapter. Participants knew beforehand they would participate in two experiments, but the second was described only once the first was over.

b. See Battiston et al. (2018) for a more detailed description of experimental procedures.

c. The reported outcome under secrecy is missing for five subjects: for them, the "mean" only includes the reported outcome under ex post patrol scrutiny.

Importantly, in three randomly drawn sessions/troops, subjects had earnings paid with individual vouchers, as is standard in the experimental literature on cheating, while in the other three sessions/troops, payments were cumulated at the patrol level and paid with collective vouchers (in a between-individual treatment). In both cases, vouchers were to be spent at the local scouting store, selling both goods for private, individual use (e.g., backpacks, uniforms, sleeping bags) or goods for public, collective use (e.g., tents, pots, and other team equipments). Battiston et al. (2018) have already shown that this treatment has no discernible effect: in what follows, we pool the results from all six sessions unless specified otherwise.

Answers from the questionnaire (see the Appendix) cover socio-demographic information (gender, age, whether any of the parents was born outside Italy, household size) as well as several individual characteristics that could affect the propensity to cheat, regrouped in four main categories:

1. Trust in other people, with questions adapted from the 2008 European Value Survey, including
   - a general Yes/No question about trust in other people, and
   - five more detailed questions specifying the recipients of trust (e.g., people in general vs member of one's troop/patrol) and admitting responses ranging from 0 to 10, where larger values denote higher levels of trust.[d] The choice to include detailed questions specifying the recipients of trust derives from the fact that the literature on trust and misbehavior generally finds a differential effect of *general* trust, i.e., trust toward unknown members of the society, vs *particular* trust. While confidence in unknown others is widely recognized as an essential component of positive social capital, since it leads to widespread cooperation (Putnam, 2001) with a resulting positive effect in terms of social and economic development (e.g., Adhikari and Goldey, 2010), confidence *only* in known people is usually conducive to negative social capital (Banfield, 1958) and it can constitute a burden in terms of economic development. As a matter of example, particular trust has been shown to be conducive to corruption (Uslaner, 2004), while high levels of interpersonal trust have been found to reduce corruption (Bjørnskov, 2006);
2. Propensity to break the rules to improve the condition of other individuals, depending on their identity (e.g., family member, patrol members, or people met for the first time), measured from 1 (*low propensity*) to 4 (*high propensity*)[e];

d. In what follows we consider as "trust_takeadv" the *complement to 10* of the answer to the question "how much do you agree that most people would try to take advantage of you if they had the chance?", for which larger values denoted *lower* trust.

e. Notice that, for ease of exposition, we analyze the *complement to 5* of answers to the questions reported in the Appendix. Hence, larger values correspond to a larger propensity to break the rules.

3. Personality traits, investigated through a revised Italian version of the Ten-Item Personality Inventory (Chiorri et al., 2015). For each of the "Big Five" traits (extraversion, agreeableness, conscientiousness, neuroticism, and openness to experience), two questions were proposed: one directly asking about the trait, and one asking about the counterpoised trait. Possible answers to each question range from 1 (*completely disagree*) to 7 (*completely agree*);
4. Risk propensity, measured with a reduced version of the Domain-Specific Risk-Taking (DOSPERT) Scale (Blais and Weber, 2006), including questions about risk attitudes in the recreational, financial, ethical, health, and social domains. We extracted out of the original questions two from each domain. The scale goes from 1 to 7, where 1 represents a low risk propensity and 7 a high risk propensity. Although we are aware of the fact that risk aversion can be more effectively measured through laboratory experiments, we preferred not to further complicate the experimental design and to introduce a possibility of hedging. We refer the reader to the existing literature on the correlation between experimental and questionnaire measures of risk aversion (e.g., Attanasi et al., 2018).

In total, we consider 38 variables extracted from the questionnaire: their list and descriptive statistics are provided in Table 1.

The winning rate is $\pi=0.541$: a one-sided *t*-test shows this is significantly higher ($p=0.067$) than the objective probability of extracting €10 ($\pi=0.5$). 25 individuals present at least one missing value for the variables of interest and are hence dropped from the subsequent analysis. We verify that the propensity to cheat for dropped individuals is not significantly different than for other individuals.

## 3. Analysis

Our data set includes a large number of variables, which are purposely strongly correlated among them. This is true for instance for the 10 questions concerning risk aversion, and for the pairs of questions concerning the "Big Five" personality traits.

Rather than basing our analysis on an arbitrary selection of variables and on ad-hoc independence assumptions, we run a PCA. We use this technique with the aim to reduce the dimensionality of the data while capturing common moments, defined by linear combinations of individual variables. Importantly, our variables can be seen as regrouped in clusters (risk, trust, …) but at the same time are of quite different nature from one cluster to another. That is, it is reasonable to expect that different components will correspond, at least approximately, to such clusters—while it is unlikely that a single component explains most of the variability. Identifying a reduced number of important components will then allow us to analyze how they shape the individual propensity to cheat.

**TABLE 1** Descriptive Statistics for Explanatory Variables Involved in the Analysis

| | Count | Mean | Std | Min | Median | Max |
|---|---|---|---|---|---|---|
| male | 158 | 0.513 | 0.501 | 0 | 1 | 1 |
| age | 158 | 14.316 | 1.216 | 12 | 14 | 16 |
| foreign | 160 | 0.069 | 0.254 | 0 | 0 | 1 |
| hhsize | 159 | 4.824 | 1.675 | 2 | 5 | 20 |
| trust | 158 | 0.620 | 0.487 | 0 | 1 | 1 |
| trust_general | 160 | 5.956 | 1.760 | 1 | 6 | 10 |
| trust_troop | 160 | 7.900 | 1.668 | 1 | 8 | 10 |
| trust_patrol | 160 | 8.681 | 1.623 | 2 | 9 | 10 |
| trust_helpful | 160 | 6.356 | 1.944 | 0 | 6 | 10 |
| trust_takeadv | 160 | 4.956 | 2.318 | 0 | 5 | 10 |
| rule_family | 159 | 3.660 | 0.645 | 1 | 4 | 4 |
| rule_neighbors | 160 | 2.181 | 0.816 | 1 | 2 | 4 |
| rule_known | 159 | 3.333 | 0.709 | 1 | 3 | 4 |
| rule_unknown | 157 | 1.911 | 0.779 | 1 | 2 | 4 |
| rule_oneself | 158 | 3.228 | 0.874 | 1 | 3 | 4 |

*(Continued)*

**TABLE 1** Descriptive Statistics for Explanatory Variables Involved in the Analysis—cont'd

| | Count | Mean | Std | Min | Median | Max |
|---|---|---|---|---|---|---|
| rule_oth_religion | 159 | 2.943 | 0.859 | 1 | 3 | 4 |
| rule_oth_nation | 159 | 3.075 | 0.776 | 1 | 3 | 4 |
| rule_patrol | 160 | 3.300 | 0.734 | 1 | 3 | 4 |
| personality_extroverted | 158 | 4.259 | 1.817 | 1 | 5 | 7 |
| personality_difficult | 156 | 3.269 | 1.739 | 1 | 3 | 7 |
| personality_trustworthy | 158 | 5.329 | 1.239 | 1 | 6 | 7 |
| personality_worried | 158 | 3.778 | 1.917 | 1 | 4 | 7 |
| personality_open | 159 | 5.503 | 1.466 | 1 | 6 | 7 |
| personality_reserved | 159 | 3.277 | 1.876 | 1 | 3 | 7 |
| personality_understanding | 158 | 5.177 | 1.426 | 1 | 5 | 7 |
| personality_disorganized | 158 | 3.722 | 1.777 | 1 | 4 | 7 |
| personality_calm | 157 | 4.599 | 1.454 | 1 | 5 | 7 |
| personality_traditionalist | 159 | 3.799 | 1.757 | 1 | 4 | 7 |
| risk_recreational_I | 159 | 3.541 | 1.824 | 1 | 4 | 7 |
| risk_financial_I | 156 | 3.455 | 1.546 | 1 | 4 | 7 |
| risk_financial_II | 159 | 1.950 | 1.504 | 1 | 1 | 7 |
| risk_ethical_I | 158 | 2.525 | 1.599 | 1 | 2 | 7 |

| | | | | | | |
|---|---|---|---|---|---|---|
| risk_health_I | 158 | 2.734 | 1.940 | 1 | 2 | 7 |
| risk_social_I | 157 | 4.261 | 1.614 | 1 | 4 | 7 |
| risk_recreational_II | 158 | 4.418 | 2.212 | 1 | 5 | 7 |
| risk_health_II | 159 | 4.057 | 1.887 | 1 | 4 | 7 |
| risk_social_II | 158 | 4.481 | 1.847 | 1 | 5 | 7 |
| risk_ethical_II | 158 | 3.095 | 2.006 | 1 | 3 | 7 |
| | | | | | | |

Of the 38 components returned by the PCA decomposition (same as the number of input variables, by design), 13 correspond to eigenvalues larger than 1—meaning that each of them explains more variability than the average individual variable—and 5 components correspond to eigenvalues larger than 2 (see Fig. 1). Given our goal of tracing back the cheating behavior to a limited number of easily interpretable individual traits, we focus on the latter five components—which together explain 38.24% of variance in the data.

We can interpret the main components by looking at their *loading factors* (presented in Table 2), that is, at the role of each input variable in their composition. The results of this analysis reflect the structure of the questionnaire, but at the same time provide interesting insights about the interrelation between variables. In particular, some clear features can be identified among the most important components.

- The section of the questionnaire concerning risk attitudes is quantitatively important (10 questions) and considers a relatively narrow aspect of personality—propensity to risk. Hence, it is not surprising that the first component is mostly related to *risk propensity*: risk variables all bear loading factors which are positive, and in some cases large. Nevertheless, the magnitude of the loading factors varies significantly, from 0.096 (risk_financial_II)[f] to 0.301 (risk_health_II).[g] Concerning personality, in Fig. 2, we can notice that

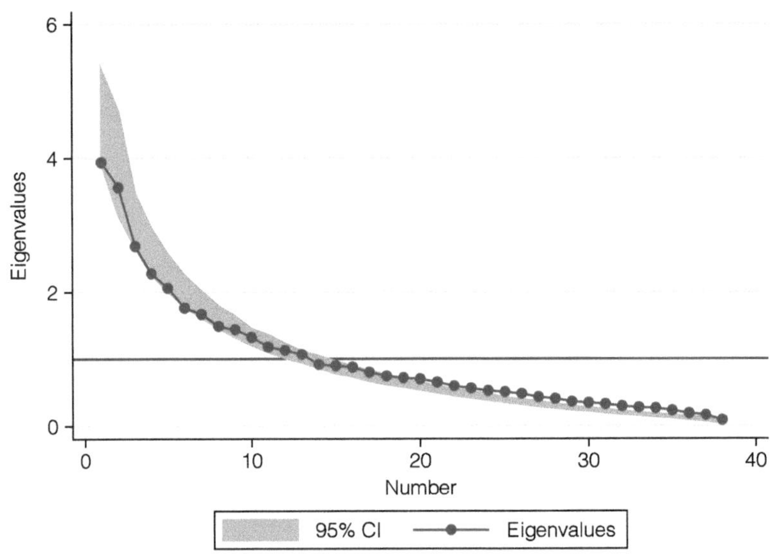


**FIG. 1** Scree plot of PCA components. *Note*: Each *dot* corresponds to a PCA component, ranked according to the corresponding eigenvalue. A larger eigenvalue denotes a higher explanatory power for the associated component. The *horizontal line* denotes the value of 1—the threshold value above which a component explains more than the average original variable. 13 components have an eigenvalue larger than 1, and 5 larger than 2.

f. Propensity to "Betting a day's income on the outcome of a sporting event".
g. Propensity to "Walking home alone at night in an unsafe area of town".

**TABLE 2** Loading Factors for Main PCA Components

| | Comp1 | Comp2 | Comp3 | Comp4 | Comp5 |
|---|---|---|---|---|---|
| male | 0.058 | −0.131 | 0.059 | −0.328 | −0.114 |
| foreign | 0.06 | −0.018 | −0.072 | 0.044 | −0.18 |
| age | 0.227 | −0.053 | 0.163 | −0.029 | −0.017 |
| hhsize | −0.023 | 0.081 | −0.043 | 0.161 | −0.077 |
| trust | −0.12 | 0.182 | 0.207 | 0.082 | 0.02 |
| trust_general | −0.086 | 0.238 | 0.269 | 0.091 | −0.055 |
| trust_troop | −0.145 | 0.281 | 0.264 | 0.023 | 0.017 |
| trust_patrol | −0.091 | 0.28 | 0.243 | −0.005 | −0.031 |
| trust_helpful | −0.107 | 0.224 | 0.249 | 0.013 | −0.008 |
| trust_takeadv | −0.191 | 0.16 | 0.116 | −0.031 | 0.01 |
| rule_family | 0.119 | 0.205 | −0.278 | −0.286 | −0.055 |
| rule_neighbors | −0.104 | 0.135 | −0.172 | 0.145 | −0.043 |
| rule_known | 0.147 | 0.341 | −0.23 | −0.1 | −0.004 |
| rule_unknown | 0.068 | 0.074 | −0.09 | 0.313 | 0.018 |
| rule_oneself | 0.192 | 0.154 | −0.242 | −0.18 | −0.019 |
| rule_oth_religion | 0.117 | 0.319 | −0.23 | 0.147 | 0.086 |

*(Continued)*

**TABLE 2** Loading Factors for Main PCA Components—cont'd

| | Comp1 | Comp2 | Comp3 | Comp4 | Comp5 |
|---|---|---|---|---|---|
| rule_oth_nation | 0.059 | 0.343 | −0.231 | 0.141 | −0.043 |
| rule_patrol | 0.155 | 0.287 | −0.197 | −0.003 | −0.162 |
| personality_extroverted | 0.183 | 0.079 | 0.263 | −0.014 | −0,022 |
| personality_difficult | 0.219 | −0.112 | −0.052 | 0.208 | 0.175 |
| personality_trustworthy | −0.103 | 0.068 | −0.067 | −0.032 | 0.54 |
| personality_worried | −0.101 | −0.068 | −0.074 | 0.396 | 0.02 |
| personality_open | 0.143 | 0.112 | 0.183 | −0.054 | 0.288 |
| personality_reserved | −0.091 | −0.136 | −0.214 | 0.305 | 0.068 |
| personality_understanding | −0.191 | 0.128 | −0.017 | 0.057 | 0.289 |
| personality_disorganized | 0.209 | −0.054 | 0.137 | 0.199 | −0.209 |
| personality_calm | −0.025 | 0.017 | −0.036 | −0.237 | 0.24 |
| personality_traditionalist | −0.105 | −0.15 | −0.122 | −0.097 | 0.286 |
| risk_recreational_I | 0.24 | 0.011 | 0.037 | −0.082 | 0.194 |
| risk_financial_I | 0.181 | 0.022 | 0.044 | 0.018 | 0.079 |
| risk_financial_II | 0.096 | 0.002 | 0.053 | 0.064 | −0.105 |

| | | | | | |
|---|---|---|---|---|---|
| risk_ethical_I | 0.11 | −0.027 | 0.021 | 0.276 | 0.046 |
| risk_health_I | 0.261 | −0.013 | 0.095 | 0.089 | −0.008 |
| risk_social_I | 0.178 | −0.021 | 0.091 | 0.215 | 0.305 |
| risk_recreational_II | 0.267 | 0.06 | 0.105 | −0.099 | 0.248 |
| risk_health_II | 0.301 | 0.026 | 0.143 | −0.002 | −0.096 |
| risk_social_II | 0.265 | 0.039 | 0.116 | 0.073 | 0.059 |
| risk_ethical_II | 0.215 | −0.186 | −0.08 | 0.014 | 0.015 |

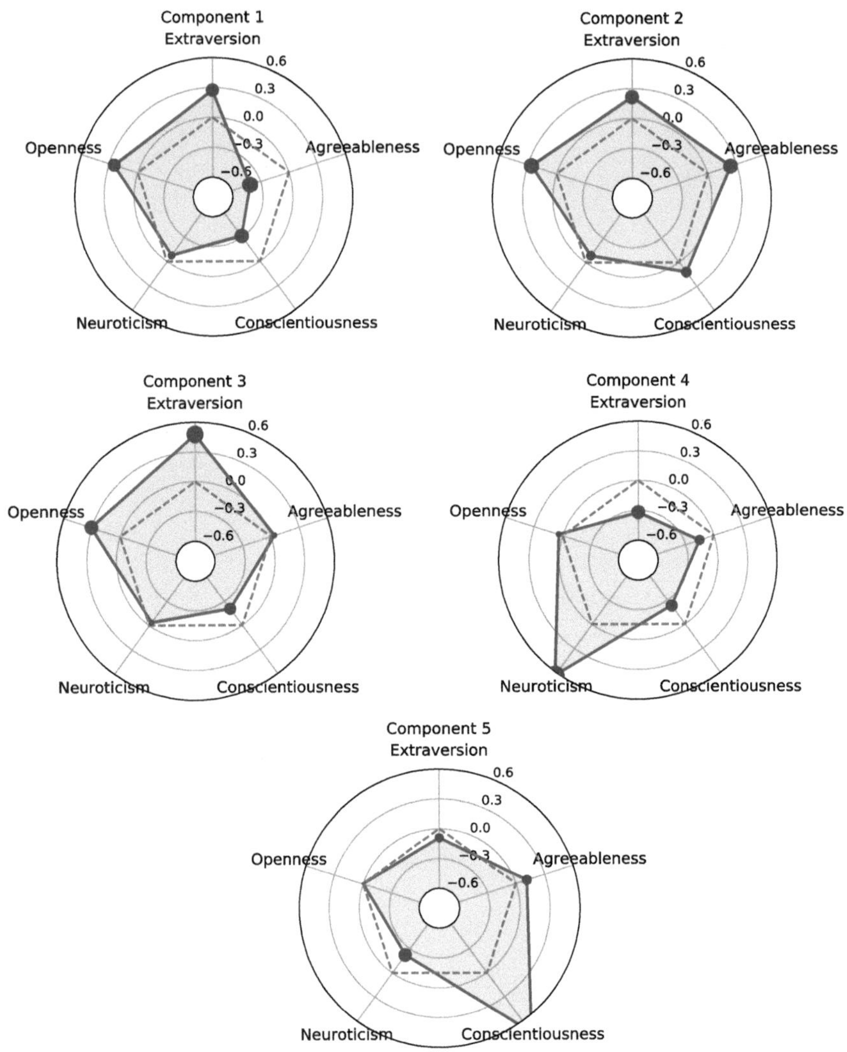


**FIG. 2** Summary of personality traits related to the first five PCA components. *Note*: Each "trait score" is calculated as the loading factor for one question of the "personality" section minus the loading factor for the opposed question (see Section 2 for details). *Dashed pentagons* indicate value 0 (expected location of *bullets* if, e.g., answers to personality questions were random); the size of *bullets* indicates absolute value of the trait score (i.e., their importance).

this first component is positively related to extraversion and openness, and negatively to conscientiousness and agreeableness, in accordance with the existing literature on the relationship between the Big Five and risk attitude (Nicholson et al., 2005) and with what the intuition would suggest for less risk averse individuals. No clear relation is found with the last of the Big

Five traits, that is, neuroticism (obtaining a score close to 0). Notice, indeed, that such score is the combination of two questionnaire items[h] which, while being conceived as counterpoised in the Ten-Item Personality Inventory (Chiorri et al., 2015), can be expected to have a similar, negative, relation to risk. In fact, this is, among the 10 personality questions, the only pair of questions which do *not* have opposite loading coefficients for the first component (−0.101 and −0.025, respectively). In addition, the attitude toward risk correlates positively with the propensity to break the rules, and negatively to the measures of trust. Consistently with the existing literature, it also correlates positively with being a male (although the absolute value of the loading factor is small) (Miller, 2011) and with age (Duell et al., 2018).

- If the first component was clearly related to the questionnaire section concerning risk, the second component prominently features variables from the section concerning trust and from the section concerning the propensity to break the rules: all loading factors for the related variables are positive, and most of them are larger than 0.2 (see Table 2).
- At a first sight, the fact that this second component relates positively both to measures of trust *and* to propensity to break the rules might seem odd—given that the two sections mostly had opposite signs in the first component. But this is instead a natural consequence of the fact that components of PCA analysis are *uncorrelated* (if they were not, their informational content would overlap, and their explanatory power would not be maximized). Hence, the second component is capturing the main feature of data which is *not explained* by the first component: namely, that, controlling for risk attitudes, subjects with higher levels of trust are more inclined to break the rules. Interestingly, the second plot in Fig. 2 shows that this component mostly correlates with *positive* traits: in fact, all pairs of personality-related variables have opposite signs, and the largest loading factor (in absolute value) is the −0.150 for "traditionalist, routine-bound." Thus, this component seems to capture a dimension of freedom and *self-confidence* which is orthogonal to risk aversion.
- While the third, fourth, and fifth components have significantly lower explanatory power, they are worth surveying as they are each strongly related to—almost dominated by—a different personality trait from the Big Five (see Fig. 2). Component 3 is related to extraversion, openness, and trust, denoting an *outwards* oriented personality. Component 4 is related to high levels of neuroticism, low extraversion and in general a *reserved* and anxious attitude, which seems to be more common among female subjects (see the coefficient of −0.328 for "male"). Component 5 is instead strongly related to conscientiousness, and in particular it presents a very large loading factor (0.540) for trustworthiness, signaling a *reliable* person. It is worth mentioning that only two of the five pairs of personality questions have

h. Being "Worried, anxious" (question 4) and being "calm, emotionally stable" (question 9).

matching signs, and that, among components considered so far, this is the one presenting the largest absolute value for the loading factor of "foreign" (−0.180): notice, however, from Table 1, that this variable is strongly unbalanced, taking value 1 for less than 7% of the sample.

Fig. 3 represents the loading factors for each variable for the first two components. It allows for an easy spatial characterization of the different realms covered by our questionnaire. Indeed, we can observe that, with the exception of the personality questions (which are meant to be strongly differentiated), each family of questions occupies a specific area of the plane. Variables from sections "trust" and "rule" are well identified in terms of each of the two main components; instead, "risk" variables, which form the backbone of component 1, *risk propensity*, are not strongly related to component 2, *self-confidence*: recall that the two components are orthogonal by design.

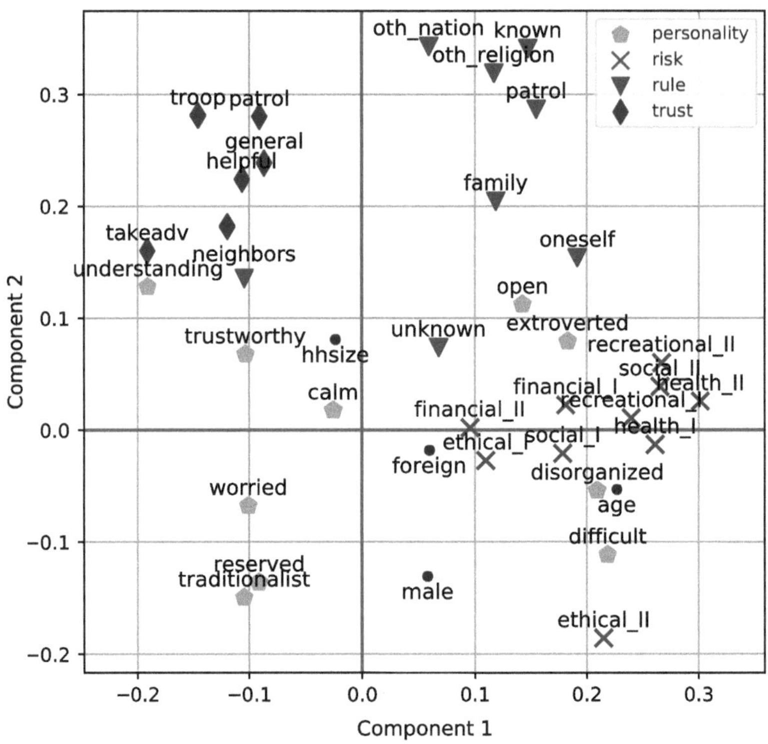


**FIG. 3** Factor loadings for the first two components. *Note*: *Graphic representation* of the first two columns from Table 2, characterizing the two main components. Each *marker* denotes 1 of the 38 original variables employed in the analysis, with the *shape* denoting the section of the questionnaire (according to the legend), and the *label* identifying the specific item. For instance, the *triangle* with label "oneself" denotes the loading factors for the "rule_oneself" variable. The *rhombus* without label refers to the simple ``trust" variable; simple dots correspond to the general demographic variables.

## 3.1 Linear analysis

Having identified the main components of the questionnaire data, we are left with a reduced number of variables which can explain a large share of the data variability, and which can be used to explain the propensity to cheat, by regressing the reported outcomes from the cheating experiment on the components themselves. Results are presented in Table 3, Column (1). Importantly, since components are uncorrelated by design, results are robust to the inclusion of further components. Similarly, results are qualitatively unchanged if only the

**TABLE 3** Results From PCA-Based Linear Specifications

| | (1) | (2) | (3) | (4) |
|---|---|---|---|---|
| | Full | Full | Individual | Patrol |
| pca1—risk propensity | 0.010 | 0.009 | 0.003 | 0.016 |
| | (0.011) | (0.012) | (0.020) | (0.013) |
| pca2—self-confidence | 0.038** | 0.037** | 0.048 | 0.033 |
| | (0.016) | (0.016) | (0.028) | (0.020) |
| pca3—outwards | 0.000 | 0.002 | −0.012 | 0.026 |
| | (0.018) | (0.017) | (0.027) | (0.026) |
| pca4—reserved | 0.003 | 0.006 | −0.000 | 0.009 |
| | (0.020) | (0.021) | (0.033) | (0.027) |
| pca5—reliable | 0.003 | 0.003 | 0.010 | −0.011 |
| | (0.022) | (0.023) | (0.028) | (0.035) |
| PatrolPayment | | −0.026 | | |
| | | (0.071) | | |
| _cons | 0.530*** | 0.543*** | 0.537*** | 0.509*** |
| | (0.034) | (0.033) | (0.033) | (0.062) |
| $R^2$ | 0.046 | 0.048 | 0.056 | 0.060 |
| $N$ | 135 | 135 | 66 | 69 |

*Note*: Clustered standard errors (at the patrol level) in *parentheses*. Columns (3) and (4) disaggregate the analysis based on the recipients of payments. $^{*}p<0.10$, $^{**}p<0.05$, $^{***}p<0.01$.

first two components—which are characterized by eigenvalues larger than 3—are included in the analysis.

Contrary to what one might expect, the first component, *risk propensity*, is not significant ($p=0.383$). This might seem even more surprising because, as already observed, seven out of eight questions concerning the propensity to break the rules have a positive loading factor for such component. However, we can observe that our experiment—as well as most experiments on cheating in the literature—did not involve any *uncertainty* regarding the probability of being observed by the experimenter or being punished. This can explain the apparent inconsistency of our results with those reported by Bucciol et al. (2013, 2019), who find, respectively, that bus passengers traveling without a valid ticket and students frequently cheating in written exams (contexts which involve a risk of being caught and sanctioned) are more risk tolerant. On the other hand, the propensity to break the rules takes a more central role in the second component, *self-confidence* (see Table 2), which is instead strongly significant ($p=0.027$). That is, once removing uncertainty from the decision-making context, a self-confident attitude is a crucial explanation of the propensity to cheat.

It is important to remember that participants were subject to a between-individual treatment that potentially shaped their decision to cheat: in three troops, payments were at the individual level, while in the remaining three troops, they were aggregated in a voucher assigned to each patrol (see Section 2). As already mentioned, this treatment did not affect the propensity to cheat. This is visible in Column (2) of Table 3: the coefficient for the "PatrolPayment" variable is not significant ($p=0.717$), while other coefficients are virtually unchanged—in particular, the second PCA component, *self-confidence*, is still strongly significant. We further control for a possible interaction between the treatment and the individual characteristics, i.e., for personality traits having different effects depending on the beneficiary of the lie, by running the analysis separately on sessions with individual payments (Columns (3)) and sessions with patrol payment (Column (4)). Although the significance of the second component disappears ($p=0.112$ and 0.116, respectively) due to the smaller sample sizes, we can see that both the sign and the magnitude of the coefficient are consistent with our previous results.

For completeness, Table 4 summarizes the results for several model specifications, in which the outcome is regressed on the constant and a single variable at a time. In line with results presented in Table 3, we find no relation between the propensity to cheat and our treatment variation (PatrolPayment). None of the personality variables is significant after adopting a Bonferroni correction,[i] confirming the important role of the PCA in identifying traits that explain the pro-

i. Multiple hypothesis testing can increase the probability of incorrect rejection of true null hypotheses (type I error). The Bonferroni correction neutralizes this risk by testing each hypothesis, for a given desired significance level $\alpha$, at a level of $\frac{\alpha}{m}$, where $m$ is the total number of hypotheses to be tested.

**TABLE 4 Results for Different Model Specifications**

| | Coeff | SE |
|---|---|---|
| male | −0.089 | (0.067) |
| foreign | −0.032 | (0.120) |
| age | −0.041 | (0.024) |
| hhsize | 0.020 | (0.013) |
| trust | −0.015 | (0.061) |
| trust_general | 0.023 | (0.017) |
| trust_troop | 0.020 | (0.021) |
| trust_patrol | 0.029 | (0.023) |
| trust_helpful | 0.002 | (0.016) |
| personality_extroverted | −0.008 | (0.014) |
| personality_difficult | −0.006 | (0.019) |
| personality_trustworthy | 0.007 | (0.026) |
| personality_worried | −0.012 | (0.017) |
| personality_open | 0.023 | (0.021) |
| personality_reserved | −0.029** | (0.013) |
| personality_understanding | 0.012 | (0.022) |
| personality_disorganized | −0.004 | (0.013) |
| personality_calm | 0.000 | (0.019) |
| personality_traditionalist | −0.020 | (0.021) |
| risk_recreational_I | 0.009 | (0.015) |
| risk_financial_I | 0.011 | (0.019) |
| risk_financial_II | 0.049** | (0.019) |
| risk_ethical_I | −0.001 | (0.018) |
| risk_health_I | 0.007 | (0.019) |
| risk_social_I | −0.002 | (0.016) |
| risk_recreational_II | 0.010 | (0.014) |
| risk_health_II | 0.018 | (0.013) |
| risk_social_II | 0.017 | (0.017) |

*(Continued)*

**TABLE 4** Results for Different Model Specifications—cont'd

| | Coeff | SE |
|---|---|---|
| risk_ethical_II | 0.006 | (0.014) |
| trust_takeadv | 0.020* | (0.010) |
| rule_family | 0.040 | (0.038) |
| rule_neighbors | 0.030 | (0.031) |
| rule_known | 0.053 | (0.035) |
| rule_unknown | 0.041 | (0.027) |
| rule_oneself | 0.047 | (0.031) |
| rule_oth_religion | 0.061* | (0.035) |
| rule_oth_nation | 0.048 | (0.046) |
| rule_patrol | 0.020 | (0.027) |
| PatrolPayment | −0.031 | (0.069) |

*Note*: Clustered standard errors (at the patrol level) in *parentheses* (no variable is significant after applying Bonferroni correction). $^{*}p<0.10$, $^{**}p<0.05$, $^{***}p<0.01$. Each regression is run on 135 observations.

pensity to cheat. More specifically, the PCA improves our analysis both because it allows the identification of traits which are the composition of different variables, and because thanks to the dimension reduction it alleviates the problem of multiple hypotheses testing. It might still worth noticing that variables for which the relation is significant (without Bonferroni correction) all have loading coefficients larger than 0.1 in PCA component 2, related to self-confidence, with the exception of "risk_financial_II," which is the risk variable presenting the lowest loading factor in the PCA component 1, related to risk aversion.

## 3.2 Nonlinear analysis

The analysis run so far focuses on the importance of single traits in explaining cheating behavior and accounts, through the PCA transformation, for the strong collinearity characterizing the original data. However, it does not explore the possible interaction effects between different variables. Indeed, given that PCA components are orthogonal among them, there is no obvious candidate interaction term which could be introduced in the analysis. At the same time, even limiting to the five main components, the possible interaction terms amount to 10, which would make a linear analysis difficult to interpret and prone to spurious results. In what follows, we therefore apply more flexible methods that allow us to predict cheating behavior in a theory-agnostic way, and to compare the results with what we found so far.

Decision tree classifiers are a very general technique which is extremely popular in the machine learning literature and practice, in particular, when the number of available features is large compared to the number of observations. Given a Boolean outcome variable—defining two *classes* within the sample—and a potentially large number of explanatory variables, a decision tree is built by splitting the sample according to the variable and threshold value that best separate the two classes, and by iterating the analysis on each of the two subsamples separately. In other terms, the sample is ultimately partitioned in a number of subsamples such that the *impurity* of each (typically identified with the Gini index of the outcome variable within the subsample) is minimized.

In a general sense, the decision tree technique also achieves dimensionality reduction, since it selects the variables that best explain the outcome. However, to the extent that PCA components capture actual traits of experiment participants more succinctly than original variables, the same should hold for their interaction effects; hence, ceteris paribus, a decision tree based on the PCA components, should outperform a decision tree based on the original variables.

Decision trees potentially allow for a very large number of degrees of freedom but, given the limited number of observations in our sample, in what follows we focus on trees including only two levels—i.e., three branching points. We safeguard against the risk of *over-fitting* by testing the out-of-sample prediction power of our models. To this aim, we implement a *cross-validation* procedure: we randomly split multiple times the population in two disjunct samples, using one sample to train the model (i.e., build the regression tree), and the other to validate it (i.e., predict the outcome variable). The prediction power of a model is then computed as the average fit over the different iterations.

Concerning the outcome variable, given our focus on *classification* of subjects, we refrain from recurring to the mean of the two individual decisions, as done in Section 3.1, since that results in a variable which can assume three values (0, 0.5, 1)—and considering them as mere categories would disregard the important fact that they are ordered. Hence, we include both reported outcomes of each individual separately. The potential pitfall related to this approach is that, to the extent that the two reported outcomes of each individual are correlated, using (a sample including) one of the two to predict the other introduces again a risk of over-fitting. We solve this problem by ensuring that, in the cross-validation procedure, the two samples never have individuals in common—that is, the random subsample selection is made at the individual, rather than at the observation, level.

A leave-one-out procedure (in which each individual in the sample is in turn removed from the training set and the rest of the sample is used to predict its outcome) returns a pseudo-$R^2$ of 0.544 when using the 38 original variables, and of 0.581 when using the five main PCA components.[j] Fig. 4 plots the results of

j. Consistently with the linear analysis above, in what follows we limit our analysis to the first 5 components.

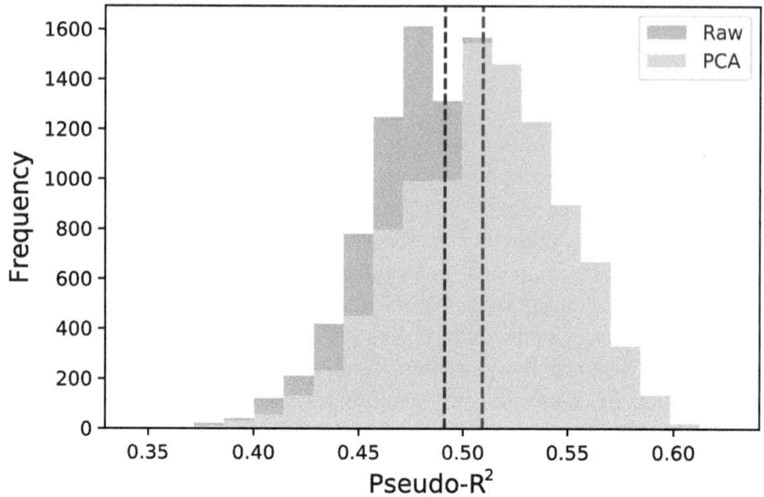


**FIG. 4** Distribution of pseudo-$R^2$ from depth 2 classification trees. *Note*: Results from 10,000 iterations of twofolds cross-validation. In order to guarantee balancedness of the samples, each pair (training sample, testing sample) was subsequently reversed and reused. Notice that the distribution is concentrated in a limited number of values, as the pseudo-$R^2$ is the result of the normalization of an integer number (the number of observations which were correctly classified).

10,000 iterations of twofolds cross-validation: the prediction based on the five main PCA components performs systematically better than the prediction based on the original variables ($p=0.000$ from a Mann–Whitney $U$ test).

Fig. 5 features the structures obtained when training the tree on the entire sample. The color of each node is related to the predicted value of the outcome variable, with blue and red denoting, respectively, more and less cheating. Each node is characterized by a Gini index, a sample size, and two values, indicating, respectively, the in-sample frequency of reporting "€0" and "€10," weighted so that the two classes have equal mass in the overall sample (root node). Finally, each branching (nonleaf) node reports, at the top, the variable and the threshold which determine the sample split between the two children nodes—i.e., the split which minimizes the Gini index of each subsample.

In the decision tree for PCA components (Fig. 5A), component 2, *self-confidence*, is placed in the root branch, consistently with its preeminence in the linear analysis presented above: as can be read in the two children nodes, we confirm results from Section 3.1 that more self-confident individuals (comp2 > 0.4865) tend to cheat more. This is a robust result, as it also happens in 65.6% of cases in the twofolds cross-validation exercise. The branching nodes at the second level also constitute the most common structure observed in the twofolds cross-validation. On the left, in the subsample of individuals with a relatively low self-confidence, we observe that those with lower *risk propensity* (comp1 ≤ 2.4033) tend to report "€10" less often than the risk lovers. On the right, in the subsample of more self-confident individuals, component 4,

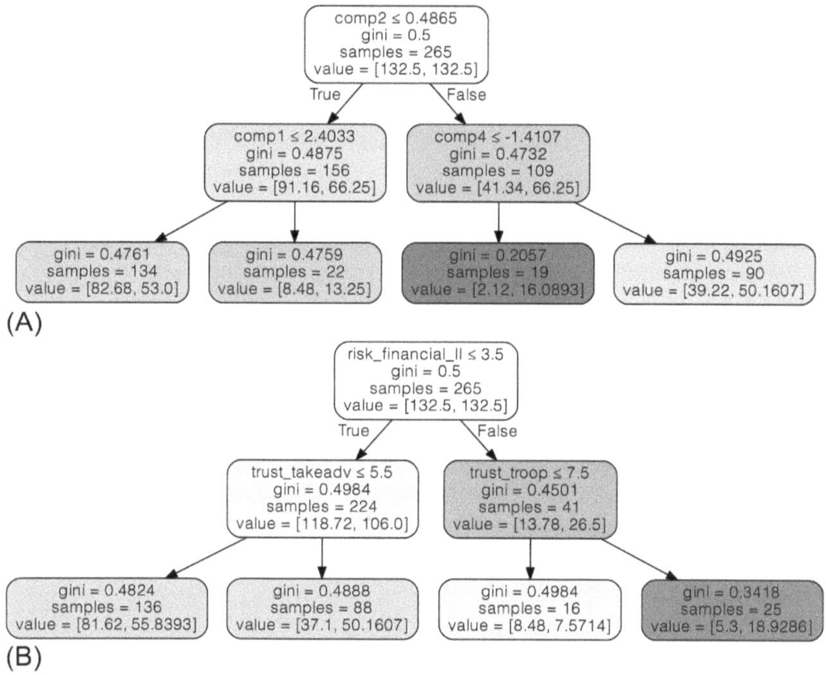


**FIG. 5** Depth 2 decision tree structure. *Note*: Decision trees trained on the entire sample, employing the five main PCA components (A) or original variables (B). Each branching node is identified by the condition that separates the two children nodes. In addition, each node reports the Gini index, size, and outcome frequencies for the subsample it represents. Frequencies are weighted in such a way as to have both outcomes (0 and 10) equally represented (in the root node), as unbalanced samples otherwise result in biased decision trees. This explains why the elements of "value" are not integer numbers.

*reserved*, determines the subsequent sample splitting. The fact that this is the most important component to be strongly related to gender (being more prominent for females) suggests that women (comp4 > 1.4107) tend to cheat less.

The decision trees for the original variables are not only less powerful predictors, but they are also much less stable. The structure featured in Fig. 5B is among the most frequently observed in the twofold cross-validation exercise, but there is a large variability—the variable "risk_financial_II" is the root tree in only 8.37% of cases. Nevertheless, it is instructive to observe once more that such variable is precisely the one, among questions related to risk, that had the *lowest* loading factor in the PCA component 1.

## 4. Conclusion

In this chapter we focus on the role played by personality traits in terms of cheating behavior.

We exploit data from a detailed questionnaire and a cheating experiment to study the determinants of cheating in adolescents aged 12–16. Through a PCA analysis, we identify the traits of participants that best summarize the data variability: we clearly identify a first component related to risk propensity and a second component related to self-confidence. We show that, differently from what one might expect, risk propensity is not a strong overall predictor of cheating behavior. Instead, self-confident subjects tend to cheat significantly more. Interestingly, the beneficiary of the payment (the individual or the patrol)—i.e., our between-individual treatment—does not affect the propensity to cheat, neither the role of different individual traits in explaining this propensity.

Through the use of decision tree classifiers we confirm results found in linear analysis that self-confidence (PCA component 2) is the driving predictor of the propensity to cheat. Looking at the subsequent level in the tree, we also see that, *among less self-confident subjects*, a specific measure of propensity toward risk does explain a larger propensity to cheat. We show that, in general, the PCA approach makes decision tree classifiers significantly more accurate and stable than when individual variables are used.

## Appendix. Questionnaire

Below is the translation from Italian of the questionnaire that participants answered at the end of the experimental session. Each question is accompanied by the label of the corresponding variable, in square brackets. Asterisks denote questions for which answers were rescaled or combined in the analysis—see main text for details.

- Assigned totem:
- Year of birth *[age]*
- Place of birth:
- Generally speaking, would you say that most people can be trusted or that you can't be too careful in dealing with people?
  □ Yes □ No (you can't be too careful) *[trust]*
  *[Each of the following six questions was followed by check boxes with numbers from 0 to 10]*
- From 0 to 10, how much do you tend to trust people in general? *[trust_general]*
- From 0 to 10, how much do you tend to trust members of your troop? *[trust_troop]*
- From 0 to 10, how much do you tend to trust members of your patrol?*[trust_patrol]*
- From 0 to 10, how much do you agree that most people would try to take advantage of you if they had the chance? *[trust_takeadv*]*
- From 0 to 10, how much do you agree that most of the time people try to be helpful? *[trust_helpful]*
- From 0 to 10, taking all things together, how happy would you say you are?
- Was your father born in Italy? □ Yes □ No *[foreign*]*

- Was your mother born in Italy? □ Yes □ No *[foreign*]*
- How many people are in your family, including you? *[hhsize]*
- For each of the following groups of people, how willing would you be to break the rules in order to improve their condition?

  *[Each of the following items was followed by check boxes with numbers from 1–4, where 1 was labeled as "very willing" and 4 as "definitely not willing"]*

  - Your family *[rule_family*]*
  - Your neighbors *[rule_neighbors*]*
  - Someone you know well *[rule_known*]*
  - Someone you meet for the first time *[rule_unknown*]*
  - Yourself *[rule_oneself*]*
  - Someone of a different religion than yours *[rule_oth_religion*]*
  - Someone of a different nationality than yours *[rule_oth_nation*]*
  - Your patrol *[rule_patrol*]*
- Please read the following personality traits and rate how well each pair of adjectives describes you. Even if you think that one characteristic describes you better than the other, using the following scale:

  *[A 7-item Likert scale was used. Each of the following items was followed by check boxes with numbers from 1 to 7.]*
  1. extroverted, exuberant *[personality_extroverted]*
  2. difficult, adversarial *[personality_difficult]*
  3. trustworthy, self-disciplined *[personality_trustworthy]*
  4. worried, anxious *[personality_worried]*
  5. open to new experiences, with many interests *[personality_open]*
  6. reserved, silent *[personality_reserved]*
  7. understanding, affectionate *[personality_understanding]*
  8. disorganized, absent-minded *[personality_disorganized]*
  9. calm, emotionally stable *[personality_calm]*
  10. traditionalist, routine-bound *[personality_traditionalist]*

- For each of the following statements, please indicate the likelihood that you would engage in the described activity or behavior if you were to find yourself in that situation. Provide a rating from Extremely Unlikely to Extremely Likely, using the following scale:
  *[A 7-item Likert scale was used. Each of the following items was followed by check boxes with numbers from 1 to 7. Labels in square brackets are provided for reference and did not appear in the printed questionnaire.]*
  1. Going down a ski run that is beyond your ability. *[risk_recreational_I]*
  2. Investing 10% of your annual income in a start-up. *[risk_financial_I]*
  3. Betting a day's income on the outcome of a sporting event. *[risk_financial_II]*
  4. Revealing a friend's secret to someone else. *[risk_ethical_I]*
  5. Riding a motorcycle without a helmet. *[risk_health_I]*

6. Speaking your mind about an unpopular issue in a patrol meeting. *[risk_social_I]*
7. Bungee jumping off a tall bridge. *[risk_recreational_II]*
8. Walking home alone at night in an unsafe area of town. *[risk_health_II]*
9. Moving to a city far away from your parents. *[risk_social_II]*
10. Not returning a wallet you found that contains €200. *[risk_ethical_II]*

## References

Abeler, J., Nosenzo, D., Raymond, C., 2018. Preferences for truth-telling. Econometrica . Forthcoming.

Adhikari, K.P., Goldey, P., 2010. Social capital and its downside: the impact on sustainability of induced community-based organizations in Nepal. World Dev. 38 (2), 184–194. Elsevier.

Ashton, M.C., Lee, K., 2007. Empirical, theoretical, and practical advantages of the Hexaco model of personality structure. Pers. Soc. Psychol. Rev. 11 (2), 150–166. Sage Publications Sage CA: Los Angeles, CA.

Attanasi, G., Georgantzís, N., Rotondi, V., Vigani, D., 2018. Lottery-and survey-based risk attitudes linked through a multichoice elicitation task. Theor. Decis. 84 (3), 341–372. Springer.

Banfield, E.C., 1958. The Moral Basis of a Backward Society. 3 Glencol, New York, p. 4.

Barr, A., Michailidou, G., 2017. Complicity without connection or communication. J. Econ. Behav. Organ. 142, 1–10. Elsevier.

Battiston, P., Gamba, S., Rizzolli, M., Rotondi, V., 2018. Lies have long legs. Cheating, Public Scrutiny and Loyalty in Teams." (Working Paper).

Baughman, H.M., Jonason, P.K., Lyons, M., Vernon, P.A., 2014. Liar liar pants on fire: cheater strategies linked to the dark triad. Personal. Individ. Differ. 71, 35–38. Elsevier.

Bjørnskov, C., 2006. The multiple facets of social capital. Eur. J. Polit. Econ. 22 (1), 22–40. Elsevier.

Blais, A.-R., Weber, E.U., 2006. A domain-specific risk-taking (DOSPERT) scale for adult populations. Judgm. Decis. Mak. 1 (1), 33–47.

Brown, S., Taylor, K., 2014. Household finances and the 'big five' personality traits. J. Econ. Psychol. 45, 197–212. Elsevier.

Bucciol, A., Piovesan, M., 2011. Luck or cheating? A field experiment on honesty with children. J. Econ. Psychol. 32 (1), 73–78. Elsevier.

Bucciol, A., Landini, F., Piovesan, M., 2013. Unethical behavior in the field: demographic characteristics and beliefs of the cheater. J. Econ. Behav. Organ. 93, 248–257.

Bucciol, A., Cicognani, S., Montinari, N., 2019. Cheating in academia: the relevance of social factors. In: Bucciol, A., Montinari, N. (Eds.), Dishonesty in Behavioral Economics.

Cadsby, B., Song, F., Yang, X., 2019. Dishonesty among children: a lab-In field experiment on the impact of rural/urban status and parental migration. In: Bucciol, A., Montinari, N. (Eds.), Dishonesty in Behavioral Economics. Elsevier.

Chiorri, C., Bracco, F., Piccinno, T., Modafferi, C., Battini, V., 2015. Psychometric properties of a revised version of the Ten Item Personality inventory. Eur. J. Psychol. Assess. 31, 109–119. Hogrefe Publishing.

Cohn, A., Maréchal, M.A., 2016. Laboratory measure of cheating predicts school misconduct. Econ. J. 128 (615), 2743–2754. Wiley Online Library.

Duell, N., Steinberg, L., Icenogle, G., Chein, J., Chaudhary, N., Di Giunta, L., Dodge, K.A., 2018. Age patterns in risk taking across the world. J. Youth Adolesc. 47 (5), 1052–1072. Springer.

Fischbacher, U., Föllmi-Heusi, F., 2013. Lies in disguise—an experimental study on cheating. J. Eur. Econ. Assoc. 11 (3), 525–547. Oxford University Press.

Fletcher, J.M., 2013. The effects of personality traits on adult labor market outcomes: evidence from siblings. J. Econ. Behav. Organ. 89, 122–135. Elsevier.

Glätzle-Rützler, D., Lergetporer, P., 2015. Lying and age: an experimental study. J. Econ. Psychol. 46, 12–25. Elsevier.

Heck, D.W., Thielmann, I., Moshagen, M., Hilbig, B.E., 2018. Who lies? A large-scale reanalysis linking basic personality traits to unethical decision making. Judgm. Decis. Mak. 13 (4), 356–371. Society for Judgment; Decision Making.

Heyman, G., Lee, K., Compton, B., Zhao, L., 2019. Dishonesty in young children. In: Bucciol, A., Montinari, N. (Eds.), Dishonesty in Behavioral Economics. Elsevier.

Hilbig, B.E., Zettler, I., 2015. When the Cat's away, some mice will play: a basic trait account of dishonest behavior. J. Res. Pers. 57, 72–88. Elsevier.

Jiang, T., 2013. Cheating in mind games: the subtlety of rules matters. J. Econ. Behav. Organ. 93, 328–336. Elsevier.

Jonason, P.K., Lyons, M., Baughman, H.M., Vernon, P.A., 2014. What a tangled web we weave: the dark triad traits and deception. Personal. Individ. Differ. 70, 117–119. Elsevier.

Jones, D.N., Paulhus, D.L., 2017. Duplicity among the dark triad: three faces of deceit. J. Pers. Soc. Psychol. 113 (2), 329. American Psychological Association.

Kleinlogel, E.P., Dietz, J., Antonakis, J., 2018. Lucky, competent, or just a cheat? Interactive effects of honesty-humility and moral cues on cheating behavior. Pers. Soc. Psychol. Bull. 44 (2), 158–172. SAGE Publications Sage CA: Los Angeles, CA.

Kocher, M.G., Schudy, S., Spantig, L., 2018. I lie? We lie! Why? Experimental evidence on a dishonesty shift in groups. Manag. Sci. 64 (9), 3995–4008. https://doi.org/10.1287/mnsc.2017.2800.

Korbel, V., 2017. Do we lie in groups? An experimental evidence. Appl. Econ. Lett. 24 (15), 1107–1111. Taylor & Francis.

Maggian, V., Villeval, M.C., 2016. Social preferences and lying aversion in children. Exp. Econ. 19 (3), 663–685. Springer.

Mazar, N., Amir, O., Ariely, D., 2008. The dishonesty of honest people: a theory of self-concept maintenance. J. Market. Res. 45 (6), 633–644. American Marketing Association.

Miller, G., 2011. The Mating Mind: How Sexual Choice Shaped the Evolution of Human Nature. Anchor Books, New York.

Nga, J.K.H., Shamuganathan, G., 2010. The influence of personality traits and demographic factors on social entrepreneurship start up intentions. J. Bus. Ethics 95 (2), 259–282. Springer.

Nicholson, N., Soane, E., Fenton-O'Creevy, M., Willman, P., 2005. Personality and domain-specific risk taking. J. Risk Res. 8 (2), 157–176. Routledge.

Ostermaier, A., Uhl, M., 2017. Spot on for liars! How public scrutiny influences ethical behavior. PloS One 12 (7), 1–11. Public Library of Science.

Pfattheicher, S., Schindler, S., Nockur, L., 2018. On the impact of honesty-humility and a cue of being watched on cheating behavior. J. Econ. Psychol. Forthcoming, Elsevier.

Pierce, L., Snow, D.C., McAfee, A., 2015. Cleaning house: the impact of information technology monitoring on employee theft and productivity. Manag. Sci. 61 (10), 2299–2319. INFORMS.

Putnam, R.D., 2001. Bowling Alone: The Collapse and Revival of American Community. Simon; Schuster.

Ruffle, B.J., Tobol, Y., 2014. Honest on mondays: honesty and the temporal separation between decisions and payoffs. Eur. Econ. Rev. 65, 126–135. Elsevier.

Shalvi, S., Handgraaf, M.J.J., De Dreu, C.K.W., 2011. Ethical manoeuvring: why people avoid both major and minor lies. Br. J. Manag. 22, S16–S27. Wiley Online Library.

Uslaner, E.M., 2004. Trust and corruption. In: Lambsdorff, J.G., Taube, M., Schramm, M. (Eds.), The New Institutional Economics of Corruption. Routledge, pp. 90–106.

Chapter 2.4

# Dishonesty among university students

Simona Cicognani
*Free University of Bozen, Bozen, Italy*

## Chapter Outline



**JEL Classification:** I21, D01

## 1. Introduction and related literature

Cheating carried out by students at university is a widespread and increasing phenomenon that calls for investigation. Recent studies provide alarming trends, both in frequencies and repertoire (Bernardi et al., 2008; Jones, 2011). Researchers' attention toward cheating at university is mainly driven by the relevance of the environment in which dishonest behavior takes place: an educational context. Colleges in fact represent the last suitable setting to form future leaders in our societies (McCabe et al., 2012). Moreover, it has been pointed out that cheating at university is positively correlated with cheating in future life events, such as workplace situations (Lovett-Hooper et al., 2007; Wowra, 2007). Therefore, not only cheating by university students undermines the credibility of academia in general, but also the quality of future professionals in leading positions, who may be more likely to spread unethical behavior in case they assimilated it during their educational years.

Yet, investigating university cheating committed by students is not an easy task: one has to rely on self-reported data, given that such dishonest behavior is difficult to detect. However, the anonymity of self-reported surveys may certainly help mitigating the underreporting of illicit behaviors by students (Kerkvliet, 1994).

The first contribution on cheating by university students dates back to Drake (1941) and is based on US colleges. Since then, many researchers over the

**Dishonesty in Behavioral Economics. https://doi.org/10.1016/B978-0-12-815857-9.00007-8**

years have been trying to detect the determinants of cheating among university students. Both cheating during exams and plagiarism have been analyzed, which makes comparisons of overall cheating magnitudes difficult to undertake. However, most existing studies report very high levels of dishonest student activity, with more than half of students having committed some form of cheating at least once during their university career (Jones, 2011).

Researchers showed the relevance of both individual vs contextual factors in shaping university cheating. The formers encompass specific students' characteristics, such as age, gender, GPA, discipline of study, and intrinsic motivation for studying, whereas the latter refer mainly to the institution or environment where cheating occurs (e.g., among others: the existence of an honor code at the university, probability of detection, professors' attitude and university climate, cheating inclination by other classmates). According to Björklund and Wenestam (1999), individual factors would be the most important drivers of cheating, whereas contextual factors may simply facilitate it.

The literature has thus far vastly neglected, among contextual factors, cultural and social factors that may affect the propensity of students to commit cheating, such as the degree of trust in others, the level of opportunism in society, or the belief of importance of merit in life. This is quite surprising given the importance of trust in educational outcomes and schooling (Yamamura, 2011). Two exceptions in this regard need to be mentioned. Neville (2012) uses Google state-level queries for term-paper mills and matches these with inequality at the state level. He finds a positive correlation between the level of dishonest searches on Google and income inequality in a specific State, advocating that a higher income inequality would trigger a lower level of trust toward others and therefore cheating would occur due to the belief that others are cheating and one needs to cheat as well in order to preserve one's own competitiveness in the educational context. Differently, Bucciol et al. (2017) employ data about self-reported cheating and trust at the individual level from a big sample of Italian university students and find a positive correlation between trust in others and cheating during written exams.

In this study, we build on Bucciol et al. (2017) by extending the analysis to a sample of mostly European universities.[a] We implemented an online non-incentivized survey, accessible over 9 consecutive months through an open link. The link was advertised on web platforms of students associations. In the survey we explicitly refer to "dishonesty" as "breaking the rules of conduct during a written exam." We opted for this form of cheating instead of plagiarism for multiple reasons: (i) it is easily identifiable for students and not subject to different interpretations by them; (ii) it is taken seriously by students and it is more salient for them that it entails something illicit with respect to the case of plagiarism (Björklund and Wenestam, 1999); (iii) it is applicable to any discipline, from humanities to STEM fields.

a. Respondents based in non-European universities account for 16% of observations.

Our main contribution is twofold. On the one hand, we implement a cross-cultural study of cheating at university controlling for important cultural and social factors, unlike previous cross-cultural studies. On the other hand, we investigate the degree of detection of cheating and the degree to which cheating has proven to be useful to the student, in getting for instance a higher grade or in passing the exam. This is important for shedding light on whether the student considers this practice to be beneficial for his career, or whether s/he commits it independently on the benefits accrued from it.

The remainder of the study is structured as follows: Section 2 describes the data collected and introduces some descriptive statistics; in Section 3 we describe the econometric techniques applied and present the results. Section 4 provides concluding remarks.

## 2. Data and summary statistics

The data set is based on a non-incentivized survey, accessible online through a link open to everybody who wanted to fill it in, during the period May 2017–January 2018. The diffusion of the link was implemented through student associations (operating mainly through Facebook groups) across Europe. Almost 700 individuals completed the survey. The data set cannot be considered as representative of the European university population. Therefore, we will be cautious in drawing general conclusions from the study, also due to the self-selection of subjects intrinsic in our methodology. However, the sample is quite diversified with respect to the location of universities. The bulk of observations come from Northern Europe (24%) and Central Europe (40%), with Southern and Eastern Europe summing up to 20%, and the Americas and the rest of the world to 16% (see Fig. 1).[b]

The survey questionnaire was in English and is reported in Appendix. At the very beginning of the survey, respondents could learn the purpose of the survey ("Our aim is to study the frequency of dishonest behavior at the University"). More specifically, we clearly referred to "dishonesty" as "breaking the rules of conduct during a written exam." The survey took approximately 5–10min to be completed, and it consisted of 32 questions, divided into different sections, regarding: (i) self-reported dishonest behavior; (ii) beliefs about others' dishonest behavior; (iii) suggestions to countervail dishonest practices at university and awareness about the sanctions; (iv) trust, merit, and risk attitudes; (v) demographics and social context.

b. University location of respondents is missing in 220 instances. Moreover, Italian observations are underrepresented due to the implementation of the same questionnaire in Italian during the same time period (see Bucciol et al., 2017). Since the questionnaire was posted on European student association web pages, it is reasonable to think that observations coming from outside Europe were exchange students temporarily based in European universities at the time of the survey.

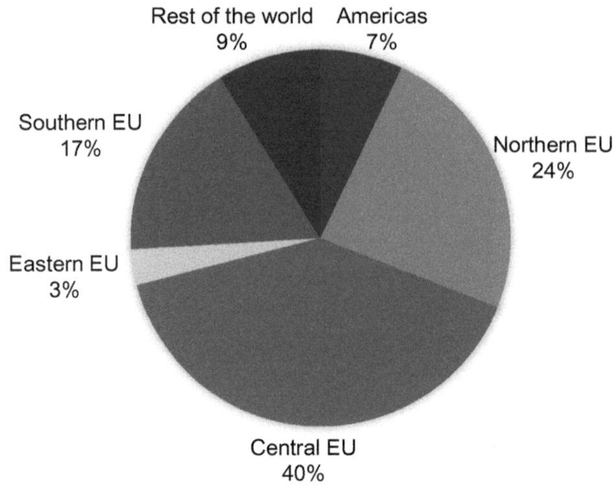


**FIG. 1** Distribution of universities locations.

In addition to diversification in the location of universities, we find quite an even distribution regarding our main dimension of interest, i.e., whether individuals behaved dishonestly during a written exam, and if so, how frequently (Q1 of the survey questionnaire). Fig. 2 displays the answers to this question: dishonesty in university written exams is a widespread circumstance, given that half of respondents report that they have cheated at least once. Among these, 37% have cheated once or twice, and 13% three times or more, and the remaining half report to have never cheated. This corroborates previous results discussed in Section 1. If we define "cheaters" as those respondents who have behaved dishonestly at least once during a written exam, the sample results as being split in two almost exact halves between cheaters and non-cheaters.

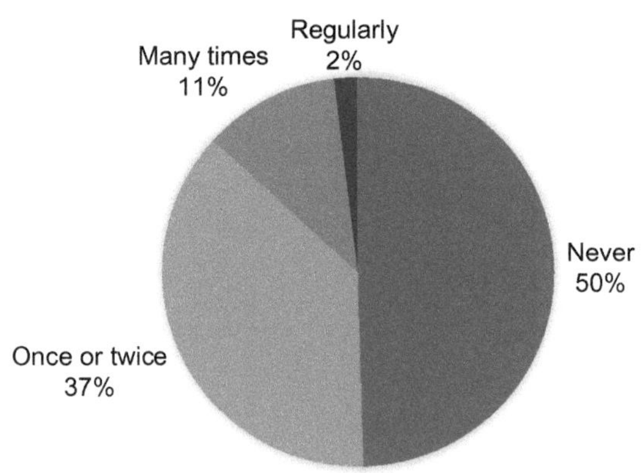


**FIG. 2** Frequency of dishonesty at exams.

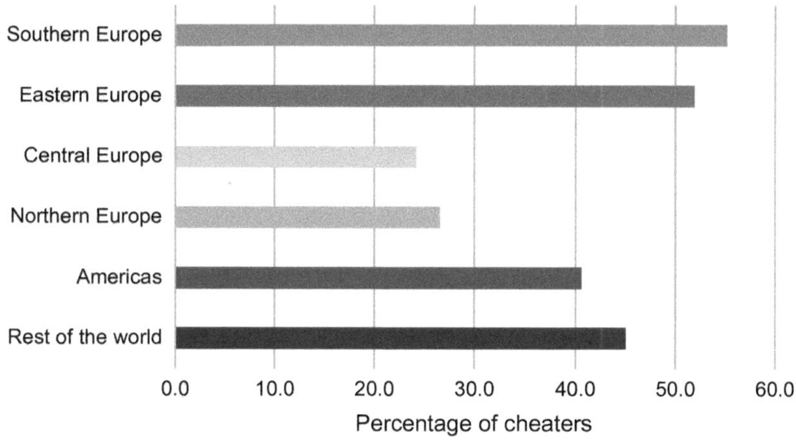


**FIG. 3** Frequency of dishonesty across geographical areas.

When we combine the definition of cheaters with the distribution of questionnaire responses across geographical areas, we find quite a heterogeneous distribution worldwide (Fig. 3). Respondents located in Southern and Eastern Europe universities exhibit the highest rates of self-reported cheating: beyond 50% of them report to have cheated at least once during their university career. In contrast, Central and Nordic European countries present rates of self-reported cheating which are about half with respect to their European counterparts, around 24% and 26%, respectively. This evidence is consistent with former cross-country studies, which show a robust higher pattern of cheating at university by Southern and Eastern European students (Miller et al., 2015; Teixeira and Rocha, 2010). Finally, the Americas locate themselves in between Southern-Eastern European countries and Northern-Central European countries in terms of self-reported cheating. A more technical analysis on the geographical determinants of cheating will be provided in Section 3, by including university location dummies in regression estimations.

In Table 1 we report the definition of the variables employed in the analysis, and in Table 2, descriptive statistics of the sample of respondents.

In addition to asking the frequency of cheating behavior as in Q1 explained above, we are interested in the ways in which dishonesty has been implemented. Building on answers to Q2, we construct two dummy variables to pinpoint two types of dishonest behavior: "ever interacted," which takes value 1 if the respondent behaved dishonestly by interacting with others during the exam, and "ever used material," which is equal to 1 if the respondent reports to have used material which is not allowed during exams. Summing up these two most frequent self-reported cheating methods, 33.6% and 16.6%, respectively, we see

**TABLE 1** Variable Definition

| Label | Definition |
|---|---|
| *Dependent variables* | |
| Ever cheated | Dummy = 1 if ever cheated (once or more) |
| Ever interacted | Dummy = 1 if cheated by interacting with others |
| Ever used material | Dummy = 1 if cheated by using material not allowed |
| No will to study | Dummy = 1 if cheated due to lack of will to study |
| *Context and social characteristics* | |
| Classmates cheated | Dummy = 1 if acquaintances cheated |
| Friends cheated | Dummy = 1 if friends frequently cheated |
| Aware of the sanction | Dummy = 1 if aware of the sanction |
| People can be trusted | Dummy = 1 if believes most people can be trusted, always or most of the time |
| People take advantage | Dummy = 1 if believes people try to take advantage, always or most of the time |
| Merit rewarded first job | Dummy = 1 if believes skills are rewarded in the first job, always or most of the time |
| *Personal characteristics* | |
| Age | Age in years |
| Female | Dummy = 1 if female |
| Not religious | Dummy = 1 if not religious |
| Risk tolerance | Risk tolerance index, from 0 to 10 |
| *University characteristics* | |
| Moved to attend University | Dummy = 1 if moved to another city/country to study |
| University in the Americas | Dummy = 1 if University located in North/Central/South America |
| University in Northern Europe | Dummy = 1 if University located in Northern Europe |
| University in Central Europe | Dummy = 1 if University located in Central Europe |
| University in Eastern Europe | Dummy = 1 if University located in Eastern Europe |
| University in Southern Europe | Dummy = 1 if University located in Southern Europe |
| Bachelor degree | Dummy = 1 if bachelor degree |
| Private university | Dummy = 1 if studied in a private university |
| Top grades | Dummy = 1 if earned top grades |
| Social sciences | Dummy = 1 if studied Social Sciences |
| STEM | Dummy = 1 if studied Hard Sciences |

**TABLE 2** Summary Statistics

| Sample | Mean All | Obs. | Mean Non-cheaters | Mean Cheaters | Test |
|---|---|---|---|---|---|
| Ever cheated (D) | 0.504 | 676 | 0 | 1 | |
| Ever interacted (D) | 0.166 | 676 | 0 | 0.328 | |
| Ever used material (D) | 0.336 | 676 | 0 | 0.666 | |
| No will to study | 0.107 | 676 | 0 | 0.211 | |
| Classmates cheated (D) | 0.254 | 676 | 0.221 | 0.287 | −1.985** |
| Friends cheated (D) | 0.136 | 676 | 0.113 | 0.158 | −1.703* |
| Aware of the sanction (D) | 0.445 | 676 | 0.618 | 0.276 | −8.952*** |
| People can be trusted (D) | 0.382 | 676 | 0.493 | 0.273 | 5.882*** |
| People take advantage (D) | 0.413 | 676 | 0.499 | 0.328 | 4.490*** |
| Merit rewarded first job (D) | 0.506 | 676 | 0.355 | 0.654 | −7.767*** |
| Age | 24.276 | 522 | 24.424 | 24.011 | 0.907 |
| Female (D) | 0.484 | 676 | 0.645 | 0.326 | 8.305*** |
| Not religious (D) | 0.377 | 676 | 0.487 | 0.270 | 5.814*** |
| Risk tolerance | 5.753 | 522 | 5.630 | 5.973 | −1.686* |
| Moved to attend University (D) | 0.642 | 676 | 0.845 | 0.443 | 10.899*** |

*Continued*

**TABLE 2** Summary Statistics—cont'd

| Sample | Mean All | Obs. | Mean Non-cheaters | Mean Cheaters | Test |
|---|---|---|---|---|---|
| University in the Americas (D) | 0.047 | 676 | 0.057 | 0.038 | 1.138 |
| University in Northern Europe (D) | 0.161 | 676 | 0.239 | 0.085 | 5.435*** |
| University in Central Europe (D) | 0.269 | 676 | 0.412 | 0.129 | 8.291*** |
| University in Eastern Europe (D) | 0.021 | 676 | 0.021 | 0.021 | 0.034 |
| University in Southern Europe (D) | 0.115 | 676 | 0.104 | 0.126 | −0.880 |
| Bachelor degree (D) | 0.294 | 676 | 0.421 | 0.561 | 7.154*** |
| Private university (D) | 0.133 | 676 | 0.155 | 0.170 | 1.676* |
| Top grades (D) | 0.419 | 676 | 0.543 | 0.296 | 6.511*** |
| Social sciences (D) | 0.430 | 456 | 0.444 | 0.403 | 0.839 |
| STEM (D) | 0.344 | 456 | 0.291 | 0.448 | −3.330*** |
| Observations | 676 | | 335 | 341 | |

*Note*: Dummy variables are marked with (D). The last column reports a test on the equality of the mean in the groups of cheaters and non-cheaters. For dummy variables, the test is a probability test. ***$p<0.01$, **$p<0.05$, *$p<0.1$.

that they account for half of dishonesty in the data.[c] Another variable of interest, that we employ as dependent variable in the regression analysis, is the dummy variable "No will" (derived from Q6 in the questionnaire), which takes value 1 if the respondent picked one among the first four available answers provided in the question, i.e., s/he behaved dishonestly during the written exam due to lack of will in studying for the exam. We can see that 21% of cheaters report to have cheated due to lack of will of study for the exam.

We now present the set of regressors employed in the analysis. Among context and social characteristics, we encompass whether the respondent thinks Classmates/Friends cheated during written exams (Q7 and Q8, respectively); whether the respondent was aware of the sanction (Q11); whether most people can be trusted (Q12) or whether they try to take advantage (Q14); and whether merit is rewarded for finding the first job compared to recommendations (Q17).

Summary statistics reported in Table 2 show not only the overall mean for the variables used in the analysis, but also the distinctive means of cheaters (those who self-report to have committed a dishonest practice at least once during a written exam) vs non-cheaters. The difference in the average between the two subsamples is compared statistically through a test on the significance. Interestingly, cheaters are more likely to report that classmates and friends cheated during exams (at the 5% and 10% significance levels, respectively), and they are significantly less likely to be aware about the sanctions taking place if caught cheating. Cheaters also have a more negative opinion on others compared to non-cheaters, in the sense that they trust others to a lesser extent and think more frequently that people behave opportunistically.

Personal characteristics of respondents show that the average respondent is 24 years old, and there is no difference in age between cheaters and non-cheaters. The sample is almost perfectly gender balanced, and females self-report to have cheated significantly less frequently than males. Moreover, it is more likely to find non-religious respondents among non-cheaters than among cheaters.

We also collected information regarding respondents' universities. Cheaters are more likely to have not moved for study reasons. We do also find some significant differences in terms of geographical location of universities: in particular, in Northern Europe the proportion of non-cheaters is much higher than cheaters, and the same applies to respondents from Central Europe.

It seems also more likely to self-report cheating for Bachelor students and for students enrolled in private universities. Respondents with top grades in their studies are significantly less likely to self-report cheating, and also there

c. The two forms of cheating considered ("Ever interacted" and "Ever used material") are not mutually exclusive: it was possible to report more than one way of cheating in Q2 of the questionnaire. However, no observation in the full sample reported both ways of cheating. The sum of "Ever interacted" and "Ever used material" adds up to 50.1%, whereas the percentage of ever cheaters is equal to 50.4%. This means that the remaining 0.3% reported a way of cheating in the category "Other" which does not belong to any of the two previously mentioned categories.

seems to be a higher proportion of cheaters among STEM students compared to non-cheaters. This statistical testing represents however *prima facie* evidence. In order to draw some more robust conclusions we implement the regression analyses outlined in Section 3.

## 3. Econometric analysis and results

In Table 3 we report results from probit regressions (average marginal effects). Regressions were run on the same specification; the only difference across the four models lies in the dependent variable employed.

In model (1), in which the dependent variable is the dummy "Ever cheated," we see that the probability to self-report a dishonest behavior during written exams increases by almost 17% if classmates are believed to cheat. Interestingly, the same does not apply to friends. Being aware of the sanction decreases the probability of cheating by about 10%. Trusting others is positively associated to self-reported cheating, a result which at a first glance seems counter-intuitive, but which was also found in Bucciol et al. (2017): cheating may not be considered against trust by the cheater, but as a way to insure him/herself against a widespread situation, in which students have to compete for higher grades in order to succeed in their future career.

Age is included as squared polynomial in the econometric specification, in order to account for possible non-linear effects of age on cheating. Regression output reports that cheating and age at the time of the degree are positively correlated up to a certain point, after which the probability to cheat decreases.[d] This result confirms previous literature contributions (Kerkvliet and Sigmund, 1999). Quite surprisingly, we do not find any geographical difference of cheating (the omitted reference category is the rest of the world, i.e., Africa, Asia, and Australia). Private universities are associated to higher self-reported levels of cheating, as well as social sciences disciplines (compared to humanities). The latter results may suggest the presence of a more competitive environment for students, although we cannot exclude the case of a higher indulgency in terms of sanctions enforcement.

In models (2) and (3) we distinguish the dishonest activity according to its way of implementation: either through interaction with other classmates or through the use of illicit material. The two types of cheating differ substantially: the first one entails the risk of being caught also on others, whereas the second one is individualistic. We note that the correlation with cheating performed by other classmates persists only in the case of "interactive" cheating, perhaps suggesting some form of self-justification with this kind of cheating, in line with Bucciol et al. (2017). Against expectations, this interactive way of cheating, which to some extent relies on the support and trust of others, is positively

d. By including also the squared term of age, divided by 100, we learn that self-reported cheating increases with age up to $100*[0.080/(2*0.156)] = 25.64$ years, and then decreases.

**TABLE 3 Probability to Behave Dishonestly (Probit Average Marginal Effects)**

| Variables | (1) Ever cheated | (2) Ever interacted | (3) Ever used material | (4) No will to study |
|---|---|---|---|---|
| *Context and social characteristics* | | | | |
| Classmates cheated | 0.166*** | 0.102** | 0.059 | 0.089** |
| | (0.049) | (0.043) | (0.039) | (0.037) |
| Friends cheated | 0.094 | 0.044 | 0.046 | −0.079* |
| | (0.058) | (0.048) | (0.043) | (0.043) |
| Aware of the sanction | −0.102** | −0.018 | −0.074** | −0.022 |
| | (0.041) | (0.036) | (0.031) | (0.031) |
| People can be trusted | 0.083* | 0.014 | 0.079** | 0.058* |
| | (0.046) | (0.040) | (0.036) | (0.035) |
| People take advantage | 0.056 | 0.088** | −0.010 | 0.086** |
| | (0.048) | (0.042) | (0.037) | (0.037) |
| Merit rewarded first job | 0.014 | −0.014 | 0.011 | 0.017 |
| | (0.042) | (0.037) | (0.032) | (0.032) |
| *Personal characteristics* | | | | |
| Age | 0.080* | 0.029 | 0.059 | 0.066** |
| | (0.044) | (0.036) | (0.040) | (0.033) |
| Age squared/100 | −0.156* | −0.061 | −0.111 | −0.114* |
| | (0.082) | (0.066) | (0.077) | (0.060) |
| Female | 0.014 | 0.012 | −0.001 | 0.009 |
| | (0.043) | (0.038) | (0.033) | (0.033) |
| Not religious | 0.052 | 0.016 | 0.022 | 0.023 |
| | (0.043) | (0.038) | (0.033) | (0.033) |
| Risk tolerance | 0.008 | −0.004 | 0.012* | −0.002 |
| | (0.009) | (0.008) | (0.007) | (0.007) |
| *University characteristics* | | | | |
| Moved to attend University | −0.039 | −0.044 | 0.027 | −0.025 |
| | (0.055) | (0.046) | (0.045) | (0.040) |

*Continued*

**TABLE 3 Probability to Behave Dishonestly (Probit Average Marginal Effects)—cont'd**

| Variables | (1) Ever cheated | (2) Ever interacted | (3) Ever used material | (4) No will to study |
|---|---|---|---|---|
| University in the Americas | −0.016 | −0.050 | 0.072 | −0.040 |
| | (0.101) | (0.084) | (0.082) | (0.073) |
| University in Northern Europe | −0.072 | −0.094 | 0.062 | −0.068 |
| | (0.086) | (0.072) | (0.072) | (0.064) |
| University in Central Europe | −0.089 | −0.113* | 0.049 | −0.088 |
| | (0.079) | (0.066) | (0.067) | (0.058) |
| University in Eastern Europe | 0.069 | −0.105 | 0.200** | 0.107 |
| | (0.126) | (0.110) | (0.093) | (0.083) |
| University in Southern Europe | 0.043 | −0.008 | 0.087 | −0.005 |
| | (0.085) | (0.070) | (0.071) | (0.061) |
| Bachelor degree | −0.050 | −0.017 | −0.028 | 0.016 |
| | (0.049) | (0.043) | (0.037) | (0.036) |
| Private university | 0.092* | 0.012 | 0.086** | 0.082** |
| | (0.051) | (0.045) | (0.038) | (0.037) |
| Top grades | −0.007 | 0.045 | −0.039 | −0.041 |
| | (0.043) | (0.038) | (0.033) | (0.032) |
| Social sciences | 0.146** | 0.132** | 0.016 | 0.040 |
| | (0.059) | (0.054) | (0.044) | (0.045) |
| STEM | 0.078 | 0.101* | −0.028 | −0.001 |
| | (0.056) | (0.052) | (0.044) | (0.043) |
| Observations | 456 | 456 | 456 | 456 |

*Note*: Standard errors in *parentheses*; ***$p<0.01$, **$p<0.05$, *$p<0.1$.

correlated with the belief that others may be opportunistic. Interestingly, this practice is less frequent in Central Europe compared to the rest of the world. Conversely, the use of illicit material seems to be more widespread in Eastern Europe. In addition, the deterrence effect of the sanction seems to exist only in the case of cheating through illicit material, as well as the positive correlation with private universities.

In the last column of Table 3, model (4) uses as dependent variable "No will." The positive correlation with the belief of classmates cheating is preserved, but in this case we also find a negative correlation with the belief of friends cheating. Most of the results of previous models find confirmation.[e]

In Table 4, we investigate whether cheating has been beneficial to the respondent, and whether it was noticed by professors (Q3 and Q4 in the survey questionnaire, respectively). In order to analyze these aspects, we need to implement a two-stage Heckman selection procedure, in which the first stage is represented by cheating, and the second one by the variables of interest (Q3 and Q4). Whereas in the first stage we do find confirmation of most of the results of Table 3, in the second stage we do not find any correlation with the regressors employed in the analysis.

In addition, we run the estimations reported in Tables 3 and 4 on the full sample of 676 observations, by not including in the estimates those variables who report high levels of missing values in the questionnaire responses (see Table 2): Risk tolerance, Age, STEM, and Social Sciences. Results are reported in Tables 5 and 6, respectively. Overall, we note that the significant results of Table 3 are confirmed, also in sign. In addition, with a higher amount of observations, we now find significant coefficients for variables that did not report any significance in the restricted sample: Friends cheated is now positively correlated with the probability of self-reporting cheating at least once, as well as with the probability of using some forbidden material during exams; female respondents are now negatively correlated to self-reported cheating (a result which confirms previous literature contributions such as, e.g., Baird, 1980; Crown and Spiller, 1998; Whitley, 1998); merit rewarded at the first job is positively correlated to cheating; if the responder has moved to a different city to attend university, the probability of cheating is lower (perhaps this signals a higher commitment in studies); respondents located in North and Central-European universities are

e. We also explored the subsidized nature of university systems at national levels, by including as regressor a dummy "Subsidized university," obtained based on OECD reports (OECD (2018a), National Student Fee and Support Systems in European Higher Education 2017/18, Eurydice; OECD (2018b), Education at a Glance 2018—OECD Indicators, Eurydice). The overall average of the new variable is 0.48, with a standard deviation of 0.50. The main results remain robust, and the variable representing Subsidized university is significant (at the 10%) only in the last model specification, indicating that when a university is located in countries in which the higher education system is subsidized, lack of will to study is more frequent as justification for cheating. Results are available upon request.

**TABLE 4** Heckman Two-Stage Process (Dishonesty Was Helpful/Was Noticed)

| Variables | (1) Helpful (selection) | (2) Helpful | (3) Noticed (selection) | (4) Noticed |
|---|---|---|---|---|
| *Context and social characteristics* | | | | |
| Classmates cheated | 0.150*** | | 0.165*** | |
| | (0.052) | | (0.050) | |
| Friends cheated | 0.121** | | 0.097 | |
| | (0.059) | | (0.061) | |
| Aware of the sanction | −0.098** | | −0.103** | |
| | (0.040) | | (0.041) | |
| People can be trusted | 0.084* | | 0.081* | |
| | (0.045) | | (0.048) | |
| People take advantage | 0.055 | | 0.055 | |
| | (0.047) | | (0.048) | |
| Merit rewarded first job | −0.003 | | 0.015 | |
| | (0.044) | | (0.043) | |
| *Personal characteristics* | | | | |
| Age | 0.080* | −0.017 | 0.080* | 0.206 |
| | (0.045) | (0.092) | (0.044) | (0.155) |
| Age squared/100 | −0.157* | 0.054 | −0.156* | −0.445 |
| | (0.082) | (0.178) | (0.082) | (0.325) |
| Female | 0.017 | 0.068 | 0.014 | −0.035 |
| | (0.043) | (0.061) | (0.043) | (0.049) |
| Not religious | 0.045 | | 0.053 | |
| | (0.043) | | (0.043) | |
| Risk tolerance | 0.009 | | 0.008 | |
| | (0.009) | | (0.009) | |
| *University characteristics* | | | | |
| Moved to attend University | −0.040 | 0.016 | −0.040 | 0.058 |
| | (0.055) | (0.067) | (0.055) | (0.076) |

**TABLE 4** Heckman Two-Stage Process (Dishonesty Was Helpful/Was Noticed)—cont'd

| Variables | (1) Helpful (selection) | (2) Helpful | (3) Noticed (selection) | (4) Noticed |
|---|---|---|---|---|
| University in the Americas | −0.019 | 0.166 | −0.015 | −0.081 |
| | (0.100) | (0.143) | (0.101) | (0.104) |
| University in Northern Europe | −0.070 | 0.032 | −0.072 | 0.016 |
| | (0.086) | (0.099) | (0.086) | (0.071) |
| University in Central Europe | −0.089 | 0.095 | −0.089 | −0.145 |
| | (0.079) | (0.093) | (0.079) | (0.095) |
| University in Eastern Europe | 0.084 | −0.011 | 0.068 | 0.012 |
| | (0.127) | (0.133) | (0.126) | (0.097) |
| University in Southern Europe | 0.043 | 0.091 | 0.043 | −0.112 |
| | (0.085) | (0.113) | (0.085) | (0.116) |
| Bachelor degree | −0.051 | 0.074 | −0.050 | 0.023 |
| | (0.048) | (0.064) | (0.049) | (0.061) |
| Private University | 0.088* | −0.026 | 0.092* | 0.078 |
| | (0.051) | (0.066) | (0.051) | (0.053) |
| Top grades | −0.008 | −0.026 | −0.007 | 0.071 |
| | (0.043) | (0.058) | (0.043) | (0.061) |
| STEM | 0.148** | 0.027 | 0.146** | 0.636 |
| | (0.059) | (0.094) | (0.059) | (125.055) |
| Social sciences | 0.082 | −0.040 | 0.078 | 0.640 |
| | (0.057) | (0.076) | (0.057) | (125.055) |
| | | | | |
| Observations | 456 | 456 | 456 | 456 |

*Note*: Standard errors in *parentheses*; ***$p<0.01$, **$p<0.05$, *$p<0.1$.

**TABLE 5 Probability to Behave Dishonestly (Probit Average Marginal Effects)—Entire Sample**

| Variables | (1) Ever cheated | (2) Ever interacted | (3) Ever used material | (4) No will to study |
|---|---|---|---|---|
| *Context and social characteristics* | | | | |
| Classmates cheated | 0.125*** | 0.129*** | 0.008 | 0.080*** |
| | (0.041) | (0.033) | (0.037) | (0.028) |
| Friends cheated | 0.086* | 0.011 | 0.074* | −0.062* |
| | (0.049) | (0.039) | (0.043) | (0.034) |
| Aware of the sanction | −0.136*** | −0.005 | −0.118*** | 0.002 |
| | (0.032) | (0.028) | (0.029) | (0.024) |
| People can be trusted | −0.024 | 0.058* | −0.048 | 0.052** |
| | (0.036) | (0.030) | (0.032) | (0.026) |
| People take advantage | −0.050 | 0.095*** | −0.119*** | 0.083*** |
| | (0.037) | (0.031) | (0.032) | (0.027) |
| Merit rewarded first job | 0.086*** | −0.044 | 0.099*** | −0.008 |
| | (0.033) | (0.029) | (0.028) | (0.024) |
| *Personal characteristics* | | | | |
| Female | −0.072** | 0.026 | −0.085*** | 0.006 |
| | (0.033) | (0.029) | (0.028) | (0.025) |
| Not religious | 0.027 | 0.019 | −0.000 | 0.024 |
| | (0.037) | (0.032) | (0.033) | (0.027) |
| *University characteristics* | | | | |
| Moved to attend University | −0.176*** | 0.027 | −0.143*** | 0.030 |
| | (0.039) | (0.035) | (0.033) | (0.030) |
| University in the Americas | −0.104 | −0.024 | −0.038 | −0.002 |
| | (0.079) | (0.065) | (0.072) | (0.056) |
| University in Northern Europe | −0.176*** | −0.085* | −0.062 | −0.036 |
| | (0.053) | (0.048) | (0.048) | (0.041) |

**TABLE 5** Probability to Behave Dishonestly (Probit Average Marginal Effects)—Entire Sample—cont'd

| Variables | (1) Ever cheated | (2) Ever interacted | (3) Ever used material | (4) No will to study |
|---|---|---|---|---|
| University in Central Europe | −0.174*** | −0.105** | −0.066 | −0.068* |
| | (0.050) | (0.045) | (0.046) | (0.039) |
| University in Eastern Europe | −0.026 | −0.077 | 0.095 | 0.098 |
| | (0.105) | (0.088) | (0.086) | (0.065) |
| University in Southern Europe | −0.082 | 0.002 | −0.060 | 0.026 |
| | (0.058) | (0.048) | (0.051) | (0.041) |
| Bachelor degree | −0.119*** | 0.001 | −0.108*** | 0.004 |
| | (0.036) | (0.031) | (0.033) | (0.026) |
| Private university | 0.049 | 0.016 | 0.046 | 0.068** |
| | (0.044) | (0.038) | (0.040) | (0.030) |
| Top grades | −0.058 | 0.043 | −0.082** | −0.022 |
| | (0.036) | (0.031) | (0.032) | (0.026) |
| Observations | 676 | 676 | 676 | 676 |

*Note*: Standard errors in *parentheses*; ***$p<0.01$, **$p<0.05$, *$p<0.1$.

less involved in self-reported cheating; finally, being enrolled in a Bachelor degree compared to a Master degree is negatively associated to cheating.

We run estimations on the whole sample also in the case of econometric specifications presented in Table 4: results are reported in Table 6. Also in this case the higher numerosity of the sample enhances the significance of coefficients. The cheating stage (model (1) and (3)) mostly confirms results obtained in Table 5, based on the full sample of respondents. Among the most relevant differences in the second stage of Table 5 compared to estimations run in Table 4, we find that: females, those who moved to attend university and enrolled in a bachelor degree, are more likely to report that cheating during exams was useful; as regards cheating being noticed, this is positively correlated to moving to attend university and with the respondent obtaining top grades.

**TABLE 6** Heckman Two-Stage Process (Dishonesty Was Helpful/Was Noticed)—Entire Sample

| Variables | (1) Helpful (selection) | (2) Helpful | (3) Noticed (selection) | (4) Noticed |
|---|---|---|---|---|
| *Context and social characteristics* | | | | |
| Classmates cheated | 0.124*** | | 0.108*** | |
| | (0.041) | | (0.041) | |
| Friends cheated | 0.093* | | 0.111** | |
| | (0.052) | | (0.047) | |
| Aware of the sanction | −0.133*** | | −0.138*** | |
| | (0.032) | | (0.031) | |
| People can be trusted | −0.023 | | −0.029 | |
| | (0.036) | | (0.035) | |
| People take advantage | −0.048 | | −0.055 | |
| | (0.037) | | (0.035) | |
| Merit rewarded first job | 0.081** | | 0.082** | |
| | (0.035) | | (0.032) | |
| *Personal characteristics* | | | | |
| Female | −0.073** | 0.177*** | −0.068** | −0.016 |
| | (0.033) | (0.048) | (0.033) | (0.062) |
| Not religious | 0.026 | | 0.034 | |
| | (0.037) | | (0.036) | |
| *University characteristics* | | | | |
| Moved to attend University | −0.180*** | 0.343*** | −0.177*** | 0.303*** |
| | (0.040) | (0.046) | (0.038) | (0.088) |
| University in the Americas | −0.108 | 0.393*** | −0.107 | 0.017 |
| | (0.079) | (0.127) | (0.078) | (0.124) |
| University in Northern Europe | −0.176*** | 0.037 | −0.177*** | 0.128 |
| | (0.053) | (0.083) | (0.052) | (0.088) |

**TABLE 6** Heckman Two-Stage Process (Dishonesty Was Helpful/Was Noticed)—Entire Sample—cont'd

| Variables | (1) Helpful (selection) | (2) Helpful | (3) Noticed (selection) | (4) Noticed |
|---|---|---|---|---|
| University in Central Europe | −0.175*** | 0.021 | −0.173*** | −0.094 |
| | (0.050) | (0.084) | (0.050) | (0.102) |
| University in Eastern Europe | −0.025 | −0.012 | −0.024 | 0.040 |
| | (0.105) | (0.141) | (0.105) | (0.143) |
| University in Southern Europe | −0.087 | 0.249*** | −0.082 | −0.082 |
| | (0.059) | (0.079) | (0.058) | (0.095) |
| Bachelor degree | −0.120*** | 0.136** | −0.122*** | 0.116 |
| | (0.036) | (0.059) | (0.036) | (0.072) |
| Private University | 0.047 | 0.058 | 0.047 | 0.093 |
| | (0.045) | (0.072) | (0.044) | (0.074) |
| Top grades | −0.060* | 0.023 | −0.062* | 0.130** |
| | (0.036) | (0.058) | (0.036) | (0.066) |
| Observations | 676 | 676 | 676 | 676 |

*Note*: Standard errors in *parentheses*; ***$p < 0.01$, **$p < 0.05$, *$p < 0.1$.

## 4. Conclusion

This study aimed at investigating the phenomenon of cheating at universities, which represents a growing phenomenon in real life, yet under-investigated in the economic literature. The need to explore this phenomenon is driven by the fact that college environments represent important places where future leaders in our societies interact with each other and get educated.

Through the implementation of a web-based survey across European universities, we investigate the diffusion of cheating (rule violations) during written exams. We are interested in studying the diffusion of the phenomenon and whether dishonest behaviors during exams are characterized by a geographical distribution, perhaps due to different social norms and competitive levels across countries.

Our results, based on a total of almost 700 observations, highlight that cheating is a severely widespread phenomenon, since half of respondents report to have committed cheating in a written exam at least once during their university career. Cheaters are more likely to believe that their classmates also cheated, to think that most people can be trusted, to attend private universities and less likely to be aware of the sanctions connected to cheating.

Our survey allows us to disentangle two types of cheating: one which involves interaction with other classmates, and another one which relies on the use of illicit material. Only the interactive cheating seems to be correlated with the belief of other classmates cheating, and also with the belief that people try to take advantage, whereas the awareness of the sanctions seems to affect (negatively) only the use of illicit material. The two distinct types of cheating call for different targeted policies, given the varying relationship with cheating by other classmates.

Overall, we do not find significant differences across geographical locations of universities, although interactive cheating seems less widespread in Central Europe whereas the use of illicit material is more common in Eastern Europe. The absence of geographical patterns regarding cheating at university may be explained by the inclusion of social and cultural factors among the regressors, which may capture some idiosyncratic characteristics of different origins.

Awareness of the sanctions seems to play an important role in cheating practices, by substantially lowering the probability of cheating. This result corroborates previous findings: cheaters are found to have lower knowledge of departmental rules about cheating than non-cheaters (Jackson et al., 2002). Along these lines, reading and signing an honor code about ethical practices at university, which also mentions the consequences of cheating, has been proven to be effective in reducing cheating (McCabe, 2005; Shu et al., 2011). The intuition is that when unethical behavior is made more salient, people may be more susceptible to their own moral standards, and also they may better take into account consequences attached to their unethical behavior (Gino et al., 2009). This result is particularly important when reasoning in terms of policy implications, since the introduction of honor codes at universities represents a cheap and effective policy intervention.

Future research should be devoted to tackling the profile of the cheater also in relation to his/her social context, and also to solve the sample selection problems which characterizes our analysis, perhaps imposing the completion of the survey in an anonymous setting before students complete their university studies.

## Appendix. Online questionnaire[f]

SURVEY ON DISHONESTY IN THE UNIVERSITY

The survey is addressed to current and former university students and is part of a research project being carried out by the Universities of Bologna and Verona in Italy.

---

f. Text in italics is not part of the questionnaire.

Filling out the survey will take <10 min.

Please answer the questions honestly. Your answers will be anonymous and there is no way for us to trace your answers to your identity. The answers will be used for scientific research purposes only. They will be presented and discussed in an aggregate way.

If you have any doubts or questions, or you want to be updated on the results of this project, we invite you to contact. *[Here the name and email address of one of the researchers was written.]*

It is important that as many people as possible fill out this survey. Please share the link with your friends!

THANK YOU FOR YOUR PARTICIPATION!
Our aim is to study the frequency of dishonest behavior at the university. In this survey, by dishonest behavior we mean breaking the rules of conduct during a written exam (i.e., copying from different sources, speaking with other students, etc.).

**Q1**. Have you ever behaved dishonestly during an exam?

- □ Never
- □ Once or twice
- □ Many times
- □ Regularly

*[If "Never": go to Q7]*

**Q2**. In which way did you behave dishonestly? (more than one answer is possible)

- □ I used materials which are not allowed (books, notes on paper or written on the body, cheat sheets)
- □ I used my phone to search for information
- □ I interacted with one or more classmates during the exam
- □ I asked another person to take the exam in my place
- □ Other: ___________

**Q3**. Was your behavior of any help?

- □ No, I did not benefit from it eventually
- □ Yes, in this way I answered to what I did not know and I was thus able to pass the exam
- □ Yes, in this way I answered to what I did not know and I was able to obtain a higher grade
- □ Other: ___________

**Q4**. Have the professors ever noticed your dishonest behavior?

- □ No, they never noticed it
- □ Yes, they noticed it sometimes
- □ Yes, they noticed it regularly

**Q5**. If the professors noticed it, what measure did they take?
- □ They never noticed it
- □ They did not take any measures
- □ I had to skip one or more exam session
- □ I was summoned to the law office/executive board/dean
- □ I got expelled from the University
- □ Other: ___________

**Q6**. Why did you behave dishonestly?
- □ The course was too difficult
- □ I did not have enough time to study everything
- □ There was too much to study
- □ I did not like the course/I found it useless
- □ I had studied but I did not feel self-confident
- □ To improve my performance
- □ Other: ___________

**Q7**. Do you think that dishonest behavior during the exams is frequent among your classmates?
- □ No, it happens rarely (I never noticed it or heard about it in fewer than three exams)
- □ No, it happens quite rarely (I noticed it or heard about it in fewer than half of the exams)
- □ Yes, it happens quite frequently (I noticed it or heard about it in more than half of the exams)
- □ Yes, it happens frequently (I noticed it or heard about it in every exam or almost every exam)

**Q8**. Do you think that dishonest behavior during the exams is frequent among your friends?
- □ No, it happens rarely (I never noticed it or heard about it in fewer than three exams)
- □ No, it happens quite rarely (I noticed it or heard about it in fewer than half of the exams)
- □ Yes, it happens quite frequently (I noticed it or heard about it in more than half of the exams)
- □ Yes, it happens frequently (I noticed it or heard about it in every exam or almost every exam)

**Q9**. If you have ever witnessed dishonest behavior during the exams among your classmates, what was the effect on you?
- □ None, I prefer to behave honestly regardless of the others
- □ I was bothered but I did not report it to the professor
- □ I was bothered and I reported it to the professor
- □ Other: ___________

**Q10**. How do you think the problem of dishonesty during the exams could be solved?

- □ By increasing the punishment
- □ By providing different versions of the text of the exam
- □ By decreasing the material of the teaching program
- □ By offering (or increasing the number of) practice exercises or mock examinations in class
- □ By providing more information to the students regarding the immorality of this behavior
- □ By introducing a compulsory oral exam after the written examination
- □ By increasing the knowledge about the punishment
- □ Other: ___________

**Q11**. Do you know what the sanctions are for those who behave dishonestly during an exam?

- □ Yes, I read them in the University rules
- □ Yes, they were explained by the professors
- □ No
- □ I am not sure
- □ Other: ___________

In this section you will find questions about your view on several topics.

**Q12**. In general, do you think that you can trust most people?

- □ No, you always have to be careful
- □ No, you have to be careful most of the times
- □ Yes, you can trust most people most of the times
- □ Yes, you can always trust most people

**Q13**. How much do you trust these groups?

| | Not at all | A little | Quite enough | A lot |
|---|---|---|---|---|
| Family | □ | □ | □ | □ |
| Neighbors | □ | □ | □ | □ |
| Acquaintances | □ | □ | □ | □ |
| Church | □ | □ | □ | □ |
| Political parties | □ | □ | □ | □ |
| Institutions | □ | □ | □ | □ |

**Q14**. In general, do you think that most people try to take advantage of others when given the chance to do so?

- □ No, they always behave in a fair way
- □ No, they behave in a fair way most of the times
- □ Yes, they try to take advantage of others most of the times
- □ Yes, they always try to take advantage of others

**Q15**. Generally speaking, do you think that merit is rewarded in the public sector and in the private sector?

| | Yes, always | Yes, most of the times | No, only some of the times | No, never |
|---|---|---|---|---|
| Public sector | ☐ | ☐ | ☐ | ☐ |
| Private sector | ☐ | ☐ | ☐ | ☐ |

**Q16**. Do you consider yourself a person who is willing to take risks or a person that avoids taking risks? Mark one of the underlying numbers, where 0 means "absolutely not willing to take risks" and 10 means "totally willing to take risks"

| | 0 | 1 | 2 | 3 | 4 | 5 | 6 | 7 | 8 | 9 | 10 | |
|---|---|---|---|---|---|---|---|---|---|---|---|---|
| Absolutely not willing to take risks | ☐ | ☐ | ☐ | ☐ | ☐ | ☐ | ☐ | ☐ | ☐ | ☐ | ☐ | Totally willing to take risks |

**Q17**. How much do you think merit matters for finding one's first job compared to other factors like references and recommendations? Mark one of the underlying numbers, where 0 means "Not at all" and 10 means "A lot"

| | 0 | 1 | 2 | 3 | 4 | 5 | 6 | 7 | 8 | 9 | 10 | |
|---|---|---|---|---|---|---|---|---|---|---|---|---|
| Not at all | ☐ | ☐ | ☐ | ☐ | ☐ | ☐ | ☐ | ☐ | ☐ | ☐ | ☐ | A lot |

You are almost done with the questionnaire. Please answer some final sociodemographic questions.

**Q18**. How old are you?

- ☐ Between 18 and 20
- ☐ Between 21 and 23
- ☐ Between 24 and 26
- ☐ Between 27 and 29
- ☐ Between 30 and 32
- ☐ Between 33 and 35
- ☐ Between 36 and 38
- ☐ Between 39 and 41
- ☐ Between 42 and 44
- ☐ Between 45 and 47
- ☐ Between 48 and 50
- ☐ Between 51 and 53
- ☐ Between 54 and 56
- ☐ Between 57 and 59

- □ Between 60 and 62
- □ Between 63 and 65
- □ Between 66 and 68
- □ Between 69 and 71
- □ Over 71

**Q19**. What is your gender?

- □ Male
- □ Female

**Q20**. In which country did you spend most of your life?

- □ Argentina
- □ Australia
- □ Austria
- □ Belgium
- □ Brazil
- □ Bulgaria
- □ Canada
- □ China
- □ Croatia
- □ Cyprus
- □ Czech Republic
- □ Denmark
- □ Estonia
- □ Finland
- □ France
- □ Germany
- □ Greece
- □ Hungary
- □ India
- □ Ireland
- □ Italy
- □ Japan
- □ Latvia
- □ Lithuania
- □ Luxembourg
- □ Malta
- □ Mexico
- □ Netherlands
- □ Poland
- □ Portugal
- □ Romania
- □ Slovakia
- □ Slovenia
- □ South Korea

- □ Spain
- □ Sweden
- □ United Kingdom
- □ United States of America
- □ Other: ___________

**Q21**. Did you move to a different city from the one where you grew up in order to attend the University?

- □ Yes, I moved to a new city in the same country
- □ Yes, I moved to a new city in a different country
- □ No, I studied in the same city where I grew up
- □ Other: ___________

**Q22**. Where is your University located? Please indicate the country

- □ Argentina
- □ Australia
- □ Austria
- □ Belgium
- □ Brazil
- □ Bulgaria
- □ Canada
- □ China
- □ Croatia
- □ Cyprus
- □ Czech Republic
- □ Denmark
- □ Estonia
- □ Finland
- □ France
- □ Germany
- □ Greece
- □ Hungary
- □ India
- □ Ireland
- □ Italy
- □ Japan
- □ Latvia
- □ Lithuania
- □ Luxembourg
- □ Malta
- □ Mexico
- □ Netherlands
- □ Poland
- □ Portugal
- □ Romania

□ Slovakia
□ Slovenia
□ South Korea
□ Spain
□ Sweden
□ United Kingdom
□ United States of America
□ Other: ___________

**Q23**. Which year did you begin your University studies in?
□ Before 2010
□ 2010
□ 2011
□ 2012
□ 2013
□ 2014
□ 2015
□ 2016
□ 2017

**Q24**. What level is your current degree? If you are not currently studying, answer with the highest level you have obtained.
□ Bachelor's degree
□ Master's degree or Advanced degree
□ Single cycle degree (i.e., Med school or Law school)

**Q25**. When do you expect to finish/did you finish your University studies?
□ Before 2000
□ Between 2000 and 2009
□ Between 2010 and 2016
□ 2017
□ 2018
□ 2019
□ 2020
□ 2021
□ 2022

**Q26**. Is the University that you are/were attending private or public?
□ Private
□ Public

**Q27**. What is/was your field of studies?
□ Agricultural
□ Architecture
□ Economics
□ Law
□ Engineering

- ☐ Literature or History
- ☐ Medicine
- ☐ Psychology
- ☐ Science or Biotechnology
- ☐ Political Science
- ☐ Mathematics or Physics
- ☐ Foreign Languages
- ☐ Other: ___________

**Q28**. Why did you enroll in the course that you are attending/attended?

- ☐ Because I found it interesting
- ☐ Because I thought it could increase the chance of finding a job after the graduation
- ☐ I was driven by my family or friends
- ☐ Other: ___________

**Q29**. What is your grade average? Please indicate using the international ECTS scale (letters A-B-C-D-E, where A is the top grade and E is the bottom grade).

- ☐ Between E and D
- ☐ Between D and C
- ☐ Between C and B
- ☐ Between B and A
- ☐ Other: ___________

**Q30.** Who finances/financed your University studies?

- ☐ Scholarship based on income and merit
- ☐ Scholarship based on merit
- ☐ My family
- ☐ Myself working
- ☐ Other: ___________

**Q31**. Do you have a religious belief?

- ☐ No, I am atheist/agnostic
- ☐ I am Catholic/Christian
- ☐ I am Muslim
- ☐ I am Buddhist
- ☐ Other: ___________

**Q32**. How much does your religious belief influence your daily life? (mark 1 if you don't have a religious belief)

| | 1 | 2 | 3 | 4 | 5 | 6 | 7 | 8 | 9 | 10 | |
|---|---|---|---|---|---|---|---|---|---|---|---|
| Not at all | ☐ | ☐ | ☐ | ☐ | ☐ | ☐ | ☐ | ☐ | ☐ | ☐ | Very much |

Thank you for participating! Your contribution is really useful for our research!

We would be grateful if you could link the survey to your friends.

*[At the end of the questionnaire, when all the answers are submitted, a confirmation message appears on the screen with this text:]*

Thank you! We recorded all your answers. If you want to be informed on our research, please send an email to *[Here the name and email address of one of the researchers was written.]*.

## References

Baird Jr., J.S., 1980. Current trends in college cheating. Psychol. Sch. 17 (4), 515–522.

Bernardi, R.A., Baca, A.V., Landers, K.S., Witek, M.B., 2008. Methods of cheating and deterrents to classroom cheating: an international study. Ethics Behav. 18 (4), 373–391.

Björklund, M., Wenestam, C.G., 1999. In: Academic Cheating: Frequency, Methods and Causes. Paper Presented at the European Conference on Educational Research (ECER), September 22–25, Lahti, Finland.

Bucciol, A., Cicognani, S., Montinari, N., 2017. Cheating in Academia: The Relevance of Social Factors. Working Paper DSE University of Verona No. 15/2017.

Crown, D.F., Spiller, M.S., 1998. Learning from the literature on collegiate cheating: a review of empirical research. J. Bus. Ethics 17 (6), 683–700.

Drake, C.A., 1941. Why students cheat. J. High. Educ. 12 (8), 418–420.

Gino, F., Ayal, S., Ariely, D., 2009. Contagion and differentiation in unethical behavior: the effect of one bad apple on the barrel. Psychol. Sci. 20 (3), 393–398.

Jackson, C.J., Levine, S.Z., Furnham, A., Burr, N., 2002. Predictors of cheating behavior at a university: a lesson from the psychology of work. J. Appl. Soc. Psychol. 32 (5), 1031–1046.

Jones, D.L., 2011. Academic dishonesty: are more students cheating? Bus. Commun. Q. 74 (2), 141–150.

Kerkvliet, J., 1994. Cheating by economics students: a comparison of survey results. J. Econ. Educ. 25 (2), 121–133.

Kerkvliet, J., Sigmund, C.L., 1999. Can we control cheating in the classroom? J. Econ. Educ. 30 (4), 331–343.

Lovett-Hooper, G., Komarraju, M., Weston, R., Dollinger, S.J., 2007. Is plagiarism a forerunner of other deviance? Imagined futures of academically dishonest students. Ethics Behav. 17 (3), 323–336.

McCabe, D.L., 2005. Cheating among college and university students: a North American perspective. Int. J. Educ. Integr. 1 (1), 1–11.

McCabe, D.L., Butterfield, K.D., Trevino, L.K., 2012. Cheating in college: why students do it and what educators can do about it. John Hopkins University Press.

Miller, B.L., Agnich, L.E., Posick, C., Gould, L.A., 2015. Cheating around the world: a cross-national analysis of principal reported cheating. J. Crime Justice Educ. 26 (2), 211–232.

Neville, L., 2012. Do economic equality and generalized trust inhibit academic dishonesty? Evidence from state-level search-engine queries. Psychol. Sci. 23 (4), 339–345.

OECD, 2018a. National Student Fee and Support Systems in European Higher Education 2017/18. Eurydice.

OECD, 2018b. Education at a Glance 2018—OECD Indicators. Eurydice.

Shu, L.L., Gino, F., Bazerman, M.H., 2011. Dishonest deed, clear conscience: when cheating leads to moral disengagement and motivated forgetting. Pers. Soc. Psychol. Bull. 37 (3), 330–349.

Teixeira, A.A., Rocha, M.F., 2010. Cheating by economics and business undergraduate students: an exploratory international assessment. High. Educ. 59 (6), 663–701.

Whitley, B.E., 1998. Factors associated with cheating among college students: a review. Res. High. Educ. 39 (3), 235–274.

Wowra, S.A., 2007. Academic dishonesty. Ethics Behav. 17 (3), 211–214.

Yamamura, E., 2011. The role of social trust in reducing long-term truancy and forming human capital in Japan. Econ. Educ. Rev. 30 (2), 380–389.

Chapter 2.5

# Cheating in academic exams: A field study

Smadar Siev[a], Doron Kliger[b]
[a]*Ono Academic College, Faculty of Business Administration, Haifa, Israel,* [b]*Department of Economics, University of Haifa, Haifa, Israel*

## Chapter Outline



**JEL Classifications:** C91, D91

## 1. Introduction

Academic dishonesty, which includes cheating on tests, exams, and homework assignments, is a longstanding phenomenon that has become more prevalent and more socially acceptable over the years (Vojak, 2006). Statistics on the incidence of cheating are very disturbing and suggest that it is very ubiquitous. For example, in a questionnaire distributed to students at a university in the southwestern United States, more than half of the students reported cheating on exams and homework assignments (Haines et al., 1986). Other studies have found even higher rates of cheating among university students in the western and southern United States: 82% and 86%, respectively (Michaels and Miethe,

**Dishonesty in Behavioral Economics. https://doi.org/10.1016/B978-0-12-815857-9.00008-X**

1989; Stern and Havlicek, 1986). The number of college and university students engaged in cheating has been rising over the years (Davis, 1993; McCabe et al., 2001). A review of 107 studies of cheating among college students reports that, on average, 70% of the students admitted cheating (Whitley, 1998). Moreover, Pino and Smith (2003) found that 47% of respondents in a medium-size state university in the southeast of the US admitted involvement in academic dishonesty during college. Hashin (2005) found that 98% of law students in Israel admit that they did not maintain integrity in academic works and tests. Focusing on Internet plagiarism, Jones (2011) reports increased cheating rates over the years.

The overall picture suggests that academic dishonesty should not be merely of academic interest. Rather, the prevalence of the phenomenon calls for practical attention and raises the need to devise effective cheating barriers in the academic environment.

Academic dishonesty occurs in the university setting, but has consequences beyond it. As young people, students are still in the process of forming their social values and concepts, and as such they tend to be more easily influenced by new experiences and ideas. Students who are aware of the ongoing prevalence of cheating by their peers may become accustomed to it, and eventually the unethical behavior may seem normative to them and become part of their values. As a result, they are liable to adopt unethical behavior in the workplace after they graduate. Support for this idea has been provided, for example, by Nonis and Swift (2001), who found that students who believed that cheating, or a dishonest act, was acceptable were more likely to engage in these dishonest behaviors. Moreover, students who engaged in dishonest acts in college were more likely to engage in such acts in the workplace. Carpenter et al. (2004) found a strong relationship between self-reported involvement in prior academic dishonesty (high school) and self-reported involvement in present dishonest behavior (college and workplace). Their findings suggested that past deviant behavior may be an indicator of such behavior in the future. Support for these findings can be found in a survey of the Association of Certified Fraud Examiners (2016), who found that a typical organization loses 5% of its annual revenue in a given year to fraud.

Many attempts to reduce the incidence of academic dishonesty have focused on deterrence as well as using honor codes, as described in the related literature section. Priming manipulation to affect people's dishonest behavior was conducted by Mazar et al. (2008), who tested the hypothesis that drawing people's attention to their standards of integrity would encourage honest behavior. In one experiment, participants were asked to remember the Ten Commandments, and in another experiment, participants were asked to sign a statement acknowledging they were expected to adhere to an honor code. After exposure to the honesty priming manipulations, the participants performed a simple task, which was rewarded according to their degree of success. The authors found that the manipulations encouraged participants to act more honestly, compared to the control groups. One explanation of the results was that the priming manipulations increased the participants' attention to standards of integrity and thus discouraged them from cheating. Grym and Liljander (2016) aimed to replicate the experiments of Mazar et al. (2008) in a European country, as well as to examine gender differences. The authors found that the moral reminder reduced cheating rates, and that in the control group men cheated more than women.

In the current study we delve further into the mechanisms underlying cheating behavior. Specifically, we examine the effects of activating mental constructs, via priming, on cheating during exams. The main constructs we examined were the natural inclination to act honestly, sense of commitment, and the temptation to engage in cheating when such behavior is perceived as a norm. Our study has several merits with respect to the literature: (1) We conducted *a field experiment* studying real-life scenarios in undergraduate course exams (rather than conducting laboratory experiments); (2) The consequences of the participants' behavior in the setup went beyond standard payment in laboratories, as it involved success in the exams and the risk of penalty if caught cheating; and (3) We employed statements explicitly prohibiting cheating during exams, rather than encouraging integrity in general. (4) The understanding that a priming statement about the expected behavior in exams is not enough in itself, but should be accompanied by a request to adhere it; otherwise, it can achieve the undesirable effect of increasing cheating rates.

Field experiments hold significant advantages over laboratory experiments. First, the subjects (the examinees, in our case) are not aware of being scrutinized for study purposes and hence may not attempt to please the researcher. Second, the investigation is conducted in the subjects' everyday environment and therefore offers a more accurate representation of their natural behavior.

## 2. Related literature

### 2.1 Factors

Accumulated research has aimed to understand the underlying characteristics of cheaters, such as age, gender, and GPA (see Johnson and Gormly, 1972; McCabe and Trevino, 1997), as well as contextual factors, such as the probability of getting caught and the severity of punishment (see Genereux and McLeod, 1995; Johnson and Gormly, 1972; Pino and Smith, 2003). Other factors contributing to the inflated cheating rate are characteristics of the exam environment, such as a crowded room, free seating allocations, use of multiple-choice exams (e.g., Houston, 1983, 1986); students' perceptions and beliefs about the prevalence of cheating by other students (e.g., McCabe et al., 2001, 2006; McCabe and Trevino, 1993, 1997); and their perception of the exam's fairness, social norms, and pressure (Genereux and McLeod, 1995). Factors mentioned in DiBartolo and Walsh (2010) include "deterioration in moral values"; "blaming the parents and their offspring, who believe that everyone deserves an "A" grade regardless of the quality of the work"; "popular media that glamorize such behaviors as a reasonable means of getting ahead"; "more accepting attitude on the part of faculty that "cheating happens"; and "an explosion in the proliferation of various technological devices, all providing a multiplicity of opportunities to cheat."

The social factor of "helping" others may also play a role in academic cheating and even allows participants to justify to themselves and the environment its morality. Such "help" to a friend or a classmate can be perceived as altruistic behavior. Alternatively, a refusal to provide such help can be perceived as antisocial behavior. In this regard, Muñoz-Izquierdo et al. (2019) confirmed the finding of Della Vigna et al. (2016) that "respondents are concerned about their social image, so they are more likely to behave altruistically if they know that they are going to be asked to report their actions later." Gino et al. (2013) found that individuals cheated more if the unethical action increased the benefits to others, creating a situation in which dishonesty can be viewed as morally acceptable. A distinction between "individualistic" cheaters who used prohibited materials, and "social cheaters" who violated the rules interacting with others was made by Cicognani (2019). The authors found that "only social cheaters seem affected by social factors: they exhibit higher levels of trust and lower levels of perceived opportunism compared to individualistic cheaters."

## 2.2 Self-reported cheating

Numerous studies have been based on questionnaires about academic cheating that were distributed to students and faculty. Thus, participants knew the purpose of the study and voluntarily answered questions that examined their involvement in actions that could be considered academic dishonesty (e.g., Finn and Frone, 2004; LaBeff et al., 1990; McCabe, 1992; McCabe et al., 2004, 2006; Pino and Smith, 2003). Although widely accepted, conclusions of studies based on questionnaires should be considered carefully, because the data collected through this approach could be skewed. First, questionnaires rely on self-reporting (albeit anonymous) of sensitive data, so there is no certainty regarding its truthfulness. There could be several reasons for lack of accuracy in reporting: instances of cheating that were forgotten, students did not consider certain actions to be cheating, and students provided partial or distorted reporting in order to maintain a positive self-concept (e.g., Ariely and Mazar, 2006; McCabe, 1992; Sykes and Matza, 1957). Second, as noted by Finn and Frone (2004), "The representativeness of the self-selected sample may be problematic. For example, withdrawn or low-achieving students may have been less likely to volunteer for the study."

## 2.3 Attempts to reduce academic dishonesty

Many attempts to reduce the incidence of academic dishonesty have focused on deterrence. Becker (1974) suggested that theories of anomie should be abandoned in favor of addressing unethical behavior by implementing an enforcement policy that involved detection, conviction, and punishment of offenders.[a] Pino and Smith (2003) suggested that less-severe penalties serve as weak deterrents, and DiBartolo and Walsh (2010) suggested using technological approaches, such as antiplagiarism software, to enhance strategies for fraud detection. Solutions based on approaches other than deterrence have also been studied. For example, McCabe et al. (2001) found that academic integrity programs and policies that were part of the campus culture, such as honor codes, had a significant impact on student conduct. Caldwell (2010) suggested a model that combined the two approaches: creating, explaining, and integrating an academic integrity policy into the campus culture and enforcing a realistic, fair punishment when students violated it.

## 3. Research goals and method

### 3.1 Constructs

The main objective of this study was to examine if and to what extent activation of mental constructs affected and mitigated cheating in exams. The activations were carried out by means of priming, which is the process of activating certain representations or associations by exposing individuals to certain stimuli. Such activation may affect an individual's performance of near-future tasks. In the experiments we conducted, the stimuli included a combination of clarifying statements regarding accepted standards of conduct during exams, accompanied by a request to check a box confirming that the students read and understood these statements.

We assumed that the activation of three constructs would play a role in the decision whether to cheat: honesty, norms, and commitment. It was expected that reading a statement about the expected norms of conduct during an exam would activate *the natural inclination to act honestly*, and thus inhibit the desire to cheat and fortify the desire to act fairly (hereafter "the honesty construct"). However, the inclusion of a statement regarding cheating on the exam would also imply that cheating was prevalent, i.e., it would stress the *prevalence of bad social norms* and thereby activate the temptation to engage in cheating when it is perceived *as a norm* (hereafter, "the norms construct"). The third construct was *commitment*. This construct was activated by incorporating a checkbox into the priming text. Specifically, in some of the cases we requested that the examinees check a box as confirmation that they read the presented sentence. We assumed that the checkbox request (especially if complied with) would serve as

---

a. Anomie is a state of confusion, on an individual or collective level, in which social norms are unclear, weak, contradictory, or absent. It involves situations that usually result from sharp social changes that have undermined long-standing guidelines of expectations and behavior patterns. In the absence of such guidelines, members of the collective are prone to behavior that may be defined as social deviance.

a *commitment* to adhere to the text, in other words, to act fairly (hereafter: "the commitment construct"). These suppositions were corroborated by our findings, which showed that the aggregate influence of the evoked constructs ultimately determined the examinees' decision whether to cheat or not.

In order to validate our hypotheses regarding the activation of these constructs, we distributed questionnaires among a group of 41 students who did not participate in the priming experiments described here. In these questionnaires, we instructed the students to imagine that they were sitting in the classroom before the exam began and reading a priming statement as part of the exam guidelines. We asked to what extent the statements reminded them: (1) to act honestly; (2) that cheating is prohibited; (3) of the prevalence of cheating and that cheating is an option. Further, we asked whether the statements encouraged them to act accordingly or the other way around, and whether they felt that checking a box confirming that they read the statement increased their commitment to act accordingly. Some of the questionnaires included items to be rated between 1 and 5 (closed questions) and others contained open questions. We distributed questionnaires for each of the priming statements that were used in our experiments. For each statement, the questionnaires differed from each other both in the order of the questions and the order of items within each question. The results of the responses to the questionnaires supported our hypotheses regarding the activation of the described mental structures. A brief summary of the answers to the priming statement of the first experiment is in the Appendix.

## 3.2 Experimental design

The experiments were conducted over three consecutive years among business administration undergraduate students at an Israeli college, during final exams in a quantitative course. The institute's regulations stipulate that each student is entitled to take each examination on one of two dates (or both, in case of failure on the first exam). A minimum score of 60 out of 100 is required in order to pass the exam. Our experiments were conducted on the first date, which in this course is typically characterized by a 30%–40% rate of failure. The experiments were approved in advance by the relevant authorities in the institution, in accordance with the guidelines of the NIH.

Each exam had 20, equally-weighted multiple-choice questions. The exam questions were constructed in such a way that they were impossible to answer without performing written, detailed calculations. Examinees were instructed to write down their calculations in a notebook, which was provided to them for that purpose, and to mark their answers on an answer sheet attached to the exam. The written exam guidelines, as well as oral instructions given before the exam started, made clear to the examinees that any answer lacking a detailed calculation would be disregarded.

We determined cheating in the following way: An answer was coded as an act of deceit if the correct answer was marked on the answer sheet, but its related calculation was absent or mismatching. While this process of eliciting cheating incidences may not be perfect and may contain some noise, it has the advantage of keeping the detection process latent. Moreover, errors in classification would reduce the ability of detecting differences among the groups; thus, if at all, such errors increase the risk of making type-2 errors, i.e., retaining a false null hypothesis. We focused primarily on examining differences between the groups in cheating on two or three items, while cheating on one item or more than three items represents the periphery of our main measure. The exam graders did not know which priming treatment each examinee was given. Panel A in Table 1 maps the setups of the various experiments and stresses the differences between the groups within each experiment. Panel B presents the relevant hypotheses for each experiment.

It is important to note that in all the experiments, the attention of the examinees was drawn to the prohibition of cheating, except for the control group. In addition, Experiment 1 analyzes mere exposure to the priming statement vs exposure and a checkbox; Experiment 2 included a warning in the statement; and in Experiment 3 we drew the attention of the examinees to a history of past cheating. As will be detailed later on, Experiment 3 was conducted under mental stress of the examinees to succeed and obtain a score higher than 70.

## 4. Three field experiments

### 4.1 Experiment 1: attention vs attention and checkbox

#### *4.1.1 Design*

In the first exam we used a three-version between-subject design with the following text, which referred to an excerpt from the college regulations as the priming material: "During the exam, the examinee must not discuss anything with others, including technical issues, nor may (s)he copy or pass any material to other students. From the Study Regulations, Chapter 4, clause c, Item (II)."[b] The citation was printed in bold, underlined, set in an 18-point font, and placed at the center of the cover page of the exam, below the guidelines, which were printed in a 14-point font.

The three versions, which were randomly allocated to the examinees, were Attention, Attention and Checkbox (hereafter: AC), and control. The AC version instructed the examinees to confirm that they had read the sentence by checking (✓) the empty box next to the statement ("☐ Please check that you have read"). The Attention version consisted of the same excerpt, but did not ask examinees to check a confirmation box. The control version did not contain the excerpt, nor a request to check a confirmation box.

The examinees were instructed to read the exam guidelines that were printed on the cover page, and only then were they allowed to turn this page and begin solving the exam. We assumed that most of the examinees did glance at the cover page and therefore noticed the prominent priming statement. The same procedure was followed in experiments 2 and 3.

b. The chapter and section numbers have been changed to maintain anonymity.

**TABLE 1** Mapping the Experiments' Setups and Hypotheses

**Panel A. Setups**

| | | Attention | Checkbox | Warning | History |
|---|---|---|---|---|---|
| Exp. 1 | Control | | | | |
| | Attention | ✓ | | | |
| | Attention + Checkbox (AC) | ✓ | ✓ | | |
| Exp. 2 | Control | | | | |
| | Attention + Checkbox (AC) | ✓ | ✓ | | |
| | Attention + Checkbox + Warning (ACW) | ✓ | ✓ | ✓ | |
| Exp. 3 | Control | | | | |
| | Attention + Checkbox (AC) | ✓ | ✓ | | |
| | Attention + Checkbox + History (ACH) | ✓ | ✓ | | ✓ |

**Panel B. Hypotheses**

| | |
|---|---|
| Exp. 1 | H1 (honesty): C(AC) < C(control); C(Attention) < C(control) |
| | H2 (norms): C(control) < C(AC); C(control) < C(Attention) |
| | H3 (commitment): C(AC) < C(Attention) < C(control) |
| | H4 (box checking): $C(AC \mid \text{checked}) < C(AC \mid \text{not checked})$ |
| Exp. 2 | H1 (Honesty): C(AC) < C(control); C(ACW) < C(control) |
| | H2 (norms): C(control) < C(AC) < C(ACW) |
| | H3 (commitment): C(ACW) < C(AC) < C(control) |
| Exp. 3 | H1 (Attention): C (AC) = C (control) = C (ACH) |

Panel A maps the priming treatments across the three experiments. Panel B maps the hypotheses across the three experiments. *C*(*g*) denotes the cheating percentages of group *g*.

A total of 202 examinees took the exam. Of them, 61 examinees (30%) received the Attention version, 73 examinees (36%) received the AC version, and 68 examinees (34%) received the control version.

### *4.1.2 Hypotheses*

We hypothesized that the priming statement (the excerpt from the academy regulations) would evoke the *honesty* construct and the *norms* construct. In addition, we expected the request to mark the checkbox to evoke a *commitment* construct, namely, the commitment to abide by the instruction not to cheat.

We hypothesized that the activation of the honesty construct would encourage honest behavior, thereby producing lower cheating rates within the primed groups compared to those in the control group. Defining $C(g)$ as the cheating rate within group $g$, we derived the following hypothesis:

**H1 (honesty): Natural inclination to be honest:**

C(AC) < C(control); C(Attention) < C(control)

We hypothesized that the second construct, norms, would increase cheating rates, because the statement would imply that other students cheat. Otherwise, there would be no reason for the examiners to bother posting the statement. Formally, we derived the second hypothesis:

**H2 (norms): Evoking the prevalence of bad social norms:**

C(control) < C(AC); C(control) < C(Attention)

Finally, we hypothesized that the third construct, the commitment to act honestly, which was activated by the confirmation box, would lower cheating rates, especially if examinees complied with checking the box. We derived our third hypothesis:

**H3 (commitment): Evoking commitment to behave honestly:**

C(AC) < C(Attention); C(AC) < C(control)

Further, we presumed that some examinees might choose not to check the confirmation box, to avoid the commitment. We expected a difference between "checkers" and "noncheckers," in that the former would manifest lower cheating rates than the latter. Therefore, we derived our last hypothesis:

**H4 (box checking):**

C(AC | checked) < C(AC | not checked)

Note that the hypotheses were not mutually exclusive. Rather, we expected that the aggregate effect of the constructs would determine whether the examinees decided to cheat.

### *4.1.3 Results and discussion*

The three left columns in Table 2 show the cheating rates within the groups (panel A) and the statistical significance of the differences between each pair

**TABLE 2 Cheating Rates of Exp. 1: Control, Attention, and (AC) Treatments; AC Checkers and Noncheckers**

**Panel A. Cheating rates**

| | A: Control | B: Attention | C: AC | D: AC checkers | E: AC noncheckers |
|---|---|---|---|---|---|
| No. of cheaters on 1+ answers | 23 | 24 | **20** | 8 | 12 |
| percentage | 34% | 39% | **27%** | 25% | 29% |
| No. of cheaters on 2+ answers | 17 | 18 | **16** | 7 | 9 |
| percentage | 25% | 30% | **22%** | 22% | 22% |
| No. of cheaters on 3+ answers | 8 | 15 | **6** | 2 | 4 |
| percentage | 12% | 25% | **8%** | 6% | 10% |
| No. of cheaters on 4+ answers | 5 | 14 | **5** | 2 | 3 |
| percentage | 7% | 23% | **7%** | 6% | 7% |
| Number of students | 68 | 61 | 73 | 32 (44%) | 41 (56%) |

**Panel B. $z$-Statistic and its corresponding $p$-value (in parentheses)**

| | A to B | B to C | A to C | D to E |
|---|---|---|---|---|
| No. of cheaters on 1+ answers | 0.65 (0.26) | 1.47 (0.07) | 0.83 (0.2) | z=0.41 (0.34) |
| No. of cheaters on 2+ answers | 0.57 (0.28) | 1.01 (0.16) | 0.43 (0.33) | z=0.01 (0. 5) |
| No. of cheaters on 3+ answers | 1.90 (0.03) | 2.60 (0.00) | 0.70 (0.24) | z=0.54 (0.29) |
| No. of cheaters on 4+ answers | 2.50 (0.01) | 2.66 (0.00) | 0.12 (0.45) | z=0.18 (0.43) |

*Note.* Panel A shows the cheating rates for the Attention, AC and control groups. The two columns on the right present the cheating rates within the AC subsamples of checkers and noncheckers. Panel B presents the $z$-statistic (for two population proportions) and their corresponding $p$-values of the differences between the groups.

of groups (panel B). We assessed the cheating rates by counting the number of questions for which the calculations in the notebook did not match the correct answers on the reply sheet. Accordingly, the rows of panel A present the number and percentage of cheaters within each treatment group by the number of conflicting calculations, from at least one ("1+ answers") in the first row, to four or more ("4+ answers") in the last row. The lowest cheating rate, according to each assessment, is printed in bold.

Evidently, the AC group had the lowest cheating rate, the Attention group had the highest cheating rate, and the control group fell in between. Combining the statistical significances, the results suggested the following ordering of cheating rates among the groups:

C (AC) ≤ C (control) < C (Attention)

Comparing cheating rates between the control group and the Attention group show higher cheating rates in the latter. For example: 25% of the students in the Attention group cheated on 3+ answers, compared with 12% in the control group ($z = 1.9$, $p = 0.03$). We concluded that mere exposure to the priming statement caused the norms construct (H2) to dominate the honesty construct (H1).

Comparing cheating rates between the AC group and the control group demonstrates lower cheating rates in the former, which is the expected direction (H3), yet the differences were not significant. We suggest that in the AC group, the constructs acting in both directions were roughly equivalent. Specifically, the honesty and the commitment constructs, activated by the statement and the checkmark request, both of which discourage cheating (H1 and H3), were equivalent in their combined effect to the norms construct, which encouraged cheating (H2). Comparing the AC group to the Attention group demonstrates that the request to confirm by checking a box lowers cheating rates regardless if acted upon (H3). For example: 25% cheated on 3+ items in the latter group vs 8% in the former ($z = 2.6$, $p = 0.00$). It should be noted that the AC treatment had the effect of lowering the percentage of cheaters, as well as the effect of lowering the amount of cheating among the cheaters.

We expected that students who had no intention of cheating would easily comply with the request, while those who planned in advance to cheat would find it harder to check the box, if at all. Consequently, we expected to find differences in cheating rates between checkers and noncheckers. We deal with this issue toward the end of the paper in the section titled "spontaneous cheating vs planned cheating." Analysis of compliance with the checkmark request is presented in Table 2 in the two right columns. The results show that as many as 41 examinees (56% of the group) chose not to check the box. As can be seen, the cheating rates among the checkers were lower or equal to those among the noncheckers, though the differences between them were not statistically significant. So, while the results pointed in the direction suggested in H4, they did not significantly support it.

Following these analyses, we ran an OLS regression in which the dependent variable was the number of copied items and the explanatory variables were the score, dummy variables for the treatments and a dummy variable for gender. The regression equation was as follows:

$$Number\_of\_Items\_Copied = \beta_0 + \beta_1{}^{*}Score + \beta_2{}^{*}Attention + \beta_3 AC + \beta_4{}^{*}Male + \varepsilon \qquad (1)$$

Attention and AC are dummy variables reflecting the different treatments. Attention equals 1 for the Attention treatment and 0 otherwise; and so on, male equals 1 for male and 0 for female. The regression results are presented in Table 3. In addition to the OLS regression, we conducted a probit regression in which the dependent variable equals 1 in case of cheating and 0 otherwise; its results were very similar and therefore are not displayed.

In this experiment, students' abilities—as reflected by the insignificant score coefficient—do not explain cheating. We explain this result by the homogeneously, unusually low achievement level of the examinees (see Table 4). Next, mere attention to the priming statement increased cheating, as indicated by its positive and significant coefficient. The AC coefficient is negative, which is in the desirable direction of lowering cheating rates, yet it is insignificant. The positive significant coefficient of the male variable indicates that in this experiment males are more likely to cheat than females. These results support the data shown in Table 2.

To recap, Experiment 1 provided a preponderance of support for H2. The exposure to the excerpt from the study regulations about proper conduct during exams seems to have evoked the bad social norms construct and increased the cheating rates. Ostensibly, the effect was mitigated by the request to check the box, confirming that they read the excerpt, which activated the honesty and commitment constructs (H1 and H3, respectively). In other words, when examinees perceived that cheating commonly took place, they tended to act

**TABLE 3 Regressions to Assess the Priming Effect on Cheating: Exp. 1, Exp. 2, and Exp. 3**

| Exp. 1 | | Exp. 2 | | Exp. 3 | |
|---|---|---|---|---|---|
| Intercept | 0.81*** (0.29) | Intercept | 6.3* (0.78) | Intercept | 3.6 *** (0.43) |
| Score | −0.004 (0.005) | Score | −0.07*** (0.009) | Score | −0.03*** (0.005) |
| Attention | 0.57** (0.29) | ACW | 0.22 (0.67) | ACH | −0.31 (0.28) |
| AC | −0.19 (0.28) | AC | −0.49 (0.68) | AC | −0.19 (0.3) |
| Male | 0.39* (0.24) | Male | 0.49 (0.55) | Male | 0.12 (0.24) |
| *F* | 2.81 | *F* | 16.61 | *F* | 12.99 |
| Sig-F | 0.03 | Sig-F | 0.00 | Sig-F | 0.00 |
| *R* square | 0.05 | *R* square | 0.28 | *R* square | 0.36 |
| Obs | 202 | Obs | 162 | Obs | 97 |

*Note*: The table displays regression results for the three experiments, Standard error terms are in parentheses. *, **, and *** denote *p*-value at 10%, 5%, and 1%, respectively. The dependent variable is the number of items copied. The explanatory variables are score and dummy variables for the treatments and for gender.

**TABLE 4** Average Exam Grades Exp. 1

**Panel A. Average grades per group**

| | A: Control | B: Attention | C: AC |
|---|---|---|---|
| Average score on the exam | 32 | 32 | 33 |
| | A to B | B to C | C to A |
| *z*-Statistic (*p*-value) of the difference | 0.02 (0.49) | 0.26 (0.39) | 0.3 (0.38) |

**Panel B. Average grades within the groups broken down by cheaters and noncheaters**

| | A | B | C |
|---|---|---|---|
| Cheaters | 29 | 30 | 28 |
| Noncheaters | 33 | 33 | 35 |
| *z*-Statistic (*p*-value) of the difference | 0.59 (0.27) | 0.41 (0.33) | 1.03 (0.15) |

according to the maxim: "When in Rome, do as the Romans do." This tendency was mitigated by evoking a sense of honesty and a commitment to adhere to the academic code of conduct.

Table 4 presents the examinees' average scores. The average scores of the groups ranged from 32 to 33, and the differences were not statistically significant, which suggests a similar level of ability across the groups (panel A). Cheaters' average scores ranged from 28 to 30, and noncheaters' scores fell between 33 and 35 (panel B). The differences in scores were not statistically significant.

The low range of scores suggests that most of the students were not able to pass the exam on their own. Despite the similar abilities of cheaters and noncheaters, only some of the students turned to cheating. We suggest that poor preparation for the exam was not the sole consideration in deciding whether to cheat and that other considerations may have affected the decision as well.

## 4.2 Experiment 2: Attention and checkbox vs attention and checkbox and warning

### *4.2.1 Design*

The results of Experiment 1 suggested that the construct underlying H2 played a role in the examinees' decisions. Further, the results showed that the honesty and commitment constructs, underlying H1 and H3 respectively, had a possible mitigating effect. The complete picture may have been obscured because not all of the examinees in the AC group complied with checking the confirmation box. Thus, to shed further light on the examinees' decision-making process, we required all of the examinees to check confirmation boxes for all the items in the list of the exam instructions in the second experiment. One of the items in the versions distributed to the groups was the priming sentence. This design made complying with the requirement to check the boxes more extensive.

A year after Experiment 1, we conducted Experiment 2 during an exam in the same course. We devised a three-version between-subject design, with two priming sentences. The first sentence called attention to the prohibition of cheating on the exam, and the other sentence included a similar reminder, accompanied by a warning about punishment for offenders. We named them Attention and Checkbox (hereafter: AC) and Attention and Checkbox and Warning (hereafter: ACW), respectively. The control group received an exam without any priming text. The attention-priming sentence was "Please note that copying from another student or allowing others to copy is prohibited." The attention and warning priming sentence was "Please note that copying from another student or allowing others to copy is a disciplinary offense, and offenders can expect to be punished."

The priming sentences were included with the general guidelines for the exam and were distinguished from the rest of the guidelines by a larger font (14-point vs 12-point) as well as by being printed in bold and underlined. Next to each guideline was a blank square designated for a checkmark (✓), and the students were instructed to checkmark each guideline as confirmation that they read and understood it: "Please check (✓) each guideline that you have read and understood."

A total of 179 examinees attended the exam and were randomly assigned one of the versions: 61 examinees (34%) received forms with the attention-warning priming, 58 examinees (32%) received the attention-only priming, and 60 examinees (34%) served as a control group. Seventeen students (9.5% of the participants) chose not to checkmark any guidelines at all. For robustness, we analyzed the priming effect among all the students (179 students) and among the subsample of the students who checkmarked (162 students). The findings from the whole sample and for the subsample were very similar, and therefore we report only the subsample results.

### *4.2.2 Hypotheses*

Similar to the previous experiment, we hypothesized that the priming sentences would evoke two constructs, namely, the natural inclination to be honest and the prevalence of bad social norms. With respect to the latter, the attention and warning sentence was expected to imply that the problem of cheating was more acute and activate the construct more saliently. The request to checkmark the statements that appeared in the two versions was expected to activate commitment among both groups, so we performed a comparison in that respect vis-à-vis the control group. As before, $C(g)$ denotes the cheating percentages of group $g$. Thus, the formal experiment hypotheses were as follows:

**H1 (honesty): Natural inclination to be honest:**
C(AC) < C(control); C(ACW) < C(control)

**H2 (norms): Evoking the prevalence of bad social norms:**
C(control) < C(AC) < C(ACW)

**H3 (commitment): Evoking commitment to behave honestly:**
C(ACW) < C(AC) < C(control)

### *4.2.3 Results and discussion*

The findings of the experiment are presented in Table 5. Panel A shows the number and percentage of cheaters within each group, deduced by the number of inconsistent answers, from at least one ("1+ answers") in the first row, to four or more ("4+ answers") in the last row. The lowest cheating rate, according to each assessment, is printed in bold.

The results show that the group exposed to the AC priming had the lowest cheating rates, while the cheating rates in the ACW group and the control group were quite similar. Formally, the results showed the following:

C(AC) < C(control) ≈ C(ACW)

It seems that cheating on one question (out of 20) was not perceived as dishonesty, as discussed below in the summary and conclusion section. For example, 45% of the control group and 39% of the AC group cheated on at least one answer ($z = 0.65$, $p = 0.26$), whereas 38% of the control group and 27% of the AC group cheated on at least two answers ($z = 1.4$, $p = 0.08$).

Comparing the AC and the ACW groups demonstrates a lower cheating rate of the former group. For example, 27% of the AC group cheated on two or more answers, vs 38% of the ACW group ($z = 1.33$, $p = 0.09$); and 23% of the AC group cheated on three or more answers vs 32% of the ACW group ($z = 1.23$, $p = 0.11$).

We stress again that the students in the primed groups were made aware of the issue of cheating, and the students in the unprimed control group were not. In line with the hypotheses, the activated constructs influenced the decision whether to cheat in opposing directions, and therefore the cheating rates reflected the offsetting of these forces. As with the previous experiment, the combination of directing attention to the accepted norms accompanied by a checkbox yielded the lowest cheating rates, as evident in the lower cheating rates of the AC group. Thus, honesty and commitment (H1 + H3) dominated the activation of bad norms (H2). Finally, the similar cheating rates between the control group and the ACW group demonstrated that the addition of the warning to the attention formulation completely diminished the influence of the honesty construct.

Next, we conducted an OLS regression in which the dependent variable was the number of copied items and the explanatory variables were the score, dummy variables for the treatments and a dummy variable for gender. The regression equation was as follows:

$$\begin{aligned} Number\_of\_Items\_Copied = \beta_0 + \beta_1{}^{*}Score + \beta_2{}^{*}AC \\ + \beta_3{}^{*}ACW + \beta_4{}^{*}Male + \varepsilon \end{aligned} \tag{2}$$

AC and ACW are dummy variables reflecting the different treatments. AC equals 1 for the AC treatment and 0 otherwise, and so on: male equals 1 for male and 0 for female. The OLS regression results are presented in Table 3.

The results demonstrate that test score was the best predictor of cheating: Its negative significance coefficient indicates an inverse relation between cheating rates and test score, so that the stronger (weaker) the student, the less (more) he/she cheated. The AC negative coefficient and the ACW positive coefficient are in the direction shown in Table 5, yet they are not significant. When conducting regressions (not shown) of AC (ACW) and the control as dependent variables, the AC (ACW) coefficient is negative (positive) and significant. The insignificance of the male variable proves that in this sample there was no difference in the likelihood to cheat between males and females. We also conducted a probit regression in which the dependent variable equals 1 in case of cheating and 0 otherwise; its results were similar and therefore are not displayed. In summary, Table 5 shows that directing student attention to behave honestly plus a request to confirm by marking a box was the most effective way of reducing the cheating rate.

We inferred several explanations as to why the wording of the ACW condition caused students to behave according to bad social norms (H2) and dominated the inclination to act honestly (H1). First, it is possible that the longer phrase and the emphasis on cheating as an offense highlighted the prevalence of cheating. Second, when the penalty for the offense is known, the decision to commit the offense was in fact an acknowledgment that the student was willing to pay the penalty. Consequently, the decision to cheat did not harm the students' self-esteem. Third, students' past experience of not being caught and punished may have caused them to downplay the probability of punishment, resulting in a greater willingness to violate the rule (Hertwig et al., 2004; Mazar et al., 2008). Past research (Erev and Haruvy, 2013) has shown that low probability of detection (as in fraud) undermined the cognizance that violation of the law would lead to penalty.

Next, we analyzed examinees' average scores between and within the groups. The results are presented in Table 6.

Calculating the average score in each priming group (Table 6, panel A) showed that the AC group achieved the highest average score of 63, vs 56 in the control group ($z=1.2, p=0.11$) and 53 in the ACW group ($z=1.88, p=0.03$). Finding a difference in the average scores was somewhat surprising because of the random distribution of the exams. The attention reminder may have

**TABLE 5 Cheating Rates of Exp. 2: Control, AC, and ACW treatments[a]**

**Panel A. Cheating rates**

| | A: Control | B: AC | C: ACW |
|---|---|---|---|
| No. of cheaters on 1+ answers<br>percentage | 25<br>45% | **20**<br>**39%** | 24<br>43% |
| No. of cheaters on 2+ answers<br>percentage | 21<br>38% | **13**<br>**27%** | 21<br>38% |
| No. of cheaters on 3+ answers<br>percentage | 17<br>31% | **10**<br>**23%** | 18<br>32% |
| No. of cheaters on 4+ answers<br>percentage | 13<br>24% | **8**<br>**16%** | 15<br>27% |
| No. of Students | 55(100%) | 51(100%) | 56(100%) |

**Panel B. *z*-Statistic and its corresponding *p*-value for the differences between the cheating rates of the groups**

| | A to B | B to C | A to C |
|---|---|---|---|
| Cheating on 1+ answers | 0.65 (0.26) | 0.38 (0.35) | 0.28 (0.39) |
| Cheating on 2+ answers | 1.40 (0.08) | **1.33 (0.09)** | 0.07 (0.47) |
| Cheating on 3+ answers | 1.09 (0.14) | **1.23 (0.11)** | 0.14 (0.44) |
| Cheating on 4+ answers | 1.03 (0.15) | **1.40 (0.08)** | 0.38 (0.35) |

*Note.* Panel A shows the cheating rates of control, AC and ACW groups. Panel B shows the z-statistic (for two population proportions) and its corresponding *p*-value in parentheses.
[a] *The results here are only for the subsample of students who checkmarked the guidelines (91% of the whole sample).*

strengthened students' motivation not to cheat, and therefore these students relied on themselves and tried harder, resulting in them outperforming the other groups. In contrast, the students who were exposed to the ACW statement were less motivated to act honestly, and therefore they relied more on cheating than on their own abilities. This group's lower average result reflected this choice. The control group was not influenced by any of these associations, so its performance fell between the two other groups.

The average score for cheaters in the control, AC, and ACW groups was 44, 47, and 37, vs an average score of 66, 73, and 64 for noncheaters, respectively (Table 6, panel B). The differences were statistically significant. Weaker students were more motivated to cheat, as was also shown in the regression results above.

**TABLE 6** Average Exam Grades—Exp. 2

| Panel A. Average grades per group | | | |
|---|---|---|---|
| | A: Control | B: AC | C: ACW |
| Average score on the exam | 56 | 63 | 53 |
| | A to B | B to C | C to A |
| *z*-Statistic (*p*-value) of the difference | 1.2 (0.11) | 1.88 (0.03) | 0.66 (0.25) |
| **Panel B. Average grades within the groups, by cheaters and noncheaters** | | | |
| | A | B | C |
| Cheaters' average score | 44 | 47 | 37 |
| Noncheaters' average score | 66 | 73 | 64 |
| *z*-Statistic (*p*-value) of the difference | 3.26 (0.00) | 4.22 (0.00) | 4.27 (0.00) |

## 4.3 Experiment 3: Attention and checkbox vs attention and checkbox and history

### *4.3.1 Design*

In the previous experiments, we suggested that the priming text evoked two constructs that influenced students in opposing directions: the natural tendency to act honestly and the inclination to act according to bad social norms, namely, to cheat if cheating is perceived as a common behavior. In this experiment, we examined whether a priming text that emphasized the incidence of past cheating would cause the latter association to dominate, namely, to increase the incidence of cheating.

In an exam held a year later, we used only priming statements that required checking a box. The examinees were asked to confirm that they read the sentence by placing a checkmark (✓) in the empty square next to it. We distinguished between Attention and Checkbox (hereafter: AC) priming and Attention and Checkbox and History priming (hereafter: ACH)—a statement that emphasized the prevalence of past cheating. The attention-priming statement was "Please note that copying from another student or allowing others to copy is prohibited." The attention-history priming was "In light of the repeated incidents of cheating in the past, we wish to point out that copying from another student or allowing others to copy is prohibited." The control group received a form with neutral text: "Please write in a neat, clear, and readable manner."

The priming sentence was included with the general guidelines for the exam and was distinguished from the rest of the guidelines by a larger font (14-point vs 12-point) that was in bold and underlined. Next to the statement was an empty box designated for a checkmark (✓), and the students were instructed to check that they read and understood it. The cheating rates were assessed as in the previous experiments.

A total of 239 examinees attended the exam and were randomly assigned one of the treatments. Of the total, 79 examinees (33%) received forms with the AC priming, 79 examinees (33%) received the ACH priming, and 81 examinees (34%) served as a control group. Only 97 examinees (40%) completed the checkmark request ("checkers"), and 142 (60%) chose not to checkmark ("non-checkers"). According to the results, failure to check the box was by choice and not an oversight. For robustness, we analyzed the treatment's effect among all the students (239 students), among a subsample of the students who check-marked (40%), and among a subsample of the students who did not checkmark (60%). The results were similar. To maintain consistency with Experiment 2, we report only the results of the checkers' subsample.

It is important to note that in the previous two experiments, which were conducted in the same course, students needed a score of 60 (out of 100) in order to pass the exam and to continue in the regular course of study. The third experiment was conducted in a different course, in which students needed a grade of 70 or above in order to continue a prestigious course of study. As a result, the pressure to achieve a grade higher than 70 was considerable. We assumed that because the need to achieve a high score was greater, the effect of the various priming manipulations would be lower, and therefore the priming statements in this experiment would show less influence on students compared to the previous two experiments.

### 4.3.2 Hypotheses

As before, $C(g)$ denotes the cheating percentages of group $g$. We hypothesized that the two priming statements would evoke both constructs: *honesty* and *norms*, which would operate in opposing directions. Based on the results of Experiment 2, we assumed that the AC priming would decrease cheating rates vs the control group and that the ACH priming would strengthen the norms construct and hence result in increased cheating rates in that group. Under regular circumstances, our hypotheses would have been as follows:

$C\ (AC) < C\ (Control) < C\ (ACH)$

Due to the exam circumstances described above, namely the essential need to obtain a score higher than 70, we assumed that there would be no difference between the two priming manipulations in lowering the cheating rates. Therefore, we devised the following hypothesis:

**H1 (Attention):**

$C\ (AC) = C\ (Control) = C\ (ACH)$

### 4.3.3 Results and discussion

As with the previous experiments, we compared cheating rates between the groups, the results of which are presented in Table 7, and conducted an OLS regression, presented in Table 3. The regression equation was as follows:

$$Number\_of\_Items\_Copied = \beta_0 + \beta_1{}^{*}Score + \beta_2{}^{*}AC + \beta_3{}^{*}ACH + \beta_4{}^{*}Male + \varepsilon \quad (3)$$

The dependent variable was the number of copied items, and the explanatory variables were the score, dummy variables for the treatments and a dummy variable for gender. We also conducted a probit regression in which the dependent variable equals 1 in case of cheating and 0 otherwise; its results were similar and therefore are not displayed.

**TABLE 7 Cheating Rates of Exp. 3: Control, AC, and ACH Treatments**

**Panel A. Cheating rates**

| | A: Control | B: AC | C: ACH |
|---|---|---|---|
| No. of cheaters on 1 +answers<br>percentage | 15<br>42% | 11<br>42% | 16<br>46% |
| No. of cheaters on 2+ answers<br>percentage | 9<br>25% | 8<br>31% | 9<br>26% |
| No. of cheaters on 3+ answers<br>percentage | 8<br>22% | 3<br>12% | 6<br>17% |
| No. of cheaters on 4+ answers<br>percentage | 6<br>17% | 1<br>4% | 3<br>9% |
| No. of students | 36 | 26 | 35 |

**Panel B. *z*-Statistic and its corresponding *p*-value for the differences between the cheating rates of the groups**

| | A to B | B to C | A to C |
|---|---|---|---|
| No. of cheaters on 1+ answers | 0.05 (0.48) | 0.26 (0.4) | 0.34 (0.37) |
| No. of cheaters on 2+ answers | 0.5 (0.31) | 0.44 (0.33) | 0.07 (0.47) |
| No. of cheaters on 3+ answers | 1.09 (0.14) | 0.61 (0.27) | 0.54 (0.3) |
| No. of cheaters on 4+ answers | 1.57 (0.060) | 0.74 (0.23) | 1.03 (0.15) |

*Note*: Panel A shows the cheating rates for the control, AC and ACH treatments, by the number of answers copied. Panel B shows the *z*-statistic (for two population proportions) and its corresponding *p*-value in parentheses. The results here are for the subsample of students who checkmarked (40% of the whole sample).

Analysis of the cheating rates (Table 7) did not reveal differences between the treatments and thus supported H1, namely, none of the priming sentences produced an unambiguous pattern of effect on the cheating rates. This was true for the entire sample, for the subsamples of the checkers, and for the subsample of the noncheckers. Therefore, the results in Table 7 reinforced the assumption that a great necessity to succeed would reduce and even suppress the influence of the honesty construct and strengthen the effect of bad social norms. The latter effect was also reflected in the high cheating rates of more than 50% in the entire sample. The regression results (Table 3) demonstrated an expected negative relation between students' ability as reflected in their score and cheating. No differences were found between the treatments. Gender also proved to be insignificant.

Analyzing examinees' average scores (Table 8) demonstrated homogeneity in scores between the groups (panel A), and as evident from panel B, cheaters proved to be weaker students.

## 5. Spontaneous cheating vs planned cheating

In light of the prominent priming statements and the low checkmarking rate (only 40% of the examinees checkmarked, vs 91% in the second experiment), we were interested in the relation between checkmarking and cheating, and in particular whether the lack of checkmarking was the result of a conscious choice rather than an oversight. Thus, we analyzed the cheating rates (for any amount of cheating) among checkers and noncheckers. The results presented in Table 9 reveal that the students' compliance with the checkbox request proved

**TABLE 8** Average Exam Grades—Exp. 3

| **Panel A. Average grades per group** | | | |
|---|---|---|---|
| | A: Control | B: AC | C: ACH |
| Average score on the exam | 65 | 68 | 65 |
| | A to B | B to C | C to A |
| *z*-Statistic (*p*-value) of the difference | 0.73 (0.23) | 0.79 (0.22) | 0.03(0.49) |
| **Panel B. Average grades within the groups, by cheaters and noncheaters** | | | |
| | A | B | C |
| Cheaters' average score | 51 | 57 | 53 |
| Noncheaters' average score | 79 | 81 | 80 |
| *z*-Statistic (*p*-value) of the difference | 5.11 (0.00) | 5.01 (0.00) | 5.11 (0.00) |

**TABLE 9** Cheating Rates Within the Groups, Checkers, and Noncheckers

| Panel A: checkers' cheating rate | | | |
|---|---|---|---|
| | A: Control | B: AC | C: ACH |
| No. of cheaters on 1+ answers | 15 | 11 | 16 |
| Percentage | 42% | 42% | 46% |
| No. of examinees | 36 (100%) | 26 (100%) | 35 (100%) |
| **Panel B: noncheckers' cheating rate** | | | |
| | A | B | C |
| No. of cheaters on 1+ answers | 25 | 30 | 27 |
| Percentage | 56% | 57% | 61% |
| No. of examinees | 45 (100%) | 53 (100%) | 44 (100%) |
| **Panel C: $z$-Statistic and $p$-value of the differences** | | | |
| | A | B | C |
| No. of cheaters on 1+ answers | 1.24 (0.11) | 1.20 (0.12) | 1.39 (0.08) |

*Note.* This table presents the cheating rates within each priming group differentiated between checkers (panel A) and noncheckers (panel B). Panel C displays the z-statistic (for two populations' proportions) and its corresponding p-value of the difference between the groups.

to be a decisive influence in lowering the cheating rates: Cheating rates among the checkers in each of the primed groups were lower. Among the checkers, cheating rates of 42%, 42%, and 46% were found in the control, AC, and ACH groups, respectively, vs cheating rates of 56% ($z=1.24$, $p=0.11$), 57% ($z=1.20$, $p=0.12$), and 61% ($z=1.39$, $p=0.08$) among the noncheckers in the three respective groups. In light of the borderline levels of significance in the control and AC groups, we also performed a chi-square test between checking and cheating for the whole sample. This relation was found to be significant ($\chi^2=4.82$, $p=0.03$).

To further investigate the examinees' process of deciding whether to cheat, we performed additional analyses: First, we divided the sample into checkers and noncheckers and calculated the average test score within each treatment group, while further differentiating between cheaters and noncheaters (Table 10). Second, we divided the sample into two, above and below the median score, and calculated the percentage of cheaters and checkers within each group (Table 11).

Table 10 shows that the checkers' average score was clearly higher than the average score of the noncheckers: The average score was 74 vs 59 ($z=2.4$, $p=0.01$) in the control group, 75 vs 65 ($z=1.66$, $p=0.05$) in the AC group, and

**TABLE 10 Examinees' Average Test Scores Within the Groups, Checkers, and Noncheckers**

**Panel A. Checkers' average test score**

| | A: Control | B: AC | C: ACH |
|---|---|---|---|
| Checkers' average test score | 74 | 75 | 68 |
| Cheaters' average test score | 55 | 62 | 55 |
| Noncheaters' average test score | 87 | 84 | 80 |
| z-Statistic (p-value) between cheaters and noncheaters | 4.43 (0.00) | 3.03 (0.00) | 3.39 (0.00) |

**Panel B. Noncheckers' average test score**

| | A | B | C |
|---|---|---|---|
| Noncheckers' average test score | 59 | 65 | 63 |
| Cheaters' average test score | 48 | 55 | 52 |
| Noncheaters' average test score | 72 | 79 | 80 |
| z-Statistic (p-value) between cheaters and noncheaters | 2.82 (0.00) | 3.89 (0.00) | 3.7 (0.00) |

**Panel C. z-Statistic and p-value of the difference between the two subsamples**

| | A | B | C |
|---|---|---|---|
| z-Statistic (p-value) of the difference between checkers and noncheckers | 2.40 (0.01) | 1.66 (0.05) | 0.93 (0.18) |

*Note.* This table presents the average test scores for checkers (panel A) and noncheckers (panel B), differentiated further between cheaters and noncheaters within each of the priming groups. Panel C presents the z-statistic and its corresponding p-value for the difference between the groups.

68 vs 63 ($z=0.93$, $p=0.18$) in the ACH group. Another interesting result arose from comparing the scores of cheaters and noncheaters in each of the subsamples. The cheaters had statistically significant lower scores. For example, among the checkers in the ACH group (panel A), the average score of cheaters was 55 vs 80 among the noncheaters ($z=3.39$, $p=0.00$); among the noncheckers in the AC group (panel B), the average of cheaters was 55 vs 79 among the noncheaters ($z=3.38$, $p=0.00$).

Table 11 presents the sample breakdown according to the median score. Panels A and B show the percentage of cheaters and checkers within each subsample. The first finding was that the incidence of cheating among the strong examinees was much lower than that of the weaker students, namely, 29%

**TABLE 11** Rates of Cheaters and Checkers among Strong and Weak Examinees

| Panel A. Examinees above the median score (strong students) | | | |
|---|---|---|---|
| | A: Control | B: AC | C: ACH |
| No. of cheaters | 12 | 12 | 9 |
| % cheaters | 29% | 30% | 24% |
| No. of checkers | 23 | 14 | 17 |
| % checkers | 55% | 35% | 46% |
| Observations | 42 | 40 | 37 |
| **Panel B. Examinees below the median score (weak students)** | | | |
| | A | B | C |
| No. of cheaters | 28 | 29 | 34 |
| % cheaters | 72% | 74% | 81% |
| No. of checkers | 13 | 12 | 18 |
| % checkers | 33% | 31% | 43% |
| Observations | 39 | 39 | 42 |
| **Panel C: *z*-Statistic and *p*-value of the differences** | | | |
| | A | B | C |
| Between % cheaters | 3.89 (0.00) | 3.95 (0.00) | 5.04 (0.00) |
| Between % Checkers | 1.94 (0.03) | 0.40 (0.34) | 0.28 (0.39) |

*Note.* This table presents the sample breakdown according to the median score. Panels A and B show the percentage of cheaters and checkers within each subsample. Panel C present the *z*-statistic and its corresponding *p*-value for the difference between the groups.

vs 72% ($z$=3.89, $p$=0.00), 30% vs 74% ($z$=3.95, $p$=0.00), and 24% vs 81% ($z$=5.04, $p$=0.00) in the control, AC, and ACH groups, respectively. This finding supports the conclusion from the previous experiment that weaker students cheat more, probably due to the fact that their ability to pass the exam by honest means was quite low.

The second finding was that there was no difference in the percentage of checkers (and therefore also in the percentage of noncheckers) among strong and weak students in the primed groups: 35% vs 31% ($z$=0.4, $p$=0.34) in the AC group, and 46% vs 43% ($z$=0.28, $p$=0.39) in the ACH group. We interpreted this finding in light of the correlation between nonchecking and cheating. The similarity in the (non)checkers' rate implied a close similarity in the (dis) honest examinees' percentage. Thus, we concluded that there was no difference in the *marginal propensity to cheat* among strong and weak examinees, to wit, in the entire group of examinees. Nonetheless, this propensity was prevalent among more than half of the population: 57% of examinees in the AC group and 61% in the ACH group (Table 9).

Based on the findings reported in Tables 10 and 11, we inferred the following decision-making process to explain (non)checking and cheating: We assumed that the act of (non)checking constituted an internal statement of the intention (not) to act honestly. Thus, nonchecking was a conscious choice, the checkers' act of cheating was spontaneous, and the noncheckers' act of cheating was planned.

The decision-making process of weak students and strong students may have proceeded in the following way: (1) Weak students arrive at the exam. They are well-aware of their inadequate understanding of the material covered by the exam and therefore plan in advance to cheat. When asked to checkmark, they do not comply with the request in order to avoid a future possible conflict that may arise between checkmarking, which evokes an internal commitment not to cheat, and their actual behavior of cheating. During the exam, if they are unable to handle the exam on their own, they cheat as originally planned. If they realize that they are able to handle the exam, they choose not to cheat; (2) Strong students arrive at the exam, confident in their ability to succeed, and therefore they have no intention to cheat. When they are asked to checkmark, they have no reservations in complying with the request and therefore check the boxes. During the exam, if they handle the exam well, they do not cheat. Alternatively, if they realize that they are unable to answer on their own, they then chose to cheat, and in that sense the cheating is spontaneous and unplanned. Differences in motivation between planned and spontaneous academic dishonesty have been described by Genereux and McLeod (1995).

Another point worthy of note was the similar behavior of the control group and the two other primed groups. The neutral opening sentence given to the control group should not have triggered any future conflict between (present) checking and (future) cheating. Yet even in the control group, the cheating rates were lower and scores were higher among those who checkmarked. The similar behavior of the checking students could be explained by the trait of conformity or by the inclination to work in an orderly or disciplined manner in general. These students were asked to checkmark and therefore they did, regardless of the content. The same disposition that led examinees to behave in a disciplined manner also led them to learn in a more organized way, which improved their chances of success, as reflected in the average scores.

## 6. Summary and conclusions

Reports of fraud in government as well as in public and private organizations are commonplace in the media, and their prevalence suggests that dishonesty and corruption have become an increasingly integral part of life. It seems that no organization, including academic institutions (see the many studies cited above), is immune to dishonest behavior. The high prevalence of dishonesty can cause a continuous adjustment of individuals' ethical values and may result in a permanent blurring of the line between what is viewed as acceptable behavior and unethical behavior. Behaviors that once were unequivocally perceived as dishonest are now viewed more tolerantly. Supporting evidence for this shift in the context of academic dishonesty in particular can be found in McCabe et al. (2001), who found that the number of students who cheated on tests has increased constantly over the years, even among institutions with an honor code. Accordingly, academic dishonesty is a social and ethical problem that has only intensified with time. Especially worrisome is the tendency to cheat that was found greater among students studying business administration and economics than among students in other majors, as the former are or will be managers, and as such will outline and model the policy of the organization in which they operate (see López-Pérez and Spiegelman, 2019; Muñoz-Izquierdo et al., 2019).

Our study examined the effect of activating certain mental and emotional constructs, via priming, on cheating on exams. Examinees were exposed to priming statements just before taking an exam, stating that cheating was prohibited and in some of the treatments were directed to checkmark a box confirming that the preliminary statement was read and understood.

Our findings were as follows: (1) A priming statement lowered cheating rates when it was accompanied by a commitment to adhere to it. When students were exposed to the same statement and no such commitment was requested, cheating rates increased; (2) A priming statement about expected norms accompanied by a checkbox decreased cheating rates. However, adding a warning about the punishment for offenders increased cheating rates; (3) When the motivation to achieve a high score was strong, the priming manipulations were not effective in lowering the cheating rates; (4) In all of our experiments, students restricted the extent of their cheating or the extent of their dishonesty. It can be seen that as the number of copied answers increased, fewer examinees participated in cheating. For example, in Experiment 1 (Table 2), out of the 68 examinees in the control group, 23 engaged in cheating but only 17 of them cheated on more than two answers, only eight cheated on more than three, and so forth. (See also Experiment 2—Table 5 and Experiment 3—Table 7.) This phenomenon may be attributed to the examinees' perception of cheating on "just a few" answers as "light" and less offensive than "heavy" cheating on more answers. It could be explained by what Mazar et al. (2008) called "categorization flexibility," whereby people categorize some of their actions and a certain amount of dishonesty in more palatable terms. That is to say, when people cheat up to a certain extent, they can avoid or ignore negative signals that may affect their self-concept, thus preventing a negative change in their self-image. In the context of the present study, we inferred that cheating on one question was not perceived as dishonest and therefore did not negatively affect the student's self-image, whereas cheating on many questions would have been more problematic in this sense, and therefore its frequency decreased. (5) Cheating rates among weaker students were found to be dozens of percentage points higher than among the stronger students. Weaker students cheated more, probably because without cheating their chances of passing the exam were quite low. In this context, we distinguished between planned and spontaneous cheating. We suggest that students who planned to cheat chose not to comply with the checkmark request so as to avoid a future possible conflict that would arise between checking and cheating.

Some limitations are worth mentioning. First, the actual cheating rates may have been higher. Cheating was determined by noting an absent or incorrect calculation in the notebook and a correct answer on the answer sheet. We stress, again, that our goal in establishing our "cheating-detecting algorithm" was to construct an unequivocal process that can be repeated and that precludes the involvement of personal impressions, which could lead to biases in measurement. It should be noted that the "noise" that is embedded in our process is homogeneous across the groups. Moreover, errors in classification would reduce the ability of detecting differences among the groups; thus, if at all, such errors increase the risk of making type-2 errors, i.e., retaining a false null hypothesis. Second, in spite of the prominence of the priming statements and the exam supervisors' guidance to read the instructions before the exam started, it is possible that some examinees did not checkmark because they missed the statements/instructions, and not because they made a conscious choice not to checkmark. Third, the examinees' ages ranged between 25 and 50. Thus, there may have been differences in the moral development and maturity of the examinees and therefore differences in the influence of priming.

To summarize, we offer some conclusions and practical implementations. Using priming by means of supplying a preliminary text alluding to the accepted moral norms of behavior and requesting the examinees to commit to adhere to the text can be effective in reducing the incidence of cheating. Although priming's limited scope of success makes it insufficient as a sole solution and certain priming manipulations may induce the opposite effect, we would nonetheless recommend the use of a priming text because it is costless and easy to implement. Further research is needed to assess the effect of differently worded priming statements and a clear request from examinees to sign a pledge not to cheat, as well as to investigate whether such methods lose their effectiveness with repeated use over time.

## Appendix

In the first experiment, the priming statement was "*During the exam, the examinee must not discuss anything with others, including technical issues, nor may (s)he copy or pass any material to other students.*"

The questionnaire was distributed among 41 students. Twenty received closed questions and 21 received open questions. Eighty-nine percent of the respondents to the closed questions replied that the statement reminded them that cheating is forbidden and 84% replied that the statement reminded them to act honestly. Fifty-eight percent of the respondents were reminded that cheating is an option and 74% were reminded that cheating exists. Among 79% of the respondents, the statement aroused the desire to act according to it, namely to act honestly, and among 63% of the respondents the statement aroused the desire to act in the opposite way, namely to cheat. Regarding the question if checking a box, i.e., confirming that they read the statement, encouraged their commitment to act accordingly, 42% answered positively; 11% answered negatively, and the rest did not answer.

Among the respondents to the open questionnaires, 72% pointed out that they agree with the statement that students should act honestly and that cheating is an offense. Eleven percent replied that the statement encouraged them to act in the opposite way, namely to cheat, and the rest replied that the statement had nothing to do with them.

Fifty-two percent of the participants acknowledged that checking a box, i.e., confirming that they read the statement, caused them to feel committed to act according to it, 28% replied that they feel committed not to cheat with or without a checkbox, and the rest did not reply.

The students' answers to the above questionnaire and to the other questionnaires which are not presented here supported our assumptions regarding the existence and activation of the mental constructs among those who were exposed to priming statements.[c]

## References

Ariely, D., Mazar, N., 2006. Dishonesty in everyday life and its policy implications. J. Public Policy Mark. 25 (1), 1–19.

Association of Certified Fraud Examiners. *Report to the nations on occupational fraud and abuse: 2016 global fraud study*. Association of Certified Fraud Examiners. https://www.acfe.com/uploadedFiles/ACFE_Website/Content/rttn/2012-report-to-nations.pdf

Becker, G.S., 1974. Crime and punishment: an economic approach. In: Becker, G.S., Landes, W.M. (Eds.), Essays in the Economics of Crime and Punishment. Columbia University Press, New York, pp. 1–54.

Caldwell, C., 2010. A ten-step model for academic integrity: a positive approach for business schools. J. Bus. Ethics 92 (1), 1–13.

Carpenter, D.D., Harding, T.S., Finelli, C.J., Passow, H.J., 2004. Does academic dishonesty relate to unethical behavior in professional practice? An exploratory study. Sci. Eng. Ethics 10 (2), 311–324.

Cicognani, S., 2019. Cheating in academia: the relevance of social factors. In: Bucciol, A., Montinari, N. (Eds.), Dishonesty in Behavioral Economics. Academic Press.

Davis, S.F., 1993, March. Cheating in college is for a career: academic dishonesty in the 1990's. In: Paper presented at the annual meeting of the Southeastern Psychological Association, Atlanta, GA.

Della Vigna, S., List, J.A., Malmendier, U., Rao, G., 2016. Voting to tell others. Rev. Econ. Stud. 84 (1), 143–181.

c. Detailed results for the unreported questionnaires will be provided upon request.

DiBartolo, M.C., Walsh, C.M., 2010. Desperate times call for desperate measures: where are we in addressing academic dishonesty? J. Nurs. Educ. 49 (10), 543–544.

Erev, I., Haruvy, E., 2013. Learning and the economics of small decisions. In: Kagel, J.H., Roth, A.E. (Eds.), Handbook of Experimental Economics 2, pp. 1–136.

Finn, K.V., Frone, M.R., 2004. Academic performance and cheating: moderating role of scholl identification and self-efficacy. J. Educ. Res. 97 (3), 115–122.

Genereux, R.L., McLeod, B.A., 1995. Circumstances surrounding cheating: a questionnaire study of college students. Res. High. Educ. 36 (6), 687–704.

Gino, F., Ayal, S., Ariely, D., 2013. Self-serving altruism? The lure of unethical actions that benefit others. J. Econ. Behav. Organ. 93, 285–292.

Grym, J., Liljander, V., 2016. To cheat or not to cheat? The effect of a moral reminder on cheating. Nord. J. Bus, 65.

Haines, V.J., Diekhoff, G.M., Labeff, E.E., Clark, R.E., 1986. College cheating: immaturity, lack of commitment, and the neutralizing attitude. Res. High. Educ. 25 (4), 342–354.

Hashin, Y., 2005. Academic honesty in high education institutions in Israel. Al-Hagova 5, 17–19. http://www2.colman.ac.il/al_hagova/5/yual_hashin.pdf. In Hebrew.

Hertwig, R., Barron, G., Weber, E.U., Erev, I., 2004. Decisions from experience and the effect of rare events in risky choice. Psychol. Sci. 15, 534–539.

Houston, J.P., 1983. Alternative test forms as a means of reducing multiple-choice answer copying in the classroom. J. Educ. Psychol. 75 (4), 572–575.

Houston, J.P., 1986. Classroom answer copying: roles of acquaintanceship and free versus assigned seating. J. Educ. Psychol. 78 (3), 230–232.

Johnson, C.D., Gormly, J., 1972. Academic cheating: the contribution of sex, personality, and situational variables. Dev. Psychol. 6 (2), 320–325.

Jones, D.L., 2011. Academic dishonesty: are more students cheating? Bus. Commun. Q. 74 (2), 141.

LaBeff, E.E., Clark, R.E., Haines, V.J., Diekhoff, G.M., 1990. Situational ethics and college student cheating. Sociol. Inq. 60 (2), 190–198.

López-Pérez, R., Spiegelman, E., 2019. Do economists lie more? In: Bucciol, A., Montinari, N. (Eds.), Dishonesty in Behavioral Economics. Academic Press.

Mazar, N., Ariely, D., Amir, O., 2008. The dishonesty of honest people: a theory of self-concept maintenance. J. Mark. Res. XLV, 633–644.

McCabe, D.L., 1992. The influence of situational ethics among college students. Sociol. Inq. 62 (3), 365–374.

McCabe, D.L., Trevino, K.L., 1993. Academic dishonesty honor codes and other contextual influences. J. High. Educ. 64 (5), 522–538.

McCabe, D.L., Trevino, K.L., 1997. Individual and contextual influences on academic cheating: a multi campus investigation. Res. High. Educ. 38 (3), 379–396.

McCabe, D.L., Trevino, L.K., Butterfield, K.D., 2001. Cheating in academic institutions: a decade of research. Ethics Behav. 11 (3), 219–232.

McCabe, D.L., Butterfield, K.D., Trevino, L.K., 2004. Academic integrity: how widespread is cheating and plagiarism? In: Allena, T., Karp, D.R. (Eds.), Restorative Justice on the College Campus: Promoting Student Growth and Responsibility, and Reawakening the Spirit of Campus Community. Charles C. Thomas Publisher Ltd., Springfield, IL, pp. 124–135.

McCabe, D.L., Butterfield, K.D., Trevino, L.K., 2006. Academic dishonesty in graduate business programs: prevalence, causes, and proposed action. Acad. Manag. Learn. Educ. 5 (3), 294–305.

Michaels, J.W., Miethe, T.D., 1989. Applying theories of deviance to academic cheating. Soc. Sci. Q. 70 (4), 870–885.

Muñoz-Izquierdo, N., Gil-Gómez de Liaño, B., Rin-Sánchez, F.D., Pascual-Ezama, D., 2019. Cheating and altruism by discipline. In: Bucciol, A., Montinari, N. (Eds.), Dishonesty in Behavioral Economics, Academic Press.

Nonis, S., Swift, C.O., 2001. An examination of the relationship between academic dishonesty and workplace dishonesty: a multicampus investigation. J. Educ. Bus. 77 (2), 69–77.

Pino, N.W., Smith, W.L., 2003. College students and academic dishonesty. Coll. Stud. J. 37 (4), 490–500.

Stern, E.B., Havlicek, L., 1986. Academic misconduct: results of faculty and undergraduate students surveys. J. Allied Health 15 (2), 129–142.

Sykes, G.M., Matza, D., 1957. Techniques of neutralization: a theory of delinquency. Am. Sociol. Rev. 22 (6), 664–670.

Vojak, C., 2006. What market culture teaches students about ethical behavior. Ethics Educ. 1 (2), 177–195.

Whitley, B.E., 1998. Factors associated with cheating among college students: a review. Res. High. Educ. 39 (3), 235–274.

Section 3

# Dishonesty, individual, and social preferences

Chapter 3.1

# Do economists lie more?

Raúl López-Pérez[1], Eli Spiegelman[2]
[1]*Institute of Public Goods and Policies (IPP), Spanish National Research Council (CSIC), Madrid, Spain,* [2]*CEREN, EA 7477, Burgundy School of Business - Université Bourgogne Franche-Comté, Dijon, France*

## Chapter Outline



**JEL Classification:** C70, C91, D03, D64

## 1. Introduction

A relatively recent experimental literature shows that people sometimes tell the truth when this is costly for them (Erat and Gneezy, 2012; Fischbacher and Heusi, 2013; Gneezy, 2005; López-Pérez and Spiegelman, 2013; Lundquist et al., 2009). This evidence contrasts with the standard homo economicus view that all agents are self-interested money-maximizers, and suggests that people's preferences in this regard are significantly more complex. In particular, it has been suggested that some people have a preference for being honest and dislike lying (e.g., Ellingsen and Johannesson, 2004; Kartik, 2009; López-Pérez, 2012). An ability to predict and foster such *lie aversion* would be of great benefit in many economic settings. Therefore, an examination of the extent to which lie aversion correlates with sociodemographic indicators such as gender, field of study (major), and religiosity seems warranted.[a] In order to investigate these potential covariates, we consider an experiment that isolates lie aversion from other motivations mentioned in the literature.

a. We define a lie as any statement describing a state of the world at odds with one's beliefs. Lie aversion is conceived as a psychological cost that people suffer if they lie, *irrespectively of the consequences of the lie.*

**Dishonesty in Behavioral Economics. https://doi.org/10.1016/B978-0-12-815857-9.00003-0**

Some of the indicators cited are potential candidates to correlate with lie aversion. For instance, many religions expressly condemn lies; one might therefore expect people with strong religious beliefs to be lie-averse. Regarding differences in honesty across genders, Dreber and Johannesson (2008) and Erat and Gneezy (2012) find differences between men and women in sender-receiver games. Yet this difference appears to be a subtle one, as Lundquist et al. (2009), Holm and Kawagoe (2010), and Childs (2012) observe no correlation between gender and honest behavior. Finally, a relationship between major and honesty is (indirectly) suggested by lab studies reporting that economics students conform more closely to homo economicus "ideals"—see Marwell and Ames (1981) on public-good experiments or Frank et al. (1993, 1996) in a Prisoners' Dilemma context. More specifically related to our study, economics students in Lundquist et al. (2009) and Lewis et al. (2012) lied more often than subjects from other fields; see also Chapter 3.2 in this book for a similar result regarding cheating.[b]

Importantly, our analysis controls for a potential effect of beliefs on preferences and honest behavior. In effect, it has been argued (Cialdini et al., 1990; Bicchieri, 2005; López-Pérez, 2012; Erat and Gneezy, 2012; see also Chapters 2.3 and 2.4 in this book) that normative behavior, including honest behavior, may be sensitive to expectations about how others will act. That is, people may be more likely to comply with an honesty norm if they expect many others to respect it as well. Since we elicit the expectations for truth-telling, we can clarify whether, say, a potential correlation between major and honesty is due to subjects from different majors having different expectations.

Our results indicate that Business and Economics (B&E) students are more likely to lie in our experiment than are students from other fields. Although we find that expectations are highly significant predictors of honesty and that B&E students tend to be pessimistic in their expectations of honest behavior, the correlation between major and truth-telling still persists when we control for expectations econometrically. Overall, gender and religion lack predictive value. However, the picture regarding gender is substantially more complex than that of religion: While female and male students are equally honest overall, we observe that female B&E students are significantly less honest than female students from other fields, whereas the same is not true for male students. In other words, the differences observed across majors in terms of honesty seem to be generated by the differences between the female students. We discuss later this issue in more detail.

The rest of the chapter is structured as follows. The next section describes our experimental design and procedures. In turn, Section 3 reports the results from our experiment. Section 4 concludes with a discussion of our main results.

---

b. It is worth noting that contagion effects (see Chapter 3.5 of this book), may amplify discipline-based differences. Students in a particular department may interact preferentially with others from the same department, resulting in the formation of local norms of behavior that may well include reduced perceived importance of honesty, at least in some situations.

## 2. Experimental design and procedures

The decision problem considered in our experiment is extremely simple. A random process with common-knowledge distribution generates a colored circle (blue or green, henceforth called the *signal*) on a computer screen.[c] A "sender" observes the signal and sends a message to a "receiver," indicating either "The blue circle has appeared" or "The green circle has appeared." The sender earns €14/15 for saying the color is "blue"/"green," irrespective of the true color. Consequently, she faces a dilemma between honesty and material interest if the signal happens to be blue (we discuss the reasons for the small cost of honesty below). The receiver, in turn, receives a payoff of €10 irrespective of either the message or the true color. In fact, he is uninformed of the true color, and hence cannot verify whether the message received is false or true. The whole previous description is common knowledge. Fig. 1 depicts the decision tree; the upper payoffs are the sender's, and $p$ denotes the probability of the blue signal.

We conducted 20 computerized sessions at the Universidad Autónoma de Madrid, with a total of 258 participants. The software used for our sessions was z-Tree (Fischbacher, 2007). After being seated at a visually isolated computer terminal, each participant received written instructions that described the decision problem (the appendix includes them, translated from Spanish to English). Subjects read the instructions at their own pace and we answered their questions in private. We used neutral language and avoided terms such as "lie."

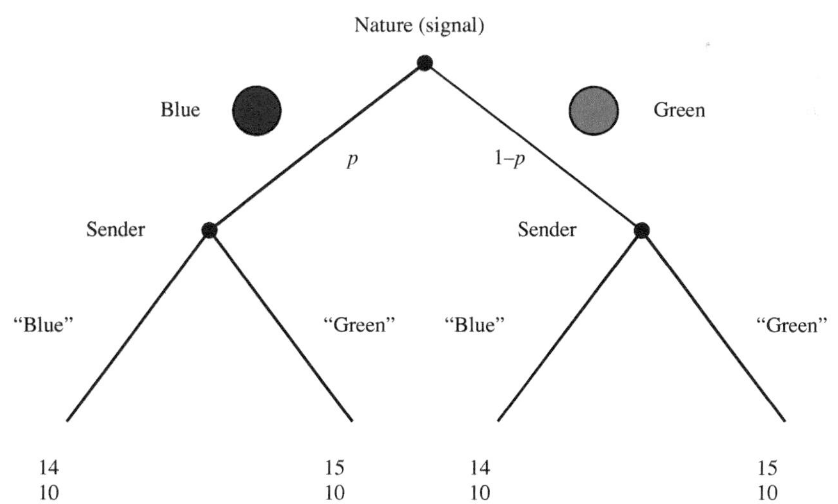


**FIG. 1** Decision tree.

c. In order to test an unrelated set of hypotheses, we considered two treatments, varying the probability of the blue signal (0.25 vs 0.75). Since there are no significant differences in honesty rates across treatments (see López-Pérez and Spiegelman, 2013 for details), all results are pooled across those treatments.

Understanding of the instructions was checked by means of a questionnaire (also available in the appendix) that all subjects had to answer correctly before moving on to decisions.

Each session then consisted of a number of steps. In chronological order: First, all participants chose in our decision problem as if they were senders. We used the strategy method; that is, before knowing the actual realization of the random signal, subjects indicated what message they would send for each possible realization of the signal (blue/green). In this manner, we maximized the amount of data gathered.[d] Second, we elicited first- and second-order beliefs from all subjects in an incentive-compatible manner. More precisely, first-order beliefs refer to beliefs about the proportion of subjects who send the "green" message when the signal is blue, that is, the percentage of subjects who lie in that situation. Second-order beliefs are beliefs about the average first-order beliefs reported by other subjects. In this chapter we only make use of data on first-order beliefs, referring to them simply as *beliefs*. Third, participants were anonymously matched in pairs and one subject in each pair was randomly selected as the real sender, the other as the receiver. Fourth, the color of the circle was generated based on the relevant probability (conditional on treatment), the sender informed of the actual color, and the message previously selected by that sender sent to the corresponding receiver. Fifth, we collected several sociodemographic variables from the participants, including gender, major, religiosity and political ideology. Sixth, subjects were reminded of the choice they made in the eventuality of a Blue signal, and asked to provide an open-form explanation for the choice. Finally, they were paid in private by an assistant who was not informed about the details of the experiment. Each session lasted approximately 40 min, and on average subjects earned €12.70.

Our design separates the lie-averse and nonlie-averse types, allowing us to investigate the correlations of our sociodemographic variables with pure lie aversion Clearly, lie-averse senders should say "blue"/"green" if the signal was "blue"/"green."[e] In contrast, senders who do not care about telling lies should arguably exhibit different behavior. In fact, there seems to be no other plausible reason to always (i.e., for any realization of the signal) announce the true color than a preference for honesty. For instance, a selfish sender should always announce "green." The same is true even if the sender is altruistic: There is no altruistic reason to tell the truth as the receiver always gets €10, even if he is deceived. Similarly, guilt-aversion as in Charness and Dufwenberg (2006) is irrelevant because the receiver's payoff expectations are fixed—he gets €10

d. We have run a control treatment to check for possible effects of the strategy method on behavior, and we observe no significant effect (López-Pérez and Spiegelman, 2013).

e. A key point here is that the cost of telling the truth is rather small (€1). We calibrated this low value to the low harm of the lie, which concerns neither the sender nor the receiver personally, will have no future consequences and has no material influence on the receiver. Given this, even a lie-averse sender could decide not to tell the truth if the cost of that behavior was high, making it impossible to discriminate between lie-averse and nonlie-averse agents.

anyway. In addition, models of inequity aversion like Fehr and Schmidt (1999) and Bolton and Ockenfels (2000) assume that aversion to advantageous inequity is never so strong that people would "hurt" themselves to reduce such inequity; hence these models per se do not predict truth-telling. Finally, Utikal and Fischbacher (2013) identify a desire to appear honest, rather than to actually be honest, at least among some subsets of the population. Because in this case the incentive is the same regardless of the color of the circle, anyone who told the truth when the circle was blue for this reason would also lie when the circle was green, minimizing payoff and lying to look honest. Therefore, our use of the strategy method allows us to investigate this behavior. In short, it seems safe to assume that any sender who always announces the true color has a preference for honesty.

## 3. Results

Let strategies be specified such that (G, B) indicates the message vector ("Green if signal is green," "Blue if signal is blue"), and so on. In the full sample ($N$=258), 50.78, 38.76, 8.14, and 2.33% of the subjects, respectively, chose the message vector (G, G), (G, B), (B, B), and (B, G). That is, the most frequent choices (89.53% of the total) correspond to the "payoff maximizing" (G, G) and "honest" (G, B) strategies, while other strategies are much less frequently chosen. A total of 21 subjects chose the "payoff minimizing strategy" (B, B), and 6 chose the "pathological" (B, G) strategy. Table 1 shows an overall picture of the demographics of the three main behavioral groups—to simplify the table, we do not include the small group of (B, G) subjects. More precisely, Table 1 offers data for each group about the distribution of majors, average (first-order) beliefs, gender distribution, and average religiosity and political ideology, both measured on a scale from 1 to 10, where 1 means not religious and extreme left, respectively, and 10 indicates deeply religious and extreme right, respectively. We note that the information on field of studies was collected with an open-ended question, and is classified based on the answers received. Our classification largely follows the International Standard Classification of Education (UNESCO, 2011). One difference is, in that system, social and behavioral sciences are grouped together, so psychology and economics should be in the same category, while Business Administration is a separate group. Our a priori interest in economics majors, confirmed by the empirical difference in their behavior, lead us distinguish between the former two, and we follow the literature cited above in grouping business and economics in a single behavioral group, which we refer to as B&E.

The table shows that overall there was relatively little sociodemographic difference between the honest and maximizing groups. Minimizers appear distinct (more males, more religious, and farther to the right), but the small numbers leave the statistics inconclusive. On the other hand, there is a significant relationship between program of study (major) and strategy (Pearson Chi-square (4)=15.63; $p$=0.004), and a quite remarkable difference between maximizers

**TABLE 1** Demographic Breakdown of Nonpathological Subjects

| Strategy | *N* | B&E | Hum | Other | Beliefs | Male | Religion | Politics |
|---|---|---|---|---|---|---|---|---|
| Honest (G,B) | 100 | 18 | 37 | 44 | 53.86 | 0.444 | 3.34 | 4.4 |
| | | | | | *(2.928)* | *(0.05)* | *(0.277)* | *(0.182)* |
| Maximizer (G,G) | 131 | 50 | 26 | 55 | 84.53 | 0.489 | 3.56 | 4.878 |
| | | | | | *(1.693)* | *(0.044)* | *(0.228)* | *(0.161)* |
| Minimizer (B,B) | 21 | 9 | 4 | 8 | 50.81 | 0.762 | 4.05 | 5.286 |
| | | | | | *(6.586)* | *(0.095)* | *(0.603)* | *(0.448)* |
| Total | 251 | 77 | 67 | 107 | 69.55 | 0.496 | 3.52 | 4.722 |
| | | | | | *(1.836)* | *(0.032)* | *(0.169)* | *(0.118)* |

*Notes*: Columns B&E, Hum, and Other, respectively, show the number of subjects from Business & Economics, Humanities, and other majors choosing the corresponding strategy. One (honest) subject reported no major, which affects the totals in these columns. For the rest of variables, we report the mean of 252 "nonpathological" subjects and *standard error* (in italics) conditional on strategy choice. Religion: scale of 1 (not religious) to 10 (deeply religious); Politics: scale of 1 (extreme left) to 10 (extreme right).

and the rest in terms of stated first-order beliefs (Mann–Whitney $p=0.000$). Interestingly, while minimizers are closer to the maximizers in their politics, religion and major status, they state beliefs similar to the honest.

Because major appears predictive of behavior, Table 2 shows the percent of subjects from each major choosing the "honest" strategy (Table A1 in the appendix also provides sociodemographic data on the average subject from each major). Since many of the majors were represented by only a few individuals, however, we generally group them together in the analysis. Therefore the "main groups" classification on the bottom of the table sets B&E students apart. It also separates Humanities students, who comprised the largest single group, and were also behaviorally distinct (see below).

Table 2 shows a significant variation in honesty rates across majors, ranging from more than 50% among humanities and law students to less than 25% among engineers and economists.[f] On a more aggregate level, only 22.8% of the B&E subjects chose strategy (G, B), while 45.5% of the (pooled) non-B&E subjects did so, a significant difference (Mann–Whitney test; $p$-value$=0.001$). Among those other subjects, the highest rate of honesty was found in the humanities. The average rate of the "honest" profile outside the humanities (i.e., including B&E) was 33.5%; for the humanities it was 52.9% (Mann–Whitney $p$-value$=0.004$).

Thus our data seem to corroborate the pattern discussed above, that B&E students are less likely to be honest than are others. To further investigate this issue, Table 3 reports the results from a series of marginal effects probit regressions of honesty on our sociodemographic variables. We use the main classifications of major from Table 2. In the regressions we report, the religiosity variable is defined as a numerical value, which is statistically more powerful.[g] In addition, we consider the subjects' self-reported beliefs about deception (recall, the percentage of subjects expected to send the "green message" after the blue signal), and investigate any potential treatment effect due to the probability of the signal (see footnote [c]).

There are two important points in Table 3. *First*, beliefs are highly predictive of behavior: An increase in reported expectations of other people's dishonesty decreases the probability of an honest choice, with each percent reducing the likelihood of telling the truth oneself by about three-quarters of a percent.

f. We have received the comment that it makes sense to include engineering students in the B&E category, as "mathy thinkers." While this would only strengthen the results in this paper, we refrain from doing so because of the ad hoc nature of the adjustment, after viewing the data.

g. In alternative models not reported here, we specify religion as quartiles, which have the intuitive advantages of allowing nonlinear relationships and imposing less of an interpretation on the units of the 10-point scale. Results are analogous to those reported in Table 3. Note also that the politics variable (1 = extreme left; 10 = extreme right) was correlated with major status, and appeared to introduce collinearity problems when included in the regression. However, when included in a regression with B&E status, it has no predictive power for honesty, from which we conclude that it does not significantly mediate the B&E effect. It was therefore excluded from the regressions.

**TABLE 2** Honest Behavior, Conditional on Major

| **Major** | **Bus** | **Econ** | **Hum** | **Sci** | **Eng** | **Psych** | **Law** | **Others** | **Total** |
|---|---|---|---|---|---|---|---|---|---|
| *N* | 47 | 32 | 70 | 28 | 12 | 29 | 21 | 18 | 257 |
| (G,B) | 0.234 | 0.219 | 0.528 | 0.464 | 0.250 | 0.414 | 0.524 | 0.278 | 0.389 |
| | *(0.062)* | *(0.074)* | *(0.060)* | *(0.096)* | *(0.130)* | *(0.093)* | *(0.112)* | *(0.109)* | *(0.030)* |
| **Group** | **B&E** | | **Hum** | **Science & engineering** | | **Other soc. sci** | | **Other** | **Total** |
| *N* | 79 | | 70 | 40 | | 50 | | 18 | 257 |
| (G,B) | 0.228 | | 0.528 | 0.400 | | 0.46 | | 0.278 | 0.389 |
| | *(0.047)* | | *(0.060)* | *(0.078)* | | *(0.071)* | | *(0.109)* | *(0.030)* |

*Notes*: All subjects included except one who did not report his major ($N$=257). (G, B) denotes the percent of each category choosing the "honest" strategy; standard errors are reported in italics. *Bus*=business; *Econ*=economics; *Hum*=humanities; *Sci*=science; *Eng*=engineering; *Psych*=psychology.

**TABLE 3** Covariates of Honesty

| Outcome | (a)<br>(G,B) | (b)<br>(G,B) | (c)<br>(G,B) |
|---|---|---|---|
| B&E | −0.175** | | −0.142* |
| | (0.0690) | | (0.0761) |
| Humanities | | 0.148** | 0.0938 |
| | | (0.0733) | (0.0780) |
| Male | −0.0685 | −0.0835 | −0.0662 |
| | (0.0641) | (0.0645) | (0.0644) |
| High | 0.0413 | 0.0336 | 0.0435 |
| | (0.0649) | (0.0650) | (0.0650) |
| Religion | −0.00588 | −0.00923 | −0.00554 |
| | (0.0133) | (0.0131) | (0.0134) |
| Beliefs | −0.00738*** | −0.00755*** | −0.00734*** |
| | (0.00118) | (0.00120) | (0.00119) |

*Notes:* Marginal effects estimates on the probability of honesty versus pooled other strategies, robust standard error and the *p*-value for a zero null hypothesis. For all independent variables except Beliefs, coefficients evaluate the effect of the change of the corresponding dummy from 0 to 1. The variable Male refers to a dummy for gender. B&E and Humanities are as defined above. The variable High takes value 1 if the subject participated in the treatment in which the probability of the blue signal was 0.75. Religion is a self-report of religious conviction (1 = not at all religious; 10 = deeply religious). $N = 257$ for all regressions. Stars indicate significance *$p < 0.1$; **$p < 0.05$; ***$p < 0.01$

There are at least three possible interpretation of this correlation. To start, people might tend to respect norms only if they expect others to do so as well, as noticed in the introduction. Given our research goal, discounting the effect of beliefs is then crucial to prevent confounds (e.g., B&E subjects might lie more simply because they have particularly "pessimistic" beliefs). In a different, yet related phenomenon, people might feel some discomfort or cognitive dissonance if beliefs about "normal" behavior do not coincide with previous decisions. This would then support a tendency to manipulate their beliefs (possibly in an unconscious manner) about what constitutes such "normal" behavior. That is, the beliefs may have been effect, rather than cause, of the previous choice.[h] Finally, individuals might overestimate the extent to which others have beliefs, desires and tendencies similar to their own, the so-called (false) consensus effect. Although controlling for beliefs could lead to an underestimation of the

h. In our experiment, we asked for beliefs about other people's action after the subjects chose their own. This was done to eliminate the effect that priming social expectations might have on later behavior.

marginal effect of our sociodemographic variables on honesty if any of the last two interpretations played a role, any potential statistical significance of these variables should not be lost.

In this respect, the *second* remarkable point in Table 3 is that, even accounting for the effect of beliefs, B&E students choose the honest strategy significantly less often. It is estimated to reduce the probability of an honest strategy by as much as 18 percentage points. While a Sobel test shows that the mediation of beliefs on B&E status is significant ($p$-value$=0.025$), the direct effect remains significant, as well. None of the other determinants appear to be significant. Notice from panel (b) that humanities students, compared to pooled others (that is, when the B&E variables are not included) are significantly more honest. However, when B&E are added this effect disappears (panel (c)), while the converse does not hold: the B&E indicator remains marginally significant even with the inclusion of the Humanities variable. This pattern illustrates the phenomenon that B&E students are further away from the average than humanities students. Since B&E students are also the focus of the existing literature, we will therefore concentrate on them.

**TABLE 4** Covariates of Maximizing Behavior

| Outcome | **(d)** (G,G) | **(e)** (G,G) | **(f)** (G,G) |
|---|---|---|---|
| B&E | 0.123 | | 0.0745 |
| | (0.0789) | | (0.0853) |
| Humanities | | −0.156** | −0.129 |
| | | (0.0797) | (0.0859) |
| Male | −0.0941 | −0.0922 | −0.0994 |
| | (0.0704) | (0.0711) | (0.0711) |
| High | −0.135* | −0.133* | −0.137* |
| | (0.0700) | (0.0701) | (0.0701) |
| Religion | 0.0107 | 0.0133 | 0.0109 |
| | (0.0143) | (0.0141) | (0.0144) |
| Beliefs | 0.0117*** | 0.0119*** | 0.0117*** |
| | (0.00166) | (0.00169) | (0.00168) |

*Notes*: Marginal effects estimates on the probability of maximization versus pooled other strategies, robust standard error and the $p$-value for a zero null hypothesis. For all independent variables except Beliefs, coefficients evaluate the effect of the change of the corresponding dummy from 0 to 1. Variables are as defined in table. $N=257$ for all regressions. Stars indicate significance *$p<0.1$; **$p<0.05$; ***$p<0.01$

Although the data show that B&E students play the unconditionally honest strategy less often than do others, some caveats are in order in interpreting this result. To start, Table 4 shows results from three regressions analogous to those in Table 3, but with maximization rather than honesty on the left-hand side. Observe that the B&E variable is here not a significant predictor of maximization. This may seem to contradict our prior statement that B&E students are less likely to be honest. Yet recall from Table 1 that the typology of strategies does not reduce to honest and maximizing. A sender who believes that a "green" message will be interpreted as a probable lie, and who is sufficiently motivated to *look* honest (c.f. Utikal and Fischbacher, 2013) should choose strategy (B, B); possibly a relatively large share of subjects who engage in such perception management are B&E students. In effect, Table 1 above suggests that B&E students constitute a large share of the subjects choosing (B, B).[i]

For another caveat, it will be noticed that the "lie" in this study also increases social welfare. Suppose that some lie-averse subjects care about social efficiency (i.e., sum of payoffs) and others do not. For the first group, the cost of telling the truth is 1 Euro of personal payoff *plus* a penalty for the loss of social efficiency; for the second group is just 1 Euro of personal payoff. Suppose also that, due to selection or learning, the first group tend to end up in the B&E majors.[j] Since the cost of telling the truth in our experiment was higher for the first group, it might be that the B&E students are not less lie-averse (in the sense of lying more given a certain *fixed* cost), but lie more than other majors in our experiment because lying was socially efficient.

Yet there are several reasons to doubt this argument. Importantly, first, the regressions reported in Table 4 actually show that B&E students are no more likely than anyone else to maximize money/welfare, once beliefs are controlled. As we said before, second, Table 1 shows that B&E students were slightly more likely than other groups to choose the minimizing strategy: These subjects lie and choose inefficiently! Third, the evidence cited in the introduction from Marwell and Ames (1981) and Frank et al. (1993, 1996) is at odds with the hypothesis stated: Cooperation increases social efficiency, but economists are less cooperative. Fourth, the open-form explanations elicited at the end of the experiment do not show any particular concern by the B&E students

i. Note that the frequency of choice (B, B) is higher when the probability of blue is high. In fact, this is the only (marginally) significant difference across treatments. This corroborates the perception management interpretation, as the higher probability of the blue signal increases the chance that the green message is a lie, ceteris paribus; see López-Pérez and Spiegelman (2013).

j. Some evidence *weakly* suggests that economists are concerned about social efficiency. Fehr et al. (2006) reported that economists are significantly more likely than other majors to choose an efficient distribution than an inefficient but more egalitarian one. Yet we note that both allocations gave the *same* payoff to the decider, so that the evidence does not necessarily signal a strong concern for social efficiency.

k. Due to a computer error, three sessions of reasons were not saved. The 37% statistic refers to 40 out of 108 saved maximizers who mention this issue.

**TABLE 5 Proportions of Each Group Who Mentioned That Lie Does No Harm**

| | | Mentioned that lie does no harm | | | | Total | |
|---|---|---|---|---|---|---|---|
| | | No | | Yes | | | |
| | | *N* | % | *N* | % | *N* | % |
| Subject's major | B&E | 36 | 76.6 | 11 | 23.4 | 47 | 100 |
| | Others | 137 | 80.6 | 33 | 19.4 | 170 | 100 |
| | Total | 173 | 79.7 | 44 | 20.3 | 217 | 100 |

*Note*: Sample restricted to those for whom reasons were retained.

about social efficiency. Although nobody used the word "efficiency" exactly in their answers, 37% of those who chose the payoff-maximizing strategy spontaneously mentioned something about their choice not "harming" the receiver.[k] If we accept this justification as a proxy for efficiency concerns, then the argument above implies that the probability of mentioning the harmlessness of the lie should be greater among B&E than non-B&E subjects.[l] That is, if the result that B&E subjects lie more is driven by social efficiency concerns, then we would expect the individuals who cite this to come largely from that group. As Table 5 below shows, this is not the case. Indeed, slightly more B&E students than others make reference to the consideration, but the difference is not significant (Mann Whitney $p=0.547$).

If we focus on the maximizers, the results are even less encouraging of an efficiency explanation. A total of 36% of non-B&E maximizers mentioned the harmlessness of the choice; among B&E maximizers, the rate was 22%. This difference is great enough to reject the one-sided null that B&E maximizers care more about social efficiency than do non-B&E maximizers ($p=0.04$).[m]

On a different issue, we now pause to focus more closely on the gender effects across majors. A Chi-square analysis of major and field of study shows that the gender split varies with the major (Chi-square(4) = 12.1623; $p=0.009$). In particular, humanities and psychology (other social science) have disproportionately more women. Table 6, below, illustrates.

l. Notice that comparison across all strategies, rather than just maximizers, is more conservative. For example, if social efficiency concerns constitute the major reason for the maximizing strategy, then the rates of people citing that concern among B&E and non-B&E maximizers may be approximately the same regardless of the overall distribution of types.

m. We finally note that it seems impossible to devise an experiment where one can discriminate between lie-averse and non-lie-averse agents with absolutely no confounds due to selfishness or social preferences. In effect, discrimination requires that truth and lies lead to different outcomes; otherwise the non-lie-averse agents would be indifferent. In this respect, we believe that our design minimizes confounds.

**TABLE 6** Gender Split by Field of Studies

| Field | Female | Male | Total |
|---|---|---|---|
| Business and economics | 30 | 49 | 79 |
| | 37.97 | 62.03 | 100.00 |
| Science and engineering | 16 | 24 | 40 |
| | 40.00 | 60.00 | 100.00 |
| Humanities | 40 | 30 | 70 |
| | 57.14 | 42.68 | 100.00 |
| Psychology and Law | 20 | 9 | 29 |
| | 68.97 | 31.03 | 100.00 |
| Other | 14 | 1 | 18 |
| | 52.50 | 47.50 | 100.00 |
| Total | 127 | 130 | 257 |
| | 49.42 | 50.58 | 100.00 |

*Notes*: Number and percent of participants from each of the categories of field of study.

In this table, we see that the percent of females in Psychology is twice that in B&E. Overall, Mann–Whitney, proportion and Chi-square tests all confirm the results from the regressions above that gender is not significantly related to honesty ($p > 0.15$ for all tests). However, the field-level differences in gender balance also correlate with patterns of honesty. For instance, the field with the highest proportion of males is also that with the lowest proportion of honesty. Therefore, we run a final set of regressions interacting gender with business and economics studies, then with humanities students (the most honest category), and finally with both, to predict the honest strategy (Table 7).

In regressions (g) and (h), the field dummies are interpreted as the effects of studying in the field on females. The effect of the field on males is found with the sum of the direct field effect and the interaction. While the former are both significantly different from zero, the latter are not ($p > 0.365$ and 0.391, respectively). The implication is that the lower rates of honesty in the B&E group, and the higher rates in the humanities, are both being driven particularly by the women in the respective groups. We note that with respect to the B&E group, this goes against received wisdom of women being more honest than men (e.g., Capraro, 2017 and references therein), but that results are often more mixed in our Pareto White Lie setting than in other types of lie (c.f. Erat and Gneezy, 2012). Further, our specific interaction of lie aversion and study of business

**TABLE 7 Interaction of Gender and Field of Studies on Honesty**

| Outcome | (g) (G,B) | (h) (G,B) | (i) (G,B) |
|---|---|---|---|
| Male | −0.126* | −0.0570 | −0.108 |
| | (0.0742) | (0.0767) | (0.0963) |
| B&E | −0.294*** | | −0.259** |
| | (0.0954) | | (0.106) |
| B&E Interaction | 0.238 | | 0.220 |
| | (0.160) | | (0.173) |
| Humanities | | 0.192** | 0.110 |
| | | (0.0976) | (0.105) |
| Humanities interaction | | −0.0919 | −0.0382 |
| | | (0.132) | (0.149) |
| High | 0.0367 | 0.0299 | 0.0381 |
| | (0.0649) | (0.0652) | (0.0650) |
| Religion | −0.00464 | −0.00961 | −0.00446 |
| | (0.0134) | (0.0131) | (0.0135) |
| Beliefs | −0.00731*** | −0.00762*** | −0.00729*** |
| | (0.00119) | (0.00120) | (0.00119) |

*Notes*: Marginal effects estimates on the probability of maximization versus pooled other strategies, robust standard error and the *p*-value for a zero null hypothesis. For all independent variables except Beliefs, coefficients evaluate the effect of the change of the corresponding dummy from 0 to 1. Variables are as defined in table. $N=257$ for all regressions. Stars indicate significance $^{*}p<0.1$; $^{**}p<0.05$; $^{***}p<0.01$

and economics mirrors the results in Haucap and Müller (2014), who find that differences between economists and others in a trust game are driven by the behavior of females in the sample.

Regression (i) allows the further comparison of females and males across the two subgroups. The difference between the field dummies in regression (i) is interpreted as the difference between the females of the two groups, and is highly significant ($p=0.0035$), while the difference between sums of the respective direct and interacted effects—the difference between the male B&E and male humanities subjects—is not significantly different from zero ($p=0.2796$). Thus, not only are the differences between the most and least honest subgroups driven by the women; the men in those subgroups actually have statistically in-

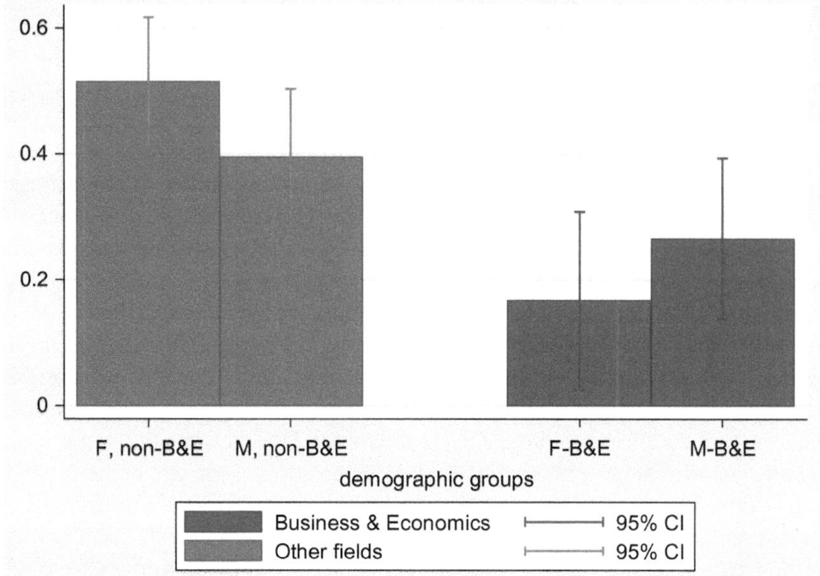


**FIG. 2** Honesty (G, B) rates among males and females in B&E vs other fields.

distinguishable honesty rates. For further analysis and illustration, Fig. 2, below, shows the (G,B) rates for male and female participants in the B&E and other categories (bounds represent confidence intervals).

We see that male versus female differences are not significant in either category (Mann–Whitney $p$-values for B&E and others = 0.3135 and 0.1095, respectively), but that the relationship between them is reversed, such that the difference between females across fields of study is much larger than the difference between males. In fact, the difference between males is not significant (Mann–Whitney $p = 0.1339$), while it is highly significant for females ($p = 0.0008$). Differences across both gender and B&E status are also significant (F-B&E vs M-non-B&E $p = 0.024$; F-non-B&E vs M-B&E $p = 0.0041$).

## 4. Conclusion

Our results show that B&E students are significantly less likely to exhibit honest behavior in our decision problem than non-B&E students, even after controlling for beliefs. In this regard, we also show that beliefs are highly predictive of behavior: People lie more if they expect others to lie as well. In contrast, we do not find significant overall differences in honesty between religious and nonreligious people.

The gender effects in our study are complex. There is no gender difference in honesty overall or within the B&E or non-B&E subgroups. However, female noneconomists are more honest than their male counterparts, while female economists are less so. The difference in males across the B&E variables is not significant. The implication is that in our experiment, the difference between B&E and non-B&E subjects is driven entirely by a marked difference in the female participants. While we would be cautious about extrapolating from these rather surprising results without further replication, this suggests that females may react to, or select into, different programs differently from males, and adds some nuance to results such as Dreber and Johannesson (2008); DJ henceforth) and Erat and Gneezy (2012); EG henceforth). *First*, there could be differences in the distribution of subjects' majors across these two studies and our study, an important issue in view of our evidence. If many female subjects come from the humanities and many male subjects come from B&E or engineering, the data may show a correlation between gender and honesty.[n] In general, our data suggests that an analysis based on gender alone can be potentially deceptive if females and males are not homogeneously distributed across majors, as seems the case in many western countries. In the game considered in DJ and some of the games in EG, *second*, altruism and honesty are interconnected. In these games, one player sends a false/true message to another player, who can use such information as a recommendation of play. Importantly, the message receiver will harm herself if she is deceived and follows the recommendation of play. If women are more altruistic (as some references cited in DJ and EG indicate), they might behave differently when communicating, even if they are not more lie-averse than men.

We close by pointing out that some of the data reported here hints at new questions for future research. For instance, we observe that around 10% of the subjects acted as minimizers, sending the blue message in any contingency. As we argue in López-Pérez and Spiegelman (2013), this behavior is partially consistent with the hypothesis that some agents expect lies to be disapproved by others, and dislike being disapproved. This would therefore be in line with Utikal and Fischbacher (2013). Interestingly, minimizers are largely male, B&E students. In this line, it might be interesting to study further potential covariates of a dislike of disapproval. Additionally, if minimization is indeed motivated by disapproval management, then it might represent a consequentialist consideration philosophically related to the maximizing behavior, with a maximand defined over both material and social outcomes. Honesty, by contrast, may be a fundamentally deontological motivation. Therefore, testing for the significant correlates of honesty against pooled maximization and minimization pits rule-based, or deontological concerns (do not lie no matter what) against consequentialist ones, and seems to find that B&E students are more behaviorally motivated by the latter. This is of course entirely consistent with the philosophi-

n. DJ and EG do not control for the subjects' major. Lundquist et al. (2009) control for both gender and major and find no significant correlation between gender and honesty, while they find that students from the Stockholm School of Economics (SSE) are significantly more likely to lie than other subjects (at the 10% level). Holm and Kawagoe (2010) do not find either a relation between gender and lying.

cal tradition from which economics springs, and may point toward promising further research questions. For another idea, note that our design aimed to prevent any confound between honesty and altruism, as we wanted to separate the purely lie-averse types. Having said this, however, we do not rule out that altruism and lie aversion might be correlated. If this were the case, lie-averse types might be more likely to lie if the truth leads to harming others (heroic examples like those of Oskar Schindler come to mind here). More within-subjects studies like Hurkens and Kartik (2009) would be useful to understand better who is more likely to be honest, and when.

## Appendix

Table A1 provides a picture of the average subject from each major, showing substantial difference between majors. Science students are the least religious, and psychology and the humanities are the majors with the greatest number of females in the sample (excluding "Other" due to its small size). Business, economics and law students are the most politically conservative, although only Business students claim to be "right of center."[o] They are also the most religious. Indeed religiosity is correlated with conservative politics in the sample, with a Spearman's rho of 0.52 ($p$-value vs independence = 0.000)

### Instructions

Thank you very much for participating in this experiment, which is financed by a research fund. Our aim is to study how people make decisions. In total, more than 40 people will participate in this study, in several sessions. There are no tricky questions, you must simply choose as you prefer. At the end of the experiment, you will be paid some money; the precise amount will depend on chance and your decisions during the experiment. It is very important that you do not talk to any other participant. If you do not follow this rule we will have to exclude you from the experiment and you will not earn any money. If you have questions, please raise your hand and we will assist you.

#### Description of the Experiment

In this experiment there are two types of participants (A and B). The basic task of each A is choosing a message for B. More precisely, toward the end of the experiment, A's computer will randomly reveal either a blue circle or a green one—the probability of a blue circle is [75% in the High treatment, 25% in the Low treatment]. A will observe the circle in the screen and then send to B one of the following two messages: (i) "the blue circle has appeared," or (ii) "the green circle has appeared." Payoffs are as follows: A will always get €14 if he/she announces that the blue circle appeared and €15 if he/she announces green. The payoff of any B is €10 in any case. We remark that B will not observe the color selected by the computer, but only receive A's message.

o. The value 5.5 would be the theoretical center-point of our scale.

**TABLE A1** Descriptive Statistics by Major

| | Full set of majors | | | | | Main groups | | | | | |
|---|---|---|---|---|---|---|---|---|---|---|---|
| **Major** | **Sex** | **Reli.** | **Poli.** | **(G,B)** | ***N*** | **Class** | **Sex** | **Reli.** | **Poli.** | **(G,B)** | ***N*** |
| Bus | 0.596 | 4.872 | 5.957 | 0.234 | 47 | B&E | 0.620 | 4.380 | 5.671 | 0.228 | 79 |
| | *(0.072)* | *(0.425)* | *(0.274)* | *(0.062)* | | | *(0.055)* | *(0.316)* | *(0.217)* | *(0.047)* | |
| Econ | 0.656 | 3.656 | 5.250 | 0.219 | 32 | | | | | | |
| | *(0.085)* | *(0.446)* | *(0.348)* | *(0.074)* | | | | | | | |
| Hum | 0.429 | 3.057 | 4.071 | 0.529 | 70 | Hum | 0.429 | 3.057 | 4.071 | 0.529 | 70 |
| | *(0.060)* | *(0.310)* | *(0.185)* | *(0.060)* | | | *(0.060)* | *(0.310)* | *(0.185)* | *(0.060)* | |
| Sci | 0.536 | 2.071 | 3.964 | 0.464 | 28 | Other | 0.472 | 3.139 | 4.444 | 0.407 | 108 |
| | *(0.096)* | *(0.349)* | *(0.339)* | *(0.096)* | | | *(0.048)* | *(0.241)* | *(0.167)* | *(0.048)* | |
| Law | 0.667 | 4.286 | 5.429 | 0.524 | 21 | | | | | | |
| | *(0.105)* | *(0.648)* | *(0.406)* | *(0.112)* | | | | | | | |
| Eng | 0.750 | 3.083 | 4.583 | 0.250 | 12 | | | | | | |
| | *(0.131)* | *(0.743)* | *(0.434)* | *(0.131)* | | | | | | | |
| Psych | 0.310 | 3.172 | 4.103 | 0.414 | 29 | | | | | | |
| | *(0.087)* | *(0.474)* | *(0.278)* | *(0.093)* | | | | | | | |
| Others | 0.222 | 3.444 | 4.500 | 0.278 | 18 | | | | | | |
| | *(0.101)* | *(0.532)* | *(0.390)* | *(0.109)* | | | | | | | |
| Total | 0.506 | 3.498 | 4.720 | 0.385 | 257 | Total | 0.506 | 3.498 | 4.720 | 0.385 | 257 |
| | *(0.031)* | *(0.167)* | *(0.116)* | *(0.030)* | | | *(0.031)* | *(0.167)* | *(0.116)* | *(0.030)* | |

Note: All subjects included except one who did not provide major information. Mean values reported over the categories at left, except for frequency, denoted *N*. Standard errors are reported in italics. Sex = percent male; *Reli* and *Poli* refer to "religion" and "politics", and are defined as in Table 1. The column (G, B) shows the percent of the sample choosing the "honest" strategy. For majors, *Bus* = business; *Econ* = economics; *Hum* = humanities; *Sci* = science; *Eng* = engineering; *Psych* = psychology. The group "Others" comprises all students who are not in Bus, Econ, or Hum.

Since we want to know the message that you would send in any possible contingency, we will proceed according to the following protocol. To start, each of you will choose as if you were an A-participant. In addition, *before* knowing the color (blue/green) selected by the computer, you must indicate the message that you would send to B in two possible cases: (a) if the blue circle were selected and (b) if the green circle were selected. Afterward, each of you will complete a short and anonymous questionnaire. Only then will your actual type be randomly determined (A or B with probability 50% each) and revealed to you. Moreover, each A-participant will be randomly matched with a different B-participant. If you happen to be A, you will see the color of the circle in the screen, and your corresponding message will be sent to B. If you are chosen to be B, you will receive the message chosen by A, and your previous responses to (a) and (b) will have no effect. Note well that you will never know the type of any other participant, nor will any other participant get to know your type. The decisions in this experiment are anonymous, that is, no participant will ever know which participant made which choice. For this reason, no participant will know the identity of the person with whom he/she is paired.
The experiment will end with another short and anonymous questionnaire. Your payment will be made in private in an adjoining office by an assistant unrelated to this study. This assistant will only know your final payoff in this experiment, but not what you actually chose in the experiment.

**Before we start the experiment, please answer the following questions. Raise your hand when you are done so that we can verify the answers**

In a hypothetical example, assume that the computer selects color ______________ (choose either "green" or "blue" to construct your own example), and that A had decided in that case to send message ______________ ____________________ (choose either "green appeared" or "blue appeared" to construct your own example).

For this hypothetical example, answer the following questions,

- What would A's payoff be? _______
- What would B's payoff be? ___________
- What would A's payoff be, if she/he had chosen the other message? ________
- What would B's payoff be, if A had chosen the other message? ____________

In addition:

- Will B ever know the color that actually appeared? Yes No
- After your type has been determined and provided that you are of type A, can you change your prior choices? Yes No
- Can A ever affect B's balance? Yes No
- Can B ever affect A's balance? Yes No
- Do A's choices affect A's balance? Yes No
- What is the probability that the circle is blue-colored? ____________

## References

Bicchieri, C., 2005. The grammar of society: The nature and dynamics of social norms. Cambridge University Press.

Bolton, G.E., Ockenfels, A., 2000. ERC: a theory of equity, reciprocity, and competition. Am. Econ. Rev. 90 (1), 166–193.

Capraro, V., 2017. Who Lies? A Meta Analysis of the Effect of Sex, Age, and Education on Honesty. (Working paper).

Charness, G., Dufwenberg, M., 2006. Promises and partnerships. Econometrica 74 (6), 1579–1601.

Childs, J., 2012. Gender differences in lying. Econ. Lett. 114, 147–149.

Cialdini, R.B., Reno, R.R., Kallgren, C.A., 1990. A focus theory of normative conduct: recycling the concept of norms to reduce littering in public places. J. Pers. Soc. Psychol. 58 (6), 1015–1026.

Dreber, A., Johannesson, M., 2008. Gender differences in deception. Econ. Lett. 99 (1), 197–199.

Ellingsen, T., Johannesson, M., 2004. Promises, threats, and fairness. Econ. J. 114, 397–420.

Erat, S., Gneezy, U., 2012. White lies. Manag. Sci. 58 (4), 723–733.

Fehr, E., Schmidt, K., 1999. A theory of fairness, competition and cooperation. Q. J. Econ. 114 (3), 817–868.

Fehr, E., Naef, M., Schmidt, K.M., 2006. Inequality aversion, efficiency, and maximin preferences in simple distribution experiments: comment. Am. Econ. Rev. 96 (5), 1912–1917.

Fischbacher, U., 2007. z-Tree: Zurich toolbox for ready-made economic experiments. Exp.Econ. 10 (2), 171–178.

Fischbacher, U., Heusi, F., 2013. Lies in disguise: an experimental study on cheating. J. Eur. Econ. Assoc. 11 (3), 525–547.

Frank, R.H., Gilovitch, T., Regan, D.T., 1993. Does studying economics inhibit cooperation? J. Econ. Perspect. 7 (2), 159–171.

Frank, R.H., Gilovitch, T., Regan, D.T., 1996. Do economists make bad citizens? J. Econ. Perspect. 10 (1), 187–192.

Gneezy, U., 2005. Deception: the role of consequences. Am. Econ. Rev. 95 (1), 384–394.

Haucap, J., Müller, A., 2014. Why are economists so different? nature, nurture and gender effects in a simple trust game. In: Dusseldorf Center for Competition Economics Paper No. 136.

Holm, H., Kawagoe, T., 2010. Face-to-face lying: an experimental study in Sweden and Japan. J. Econ. Psychol. 31, 310–321.

Hurkens, S., Kartik, N., 2009. Would i lie to you? On social preferences and lying aversion. Exp. Econ. 12, 180–192.

Kartik, N., 2009. Strategic communication with lying costs. Rev. Econ. Stud. 76, 1359–1395.

Lewis, A., Bardis, A., Flint, C., Mason, C., Smith, N., Tickle, C., Zinser, J., 2012. Drawing the line somewhere: an experimental study of moral compromise. J. Econ. Psychol. 33, 718–725.

López-Pérez, R., 2012. The power of words: a model of honesty and fairness. J. Econ. Psychol. 33, 642–658.

López-Pérez, R., Spiegelman, E., 2013. Why do people tell the truth? Experimental evidence for pure lie aversion. Exp.Econ. 16 (3), 233–247.

Lundquist, T., Ellingsen, T., Gribbe, E., Johannesson, M., 2009. The aversion to lying. J. Econ. Behav. Organ. 70, 81–92.

Marwell, G., Ames, R.E., 1981. Economists free ride, does anyone else? Experiments on the provision of public goods, IV. J. Public Econ. 15 (3), 295–310.

UNESCO, 2011. International Standard Classification of Education 2011. UNESCO Institute for Statistics, Succursale Centre-Ville Montreal, Quebec. Retrieved online at http://uis.unesco.org/sites/default/files/documents/international-standard-classification-of-education-isced-2011-en.pdf.

Utikal, V., Fischbacher, U., 2013. Disadvantageous lies in individual decisions. J. Econ. Behav. Organ. 85 (C), 108–111.

Chapter 3.2

# Cheating and altruism by discipline

Nora Muñoz-Izquierdo[1], Beatriz Gil-Gómez de Liaño[2], Francisco Daniel Rin-Sánchez[2], David Pascual-Ezama[3]

[1]*Accounting Department, CUNEF—Colegio Universitario de Estudios Financieros, Madrid, Spain,* [2]*Department of Social Psychology and Methodology, Facultad de Psicología, Universidad Autónoma de Madrid, Madrid, Spain,* [3]*Accounting and Finance Department, Facultad de Ciencias Económicas y Empresariales, Complutense University of Madrid, Madrid, Spain*

### Chapter Outline



**JEL Classification:** A12, D03, D64
**PsycINFO Classification:** 3120

## 1. Introduction

Not a single day goes by without a new case of accounting fraud, audit fraud, tax evasion, or corruption on the news. What does this mean? That someone cheated again. The underlying conflict between self-interest and social interest can be attributed to individual decisions about being honest vs behaving advantageously. If you ask yourself "Have I ever told a lie, even a very innocent one?" The (honest) answer is likely to be, "Of course, maybe even daily." This implies that cheating is undoubtedly widespread and is damaging not only individuals' own trustworthiness but also the economic principles in general,

**Dishonesty in Behavioral Economics. https://doi.org/10.1016/B978-0-12-815857-9.00010-8**

causing extraordinary financial and social costs (Mazar and Ariely, 2006). Despite the substantial body of experimental studies in the economics and social psychology literature about dishonesty (e.g. Fischbacher and Heusi, 2013; Gneezy, 2005; Houser et al., 2012; Mazar et al., 2008; Pascual-Ezama et al., 2013), there is still a need to study the intersection between the stream of research about dishonesty and the altruistic behavior.

In this chapter we investigate whether different rewards, cash penalties, and donations affect cheating behavior of university students. We focus our attention on individuals currently studying the bachelor degrees of business economics, psychology, and IT engineering. In addition, we also examine lying behavior by testing the tendency to lie about their donations, and the effect of a prior notice—telling or not in advance that they had to report donations—on lying. To address these questions, we conducted four experiments using 540 students. In Experiments 1 and 2, participants were asked to flip a white/black coin in private, so they were given the opportunity to cheat because nobody could see the outcome. In the task of Experiments 3A and 3B, recipients decided about a cash donation. A summary of the four experiments appears in Table 1, containing their purposes, task, conditions, participants, and location of each experiment.

**TABLE 1** Experiment Summary Table

| Experiment | Purpose | Experiment task and conditions | Participants and location |
|---|---|---|---|
| 1 | With the possibility of earning one chocolate truffle, examine the effect of cash penalties and donations on cheating behavior of students with different academic backgrounds | Flip a white/black coin in private (white: prize-winning side; black: prize-losing side). A chocolate truffle earned when winning, and task finished. Three conditions when losing:<br>- No penalty condition (NP) or control condition: when losing, no penalty and task finished.<br>- Penalty condition (P): when losing, a cash penalty was requested (out-of-pocket and participant was warned about it before performing the task)<br>- Altruistic penalty condition (AP): when losing, a donation was requested (out-of-pocket and participant was warned about it before performing the task) | 270 students randomly assigned (90 business economics; 90 psychologists; 90 IT engineers). In the university campus (outside the lab) |

**TABLE 1** Experiment Summary Table—cont'd

| Experiment | Purpose | Experiment task and conditions | Participants and location |
|---|---|---|---|
| 2 | With the possibility of earning €5, examine:<br>– The effect of donations on cheating behavior of students with different academic backgrounds<br>– Their tendency to lie about their donations | Flip a white/black coin in private. When losing, the task finished. When winning, the participant received €5 coins, a voluntary donation of those coins was requested and participant was asked about the money donated (participant was NOT warned about it before performing the task) | 90 students randomly assigned (30 business economics; 30 psychologists; 30 IT engineers). In the lab |
| 3A | – Examine the altruistic behavior (donations) of students with different academic backgrounds<br>– Test their tendency to lie about their donations WITHOUT a prior notice. | The participant received €5 coins, a voluntary donation of those coins was requested and participant was asked about the money donated (participant was NOT aware of it before performing the task) | 90 students randomly assigned (30 business economics; 30 psychologists; 30 IT engineers). In the lab |
| 3B | – Examine the altruistic behavior (donations) of students with different academic backgrounds<br>– Test their tendency to lie about their donations WITH a prior notice | The participant received €5 coins, a voluntary donation of those coins was requested and participant was asked about the money donated (participant was aware of it before performing the task) | 90 students randomly assigned (30 business economics; 30 psychologists; 30 IT engineers). In the lab |

Summary of all experiments, including experiment number, purpose, task and conditions, participants and location.

In Experiment 1, with a chocolate truffle reward when winning the task, we examine the effect of cash penalties and donations on cheating behavior by academic discipline. Previous literature has already suggested that there are differences in cheating behavior by academic disciplines (e.g., Bowers, 1964; Frank et al., 1993; McCabe and Treviño, 1993). Bowers (1964) found that business students and engineers were among those with the lowest rates of truth-telling, perhaps due to more demanding performance goals. Frank et al. (1993) stated that the self-interest model persuade economists to be less generous than others due to their training in profit maximizing. They argued that economists act uncooperatively in social dilemmas as a result of their training, and that economists expect others to cheat as well. Similarly, McCabe and Treviño (1993) concluded that there are significant differences in cheating behavior among students from several degrees. Concretely, they found the highest level of cheating on economists, followed by engineers, science, and humanities students. All these findings go in line with the classic approach of the standard economic model. According to this model, individuals behave as *homo economicus* (Becker, 1968; Hill and Kochendorfer, 1969; Michales and Miethe, 1989), which implies that dishonest actions are based on a simple cost–benefit analysis that depends only on two inputs: the amount to be gained and the expected punishment of being caught (Gino et al., 2009). Thus, in agreement with proponents of the standard economic model, we expect business economics students to cheat more than other students as they have paid more attention to economic models in their studies. More precisely, to add to this line of inquiry, we theorize that business economics students may cheat more than noneconomics either including or not a cash penalty when losing the task.

In addition, in Experiment 1 and regarding the effect of donations on cheating behavior, we follow the proponents of the self-concept maintenance approach. The proponents of this approach agree on the fact that business economics students are likely to cooperate in altruistic activities due to their desire to maintain a positive self-concept. Frank et al. (1993) stated that economists might be more altruistic as they have been trained in traditional communitarian ways developing voluntary support activities. Later, Yezer et al. (1996) found evidence of altruistic tendencies in economists in an experiment where students in upper level classes were more likely to return money unfairly awarded. When analyzing dues payments to professional organizations, Laband and Beil (1999) suggested that professional economists are significantly more cooperative than political scientists and sociologists. Also, Hu and Liu (2003) showed that economics degrees tend to behave more altruistically and cooperatively than noneconomics. However, other prior research supports the idea that economics students might donate less to charities (Bauman and Rose, 2011; Carter and Irons, 1991; Marwell and Ames, 1981) in accordance with the rational self-interest model, which predicts their lack of generosity and their selfishness. These mixed findings have inspired us to test how different students react when losing a task conducted in private implies the payment of an out-of-pocket donation to a nonprofit organization. As previously stated, following the most popular approach of the self-concept maintenance theory, we propose that business economics students are more altruistic than other students.

Further, we also add evidence to the core studies of the interconnection between cheating behavior and altruism with our Experiment 1 based on the self-concept maintenance approach (Gneezy et al., 2014; Mazar and Ariely, 2006; Mazar et al., 2008). Individuals try to find internal psychological reward mechanisms to self-justify unethical behaviors (Mazar and Ariely, 2006; Mazar et al., 2008). In addition, as per Gneezy et al. (2014), greater levels of altruism have a dampening effect on cheating because subjects become aware of behaving more ethically and cooperatively with others. They found that donations to charity increase after an immoral choice, so that when feelings of guilt are emphasized, individuals might refrain from breaking internal moral constraints. Gino et al. (2013) even suggested that individuals cheat more if the unethical action increased the benefits to others, creating a situation in which dishonesty can be viewed as morally acceptable. These results suggest that when altruism is made salient, individuals pay attention to their own moral standards and their self-concepts, decreasing their tendencies to engage in dishonest actions. Accordingly, we expect cheating behavior to decrease in all majors when altruism plays a role in the task performed.

We conduct Experiment 2 for various purposes. First, we verify the altruistic findings of Experiment 1 with a cash reward instead of a chocolate truffle. Second, we also add evidence to the literature about lying behavior. In line with the cost–benefit approach or standard economic model, the opinion of Lundquist et al. (2009) is that economics degrees are more likely to lie than noneconomics because economic models learned at university lead them to behave as *homo economicus*. Similarly, Lewis et al. (2012) showed that economics students are more apt to lie than noneconomics, and López-Pérez and Spiegelman (2019) indicated that business students are significantly less lie averse than those in other disciplines, as they probably expect others to lie as well because they deal with competitive environments. Following this reasoning, it is rational to believe that business economics students are going to be the group that lie the most. To the best of our knowledge, scholars have apparently ignored the connection between cheating, altruism and lying, so this lack of explanation has inspired this study to test how these three behaviors interact in different students.

Finally, our Experiments 3A and 3B contribute to understanding the ethical dilemma of lying. With their designs we study the tendency to lie about cash donations made manipulating the prior notice (not telling recipients in advance that they are going to be asked for the amount donated). Whereas in Experiment 3A the experimenter did not warn participants about the fact that they were going to be asked about the cash donated at the end, in Experiment 3B participants were aware of it before performing the task. There is recent evidence based on the self-concept maintenance approach that supports the idea that subjects are more likely to report higher private donations to charities after a lying decision (Maggian, 2019). Also, respondents are concerned about their social image, so they are more likely to behave altruistically if they know that they are going to be asked about their actions (Dellavigna et al., 2016). Thus, we expect participants to donate more when recipients know in advance that their donations are going to be questioned. In order to maintain the self-image, we also expect a tendency to lie and over report the donations when participants do not receive a prior notice.

## 2. Experiment 1: Effects of cash penalties and altruism on cheating

In the first experiment we studied the effect of cash penalties and donations on cheating behavior. Our participants were students from three different bachelor degrees. It seems that university students represent a relevant sample to analyze because cheating in educational environments, such as colleges and universities, is a widespread and growing phenomenon (Cicognani, 2019). Our experiment consisted of three conditions. The control condition or no penalty condition (NP) served as a baseline for the performance of the task—to flip a white/black coin in private—and for the magnitude of cheating, as participants were not punished for getting the bad outcome. In the second condition—penalty condition (P)—the experimenter clearly explained to participants at the onset of the experiment that, in case of losing, an out-of-pocket cash penalty had to be paid. In the final condition—altruistic penalty condition (AP)—the experimenter made it clear to participants that the cash penalty paid if losing represented a donation to a nonprofit organization. In the three conditions, participants performed the coin-toss task in private, so they had the opportunity to cheat without being exposed to anyone. Thus, for our analyses, cheating could not be determined on an individual level.

By comparing the results of the three conditions, we were able to examine the influence of two effects on cheating: cash penalties and altruism. On one hand, according to the cost–benefit approach, cheating with the exposure to a cash penalty in case of losing should have increased the tendency to behave unethical. Therefore, cheating should be higher in the penalty condition (P) than in the no penalty condition (NP). On the other hand, according to the self-concept maintenance approach, we expect lower cheating behavior after knowing that the penalty represented a donation to a nonprofit organization, in order to maintain people's self-image. Although the general behavior is to avoid cash penalties, when payments represent donations the ethical threshold gets more restrictive and people tend to be more generous. Thus, cheating should be higher in the penalty condition (P) than in the altruistic penalty condition (AP).

### 2.1 Method

#### 2.1.1 Participants

Two hundred and seventy students (52% female; $N = 141/270$) from public universities in Madrid participated in the study. They were students of three bachelor degrees: business economics ($N=90$), psychology ($N=90$) and IT engineering ($N=90$). Participants were randomly assigned to one of three conditions: control or no penalty condition (NP), penalty condition (P), and altruistic penalty condition (AP). Participants joined the experiment voluntarily and they were tempted to enroll by a visible poster which explicitly announced "Is this your lucky day? Flip a coin and win a chocolate!"

### 2.1.2 Design and procedure

The experiment consisted of a coin task replication in which every participant tossed a white/black coin in private (Pascual-Ezama et al., 2015). The ones who reported the prize-winning side (the white side) earned prize: a chocolate truffle. Since the experimenter was unable to see the toss, participants had an embedded incentive to cheat if the outcome was black. We ran the task on campus, outside the lab, on a side of the main hallway or in a corner of the cafeteria, where many students were passing nearby. The surroundings were the same in the three conditions and the answers were not distorted because participants did not perceive the task as an experiment, but more as a game or a marketing strategy for the chocolate truffles' brand.

The experimenter was located behind a desk with the poster announcing the game and he/she explained the task to students who agreed to participate. Once the experiment started, each participant (one-by-one) walked to a second desk 15 ft away to toss a white/black coin inside an empty recycling box. Thus, nobody could see the outcome. In the three conditions, if the outcome was white (the prize-winning side), the participant grabbed a chocolate truffle from another box placed in a third desk situated 6 ft further, and the experiment ended. If the outcome was black (the price-losing side), the task finished in the no penalty condition (NP). In the penalty condition (P), the participant left an out-of-pocket cash penalty of any value in a recycling box placed in the same desk as the chocolate truffles' box. Finally, in the altruistic penalty condition (AP) the out-of-pocket cash penalty was a donation to a nonprofit organization.

## 2.2 Results

### 2.2.1 Pure cheating with a chocolate truffle reward

We present the results of Experiment 1 in Fig. 1. In the no penalty condition (NP), we expected participants to over-report white coin-toss results, as they had an incentive (a chocolate truffle) to cheat and the impossibility of being caught. The null hypothesis of honest behavior is rejected at $p=0.008$ (dotted line) only for the bachelor degree in business economics. The anomalous percentage of the prize-winning side (or, as a result, the percentage of chocolate truffles taken) in business economics' students (77%; $N=69/90$) suggests that they cheat more often than noneconomics—psychologists (53%; $N=48/90$) and IT engineering students (60%; $N=54/90$). In this condition (NP), participants faced a trade-off between the joy of eating a chocolate truffle and the disutility

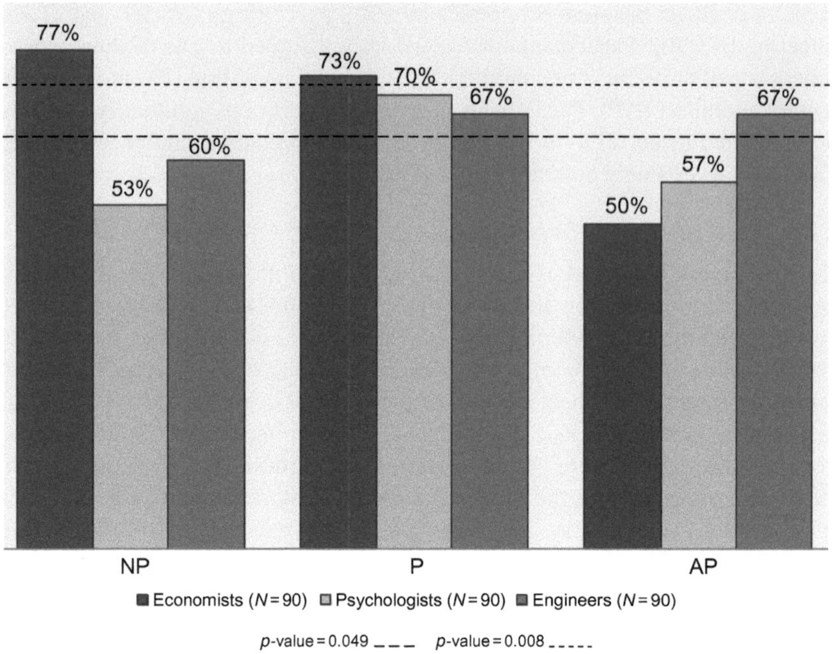


**FIG. 1** Percentage of chocolate truffles taken (prize-winning outcome) per condition and bachelor degree in Experiment 1 (Binomial significant differences). In Fig. 1, the cheating results of Experiment 1 appears. The *X* axis shows the three different conditions run in the experiment: *NP*=No penalty; *P*=Penalty; *AP*=Altruistic penalty; and the three types of participants: business economics, psychology, and IT engineering students. The *Y* axis indicates the percentage of chocolate truffles taken, that is, the number of times that participants reported the white outcome (prize-winning outcome).

of having a threatened self-concept because of cheating. While our evidence indicates that the honesty of psychology and IT engineering' students is not affected by this trade-off, the honesty of business economics students is; thus, business economics students cheat more than the others. In addition, we have examined gender differences and the results are not statistically significant.[a]

### 2.2.2 Cash penalties

In the penalty condition (P), where we included the effect of cash penalties on cheating behavior, the null hypothesis of honesty is rejected for all bachelor degrees and results are statistically significant: students of business economics degree at $p=0.008$ (dotted line), and psychology and IT engineering degrees at $p=0.049$ (dashed line), as illustrated in Fig. 1. We consider the percentage

a. There are no significant differences in gender in the four experiments of the paper; thus, men and women behave similarly according to our evidence.

of chocolates takes in all academic degrees is abnormally high, meaning that participants probably cheated. The difference of white-toss outcomes between the three different groups (business economics, psychologists, and IT engineers) is not statistically significant ($X^2=0.000$; $p=1$). Thus, when participants obtained the prize-losing outcome (black), many of them acted like winners, taking the chocolate truffle rather than paying for losing, no matter the bachelor degree. This finding shows that cash penalties persuade students to cheat.

### 2.2.3 Altruism

In the altruistic penalty condition (AP), we added the effect of altruism on cheating behavior to the experiment. The null hypothesis of behaving honestly is rejected at $p=0.049$ (dashed line) only for IT engineering students, as shown in Fig. 1. While business economics and psychology students decreased the percentage of chocolate truffles grabbed (50% or $N=45/90$, and 57% or $N=51/90$, respectively), IT engineering' students did not (67%; $N=60/90$). This result implies that the altruistic instincts of business economics and psychology students show up. Meanwhile, the behavior of IT engineers was not affected by the donation, ignoring the moral compass of helping a nonprofit organization.

## 3. Experiment 2: Effects of lying and altruistic donations

Considering only the results of Experiment 1, it seems premature to affirm that in a real-world situation cheating and altruistic behaviors are more remarkable in students in business economics than in the other students because they had the incentive of a chocolate truffle instead of real money. To ensure the reliability of the results of Experiment 1, we conducted a second experiment.

The purpose of Experiment 2 is to verify if business economics students cheat more than psychology and IT engineering students when cash incentives play a role in the design (instead of the incentive of a chocolate truffle), and if their donations are the most salient. In addition, we also compare the tendency to lie among the three academic degrees. We test the lying behavior asking participants about their donations a posteriori (at the end of the experiment).

Experiment 2 was conducted in the lab, and the task was the same as in Experiment 1: to flip a white/black coin in private. Only when winning, the participants received a cash prize that they could donate afterwards. However, in the design of this experiment, we were able to determine if participants actually cheated in the toss and the exact money they donated. This is because they had to report the outcome on a computer and they deposited their donations inside envelopes marked with invisible ink. If the findings are consistent with our Experiment 1, we expect donations from students in business economics and psychology to be higher than donations from IT engineers. In addition, it is rational to believe that the tendency to lie will go in line with the cheating behavior. Therefore, we expect lying to be higher in students in business economics, followed by psychologists and IT engineers.

## 3.1 Method

### 3.1.1 Participants

Ninety students (59% female; $N=53/90$) from public universities in Madrid joined the experiment. They were studying the bachelor degrees of business economics ($N=30$), psychology ($N=30$), and IT engineering ($N=30$). Participants enrolled in the task voluntarily, and they were paid €1 for participation.

### 3.1.2 Design and procedure

Participants received an envelope with money based on their outcome in the task, receiving the full amount when reporting the prize-winning result and no money for the prize-losing option.

Once the experimenter explained the task, each participant went to a stall (similar to a voting booth) six feet from the experimenter's desk, where there was a computer and a recycling box on a table. The computer screen presented the following message: "With your own cell phone, log in to www.rollandflip.com and flip a white/black coin. Did you get black or white?" The reason for using the participant's phone was to assure that the toss was completely private and was not registered in the computer. If the outcome was black (the price-losing side), the task ended. If the outcome was white (the prize-winning side), the participant took an envelope containing €5 coins from the recycling box and decided how much to donate to a nonprofit organization and how much to keep. The participant left the stall, went back to the experimenter's desk, and placed the envelope with the donation in a cardboard box. Finally, the participant was asked to come back to the stall and answer another question that appeared on the screen: "How many coins did you donate?" The participant was not warned about that question before performing the task. This mechanism allows us to test the lying behavior of students because their responses would be matched with their donations, as the envelopes were marked with invisible ink.

## 3.2 Results

### 3.2.1 Pure cheating with a cash reward

In Fig. 2, we provide a summary of the results of Experiment 2. The null hypothesis of honest behavior is rejected at $p=0.008$ (dotted line) for the business economics students. They over-reported white outcomes (the prize-winning side) because the percentage of chocolates taken (70%; $N=63/90$) was too high, contrary to noneconomics—psychologists (54%; $N=49/90$) and IT engineers (52%; $N=47/90$). This finding goes in agreement with the evidence of Experiment 1, suggesting that business economics students tend to cheat more that noneconomics, regardless of the type of earnings (nonmonetary, such as a chocolate truffle, or monetary). The honesty of psychology and IT engineering students seems not to get affected by any rewards.

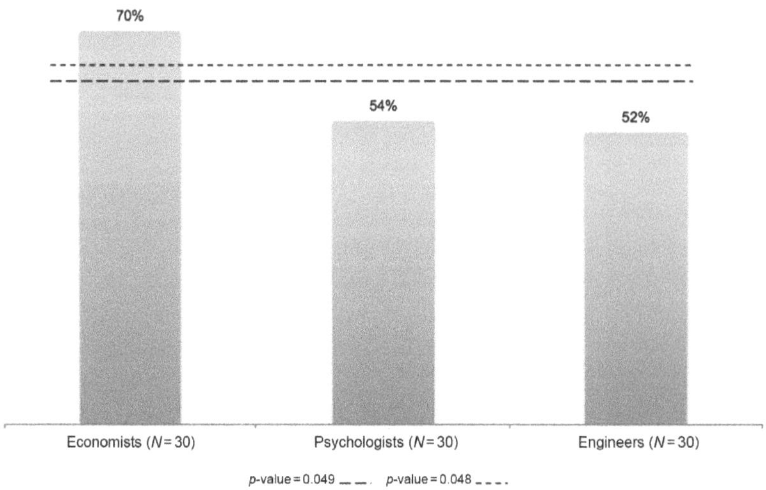


**FIG. 2** Percentage of coins taken (prize-winning outcome) by bachelor degree in Experiment 2 (Binomial significant differences). It shows the cheating results of Experiment 2. The *X* axis shows the three different types of participants: business economics, psychology, and IT engineering students. The *Y* axis indicates the percentage of rewards (cash) taken, that is, the number of times that participants reported the white outcome (prize-winning outcome).

### 3.2.2 Altruism

Donations by participants in Experiment 2 are shown in Fig. 3. This analysis only contains the winners of the task, as the cash to be donated (five €1 coins) represented the prize for winning. Business economics students donated 73% of the cash (an average of €3.67), while psychology students donated 64% (€3.21) and IT engineering students 60% (€3.01). Thus, we verify that business economics students have the highest altruistic instincts, followed by psychologists and IT engineers, in agreement with the results of Experiment 1. The difference between business economics students and noneconomics is statistically significant ($X^2=3.617$; $p=0.038$).

### 3.2.3 Lying behavior

To examine the tendency of participants to lie, we analyzed the responses to the unexpected question regarding the cash donated. For this test, we only include the winners of the task (the ones who obtained the reward, made the donation, and were questioned about the cash donated). We found that 6% of both business economics ($N=5/90$) and psychology students ($N=5/90$) reported more than what they had actually donated, while the IT engineering degree did not lie at all. Interestingly, this result validates the expectation that the degree of business economics contained the highest number of liars, although the same behavior is found in psychology students.

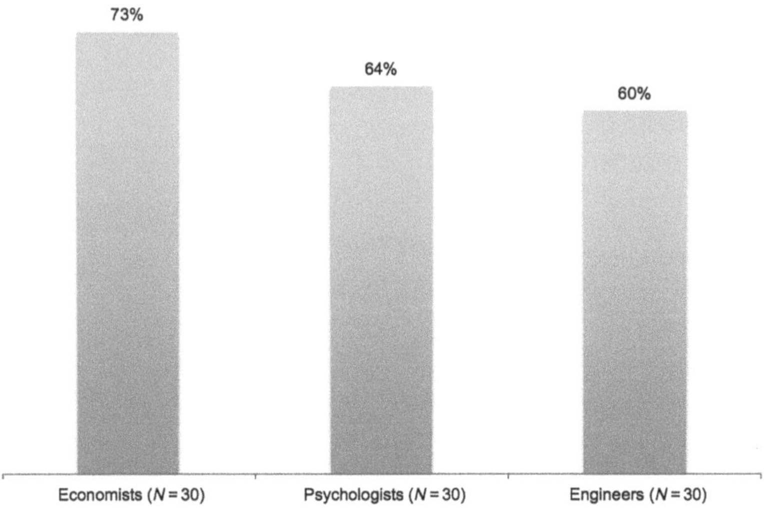


**FIG. 3** Money Donated (percentage) in Experiment 2. It shows a graph with the percentage of cash donated (out of €5) per group of participants (business economics, psychology, and IT engineering students) in Experiment 2.

# 4. Experiment 3A: Effects of pure altruism and lying behavior

To take a more in-depth look at both the altruistic and the lying behavior of individuals, and based on the interesting results found in Experiment 2, we conducted Experiments 3A and 3B. The purpose of Experiment 3A is to investigate the altruistic behavior (donations) of students enrolled in different bachelor degrees and to test their tendency to lie about their donations without any prior notice, which means without telling individuals that they will have to report the cash donated.

In Experiment 3A, there is no coin toss task so that we test altruism for all participants (not only for the task winners, as in Experiments 1 and 2). Cash was given to recipients at the beginning of the task and they decided how much to donate. If the evidence is consistent with Experiment 2, we predict that business economics students would present a stronger altruistic profile than noneconomics.

## 4.1 Method

### *4.1.1 Participants*

Similar to Experiment 2, 90 students (62% female; $N=56/90$) from public universities in Madrid enrolled in business economics ($N=30$), psychology ($N=30$), and IT engineering ($N=30$) participated voluntarily.

### 4.1.2 Design and procedure

The participant received an envelope with the five €1 coins for the donations at the beginning of the task so they do not need to leave the stall at any time. Thus, the participant decided how many coins to donate, deposited the donation inside the envelope marked with invisible ink in the box right next to the computer and answered the question about the money donated that appeared on the computer's screen at that moment without any prior awareness.

## 4.2 Results

### 4.2.1 Altruism

Cash donated by participants in Experiment 3A appears in Fig. 4. Results are similar to Experiment 2, including all individuals in this design (the honest and dishonest ones). The percentage of cash donated is higher for the business economics students than for the noneconomics, and the difference is statistically significant ($X^2=4.08$; $p=0.029$). Business economics students donated 76% (€3.8 on average), while 68% (€3.4) was donated by psychologists, and donations of IT engineers decreased to 59% (€2.9).

### 4.2.2 Lying behavior

Consistent with the lying results of Experiment 2, in response to the question about their donations, 7% ($N=6/90$) of students of the degree in business economics reported more than the amount they had really donated, 6% ($N=5/90$) of psychology students, whereas only 2% ($N=2/90$) of IT engineers lied.

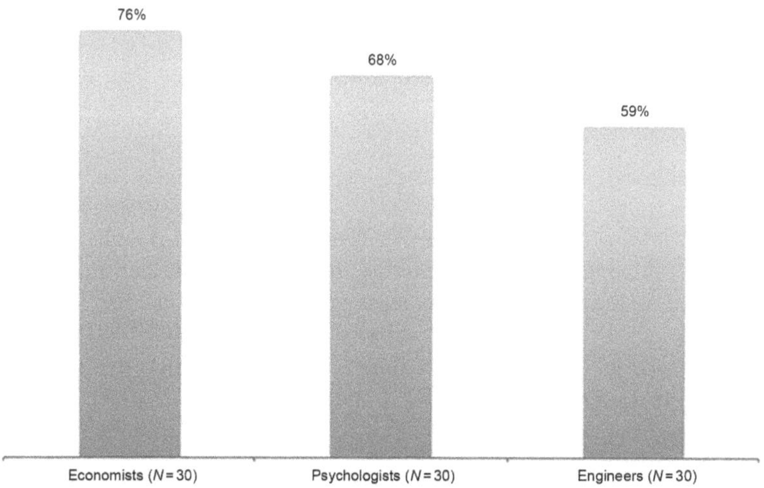


**FIG. 4** Money Donated (in percentage) in Experiment 3A. The graph in the figure includes cash donated (in percentage, out of €5) per group of participants (business economics, psychology, and IT engineering students) in Experiment 3A.

# 5. Experiment 3B: Effects of prior notice on lying behavior

The aim of Experiment 3B is to study the altruistic behavior (donations) of students enrolled in different bachelor degrees and to test their tendency to lie about their donations with a prior notice, which is telling participants in advance that they will have to report the cash donated.

Experiment 3B is similar to Experiment 3A with the exception of the prior notice. In Experiment 3B, the experimenter warned each participant at the beginning of the task that a question about the cash donated would appear on the computer after the donation. According to Dellavigna et al. (2016), respondents are concerned about their social image, so they are more likely to behave altruistically if they know that they are going to be asked to report their actions later. In line with this, we expect that the mechanism of the prior notice will increase donations. In addition, due to our results of prior experiments, we also predict that the highest donations would be granted by economists.

## 5.1 Method

### 5.1.1 Participants

Similar to Experiment 3A, 90 participants (63% female; $N=57/90$) from public universities in Madrid studying bachelor degrees in business economics ($N=30$), psychology ($N=30$), and IT engineering ($N=30$) participated voluntarily.

### 5.1.2 Design and procedure

The design of Experiments 3B and 3A matched, with one difference: in Experiment 3B, in the instructions to participants we include the question about reporting the cash donated. Therefore, participants received the envelope, performed the task in the stall, donated the cash considered, and reported the donation.

## 5.2 Results

### 5.2.1 Altruism

In Fig. 5 we illustrate the cash donated by participants in Experiment 3B. The percentage of cash was higher for business economics students than for noneconomics with statistically significant difference ($X^2=13.8$; $p<0.001$). Business economics students donated 89% of the cash earned (€4.4 on average), while psychology students donated 73% (€3.7) and IT engineers 59% (€3). Results are consistent with Experiment 3A. Participants donate slightly more in Experiment 3B, with no significant differences ($X^2=6.0$; $p=0.199$). In addition, as expected, the prior notice increased donations notably for business economics students and psychologists.

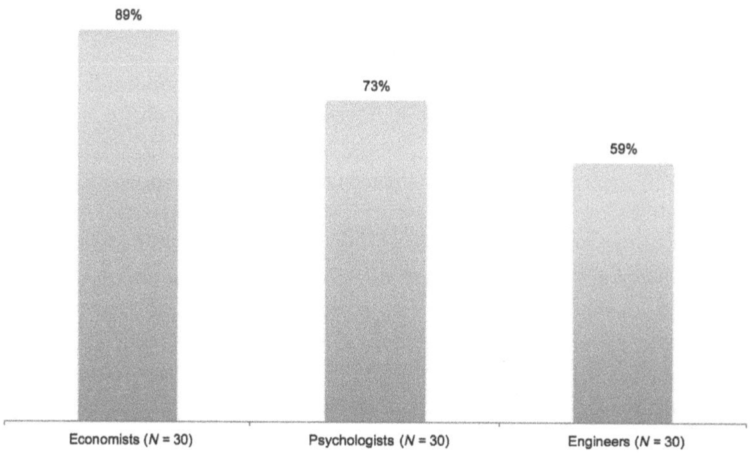


**FIG. 5** Money Donated (in percentage) in Experiment 3B. It illustrates the percentage of cash donated (out of €5) per group of participants (business economics, psychology, and IT engineering students) in Experiment 3B.

### *5.2.2 Lying behavior*

The prior notice not only increased donations but also decreased the tendency to lie. Only 2% ($N$=2/90) of business economics students and 1% ($N$=1/90) of psychologists reported more than the amount donated, whereas IT engineers did not lie, as in Experiment 2.

## 6. Discussion and general conclusion

The aim of this chapter is to examine cheating and altruistic behaviors of university students enrolled in several bachelor degrees, namely, business economics, psychology, and IT engineering. More precisely, we study the effects of different rewards (monetary and nonmonetary) and different penalties (cash penalties or penalties that represent donations to a nonprofit organization) on cheating behavior. Additionally, we also test the connection of altruistic and lying behaviors of individuals, by analyzing the tendency to lie about their donations. For these purposes, we ran four experiments using a total of 540 participants. Our results are consistent among the experiments conducted. In summary, our evidence suggests that business economics students cheat more than other individuals regardless of the rewards or the penalties, behave more altruistically donating more than others, and do not lie in general about their donations (although, if they do, they lie more than others).

Our evidence in Experiment 1 agrees with prior research that stated that individuals tend to cheat (Jacobsen et al., 2018), and this behavior is influenced by traditional economic models, based on the cost–benefit approach. The cost–benefit aspect posits that when any gain from cheating is high compared to the expected punishment, the propensity to behave dishonestly increases. Similar arguments are consistent with traditional models of agency theory in economics, which suggest that people make rational, self-interested decisions to cheat depending on incentives (Gino and Pierce, 2009; Jensen and Meckling, 1976). Accordingly, each individual is more likely to act unethically if it results in financial benefits. Business students could be more influenced by these models as they have studied them deeply in their university readings and lectures. Thus, business economics students are more academically oriented to find an equilibrium between the cost of any decision or investment and its return, and the results of Experiment 1 verify this statement.

Prior research suggested that the self-maintenance concept can lead individuals to behave more ethically (Fischbacher and Heusi, 2013; Kunda, 1990; Mazar et al., 2008; Shalvi et al., 2011) and internalized social norms could guide respondents to a preference for honesty (Pruckner and Sausgruber, 2013). When deciding whether to lie or behave ethically, individuals attempt to find the balance between obtaining the highest payoff possible and maintaining a positive self-image (Gneezy et al., 2012; Grossman, 2014; Lazear et al., 2012). In general, altruism encourages people to become more unselfish due to the self-concept maintenance theory because the possibility of donating will decrease the magnitude of cheating and increase the likelihood of altruistic behavior. This mechanism is more salient when an individual's academic background emphasizes organizational and cooperative feelings and also self-interest, profit maximizing, and maintenance of self-image in front of others, such as in the case of business economics students, as per the evidence of Experiment 1. Thus, this perspective predicts that socially oriented people or individuals who work in teams and organizations should donate more than others, and we corroborate this prediction. Altruism clearly diminishes the impact of cheating for business economics and psychology participants and enlarges donations to charity from them. This last effect is in line with Gneezy et al.'s conclusions (2014), who found that people who make an immoral choice first are more likely to donate to charity afterwards, driven by a temporal increase in guilt, which they called conscience accounting. In the case of IT engineering students, the results suggest that the altruism effect does not incentivize them to behave more ethically. This could be due to their focus in more analytical tasks, less cooperative projects or training with less attention to profit maximization. However, this result could also be driven by self-selected groups of marginal subjects in each academic degree that may not behave in the same way as average people (Houdek, 2017). Last, we corroborate these findings in Experiment 2 using different rewards when reporting the price-winning option of the task (a chocolate truffle vs a cash reward).

We also studied the likelihood of lying in Experiments 3A and 3B. By manipulating the prior notice given to participants—telling or not telling them in advance that they had to report the cash donated—we showed that a prior notice increased participants' likelihood of acting ethically. That is, individuals lie less frequently when they will be asked later about their acts. According to Dellavigna et al. (2016), respondents are concerned about their social image, so they are more likely to behave altruistically if they know that they are going to be asked to report their actions later. In addition, lying to maintain the self-image goes in line with the probability of cheating and the altruistic behavior, so that business economics students lied more than psychology and IT engineering students. Nevertheless, their altruistic behavior is stronger than that of the other groups.

The implications of these results are relevant for university staff and managers because we indicate whether or not different individuals (university students) react ethically or unethically to several situations. This work could be of interest not only for identifying unethical behaviors at the university level, but also for anticipating how to avoid unethical behaviors in the workplace, as the job market is the next step of university students' career.

Finally, the findings of our study may have implications for researchers examining ethical and unethical behaviors in individuals with different academic backgrounds. We obtain valuable evidence that business economics students seem to cheat more but behave more altruistically than psychology and IT engineering students. This may have important consequences in the real world because most of international decisions are based on a financial reasoning and made by individuals with business backgrounds. However, some economists have been criticized by social organizations for different cases of fraud or corruption, specifically salient during the global financial crisis. In this sense, our evidence might shed light on the need for studies regarding alternative models in society not only based on financial aspects but also on sociological and analytical decisions. Due to the complexity of the current economic context, the political environment and the territorial conflicts worldwide, a broader picture offered by decision-makers from different backgrounds may help to clarify the various facets of international affairs. For instance, the development of more collaborative organizations, altruistically oriented and managed by sociologists, such as the "Sharing Economy" (Schor, 2016), could notably assist in solving financial and political issues among territories.

## References

Bauman, Y., Rose, E., 2011. Selection or indoctrination: why do economics students donate less than the rest? J. Econ. Behav. Organ. 79 (3), 318–327.

Becker, S., 1968. Crime and punishment: an economic approach. In: The Economic Dimensions of Crime. Palgrave Macmillan, UK, pp. 13–68.

Bowers, W.J., 1964. Student Dishonesty and Its Control in College. Bureau of Applied Research, Columbia University, New York.

Carter, J.R., Irons, M.D., 1991. Are economists different, and if so, why? J. Econ. Perspect. 5, 171–177.

Cicognani, S., 2019. Dishonesty among University students. In: Bucciol, A., Montinari, N. (Eds.), Dishonesty in Behavioral Economics. Academic Press.

DellaVigna, S., List, J.A., Malmendier, U., Rao, G., 2016. Voting to tell others. Rev. Econ. Stud. 84 (1), 143–181.
Fischbacher, U., Heusi, F., 2013. Lies in disguise—an experimental study on cheating. J. Eur. Econ. Assoc. 11 (3), 525–547.
Frank, R.H., Gilovich, T., Regan, D.T., 1993. Does studying economics inhibit cooperation? J. Econ. Perspect. 7, 159–171.
Gino, F., Ayal, S., Ariely, D., 2009. Contagion and differentiation in unethical behavior: the effect of one bad apple on the barrel. Psychol. Sci. 20 (3), 393–398.
Gino, F., Ayal, S., Ariely, D., 2013. Self-serving altruism? The lure of unethical actions that benefit others. J. Econ. Behav. Organ. 93, 285–292.
Gino, F., Pierce, L., 2009. Dishonesty in the name of equity. Psychol. Sci. 20 (9), 1153–1160.
Gneezy, U., 2005. Deception: the role of consequences. Am. Econ. Rev. 95 (1), 384–394.
Gneezy, A., Imas, A., Brown, A., Nelson, L.D., Norton, M.I., 2012. Paying to be nice: consistency and costly prosocial behavior. Manag. Sci. 58 (1), 179–187.
Gneezy, U., Imas, A., Madarász, K., 2014. Conscience accounting: emotion dynamics and social behavior. Manag. Sci. 60 (11), 2645–2658.
Grossman, Z., 2014. Strategic ignorance and the robustness of social preferences. Manag. Sci. 60 (11), 2659–2665.
Hill, J.P., Kochendorfer, R.A., 1969. Knowledge of peer success and risk of detection as determinants of cheating. Dev. Psychol. 1 (3), 231–238.
Houdek, P., 2017. A perspective on research on dishonesty: limited external validity due to the lack of possibility of self-selection in experimental designs. Front. Psychol. 8, 1566.
Houser, D., Vetter, S., Winter, J., 2012. Fairness and cheating. Eur. Econ. Rev. 56 (8), 1645–1655.
Hu, Y.A., Liu, D.Y., 2003. Altruism versus egoism in human behavior of mixed motives. Am. J. Econ. Sociol. 62 (4), 677–705.
Jacobsen, C., Fosgaard, T.R., Pascual-Ezama, D., 2018. Why do we lie? A practical guide to the dishonesty literature. J. Econ. Surv. 32 (2), 357–387.
Jensen, M.C., Meckling, W.H., 1976. Theory of the firm: managerial behavior, agency costs and ownership structure. J. Financ. Econ. 3 (4), 305–360.
Kunda, Z., 1990. The case for motivated reasoning. Psychol. Bull. 108 (3), 480–498.
Laband, D.N., Beil, R.O., 1999. Are economists more selfish than other social scientists? Public Choice 100 (1–2), 85–101.
Lazear, E.P., Malmendier, U., Weber, R.A., 2012. Sorting in experiments with application to social preferences. Am. Econ. J. Appl. Econ. 4 (1), 136–163.
Lewis, A., Bardis, A., Flint, C., Mason, C., Smith, N., Tickle, C., Zinser, J., 2012. Drawing the line somewhere: an experimental study of moral compromise. J. Econ. Psychol. 33 (4), 718–725.
López-Pérez, R., Spiegelman, E., 2019. Do economists lie more? In: Bucciol, A., Montinari, N. (Eds.), Dishonesty in Behavioral Economics. Academic Press.
Lundquist, T., Ellingsen, T., Gribbe, E., Johannesson, M., 2009. The aversion to lying. J. Econ. Behav. Organ. 70 (1), 81–92.
Maggian, V., 2019. Negative externalities of cheating: an experiment with charities. In: Bucciol, A., Montinari, N. (Eds.), Dishonesty in Behavioral Economics. Academic Press.
Marwell, G., Ames, R.E., 1981. Economists free ride, does anyone else? Experiments on the provision of public goods, IV. J. Public Econ. 15 (3), 295–310.
Mazar, N., Amir, O., Ariely, D., 2008. The dishonesty of honest people: a theory of self-concept maintenance. J. Market. Res. 45 (6), 633–644.
Mazar, N., Ariely, D., 2006. Dishonesty in everyday life and its policy implications. J. Public Policy Mark. 25 (1), 117–126.

McCabe, D.L., Treviño, L.K., 1993. Academic dishonesty: honor codes and other contextual influences. J. High. Educ. 64 (5), 522–538.
Michaels, J.W., Miethe, T.D., 1989. Applying theories of deviance to academic cheating. Soc. Sci. Q. 70 (4), 870.
Pascual-Ezama, D., Fosgaard, T.R., Cardenas, J.C., Kujal, P., Veszteg, R., Gil-Gómez de Liaño, B., Gunia, B., Weischselbaumer, D., Hilken, K., Antinyan, A., Delnoij, J., Proestakis, A., Tira, M.D., Pratomo, Y., Jaber-López, T., Brañas-Garza, P., 2015. Context-dependent cheating: experimental evidence from 16 countries. J. Econ. Behav. Organ. 116, 379–386.
Pascual-Ezama, D., Prelec, D., Dunfield, D., 2013. Motivation, money, prestige and cheats. J. Econ. Behav. Organ. 93, 367–373.
Pruckner, G.J., Sausgruber, R., 2013. Honesty on the streets: a field study on newspaper purchasing. J. Eur. Econ. Assoc. 11 (3), 661–679.
Schor, J., 2016. Debating the sharing economy. J. Self-Gov. Manag. Econ. 4 (3).
Shalvi, S., Dana, J., Handgraaf, M.J., De Dreu, C.K., 2011. Justified ethicality: observing desired counterfactuals modifies ethical perceptions and behavior. Organ. Behav. Hum. Decis. Process. 115 (2), 181–190.
Yezer, A.M., Goldfarb, R.S., Poppen, P.J., 1996. Does studying economics discourage cooperation? Watch what we do, not what we say or how we play. J. Econ. Perspect. 10 (1), 177–186.

Chapter 3.3

# Negative externalities of cheating: An experiment with charities

Valeria Maggian
*Department of Economics, Ca' Foscari University, Venice, Italy*

## Chapter Outline



**JEL Classification:** C91, D63, D91, L31

## 1. Introduction

Recently, in an increasing number of studies (Fischbacher and F¨ollmi-Heusi, 2013; Gächter and Schulz, 2016; Weisel and Shalvi, 2015), scholars have investigated the emergence and characterization of dishonesty by means of a die-under-cup task. In the standard version of the task, participants are asked to privately roll a six-sided die twice in the cup and to report the first roll: since payment is according to reported roll, individuals are incentivized to report a higher number with respect to the actual one. In these studies, reporting a lower number than the one corresponding to the maximum payoff is considered as an evidence of lying aversion. In the great majority of these studies, however, the organizational costs associated with lying are represented by the experimental budget, which does not necessarily reflect the usual situations people encounter in the real world. In particular, lying aimed to increase the liar's payoff often imposes a cost on others. For example, when cheating on an exam, students indirectly damage their (honest) classmates, by making comparison unfairly competitive. Similarly, when cheating on taxes, citizens decrease the amount of resources available for the community.

Dishonesty in Behavioral Economics. https://doi.org/10.1016/B978-0-12-815857-9.00012-1

In this experiment, we aim to test whether people's decision to lie also depends on the identity of the victim of the unethical behavior. In particular, we investigate the effects of imposing negative externalities on a charity organization when cheating. The consequences of the dishonest behavior will thus increase the liar's payoff while reducing the amount of money donated to a charity organization.

In our *Baseline treatment*, the cost of the lie is borne by the experimental budget while in our *Charity treatment* the individual's unethical behavior decreases the budget devoted to a charity organization. Our experiment provides evidence that social concerns are activated to a similar extent when cheating on an organization with clear and explicit benevolent objectives or on an anonymous organization. Our results suggest that the identity of the receiver of the lie does not play a significant role in the decision to behave unethically.

## 2. Related literature

Individuals' decision to lie depends on several factors. First, the degree of cheating has been showed to be influenced by the extent people can maintain a self-concept of integrity: misbehavior takes place only when it does not interfere with individual's self-image of being a good and honest person (Mazar et al., 2008). Moreover, the possibility to rely on self-serving justifications for lying has also been showed to influence the decision-making process of cheating (Shalvi et al., 2012, 2015). Second, people pay attention to the consequences of their actions when lying. In particular, individuals are less likely to cheat when their personal gain comes at someone else's cost (Gneezy, 2005). When the outcome of unethical behavior is or could be shared with another person, cheating has been found to increase (Ploner and Regner, 2013; Wiltermuth, 2011). However, even when having the opportunity to tell a lie that will increase both the other's and the liar's welfare, Erat and Gneezy (2012) show, by means of a laboratory experiment, that a nonnegligible portion of individuals refrain from it, supporting the hypothesis of *pure* lie aversion.

Recent work suggests that individuals making joint decisions in groups cheat more than individuals deciding alone, because others may benefit from dishonest behavior as well (Gino et al., 2013; Weisel and Shalvi, 2015; Wiltermuth, 2011). A strong dishonesty shift is observed when examining the inclination of behaving immorally in groups rather than singularly, also when there is no payoff commonality. When allowing people to communicate, they are more likely to exchange arguments to justify misbehaviors than to comply with the honesty norm (Kocher et al., 2018).

Another factor that influences the decision to act dishonestly but that has received less attention is found on the identity of the person or of the group of people who bears the consequences of unethical behavior. Amir et al. (2016) provide evidence that framing is important in this context. They show that the minor the harm caused by the lie, the higher the tendency to cheat to individuals, independently on whether they are part of a group or not. However, this applies only when the cost of the lie to each individual in the group is made explicit; differently, if the harm cause by the lie is expressed in global terms, cheating toward groups increases. Meub et al. (2016) found that participants in their lab experiment were less likely to report false numbers to get a higher payoff when rolling a fair die if negatively affecting another subject rather than the experimenter.

The addressee of the immoral behavior seems thus to affect the occurrence of cheating, even if it is not clear through which channels. On the one hand, the experimenter only represents a faceless organization evoking minor social concerns, possibly increasing individuals' propensity to lie with respect to a situation where a real person is negatively affected by the unethical decision. On the other hand, the individual sense of responsibility might be watered down by the fact that all subjects participating in an experimental session are taking the same decision when cheating on the experimenter, while each one of them is the only accountable for dishonestly decreasing the other's payoff. Our experiment allows us to disentangle between these two forces, since the individual's decision to lie is fully comparable between our Baseline and Charity treatment.

Cojoc and Stoian (2014) take a dynamic point of view on cheating and investigate how having the opportunity to donate to a charity in the future affects the likelihood of engaging in dishonest behavior (at the expense of the experimenter) in the present. They observe that, with respect to a baseline condition where participants were not aware of the opportunity to donate, people were more likely to act dishonestly, but both honest and dishonest individuals were donating a lower amount. With a similar experimental design, Gneezy et al. (2014) found that subjects who are not given an opportunity to donate to a charity were more honest than subjects who can donate. However, in both studies, there is no trade-off between the decision to act dishonestly and the decision to donate. One can misbehave and take the money from the experimenter in order to donate them to the charity. Differently, in our experiment the focus is on the analysis of behavior when being aware that the dishonest act will necessarily decrease the amount devoted to a charity organization so that there is no room for self-serving justifications.

## 3. Experimental design

Our experiment consists of two parts. Part one is divided into five stages. In part one, subjects were randomly assigned into groups composed by six men and six women and participated in a multistage tournament (similar to Niederle et al., 2013).[a] No information about previous payoff was given until the very end of the experiment.

---

a. The objective of the study implemented in the first part of the experiment was to investigate the effects of gender quotas in promoting women's participation to competition at the last step of a multistage tournament, resembling a career ladder. Results of this study are presented in the working paper "Getting to the Top: A Laboratory Experiment on the Impact of Gender Quotas in a Multi-Stage Tournament" by Maggian et al. (2017).

In part two, we investigate the effects of making explicit the negative externalities of cheating on subjects' behavior, when implementing a variation of the die under-the-cup task (Shalvi et al., 2011).[b] In our experiment, reporting an odd number results in getting €4 while reporting an even number results in getting €1. Our experiment consists in two treatments. In our Baseline treatment, subjects were first instructed to roll the die and, only after having reported the outcome, they were informed about the charity. In particular, subjects were informed that €400 were devoted to the second part of the (Baseline) experiment and that once all the 96 participants had been paid according to their report, the remaining amount would have been donated to a charity. In the Charity treatment, the only difference, with respect to the Baseline treatment, is in the order of the instructions: before rolling the die, participants were informed about the charity and the donation's procedure so that, when making their reporting decision, they were aware of the negative externality imposed on it. In both treatments, each subject was given the opportunity to select to which charity to donate the money, by selecting one out of the five most known charities in France or by adding one more charity organization to the list. Participants were aware that the most voted charity would have received the money, once the experimental sessions were done.[c] Finally, as a last step of the experimental session, each individual was asked to answer some questions regarding his own average charitable behavior. In particular, we investigate whether (i) subjects were used to donate to charities, (ii) the average amount per year eventually donated, and (iii) the reasons why they might have decided not to donate to charities.

The experiment was conducted using z-Tree (Fischbacher, 2007), at GATE-LAB, the experimental laboratory of GATE (Lyon, France). 192 Subjects were recruited using HROOT (Bock et al., 2014) from September to December 2016. Both treatments were run in a between-subjects design and none participated in more than one treatment. Subjects were randomly assigned to treatments. Subjects received a show-up fee of €5 plus their earnings from one randomly selected stage between 1 and 4, their earnings from stage 5 (test for risk aversion (Crosetto and Filippin, 2013)), and from the die under-the-cup task.

## 4. Experimental results

In both the Baseline and the Charity treatment subjects reported a significantly higher number of odd numbers than 50% (binomial test, $p=0.000$). In particular, the proportion of individuals reporting an odd number is equals to 80.21% independently on the treatment.[d]

---

b. See the Experimental Instructions (originally in French) in the Supplementary Material in the online version at https://doi.org/10.1016/B978-0-12-815857-9.00012-1.

c. In particular, participants were informed that the receipt of the donation would have been made available on the researcher's website once the experimental sessions were over. The complete web address and the exact date were communicated to each participant at the end of the experiment.

d. If everyone would have had reported the roll of the die honestly, we should have devoted about 320 out of €800 to the charity. However, after having paid all 192 participants according to their report, we finally donated €146 to the Charity. The most voted one was Médecins sans frontiers.

We observe no difference in behavior with respect to the treatment. Subjects respond to incentives in the same way, no matter the identity of the one bothering the consequences of their misconduct.

In the following we investigate whether personal characteristics or individual's charitable behavior in private life may further explain the observed behavior.

In the literature, there is some evidence of males being more dishonest than females, when having the opportunity to increase personal gain (Dreber and Johannesson, 2008; Friesen and Gangadharan, 2012). Fig. 1 displays the proportion of men and women reporting an odd number in the die-under-the-cup task under the Baseline and Charity treatment. Our findings are in line with recent studies providing evidence of no gender effect in unethical behavior (Abeler et al., 2014; Barkan et al., 2012; Belot and Schröder, 2013; Cadsby et al., 2010; Gino and Margolis, 2011; Gino and Pierce, 2009; Gravert, 2013; Holm and Kawagoe, 2010). We observe no significant difference in neither of the treatment with respect to gender (Chi-square test. Baseline treatment, $p=0.442$; Charity treatment, $p=0.798$).

As a further step, we examine whether individuals' charitable behavior in their private life might have affected their choices in the Charity treatment. On the one hand, a person who is already donating a lot to charities might be more tempted to misreport the roll of a die to increase her personal gain. On the other hand, it is also possible that people with stronger other regarding preferences, possibly signaled by their donating behavior, are also less likely to act dishonestly (Maggian and Villeval, 2016). It is important to note, however, that the

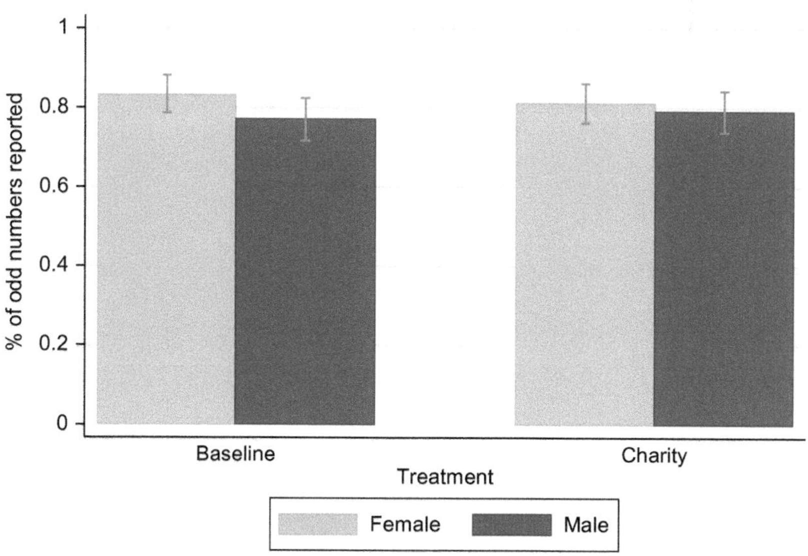


**FIG. 1** Proportion of men and women reporting an odd number in the die under-the-cup task, by treatment.

information provided by individuals on the final questionnaire is self-reported, thus nonverifiable. As a consequence, we are aware that one might have exaggerated her donating behavior in order to appear a good person with respect to the experimenter.

Table 1 reports the marginal effect of reporting an odd number between the Charity and the Baseline treatment with respect to a series of independent variables. Our set of probit regressions confirms our previous analysis with respect to the gender of our participants: the female variable is never significant. Interestingly, in model (3) we observe that the more often individuals donate to charities the lower the probability to report an odd number. Moreover, the donated amount positively affects individual's likelihood to report an odd number, also when considering its logarithmic transformation, as shown by the significant coefficient of "log of the donated amount" variable in model (4).

**TABLE 1 Determinants of Unethical Behavior**

| *Dependent variable* | 1 if an odd number is reported, 0 otherwise | | | |
|---|---|---|---|---|
| *Independent variables* | (1) | (2) | (3) | (4) |
| *Charity* | $1.11 \times 10^{-16}$ | 0.000 | 0.006 | 0.007 |
| 1 if Charity, 0 if Baseline | (0.057) | (0.057) | (0.054) | (0.071) |
| *Female* | | −0.042 | 0.036 | 0.089 |
| 1 if Woman, 0 otherwise | | (0.057) | (0.054) | (0.073) |
| *Previously donated*<br>0="Never"; 1="Less than two times per year"; 2="Between 2 and five times per year"; 3="More than five times per year" | | | −0.109*<br>(0.054) | −0.150**<br>(0.068) |
| *Donated amount*<br>Continuous variable from 0 to 500 | | | 0.004**<br>(0.002) | |
| *Log of the donated amount* | | | | 0.084*<br>(0.044) |
| *Observations* | 192 | 192 | 192 | 108 |
| *Pseudo $R^2$* | 0.000 | 0.769 | 0.038 | −0.068 |
| *LR chi2* | 0.00 | 0.53 | 7.33 | 6.88 |
| *Prob > chi2* | 1.000 | 0.003 | 0.119 | 0.1425 |

*Notes:* The table reports marginal effects of the respective independent variables on the probability of reporting an odd number. Standard errors in *parentheses*. Significance levels: *$p<0.10$; **$p<0.05$; ***$p<0.01$.

A Chow test provides evidence that the coefficients estimated over the Baseline treatment are not different than the coefficients estimated over the Charity treatment ($p=0.325$).

In all models, if we include a series of dummy variables for the field of study of our participants, we observe that results are unchanged.[e] This evidence differs with respect to the results presented in Chapter 3.2. The authors found, in their experiment 1, that asking participants to donate a value of any coin to a nonprofit organization when privately tossing a coin and getting the prize-losing side diminishes the impact of cheating for business economics and psychology participants, but not for engineering students. However, in their experiment, there is no trade-off between cheating or being honest and donating to the nonprofit organization, since one may still decide (not) to donate when tossing a coin and getting the prize-winning (losing) side. In our study, cheating automatically reduces the amount of money donated to the charity and increases the payoff of the individual, so that the negative externalities of cheating are made salient.

## 5. Conclusion

We conduct an experiment in the laboratory to examine the effect on the individuals' willingness to lie of imposing negative externalities of cheating on a charity organization. Our results reveal no significant difference on unethical behavior with respect to the identity of the victim who bears the cost of the lie (the experimental budget vs the amount devoted to a charitable organization).

Our findings are consistent with the hypothesis that individual sense of responsibility might be watered down when cheating on an organization. Individuals are found to be more likely to act unethically than when harming another subject, since in the latter situation each individual is the only accountable for dishonestly decreasing the other's payoff. When the identity of the receiver of the lie is an organization, no matter whether an impersonal one (i.e., the experimental institution) or one evoking a well-defined social concern (i.e., a charitable organization), people perceive it in a more global and impersonal fashion. Consequentially, as suggested by recent research (Amir et al., 2016; Kogut and Ritov, 2005; Slovic, 2007), the individual's level of caring is diminished, due to the greater psychological distance, and subjects are less likely to take into account the externalities associated with their (immoral) actions on them.

The results of this chapter emphasize that the cost imposed on others associated with one's self-serving behavior is not necessarily perceived different depending on the identity of the victim, when it consists in an organization. Policies designed to limit unethical actions should take into account whether to

e. Participants in our experiment were studying for attending six different bachelor degrees courses: Economics ($n_B=6$ and $n_C=7$ in the Baseline and Charity treatment, respectively), Management ($n_B=36$ and $n_C=37$), Engineering ($n_B=40$ and $n_C=39$), Sociology ($n_B=1$ and $n_C=0$), Medicine ($n_B=4$ and $n_C=2$), or other disciplines ($n_B=9$ and $n_C=11$).

inform individuals about the negative externalities they are causing, avoiding referring to global and impersonal terms.

## Acknowledgments

The authors gratefully acknowledge the financial support of the Jan Wallander and Tom Hedelius Foundation, Handelsbanken, Sweden (Research Grant P2016-0126):1 for founding the experiment and the French National Research Agency (ANR, FELIS Grant, ANR-14-CE28-0010-01) for support on the implementation of the research. The author's contribution was performed within the framework of the LABEX CORTEX (ANR-11-LABX-0042) of Université de Lyon, within the program Investissements d'Avenir (ANR-11-IDEX-007) operated by the French National Research Agency (ANR). We thank Natalia Montinari, Antonio Nicolò, and Marie Claire Villeval for useful discussions and Claire Rimbaud, Alice Solda, and Quentin Thévenet for their laboratory assistance

## References

Abeler, J., Becker, A., Falk, A., 2014. Representative evidence on lying costs. J. Public Econ. 113, 96–104.

Amir, A., Kogut, T., Bereby-Meyer, Y., 2016. Careful cheating: people cheat groups rather than individuals. Front. Psychol. 7, 371.

Barkan, R., Ayal, S., Gino, F., Ariely, D., 2012. The pot calling the kettle black: distancing response to ethical dissonance. J. Exp. Psychol. Gen. 141 (4), 757–773.

Belot, M., Schröder, M., 2013. Sloppy work, lies and theft: a novel experimental design to study counterproductive behaviour. J. Econ. Behav. Organ. 93, 233–238.

Bock, O., Baetge, I., Nicklisch, A., 2014. hroot: Hamburg registration and organization online tool. Eur. Econ. Rev. 71, 117–120.

Cadsby, C.B., Song, F., Tapon, F., 2010. Are you paying your employees to cheat? An experimental investigation. B.E. J. Econom. Anal. Policy 10 (1), 1–32.

Cojoc, D., Stoian, A., 2014. Dishonesty and charitable behavior. Exp. Econ. 17 (4), 717–732.

Crosetto, P., Filippin, A., 2013. The "bomb" risk elicitation task. J. Risk Uncertain. 47 (1), 31–65.

Dreber, A., Johannesson, M., 2008. Gender differences in deception. Econ. Lett. 99 (1), 197–199.

Erat, S., Gneezy, U., 2012. White lies. Manag. Sci. 58 (4), 723–733.

Fischbacher, U., 2007. z-tree: Zurich toolbox for ready-made economic experiments. Exp. Econ. 10 (2), 171–178.

Fischbacher, U., F¨ollmi-Heusi, F., 2013. Lies in disguise—an experimental study on cheating. J. Eur. Econ. Assoc. 11 (3), 525–547.

Friesen, L., Gangadharan, L., 2012. Individual level evidence of dishonesty and the gender effect. Econ. Lett. 117 (3), 624–626.

Gächter, S., Schulz, J.F., 2016. Intrinsic honesty and the prevalence of rule violations across societies. Nature 531, 496–499.

Gino, F., Margolis, J.D., 2011. Bringing ethics into focus: how regulatory focus and risk preferences influence (un)ethical behavior. Organ. Behav. Hum. Decis. Process. 115 (2), 145–156.

Gino, F., Pierce, L., 2009. The abundance effect: unethical behavior in the presence of wealth. Organ. Behav. Hum. Decis. Process. 109 (2), 142–155.

Gino, F., Ayal, S., Ariely, D., 2013. Self-serving altruism? The lure of unethical actions that benefit others. J. Econ. Behav. Organ. 93, 285–292.

Gneezy, U., 2005. Deception: the role of consequences. Am. Econ. Rev. 95 (1), 384–394.
Gneezy, U., Imas, A., Madarasz, K., 2014. Conscience accounting: emotional dynamics and social behavior. Manag. Sci. 60 (11), 2645–2658.
Gravert, C., 2013. How luck and performance affect stealing. J. Econ. Behav. Organ. 93, 301–304.
Holm, H.J., Kawagoe, T., 2010. Face-to-face lying—an experimental study in Sweden and Japan. J. Econ. Psychol. 31 (3), 310–321.
Kocher, M.G., Schudy, S., Spantig, L., 2018. I lie? We lie! Why? Experimental evidence on a dishonesty shift in groups. Manag. Sci. 64 (9), 3971–4470.
Kogut, T., Ritov, I., 2005. The 'identified victim' effect: an identified group, or just a single individual? J. Behav. Decis. Mak. 18, 157–167.
Maggian, V., Villeval, M.C., 2016. Social preferences and lying aversion in children. Exp. Econ. 19 (3), 663–685.
Maggian, V., Montinari, N., Nicolo, A., 2017. Do Quotas Help Women to Climb the Career Ladder? A Laboratory Experiment. GATE—Lyon Saint-Etienne, WP, p. 1724.
Mazar, N., Amir, O., Ariely, D., 2008. The dishonesty of honest people: a theory of self-concept maintenance. J. Mark. Res. 45 (6), 633–644.
Meub, L., Proeger, T., Schneider, T., Bizer, K., 2016. The victim matters—experimental evidence on lying, moral costs and moral cleansing. Appl. Econ. Lett. 23 (16), 1162–1167.
Niederle, M., Segal, C.A., Vesterlund, L., 2013. How costly is diversity? Affirmative action in light of gender differences in competitiveness. Manag. Sci. 59, 1–16.
Ploner, M., Regner, T., 2013. Self-image and moral balancing: an experimental analysis. J. Econ. Behav. Organ. 93, 374–383.
Shalvi, S., Dana, J., Handgraaf, M.J.J., De Dreu, C.K.W., 2011. Justified ethicality: observing desired counterfactuals modifies ethical perceptions and behavior. Organ. Behav. Hum. Decis. Process. 115 (2), 181–190.
Shalvi, S., Eldar, O., Bereby-Meyer, Y., 2012. Honesty requires time (and lack of justifications). Psychol. Sci. 23 (10), 1264–1270.
Shalvi, S., Gino, F., Barkan, R., Ayal, S., 2015. Self-serving justifications: doing wrong and feeling moral. Curr. Dir. Psychol. Sci. 24 (2), 125–130.
Slovic, P., 2007. If I look at the mass I will never act: psychic numbing and genocide. Judgm. Decis. Mak. 2, 79–95.
Weisel, O., Shalvi, S., 2015. The collaborative roots of corruption. PNAS 112, 10651–10656.
Wiltermuth, S.S., 2011. Cheating more when the spoils are split. Organ. Behav. Hum. Decis. Process. 115 (2), 157–168.

Chapter 3.4

# Cheating: Perceptions and profit

Li Hao[1], Daniel Houser[2]
[1]*Economist at Convoy, Seattle, WA, United States,* [2]*Interdisciplinary Center for Economic Science, George Mason University, Fairfax, VA, United States*

## Chapter Outline



**JEL Classification:** C91, D03

## 1. Introduction

Using data initially reported by Hao and Houser (2017), this chapter provides evidence from a laboratory experiment that requiring predictions and announcements of one's own future possibly dishonest actions can deter misconduct, and specifies and estimates a model showing that this effect owes to an interaction of people's twin desires both to earn profits from cheating and to maintain a positive self-image. By "possibly dishonest actions" we refer to actions the honesty of which cannot be verified.

Despite a substantial economics literature on deception (e.g., Gneezy, 2005, and the literature we review below), and the extensive literature on signaling to self and to others (see, e.g., Andreoni and Douglas Bernheim, 2009; Ariely et al., 2009; Bénabou and Tirole, 2004), how self-image and profit incentives interact to affect decisions to cheat remains an important topic. We shed additional light on Mazar et al. (2008a,b) by conducting a novel laboratory experiment on cheating and then drawing inferences from our data by combining

Dishonesty in Behavioral Economics. https://doi.org/10.1016/B978-0-12-815857-9.00013-3

Mazar et al.'s (2008a) theory of self-image maintenance[a] with a model and estimation strategy in the spirit of Krupka and Weber (2013). We find that a possibly dishonest action taken after it is predicted is more likely to be perceived as dishonest than an equivalent action absent a prior prediction. Consequently, requiring announcements promotes honest actions among people who care about maintaining an honest image. Moreover, we find that profit incentives to cheat decrease as a possibly dishonest action becomes more likely to be perceived as dishonest, and are ultimately fully extinguished: when a possibly dishonest action is almost surely dishonest, the level of profit does not impact the likelihood one chooses to cheat.

Knowing whether predicting one's own future potentially dishonest decisions can deter dishonest behavior is important (see, e.g., Hannan et al., 2006). For example, firms often express concerns over possible employee embezzlement or contractors who log more hours than actually worked. Our results suggest that asking agents first to predict the number of hours needed for given tasks may reduce dishonesty in relation to cases where agents only report hours following task completion. Similarly, requiring traveling employees to submit their estimated travel budgets prior to their trips may reduce fraudulent travel expenses.[b]

Our investigation is based on a novel game that requires participants to predict the percent chance that a 1, 2, 3, or 4 occurs when rolling a fair four-sided die. We consider three treatments: CONTROL, PREDICT, and REPORT. In CONTROL there is no opportunity to cheat; subjects predict the outcome of a die roll, then roll a physical die, and finally are paid based on the accuracy of their predictions. PREDICT is the same except subjects roll the die privately and they knew this would be the case when they announced their predictions.[c] In REPORT subjects keep their predictions private until after they and the experimenter observe the die-roll outcome.[d]

To understand how potential behavioral differences arise between the two cheating treatments, consider three types of play.[e] First, individuals who are

a. Mazar et al. (2008a,b) use the term "self-concept" maintenance. We use the terms "self-concept" and "self-image" interchangeably.

b. These types of precommitment effects may work through, for example, guilt aversion (Charness and Dufwenberg, 2006) or social pressure (DellaVigna et al., 2012). Any effect may be weaker among those who experience less guilt from lying, as may arise for example in environments where the norm is to lie (e.g., white lies).

c. The possibility to cheat was not explicitly announced. However, that the die roll would be private was emphasized three times in the instructions. Hard copy instructions were in front of the subjects during the entire experiment, and were also read aloud by the experimenter.

d. Like most of the economics literature in this area, we are not able to identify whether any specific individual cheated and our inferences are based on aggregative analyses. An alternative approach is suggested by Cadsby et al. (2010), who employs a design that enables cheating detection at the individual level.

e. For the sake of discussion, we consider only risk-neutral individuals. Note though that risk preferences are controlled due to random assignment to treatments and our analysis that compares between treatments.

averse to cheating per se would always predict the objective probabilities {25%, 25%, 25%, 25%} and obtain a guaranteed amount regardless the outcomes in both PREDICT and REPORT. Second, absolute profit maximizers in both treatments would predict {100%, 0%, 0%, 0%}, which they would make sure perfectly match the outcomes to obtain the maximum earnings. In contrast, the third type, those who would cheat for profit but also act to maintain their honest image, will avoid making cheating decisions that place their self-image in jeopardy. In particular, this third type might cheat less in PREDICT than REPORT if, for example, they believe a possibly dishonest prediction announced in advance of a winning die roll in PREDICT is more likely to be perceived as cheating than an equally "lucky" prediction made immediately (perhaps impulsively) after observing the die roll outcome in REPORT.[f]

Comparing decisions between PREDICT and REPORT enables us to shed light on whether cheating can be deterred if intent to cheat must be revealed *before* a potentially dishonest act. In particular, these treatments allow us to hold fixed the profit incentive for cheating while varying the probability that the possibly dishonest action is perceived to be dishonest. Following Mazar et al. (2008a,b) and Mazar and Ariely (2008), we argue that any differences in behavior between PREDICT and REPORT are connected to differences in the way behaviors are perceived between those two treatments, and the implications this can have for one's self-image.

To provide evidence on this argument, we collected opinions from independent evaluators regarding whether a possibly dishonest decision was in fact cheating in REPORT and PREDICT. We find, ceteris paribus, the equivalent possibly dishonest action was either at least as or more likely to be perceived as dishonest in PREDICT than REPORT.[g] Importantly, while these perceived differences are subtle (see Fig. 1), we show they nevertheless can explain our finding of substantially more cheating in REPORT than PREDICT.

We combine these perceptions data with decisions from our cheating treatments using a modeling strategy inspired by Krupka and Weber (2013). Doing so reveals that honest actions are more likely when a potentially dishonest action is more likely to be perceived as dishonest. With respect to profit incentives, when self-image is not a concern (when a possibly dishonest act is not perceived as dishonest), the greater the profit gain from cheating, the more likely the participant is to cheat. We found, however, that self-image mitigates this effect. In

f. Such a belief may be connected to the social and legal distinction between premeditated and impulsive transgressions. Much evidence shows deceivers with no evidence of having cheated intentionally are more likely to be forgiven and avoid retribution (Von Hippel and Trivers, 2011). The attribution of intent is also critical in dealing with deception and fraud (Schweitzer et al., 2006; Stouten et al., 2006). This is codified in law by punishing premeditated crimes more severely than crimes of passion.

g. It is worth noting that, to our knowledge, the use of external evaluators to assess the appearance of honesty, and thus to provide evidence on the source of the differences in behaviors we find, is novel to our study.

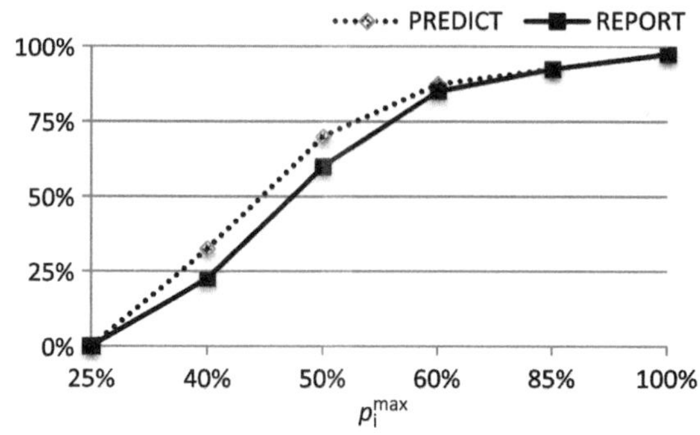


**FIG. 1** Fraction of evaluators who think the person cheated in PREDICT/REPORT. *Notes*: There are $n=40$ evaluators in this figure. Eight evaluators are dropped from this analysis due to irrational or inconsistent responses: they either stated that objectively true predictions ($p_i^{max}=25\%$) looked dishonest, or that lower $p_i^{max}$ looked more dishonest than a higher $p_i^{max}$. The *x*-axis indicates the scenario $p_i^{max}$, and the *y*-axis is the fraction of evaluators who believe the decision maker cheated in the given scenario in the PREDICT or the REPORT treatments. The data show that the same action in PREDICT treatment is persistently perceived to be more dishonest than in the REPORT treatment. These perception data are drawn from evaluators' direct assessment (Decision Sets A and B) on whether a person cheated in the given scenario. The relative assessment from evaluators' responses in Decision Set C (reported in fig. 2b in Hao and Houser, 2017) is consistent with this story in that significantly more evaluators viewed identical actions as more likely to be dishonest in PREDICT than in REPORT. The relative assessment was intended to break ties in that it asked, between PREDICT and REPORT, in which treatment was the person more likely to have been dishonest.

particular, the positive profit effect on the likelihood to cheat becomes smaller as an action becomes more likely to be perceived as dishonest. This effect is strong: when an action is nearly certain to be perceived as dishonest, we find the effect of profit on the likelihood of cheating has negligible effect size and is statistically zero.

This chapter proceeds as follows. Section 2 reviews related literature; Section 3 describes the design of the experiment; Section 4 specifies our hypotheses; Section 5 reports the results; and the final section concludes the chapter.

## 2. Literature review

Recent years have seen substantial research interest in cheating behavior. Gneezy (2005) showed that people exhibit a consequence-mediated aversion to lying. He reports data from a sender-receiver game where only Player 1 was informed about the monetary consequences of the two options, and Player 2 chose which option should be implemented based on the message sent from Player 1. Hence, Player 1 could either: (i) tell the truth and obtain Option A, in which his payoff was lower than Player 2s; or (ii) lie and obtain Option B for a slight monetary gain at a greater cost to Player 2. In an otherwise identical dictator game, Player 1 chose between Options A and B; Player 2 had no choice but to accept the payoff division. Gneezy (2005) reported that the proportion of Option B was significantly lower in the sender-receiver game than in the dictator game, suggesting an aversion to lying as opposed to pure preferences over monetary allocations. In addition, Gneezy (2005) found that people lie less when lying results in greater costs to others.

Gneezy's (2005) findings stimulated substantial subsequent studies (see, e.g., Gibson et al., 2013; Hurkens and Kartik, 2009; Lundquist et al., 2009; Rode, 2010; Sánchez-Pagés and Vorsatz, 2007, 2009). For example, data reported by Gibson et al. (2013) showed heterogeneity in preference for truthfulness. Lundquist et al. (2009) found that lying aversion is greater when the size of the lie (i.e., the difference between the truth and the lie) is greater. In their experiment, Player 1 reported his type to Player 2, who decided whether to enter into a contract with Player 1. Upon completing the contract, Player 1 always gained. Player 2 gained if Player 1s type was above threshold, but otherwise lost. The authors found that the further was Player 1s type from threshold, the less likely was he to lie.

Mazar et al. (2008a) proposed an influential theory of self-concept maintenance, which provides an explanation for incomplete cheating. In particular, people only cheat to the level that allows them to delude themselves of their own integrity. The authors suggest two mechanisms that facilitate self-concept maintenance: (i) inattention to moral standards; and (ii) categorization malleability. In one of their well-known experiments, subjects self-reported their own performance on a real-effort task and were paid accordingly. However, some subjects were asked to write down the 10 Commandments before the task, while others were not. They found those who were reminded of moral standards lied substantially less, thus supporting their theory of self-concept maintenance.

Fischbacher and Föllmi-Heusi (2013) report data from a novel experiment where subjects rolled a six-sided die privately and self-reported the first roll. The outcome of the first roll was the amount of payment they received for the experiment. The fraction of self-reported highest payoff outcomes was significantly higher than one-sixth, as expected; however, the fraction of the second highest payoff was also significantly higher than one-sixth. This is a type of "incomplete cheating," which the authors speculate might be due to greed aversion and the desire to appear honest.

Building on Fischbacher and Föllmi-Heusi (2013) and Jiang (2013) reported two treatments. One, the "throw-first" treatment, involved subjects first rolling a six-sided die and obtaining outcome X, and then subjects choosing between earning either X euros or 6-X euros. In the second treatment, "report-first," subjects chose the earning scheme prior to rolling the die. Jiang (2013) reported that subjects cheated more in "throw-first" than in "report-first," a result that is broadly consistent with our own.

Our contribution to this literature is quite distinct from others'. As noted, building from both Mazar et al. (2008a) and Krupka and Weber (2013), we specify a new model that captures the balance between the desire to cheat for profit and the preference to maintain a positive self-image. We estimate this model using both decisions from our cheating treatments and beliefs we elicited regarding the likelihood that possibly dishonest decisions are dishonest. Our estimates provide novel quantitative inferences about the individual and joint effect of self-image and profit incentives on dishonest behavior, as discussed below.

## 3. Experiment design[h]

### 3.1 Procedures

Subjects were recruited via email from registered students at George Mason University. Upon arrival, subjects were seated in individual cubicles, separated by partitions, so that others could not observe their actions. Sessions lasted 40 min on average, and earnings ranged between $6.25 and $25, in addition to a show-up bonus of $5.

### 3.2 Design

We conducted three treatments with die rolls: CONTROL, REPORT, and PREDICT. After these treatments, a final group of subjects were asked to evaluate whether participants in given scenarios from REPORT and PREDICT treatments appeared to have cheated. We used a between-subject design: nobody participated in more than one session and nobody who participated in any die-roll session participated in any evaluation session. All instructions and decisions sheets are provided in Appendix A in Hao and Houser (2017).

#### *3.2.1 CONTROL treatment*

This treatment involved two stages. In the first stage, the subject predicted the percent chance that each face of a fair four-sided die would turn up in a single roll, and then submitted his/her prediction to the experimenter on paper. The individual probabilities had to be between 0% and 100% (inclusive), and the four probabilities had to add up to exactly 100%.

In the second stage, the subject rolled a fair four-sided die. The experimenter observed and recorded the outcome. Subjects earned more for accurate prediction, according to a quadratic scoring rule detailed in the next section.

#### *3.2.2 PREDICT treatment*

Identical to CONTROL, except that the die roll in the second stage was private, and the subject knew before he made predictions that his rolling would not be monitored by the experimenter. They were encouraged to roll the die privately

h. Additional detail regarding the experiment design, including instructions, can be found in Hao and Houser (2017).

as many times as they wished, but to remember the first roll and report it to the experimenter via paper.[i]

### 3.2.3 REPORT treatment

Identical to CONTROL, except that in the first stage, the subject was asked to report his predictions *after* the die roll outcome was observed and recorded in the second stage. This reporting was assisted by a spreadsheet open on each subject's computer on which their predictions could be displayed for their own use. Thus, in "PREDICT" subjects saw several die rolls and reported one, while in "REPORT" subjects saw several distributions and reported one.

Several features of our design are worth noting. First, in the PREDICT treatment, as it was emphasized three times that the die roll would be private—at the beginning, the middle, and the end of the instructions. Hard copy instructions were available during the entire experiment. In addition, the experimenter illustrated the experiment with five examples, including the earnings-maximizing strategy. A comprehension quiz was conducted, and subjects were required to answer all questions correctly before proceeding to the experiment. Also, it is worth emphasizing that subjects were given no time pressure to make their decisions, and we observed no difference in the actual total time spent on decision-making between the two cheating treatments.

We used fair dice and made sure subjects understood this; thus, predictions that differed from the objective distribution could not be attributed to suspicions that the dice might be biased. While we emphasized the dice were fair, we also indicated it was fine to play hunches if they believed certain outcomes were more likely than others. The goal was to ensure subjects did not feel pressure from the experimenters to choose the objectively true distribution.[j]

Finally, recall that the goal of our design is to compare treatments where the monetary incentives to cheat are identical and yet there is variation in the perception that one has cheated. The manipulation we use to obtain this is intentionally subtle; nevertheless, as reported below, it produces reliable differences in perceptions that a possible cheat was in fact a cheat.

### 3.2.4 Evaluation sessions

Subjects were recruited to serve as independent evaluators of whether a participant in a given scenario from the die-roll treatments appeared honest or not. These evaluators received detailed debriefing about the PREDICT and REPORT treatments, including the original instructions.

The evaluation task was divided into decision sets A, B, and C. Decision sets A and B consisted of evaluating 12 scenarios, where highest-payoff outcomes

---

i. To minimize differences, subjects in all three treatments were asked to roll the die as many times as they wished. The only difference is that the first roll in CONTROL and REPORT treatments was observed and recorded by the experimenter.

j. Note that identical words were used in all treatments.

were obtained in all cases. Scenarios 1–6 (Decision Set A) were from the PREDICT treatment, and differed only according to $p_i^{max}$ values, which were 50%, 60%, 40%, 25%, 85%, and 100%, respectively.[k] Scenarios 7–12 (Decision Set B) were from the REPORT treatment, repeating the same sequence of $p_i^{max}$ as the first six scenarios. We used "Experiment 1" and "Experiment 2" for the "PREDICT" and "REPORT" treatments, respectively. For example, the first scenario was as below:

> *Scenario 1: In Experiment 1, a participant first revealed his or her prediction that outcome* **2** *would occur with* **50%** *chance, and that was the highest probability the participant placed on any outcome. The participant then rolled the die privately and reported that the die roll was* **2**.
>
> *Question 1: Do you think the majority of people in this room believe that this participant cheated?*
>
> *("Yes" or "No")*

Decision Set C included six questions asking evaluators to directly compare identical scenarios between the two treatments, e.g., "*If your answers in* ***Scenarios 1 and 7*** *are the same, do you think the majority of people in this room believe that the participant is more likely to have cheated in Scenario 1 or in Scenario 7?*" Subjects could choose among three answers: "Scenarios 1," "Scenarios 7," and "equally likely."

After the evaluation was complete, and following a procedure suggested by Xiao and Houser (2005) and Houser and Xiao (2011), one question from each of the three sets of six was randomly selected for payment. Subjects earned $5 for each answer that was in agreement with the majority of the evaluators in the room for the selected questions.

## 3.3 Earnings in the die-roll experiment

In the die-roll experiment, each subject's first-stage probabilistic prediction was compared with the relevant roll in the second stage. Earnings were calculated according to the following quadratic scoring rule, which rewards prediction accuracy.

$$\text{Earnings} = \$25 - \$12.5\sum_{i=1}^{4}(\chi_i - p_i)^2 \quad (1)$$

where $i$ indexes the four faces of the die: $i \in \{1,2,3,4\}$, and $p_i$ is the probability that the subject assigned to face $i$. The indicator $\chi_i$ is 1 if face $i$ is the outcome of the roll, and 0 otherwise (so we have $\sum_{i=1}^{4}\chi_i = 1$). In the first stage,

k. We chose six values for $p_i^{max}$ that spanned from its minimum value of 25% to its maximum 100%. We randomized the order in which they were presented to subjects. Note that $p_i^{max}$ = 25% indicates objective predictions, and evaluators should not have viewed this prediction as dishonest. We included this one to verify that subjects understood the experiment.

the subject submitted a vector of four probabilities: $p=(p_1,p_2,p_3,p_4)$, where $0 \le p_i \le 1, \text{and} \sum_{i=1}^{4} p_i = 1.$[l]

Therefore, subjects could earn as low as US \$0, when they predicted 100% on a wrong face of the die, and as high as US \$25, when they predicted 100% on the correct face. Note that an honest prediction implies guaranteed earnings of US \$15.625, which is the objective prediction with 25% on each face.

Quadratic scoring rules are widely used incentive-based mechanisms for eliciting subjective probabilities in experimental studies (see e.g., Andersen et al., 2014; Nyarko and Schotter, 2002). Kadane and Winkler (1988, p. 359) showed that an expected utility maximizer would report truthfully, under conditions including that the individual's utility is linear in money.[m]

To facilitate subjects' understanding of the payoffs we provided an interactive Excel spreadsheet in which subjects could type in any probabilistic prediction and view the payoffs associated with any outcome.[n]

It is worth reiterating that this sheet was available to subjects during the entire experiment. In particular, subjects in REPORT made a number of distributions and reported one to the experimenter. This is a direct analogy to PREDICT where subjects made a number of die rolls and reported one to the experimenter.

# 4. Model and hypotheses

## 4.1 Model

In the spirit of Krupka and Weber (2013),[o] in this section we describe a choice model for PREDICT and REPORT. Following Mazar et al. (2008a), we assume agents balance the profit gain from cheating with the self-image cost of being perceived (by themselves or others) as dishonest. Formally, let $A=\{a_1,\ldots,a_K\}$ represent the set of $K$ possible actions available to the agent. Let $\pi(a_j)$ denote the profit gain from taking action $a_j$, and $P(a_j)$ a measure of the agent's belief that the action if taken will be perceived as dishonest. Then, the agent's utility from selecting an action $a_j$ is represented as follows:

$$u(a_j)=V(\pi(a_j))+\gamma_1 P(a_j)+\gamma_2 \pi(a_j) P(a_j)+\varepsilon_j \tag{2}$$

l. The payoff function further demonstrates that PREDICT and REPORT are identical to those who do not value appearing honest: one either cheats on $\chi_i$ or cheat on $p_i$, for any given level of intrinsic aversion to lying.

m. This also requires an additional assumption, the no-stakes condition, which is not violated here because subjects' wealth outside the laboratory experiment is independent of the outcome of the die roll.

n. For a screenshot of the interactive spreadsheet, please see figure 1 in Hao and Houser (2017). We thank Zachary Grossman for providing us the original version of this tool.

o. Using a model similar to the one developed here, Krupka and Weber (2013) show that the tension between obeying social norms and earning profits affects behavior in dictator games. In particular, they find participants are systematically willing to sacrifice money in order to behave in socially appropriate ways.

The first term in Eq. (2) is the utility $V$ derived from the pecuniary return $\pi$ associated with action $a_j$. We assume $V(\bullet)$ is concave and increasing in $\pi(a_j)$. The second term in (2), $\gamma_1 P(a_j)+\gamma_2\pi(a_j)P(a_j)$, is the nonpecuniary cost from being perceived as dishonest (by self or others). We assume that agents have unbiased beliefs about the likelihood their actions are perceived as dishonest. That is, for any action, agents know the likelihood that observers (including themselves) believe the possibly dishonest action is actually dishonest. Considering only the first term $\gamma_1 P(a_j)$, reflecting the case that a cheating action $j$ has no pecuniary return ($\pi(a_j)=0$), then $\gamma_1=0$ implies that an agent is unconcerned about the appearance of honesty (does not update their self-image negatively, regardless of the perception of the action), while $\gamma_1<0$ holds for agents who incur a cost from appearing dishonest to themselves or others.

Consider now $\gamma_2\pi(a_j)P(a_j)$, the interaction of the perception of dishonesty with the profit from the action. This term allows self-image updating to vary according to the profit gain from the action. In particular, if $\gamma_2<0$ and $P(a_j)>0$ (so the agent believes the action may be perceived as dishonest) then the appearance of dishonesty has a more negative impact on utility when the profit gain is greater. Mazar et al. (2008a) argue this can occur due to the limits of "categorization"[p]: cheating for little benefit may require little negative updating to one's self-image, while larger negative updating may be unavoidable when cheating for larger profits.)

Finally, $\varepsilon_j$ is assumed to be a random utility component identically and independently distributed over alternatives and agents.

Let $A=\{a_1,\ldots,a_K\}$ represent an agent's choice set. We assume that an agent chooses alternative $k$ if and only if $u(a_k)>u(a_j)\forall j\neq k$.

Under conditions detailed below, this model's parameters can be estimated using the data from our experiment. In particular, by combining data across treatments we obtain variation in the perception of cheating at any given level of profit gain. This allows us to draw inferences regarding the elasticity of honest behavior with respect to profit gains, the image cost of dishonesty, and their interaction.

## 4.2 Hypotheses

### 4.2.1 *Self-image*

Our hypotheses are based on self-image maintenance (Mazar et al., 2008a). When a person who values appearing honesty signals an intent to cheat, in our case by making decisions that seem dishonest, their self-image is jeopardized. One reason relates to "categorization," which refers to people's ability to interpret some dishonest actions in a way that avoids updating one's self-image negatively. While an honest person may be able to rationalize an impulsive small-scale deception, it may be much more difficult to do so if that same

p. See Hypotheses below for further discussion of categorization.

deception is planned.[q] In part, this difficulty arises because "premeditated" deception violates social norms (and sometimes legal statutes). People view negatively those who engage in planned deception, and it may be difficult to maintain a positive self-image knowing that one's honest appearance has been diminished in the eyes of others.[r]

Relatedly, asking someone to predict their future behavior may direct their attention on the relevant moral norm or standard to a greater degree than occurs when actions are more impulsive. People are more likely to update their self-image negatively when their actions violate a moral standard to which they are closely attending (Mazar et al., 2008a). Moreover, a focus on relevant standards could lead to increased feelings of guilt after choosing to plan to cheat. Increased anxiety may also occur, stemming from the discomfort tied to sending a dishonest signal and then remaining under scrutiny (by oneself or others) for a period of time. All of these effects would suggest that cheating in PREDICT would not be greater than in REPORT.

### 4.2.2 Definitions

We define terms prior to stating hypotheses. We say a prediction is an "**objective prediction**" if it is identical to the objective distribution (25%, 25%, 25%, 25%). When predictions are not objective, we denote the (not necessarily unique) highest assigned probability by $p_i^{max}$, and we call its corresponding outcome(s) the "**highest-payoff outcome(s)**." The highest probability and its corresponding outcome are important because the only way to increase earnings is to concentrate greater probability mass on fewer outcomes.

We use predictions in CONTROL to determine whether a prediction is "**honest-looking**." For subjects who desire to appear honest, a simple strategy is to make predictions as if they are not being monitored. Intuitively, a prediction in PREDICT would be "honest-looking" if it did not differ from predictions in CONTROL. The highest probability $p_i^{\max}$ is a key determinant of an honest-looking prediction: $p_i^{\max}=25\%$ is objectively true and honest, while many would likely question the honesty of one who claims a $p_i^{\max}=100\%$. To determine the point at which $p_i^{\max}$ begins to look dishonest, we examine the distribution of $p_i^{\max}$, and find that 99th percentile is 50%; thus, the vast majority of subjects (69 out of 70) in CONTROL stated 50% or less as the highest probability $p_i^{\max}$. We

q. Mazar et al. (2008a,b) suggest it is easier to avoid negative self-concept updating after stealing a friend's $0.10 pencil than it would be after stealing that amount from her pocket. Similarly, one can likely more easily maintain self-concept after taking the pencil impulsively than after careful planning. In both cases, one might be able to excuse the former action, but not the latter, as something "anyone would do".

r. The value people place on maintaining an honest appearance is evidenced by the market for alibis. The company Alibi Network advertises, "*Politicians have spin doctors, celebrities have publicists, corporations have lawyers and public relations departments, investment banks have analysts, now regular people have ALIBI NETWORK.*"

therefore use 50% as the upper bound for "honest-looking" predictions.[s] We say a prediction "**honest-looking**" if it assigns no more than 50% probability to any single outcome of the die roll.

### 4.2.3 Statement of hypotheses

We are now in a position to state our hypotheses. We begin with three hypotheses that can be informed using nonparametric tests among treatments.

Our first hypothesis concerns the preference for appearing honest in PREDICT and REPORT. As noted earlier, there will be relatively more honesty in PREDICT:

**Hypothesis 1** *The fraction of honest-looking predictions in PREDICT is greater than REPORT.*

Next, following Mazar et al.'s (2008a) notion that people often want to find a balance between dishonesty and maintaining a positive self-image, we predict that people cheat to some degree in both REPORT and PREDICT. Moreover, by appealing to arguments regarding Categorization and Attention to Moral Standards, we predict that cheating will be lower in PREDICT than REPORT.

**Hypothesis 2** *Cheating occurs when given the opportunity in PREDICT and REPORT. Moreover, the level of cheating in REPORT is greater than in PREDICT.*

Our next three hypotheses refer to the model specified in Section 4.1.

**Hypothesis 3** (profit). When the cost to maintain a positive self-image is vanishingly small ($P(a_j) \to 0, \forall j$) higher profits from cheating lead to more cheating (i.e., $V$ is increasing in profit).

**Hypothesis 4** (self-image). When the profit from cheating is vanishingly small ($\pi(a_j) \to 0, \forall j$), self-image costs deter cheating (i.e., $\gamma_1 < 0$).

**Hypothesis 5** (profit and self-image). Suppose a possibly dishonest action $a_j$ has a positive probability of being perceived as dishonest ($P(a_j) > 0$). Then the greater the profit from cheating, the more difficult it is to maintain a positive self-image (i.e., $\gamma_2 < 0$).

## 5. Results

A total of 255 subjects participated in our experiment, including 48 independent evaluators, and 70, 61, and 76 subjects in CONTROL, REPORT, and PREDICT,

s. This threshold says that roughly 99% of the time, a random draw from CONTROL is no greater than 50%. In the CONTROL treatment, the top three highest $p_i^{max}$ are 57%, 50%, 50%, which are followed by a cluster between 50% and 45%. Hence, 50% seems a natural focal point with which subjects in CONTROL were comfortable. If we instead use the 95th percentile of $p_i^{max}$ in CONTROL, which is 48%, to define the upper bound of "honest-looking" predictions, 90% of predictions in *PREDICT* were "honest-looking." Moreover, 50% as the cutoff is supported by the consensus of independent evaluators (see Section 5 for details).

respectively. We draw inferences regarding whether subjects cheated by comparing their die roll outcomes to expected outcomes from a fair die.

The first subsection briefly summarizes the results detailed in Hao and Houser (2017), that predictions appear honest-looking in PREDICT but not in REPORT, while actual cheating behavior occur in both treatments. In Section 5.2, we use the combined data from the die-roll and evaluation sessions to estimate the model developed above, and show that differences between REPORT and PREDICT can be traced to the differences in the perceptions of dishonesty between the two treatments.

## 5.1 Preferences for appearing honest and for being honest

Based on predictions in the CONTROL treatment and the evaluations, we empirically define a prediction is "honest-looking" if its $p_i^{max}$ does not exceed 50%.[t] We compare the fraction of honest-looking predictions across all three treatments and report our first result.

**Result 1. (Test of Hypothesis 1).** *The fraction of honest-looking predictions in PREDICT is statistically identical to CONTROL, while the fraction of honest-looking predictions is significantly lower in REPORT: REPORT < PREDICT = CONTROL.*

*Evidence.* The fraction of the honest-looking predictions (i.e., $p_i^{max} \leq 50\%$) is 95% (72 of 76) in PREDICT, statistically identical to that of CONTROL (99%, 69 of 70; $p = 0.204$, two-sided proportion test). In contrast, this fraction is only 66% (40 of 61 subjects) in REPORT, which is significantly lower than either CONTROL or PREDICT ($p < 0.001$ in both, two-sided proportion test). We next infer and compare cheating behavior across treatments via two metrics, prediction accuracy and earnings. Cheating is evident if predictions are more accurate than chances, which also means greater profit. Hence, we compare empirical frequency of highest-payoff outcomes against their expected frequency which is 25% due to uniform distribution, or slightly higher if we adjust for ties.[u]

The ranking of the three treatments in cheating behavior is reported in Result 2, which is different from the ranking of the fraction of honest-looking predictions.

**Result 2. (Test of Hypothesis 2).** *Predictions are significantly more accurate than chances, and higher profit, in PREDICT and REPORT treatments than in CONTROL, with REPORT treatment being the highest. This suggests*

t. Our evaluation sessions provide additional evidence that an "honest-looking" prediction's $p_i^{max}$ does not exceed 50%. Once an individual's $p_i^{max}$ reaches 50%, the majority of the evaluators agreed that the she appeared to have cheated (70% in PREDICT and 60% in REPORT).

u. For example, if a subject predicts [32%, 32%, 20%, 16%], it is expected that the highest-payoff outcome (either 1 or 2) turns up with probability 50%. Hence, the expected frequency is 25% multiplied by the number of ties at $p_i^{max}$.

*the level of cheating is highest in REPORT, followed by PREDICT, and both are higher than CONTROL: REPORT > PREDICT > CONTROL.*
*Evidence (i).* The empirical frequency of highest-payoff outcomes subjects obtained was significantly higher than the expected frequency (adjusted for ties) in both PREDICT (71% vs 30%, $p<0.001$, two-sided proportion test) and REPORT (85% vs 29%, $p<0.001$, two-sided proportion test). In contrast, predictions in CONTROL were not more accurate than expected (36% vs 32%, $p=0.588$, two-sided proportion test).

*Evidence (ii).* Average earnings in REPORT are significantly higher than in PREDICT, \$19.15 and \$16.90, respectively, and both are significantly higher than \$15.26 in CONTROL ($p<0.001$ in all three pair-wised comparison, two-sided Mann–Whitney tests).[v]

## 5.2 Structural estimation

### 5.2.1 Choice space

To implement the model in Eq. (2) empirically, we assume first that agents face two alternatives: $a_1$ represents the high-payoff choice and $a_2$ the second-highest payoff alternative. We assume a binary choice set for two reasons. First, it is a reasonable characterization of the empirical choices faced by subjects: among those who predicted a nonuniform distribution (52 in PREDICT and 47 in REPORT), half of them had only two unique values (48% in PREDICT and 50% in REPORT), so they only had two alternatives. Moreover, the vast majority (96% in PREDICT and 90% in REPORT) of participants in fact obtained either the highest or second highest payoff outcome, suggesting that even when participants faced more than two alternatives they were, as a practical matter, choosing between the first and second highest available payoff outcomes.

### 5.2.2 Perceptions of dishonesty

Incentivized evaluations from independent evaluators show that the perceptions of the dishonesty of the same action differ between the two main treatments. As we described in Section 3.2, evaluators assessed the likelihood that the decision maker cheated in each of the six scenarios, where the decision maker obtained the outcome corresponding to the highest probability prediction $p_i^{max}$ at 25%, 40%, 50%, 60%, 85%, and 100%, respectively.

Fig. 1 shows the fraction of evaluators ($y$-axis) who believe the decision maker cheated in the given scenario (indicated on the $x$-axis) in the PREDICT or the REPORT treatments (Note Fig. 1 can be derived from fig. 2a in Hao and Houser, 2017). For example, in the scenario $p_i^{max}=50\%$, 70% evaluators believed the person in the scenario cheated in the PREDICT treatment, in contrast of only 60% evaluators believed the person in the identical scenario cheated in the REPORT treatment.

v. Please see table 3 and figure 4 in Hao and Houser (2017) for summary statistics and distributions of earnings.

Note that differences in perception between treatments occur when $p_i^{max}$ is between 40% and 50%. The majority of decisions from our main treatments falls within this range, and it is this that allows separate identification of the effects of profit and perception on cheating decisions. There are no perception differences at 85% and 100%, where nearly all evaluators perceived such decisions in both treatments to have been dishonest.

These perception data are drawn from evaluators' direct assessment (Decision Sets A and B) on whether a person cheated in the given scenario. The relative assessment from evaluators' responses in Decision Set C is reported in fig. 2b in Hao and Houser (2017), and the result is consistent in that significantly more evaluators viewed identical actions as more likely to be dishonest in PREDICT than in REPORT. The relative assessment was intended to break ties in that it asked, between PREDICT and REPORT, in which treatment was the person more likely to have been dishonest.

### 5.2.3 *Preference specification*

Our empirical strategy requires us to say more about the nature of the utility function. First, given a participant's predictions, the payoffs $\pi(a_k)$ associated with each outcome ($k=1$, 2) are immediately identified by Eq. (1), the payoff function used in our experiment. Next, with respect to the concern about one's image, we assume participants believe that making any choice other than the maximum payoff choice does not lead to a negative social image, so that $P(a_2)=0$. Suppose that $P(a_1)$ is the participant's subjective belief that an action would be perceived as dishonest by others, and assume this belief is *unbiased* in the sense that at equilibrium it is equal to the true fraction of observers who hold the perception that an agent who took that action has cheated. We elicited this value using an incentivized survey with independent evaluators, as described in the previous subsection.

Next, define $V(\pi(a_i))=\beta_0+\beta_1\pi(a_i)$, so that we have:

$$u(a_1)=\beta_0+\beta_1\pi\left(a_1|p_i^{max}\right)+\gamma_1 p\left(a_1|p_i^{max}\right)+\gamma_2\pi\left(a_1|p_i^{max}\right)p\left(a_1|p_i^{max}\right)+\varepsilon_1 \quad (3)$$

$$u(a_2)=\beta_0+\beta_1\pi\left(a_1|p_i^{-max}\right)+\varepsilon_2 \quad (4)$$

It follows that the agent chooses the highest payoff outcome $a_1$ if

$$\Delta u \equiv u(a_1)-u(a_2)>0,$$

or

$$\Delta u=\beta_1\left[\pi\left(a_1|p_i^{max}\right)-\pi\left(a_2|p_i^{-max}\right)\right]+\gamma_1 p\left(a_1|p_i^{max}\right)$$
$$+\gamma_2\pi\left(a_1|p_i^{max}\right)p\left(a_1|p_i^{max}\right)+\epsilon>0$$

where $\epsilon=\varepsilon_1-\varepsilon_2$.

Assuming that the random utility components are normally distributed, it is immediate that a Probit analysis can be used to estimate the structural parameters.

### 5.2.4 Results

We analyzed data from subjects who reported nonobjective predictions in PREDICT and REPORT, yielding 99 independent observations.[w] The results are reported in Table 1.

If all participants behaved honestly, then all coefficients would be statistically zero. Systematic departures from honesty are reflected by coefficients that significantly differ from zero. We indeed find that the coefficient on $\Delta\pi$ is significantly greater than zero, suggesting that the greater the profit gain from cheating (recall $\Delta\pi$ is the difference between the highest and second-highest payoffs), the more likely is a subject to choose the highest-payoff outcomes (the more likely is the subject to choose to cheat), at least when the self-image cost is low (Hypothesis 3). Second, the coefficient for *Perception* is negative (Hypothesis 4), consistent with self-image maintenance theory, although this effect is not statistically significant. However, the interaction of $\Delta\pi$ and Perception is significantly negative (Hypothesis 5), indicating that a desire to maintain one's self-image does deter cheating, and that this effect is particularly strong when the selfish gain ($\Delta\pi$) from cheating is large.

Finally, consider the overall effect of profit gains on cheating decisions, given by the coefficient of ($\Delta\pi + \Delta\pi * Perception$). When perception is equal

**TABLE 1** Effects of Profit and Self-Image on Cheating Decisions

| Probit | Coefficient | Marginal effect |
|---|---|---|
| $\Delta\pi$ | 0.312** | 0.075 |
| | [0.140] | |
| *Perception* | −0.136 | −0.033 |
| | [0.766] | |
| $\Delta\pi \times$ *Perception* | −0.185*** | −0.044 |
| | [0.053] | |
| *Constant* | −0.267* | n/a |
| | [0.115] | |
| *Number of Obs.* | 99 | 99 |

*Notes:* In *square bracket* are robust standard errors clustered at the treatment level; in *parenthesis* are standard errors computed for marginal effect holding other variables at mean. ** and *** indicate significance level at 5% and 1% level, respectively.
Dependent Variable = 1 if subject chose highest-payoff outcome, 0 otherwise.

w. All regressor variables take value zero with objective predictions. Adding those data consequently provides no information to the analysis, and they should not be pooled with the informative data. An alternative to eliminating these observations is to "dummy out" their contribution. This impacts standard error estimates and, because probits are nonlinear, can also bias coefficient estimates.

to one, meaning that an act is very likely to be viewed as dishonest, the overall coefficient is statistically insignificant ($p=0.14$) with 95% confidence interval [−0.04, 0.30]. Interestingly, one cannot reject the hypothesis that higher profit gains reduce the probability of taking possibly dishonest actions that are very likely to be perceived as dishonest.

## 6. Discussion

The influential theory of self-image maintenance proposed by Mazar et al. (2008a) suggests people balance their desire to obtain profits from cheating with their preference to maintain a positive self-image. We specified a model inspired by Krupka and Weber (2013) to capture the tension between profits and self-image, and estimated it using decision data from die-roll cheating games, augmented with evaluations from independent observers that indicated the likelihood that possibly dishonest decisions in the two treatments were in fact dishonest. The advantage to this approach is that it provides systematic variation in the perception that one's actions are dishonest at fixed levels of profit. Such belief data are central to Mazar et al.'s (2008a) theory of self-image maintenance: the more firmly one believes that a decision will be viewed as dishonest, the harder is one able to maintain a positive self-image. Consequently, with our data we were able to identify the separate quantitative effects of profit, self-image maintenance, and their interaction on cheating decisions.

We found that a possibly dishonest action taken after it is predicted is more likely to be perceived as dishonest than is an equivalent action absent prior prediction. Consequently, requiring announcements promotes honest actions among people who care about maintaining an honest image. Moreover, we found that people cheated more when profits were greater, but people also respond to self-image concerns: as the profit gain from cheating is greater, the cost of maintaining a positive self-image is greater (as the belief that a decision is perceived as dishonest becomes greater), and consequently people become less likely to cheat. Indeed, we found the profit incentive to cheat is extinguished when a possibly dishonest decision is almost certain to be viewed as dishonest. These results complement previous findings by Mazar et al. (2008a) who speculated that sufficiently large external incentives might deter cheating, as well as Krupka and Weber (2013) who reported that people will sacrifice money to remain obedient to social norms. It is worthwhile to emphasize several features of our design. First, we made an effort to ensure cognitive requirements were substantively identical between PREDICT and REPORT. We were concerned that recalling four probabilities in REPORT might be more difficult than recalling one outcome in PREDICT. Consequently, we provided subjects an interactive support tool to explore the relationship between predictions and earnings. In addition to clarifying the payoff structure, the tool served as a memory aid. In particular, when subjects finished exploring their options, they could and did leave their final predictions on screen and transcribed the four probabilities to their decision sheet.

Second, concerns regarding the subjects' understanding of the experiment deserve discussion. One is that the PREDICT group may have been worried about the possibility of being caught cheating. To address this, we emphasized three times in the instructions that the die rolls would be private. We also encouraged them to roll many times, but only to report the first roll. Finally, responses in ex-post surveys indicated subjects were aware that it was possible to cheat without detection.

Another concern is that the payoff structure (quadratic scoring rule) may have left subjects uncertain regarding the earnings-maximizing strategy. We addressed this by ensuring all participants were required to complete a quiz that assessed whether they understood how to assign probabilities to achieve maximum earnings. Participants were required to successfully complete a quiz in this regard prior to participating in the experiment.

When information between principals and agents is asymmetric, our research suggests requiring agents to predict their future actions can promote honesty and, in view of Krupka and Weber (2013), perhaps even trustworthiness and norm-obedience. More generally, predicting one's own future behavior may help to address self-control problems (i.e., cheating on oneself). For instance, to combat procrastination it may be useful to announce to friends or colleagues a self-imposed deadline for well-specified tasks (see, e.g., www.stickk.com). Similarly, when trying to achieve a healthy weight, one might be able to curb cheating by announcing plans for diet and exercise.

Substantial previous research shows people cheat yet shy away from realizing maximum earnings; our results may help to explain this puzzle of incomplete cheating. We find that the deterrence effect of self-image maintenance on cheating is greater when the profit gain from cheating is greater. Moreover, we find in both PREDICT and REPORT that an act is more likely to be perceived as dishonest when it results in higher profit. Taken together, our findings imply incomplete cheating may occur because people are not averse to being perceived as willing to cheat for small benefits, and yet prefer not to be perceived, either by themselves or others, as willing to cheat for large selfish profit gains. Further investigation of this possibility, and the role it might play in the design of institutions to deter misconduct in natural environments, defines a valuable research agenda.

## Acknowledgment

This chapter draws heavily from Hao and Houser (2017) where the experiment design and data analyzed here were originally reported. The primary difference with respect to Hao and Houser (2017) is that we provide a new structural analysis of those same data. This chapter's Section 4.1 (the structural model) and Section 5.2 (analysis based on the model) are entirely new. Some or all of other sections of this chapter originally appeared in Hao and Houser (2017).

Some of the data and analyses reported in this chapter were previously reported in the unpublished working paper "Honest Lies," by the same authors. For helpful comments we thank

David Gill, Glenn Harrison, Edi Karni, R. Lynn Hannan, Cary Deck, Salar Jahedi, Roberto Weber, Omar Al-Ubaydli, Marco Castillo, Ragan Petrie, Jo Winter, Larry White, Chris Coyne, our colleagues at ICES, George Mason University and University of Arkansas, seminar participants at CEAR, Georgia State University (2010), the ESA North-American meeting (2010, 2011), University of Fayetteville, Arkansas (2011), GSPW at George Mason University (2011), and Southern Economic Association meetings (2012), Shanghai University of Finance and Economics (2013), Southwestern University of Finance and Economics (2013). The authors are of course responsible for any errors in this chapter.

## References

Andersen, S., Fountain, J., Harrison, G.W., Rutström, E.E., 2014. Estimating subjective probabilities. J. Risk Uncertain. 48 (3), 207–229.

Andreoni, J., Douglas Bernheim, B., 2009. Social image and the 50–50 norm: a theoretical and experimental analysis of audience effects. Econometrica 77 (5), 1607–1636.

Ariely, D., Bracha, A., Meier, S., 2009. Doing good or doing well? Image motivation and monetary incentives in behaving prosocially. Am. Econ. Rev. 99 (1), 544–555.

Bénabou, R., Tirole, J., 2004. Willpower and personal rules. J. Polit. Econ. 112 (4), 848–886.

Cadsby, C.B., Song, F., Tapon, F., 2010. Are you paying your employees to cheat? An experimental investigation. B.E. J. Econ. Anal. Policy 10 (1), 1–30.

Charness, G., Dufwenberg, M., 2006. Promises and partnership. Econometrica 74 (6), 1579–1601.

DellaVigna, S., List, J.A., Malmendier, U., 2012. Testing for altruism and social pressure in charitable giving. Q. J. Econ. 127 (1), 1–56.

Fischbacher, U., Föllmi-Heusi, F., 2013. Lies in disguise—an experimental study on cheating. J. Eur. Econ. Assoc. 11 (3), 525–547.

Gibson, R., Tanner, C., Wagner, A.F., 2013. Preferences for truthfulness: heterogeneity among and within individuals. Am. Econ. Rev. 103 (1), 532–548.

Gneezy, U., 2005. Deception: the role of consequences. Am. Econ. Rev. 95 (1), 384–394.

Hannan, R.L., Rankin, F.W., Towry, K.L., 2006. The effect of information systems on honesty in managerial reporting: a behavioral perspective. Contemp. Account. Res. 23 (4), 885–918.

Hao, L., Houser, D., 2017. Perceptions, intentions, and cheating. J. Econ. Behav. Organ. 133, 52–73.

Houser, D., Xiao, E., 2011. Classification of natural language messages using a coordination game. Exp. Econ. 14 (1), 1–14.

Hurkens, S., Kartik, N., 2009. Would i lie to you? On social preferences and lying aversion. Exp. Econ. 12 (2), 180–192.

Jiang, T., 2013. Cheating in mind games: the subtlety of rules matters. J. Econ. Behav. Organ. 93, 328–336.

Kadane, J.B., Winkler, R.L., 1988. Separating probability elicitation from utilities. J. Am. Stat. Assoc. 83 (402), 357–363.

Krupka, E.L., Weber, R.A., 2013. Identifying social norms using coordination games: why does dictator game sharing vary? J. Eur. Econ. Assoc. 11 (3), 495–524.

Lundquist, T., Ellingsen, T., Gribbe, E., Johannesson, M., 2009. The aversion to lying. J. Econ. Behav. Organ. 70 (1–2), 81–92.

Mazar, N., Ariely, D., 2008. Temporal Influences on Cheating Behavior: The 'What the Hell' Effect. working paper, Sloan School of Management, Massachusetts Institute of Technology.

Mazar, N., Amir, O., Ariely, D., 2008a. The dishonesty of honest people: a theory of self-concept maintenance. J. Market. Res. 45 (6), 633–644.

Mazar, N., Amir, O., Ariely, D., 2008b. More ways to cheat—expanding the scope of dishonesty. J. Market. Res. 45 (6), 651–653.
Nyarko, Y., Schotter, A., 2002. An experimental study of belief learning using elicited beliefs. Econometrica 70 (3), 971–1005.
Rode, J., 2010. Truth and trust in communication: experiments on the effect of a competitive context. Games Econ. Behav. 68 (1), 325–338.
Sánchez-Pagés, S., Vorsatz, M., 2007. An Experimental Study of Truth-Telling in a Sender–Receiver Game. Games Econom. Behav. 61 (1), 86–112.
Sánchez-Pagés, S., Vorsatz, M., 2009. Enjoy the silence: an experiment on truth-telling. Exp. Econ. 12 (2), 220–241.
Schweitzer, M.E., Hershey, J.C., Bradlow, E.T., 2006. Promises and lies: restoring violated trust. Organ. Behav. Hum. Decis. Process. 101 (1), 1–19.
Stouten, J., De Cremer, D., Van Dijk, E., 2006. Violating equality in social dilemmas: emotional and retributive reactions as a function of trust, attribution, and honesty. Pers. Soc. Psychol. Bull. 32 (7), 894–906.
Von Hippel, W., Trivers, R., 2011. Reflections on self-deception. Behav. Brain Sci. 34 (1), 41–56.
Xiao, E., Houser, D., 2005. Emotion expression in human punishment behavior. Proc. Natl. Acad. Sci. U.S.A. 102 (20), 7398–7401.

Chapter 3.5

# An experiment on conformity in deception

Shunichiro Sasaki[1], Shoko Yamane[1], Grzegorz Mardyla[1], Kazuki Ohara[2]
[1]*Faculty of Economics, Kindai University, Osaka, Japan,* [2]*Recruit Lifestyle Co., Ltd, Tokyo, Japan*

## Chapter Outline



**JEL Classification:** C91, D63, D83

## 1. Introduction

Lying can be a feasible approach to strategic communication under asymmetric information. It is conceivable that a person who knows the true state of the world might well advance their interests by telling a lie to another person who does not know the true state of the world. In particular, the informed party could, in many contexts, directly advance their economic self-interest through the use of deceptive communication. However, many people appear to consciously and deliberately forego their potential self-interest when doing so involves lying to a less-informed party.

In an oft-cited study, Gneezy (2005) investigated experimental subjects' choices in the dictator game—where a sender subject can directly and unilaterally allocate payoffs between themselves and a receiver, and compared these choices against those in the deception game—where the sender can allocate identical

Dishonesty in Behavioral Economics. https://doi.org/10.1016/B978-0-12-815857-9.00011-X

payoffs between themselves and the receiver, but indirectly, by telling lies. He found that the proportion of self-interested payoff allocations in the dictator game was consistently greater than the corresponding proportion of self-interested lies in the deception game. As the end result is identical no matter if achieved through direct allocation or through indirect deception, Gneezy's (2005) results can only be interpreted as subjects being averse to the act of lying itself.

Aversion to lying has been observed even in situations in which lying is beneficial to both the sender and the receiver (Erat and Gneezy, 2012). Furthermore, it has been documented that lie aversion can be influenced by gender (Dreber and Johannesson, 2008; Lundquist et al., 2009),[a] by whether experiment subjects major in Economics (López-Pérez and Spiegelman, 2012; Lundquist et al., 2009), or by whether interaction is on an individual level or takes place within a group (Sutter, 2009).

Another strand of the literature, and one that is more closely related to the present study, focuses on contagion effects in lying. Innes and Mitra (2013) and Fosgaard et al. (2013) found that subjects' aversion to telling self-interested lies was weakened when they knew that their peers had told self-interested lies. These results indicate that selfish lying can be contagious. However, apart from pure self-interest motives, deception can sometimes also be altruistic, or even spiteful. Research into potential contagion effects in deceptive communication other than self-interested lying is scant. The chief purpose of the present study is to fill that void. Thus, our main research question is: Can altruistic and spiteful lies also be contagious, as selfish lies have been shown to be?

From a more general viewpoint, contagion in lying is an example of behavioral conformity. The experimental literature on conformity is vast and spans multiple disciplines. For our purposes, it is helpful to bring up a few studies, wherein it was confirmed that observing past behaviors of others influenced subjects' own behaviors. For example, in a public goods experiment, Fischbacher et al. (2001) observed that subjects were more likely to cooperate if they knew other subjects were also cooperative. In a dictator game experiment, Cason and Mui (1998) found that knowing others' allocation decisions induces other-regarding behaviors. Krupka and Weber (2009) found in a modified dictator game experiment that subjects tended to be more prosocial when they had observed many other subjects also having been prosocial. The tendency for conformity in cooperative behaviors was also confirmed in fundraising field experiments by Frey and Meier (2004), and also by Shang and Croson (2009).

These experimental results are but a few of numerous studies, in which both selfish and pro-social behaviors have been confirmed to be susceptible to contagion when subjects were given the opportunity to observe others' past choices. While most of the above-mentioned studies focus on a single specific social

a. However, no gender differences in lying were observed in Childs (2012) and Gylfason et al. (2013), nor in the selfish lies condition in Erat and Gneezy (2012).

norm or behavior, we comprehensively examine how the observation of others' behaviors influences subjects' own choices in a parsimonious two-person game framework.

Specifically, we conducted a series of dictator game and deception game experiments in which the sender in each game could allocate payoffs between themselves and the receiver for various types of payoff functions—altruistic, spiteful, and three selfish conditions. Furthermore, in an additional series of experiments we gave the subjects information on their peers' choices in past dictator and the deception games, for each type of payoff function. This setup allowed us to examine not only the differences in subjects' choices between the dictator and deception games, but also the potential influence peer information might have on subjects' choices across the various payoff functions.

Analysis of our experimental data brings about some interesting findings. First, we observe lie aversion for one of the three selfish payoff conditions. As far as conformity in lying is concerned, we have found that subjects were most likely to conform to others' selfish choices—selfish lies in the deception game and selfish payoff allocations in the dictator game. Interestingly, we also observe that subjects tend to mimic honest choices in the altruistic condition of the deception game. We also found that subjects exhibited a tendency to behave honestly when they observed others had not told spiteful lies.

These results can be explained with the inequality aversion model of Fehr and Schmidt (1999). Applying their framework, social information on others' selfish choices reduces subjects' own guilt, and likewise, knowledge that others did not tell altruistic lies raises subjects' own envy. Similarly, knowing that others did not tell spiteful lies raises subjects' guilt. However, social information on others' spiteful lies can also be considered a trigger for activating a focusing effect on the social norm of antispitefulness.

The remainder of this chapter is organized as follows: Section 2 introduces the experimental design and procedures. Section 3 presents the main results and offer an interpretation of our findings using the inequality aversion model, and we conclude in Section 4.

## 2. Experimental design and analytical framework

### 2.1 The deception game and the dictator dame

In this study, we reexamine lie aversion in a variety of payoff conditions and further to investigate potential effects social information on peers' choices has on indirect strategic communication choices (in the deception game) and on direct allocation choices (in the dictator game). All our subjects participated in both game types.

In the deception game, each subject was randomly paired with another subject. Due care was taken to ensure pairing was anonymous. Neither the subjects nor the experimenters could identify any specific player, either during or at any time after the experiment. Assignment of roles—sender or receiver—in pairs was also random and anonymous.

**TABLE 1** Payoffs and Conditions

| | | A | | B | |
|---|---|---|---|---|---|
| Payoff number | Condition | Sender (JPY) | Receiver (JPY) | Sender (JPY) | Receiver (JPY) |
| 1 | Altruistic | 1200 | 1200 | 1200 | 1600 |
| 2 | Spiteful | 1200 | 1200 | 1200 | 800 |
| 3 | Selfish 1 | 1200 | 1200 | 1600 | 800 |
| 4 | Selfish 2 | 1200 | 1200 | 1800 | 400 |
| 5 | Selfish 3 | 1200 | 1200 | 2000 | 0 |

Once the roles had been randomly assigned and subject pairs randomly formed, the computer presented a single payoff number and its corresponding payoff combination pair (A and B) to the sender subjects. These payoff combinations are reported in Table 1. While the "A" numbers always corresponded to a symmetric and equal division of payoffs between the sender and the receiver, the "B" numbers represented asymmetric and unequal, condition-dependent sender/receiver payoff pairs.

The sender subjects were then asked to send a message to the receiver subjects about the payoff number they had observed. The receivers had no information whatsoever regarding any of the payoffs or the payoff number observed by the senders. After viewing the message sent by their sender counterparts, receivers were asked to report on the payoff number they thought the sender subjects had observed.

Payoffs were determined according to whether the receivers' reported numbers matched the payoff numbers their paired senders had actually observed. If a receiver subject reported the same number that their paired sender subject had observed, the equal "A" payoffs were allocated to both subjects. If a receiver subject reported a number different from the one their paired sender subject had observed, the resultant payoffs were the unequal "B" amounts.

Senders in the deception game could lie and thus induce the receivers to report a number different from the number the senders had actually observed. By doing so, the senders could essentially effectuate the unequal B payoff amounts to be paid. The types of lies and the resulting unequal payoff pair combinations varied with different payoff numbers.

If a sender observed the payoff number 1 but then messaged a different number and the receiver subsequently reported that different number, the pair would receive payoffs B. For the number 1 payoff combination, the B amount obtained by the receiver is larger than the A amount, and it is also larger than the B amount obtained by the sender. We thus call a sender's untruthful message in this condition an "altruistic Pareto lie" because the sender's lie brings about relatively larger gains for the receiver while at the same time increasing both parties' combined total payoff. Similarly, we call a sender's untruthful message a "spiteful lie" whenever they had observed payoff number 2 but sent a message to a different effect, as it results in the amount of payoff B being smaller than that of A for the receiver while the sender's payoff is kept constant (across A and B). Furthermore, reporting any number other than 3 (or 4, or 5) whenever a sender had observed payoff number 3 (or 4, or 5) constitutes a "selfish lie" on the sender's part as the B payoff amounts for the senders are larger by JPY 400 (or by JPY 600, or by JPY 800) than the A payoff amounts for those payoff pair combinations, while at the same time the receiver B payoff is reduced, relative to A, by JPY 400 (or by JPY 800, or by JPY 1200 to JPY 0). The deception game was repeated for five rounds, for the five different payoff combination pairs. Across these five rounds, each sender subject observed all five payoff numbers in random order.

Consider a situation where a sender had observed the payoff number 1 in the deception game. If the sender reported that the number she had observed was 2 and the receiver answered that the number the sender had observed was 2, then the sender would receive JPY 1200 and the receiver would receive JPY 1600. In such a case, we regard that the sender told an altruistic lie. Consider another situation where the sender had observed the payoff number 3 in the same game. If the sender reported that the number she had observed was 3 and the receiver answered that the number the sender had observed was 3, then the sender would receive JYP 1200 and the receiver would receive JPY 1200. In such a case, we regard that the sender told the truth.

The dictator game experiment was very similar in structure to the deception game, save for the final payoffs being directly and unilaterally decided by the sender subjects' choices. Subjects were again randomly paired and assigned their sender/receiver roles, exactly as in the deception game. The computer then randomly selected and presented—only to the sender subjects—a single payoff number along with its corresponding payoff combination pair A and B (Table 1). The senders then decided on either of the A/B payoff pairs to be allocated between themselves and their paired receiver subjects. The receivers' subsequent task was to simply acknowledge the senders' rulings. The A/B payoff combinations for each payoff number were exactly identical to those in the deception game. The dictator game was also repeated for five rounds, with each sender subject observing all five payoff numbers in random order.

Consider a situation where a sender had observed the payoff number 2 in the dictator game. If the sender chose payoff B, then the sender would receive JPY 1200 and the receiver would receive JPY 800. In such a case, we regard that the sender chose the spiteful allocation. Consider another situation where the sender had observed the payoff number 4 in the same game. If the sender chose payoff A, then the sender would receive JPY 1200 and the receiver would receive JPY 1200. In such a case, we regard that the sender chose the fair allocation.

## 2.2 Measuring conformity

Our chief objective in this study is to examine the influence of social information about peer decisions on senders' strategic communication and allocation choices. To this end, we followed the *control experiment* (CE) described above with a *treatment experiment* (TE). Compared to the control, the sole modification in the treatment was the introduction of additional information about their peers' choices in the control experiment, which was made available to the sender subjects.

In the CE, the subjects simply played the deception and dictator games. After conducting all the CE sessions, we nonrandomly selected, for each payoff condition 1~5, one *reference round* (RR). Sender subjects' choices in those reference rounds were graphically summarized and shown to senders in the succeeding TE sessions. Specifically, senders in each of the five TE deception (dictator) game conditions (corresponding to the five different payoff pair combinations) were shown a pie chart revealing the proportion of subjects who had lied (had chosen payoff combination B) in the RR of the deception (dictator) game for that particular payoff condition. A sample of such peer information is depicted in Fig. 1. Senders in the TE thus faced identical tasks to those faced by the CE senders, except now they had an opportunity to survey the choices their peers had previously made.

We ran two different conditions of our TE sessions, differing in the type of peer information shown to senders. In the "*unequal*" condition (TE1), the experimenter-chosen reference round results revealed a majority of senders having lied in the deception game or having chosen the unequal B payoff combinations in the dictator game. In contrast, in the "*equal*" condition (TE2), the experimenter-chosen reference round results revealed that a peer majority having been truthful in the deception game or having chosen the symmetric and equal payoff combination pairs in the dictator game.

Straightforward comparisons of sender subjects' choices in the two treatments with their peers' choices in the control experiment enabled us to evaluate the presence and the extent of conformity effects in the deception and dictator games for various types of payoff functions.

## 2.3 Hypotheses

Given the above experimental design, we propose two primary hypotheses on subjects' behaviors.

In the previous results of the experimental study on deception cited in the introduction, it is often observed that subjects are averse to telling lies in various experimental conditions (e.g., Dreber and Johannesson, 2008; Gneezy, 2005; López-Pérez and Spiegelman, 2012; Lundquist et al., 2009; Sutter, 2009), even if lying is beneficial to both the sender and the receiver (Erat and Gneezy, 2012). From these results, we suppose that subjects are constantly averse to telling any kinds of lies. In order to examine such conjecture, we test the following hypothesis.

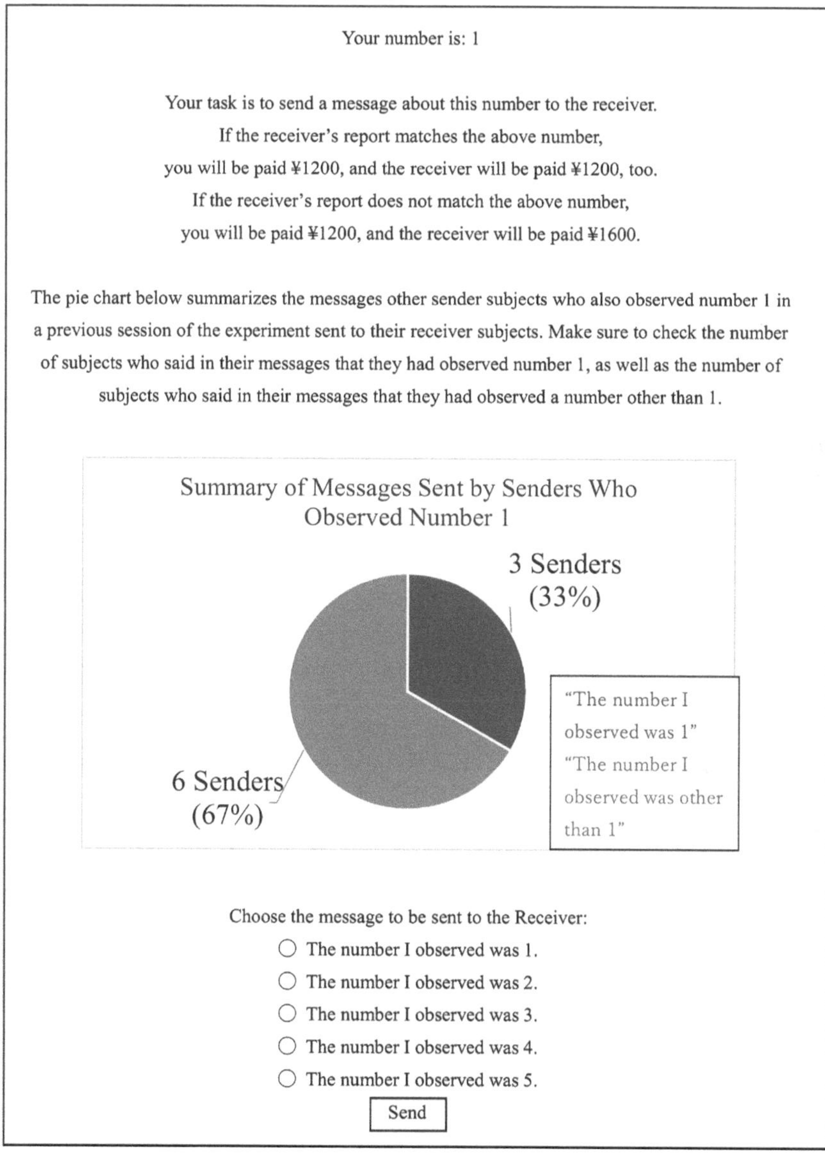


**FIG. 1** Sample of peer information.

**Hypothesis 1** Subjects are averse to lying.

We also introduced the experimental result that subjects tend to conform to others' selfish lies in Innes and Mitra (2013) and Fosgaard et al. (2013). Furthermore, a more general tendency to conform to other subjects' social preferences is confirmed in Fischbacher et al. (2001), Cason and Mui (1998),

Krupka and Weber (2009), Frey and Meier (2004), and Shang and Croson (2009). Thus, we expect that subjects in our experiments conform to not only others' lies but also others' behaviors. To examine this conjecture, we test the following hypothesis.

**Hypothesis 2** Subjects conform to others' behaviors in the deception and dictator games.

## 2.4 Experiment procedures

We conducted six sessions of the CE and six of TE, between June 2014 and December 2015. All sessions were run in the computer lab at the Faculty of Economics, Kindai University, in Japan. Subjects were undergraduate students at Kindai University; altogether 192 subjects participated in the CE sessions and 202 distinct subjects participated in the TE sessions. Detailed experimental data for each session are summarized in Table 2. At the beginning of each session, one of the experimenters read aloud the experiment instructions.[b] All subjects then played a few practice rounds, both of the deception game and of the dictator game. Having made certain that all subjects fully understood the experiment rules and procedures, main experiment sessions were commenced.

For participant payments, one round out of five was randomly selected for payout by the computer, for both the deception and dictator games. Total payments to each subject amounted to the sum of payoffs in these randomly selected two rounds, complemented with a JPY 1000 show-up fee. The average payoff across all sessions, which lasted for approximately 80 min each, was JPY 3206 (roughly equivalent to US$30).

# 3. Results

For our purposes, it suffices to examine only the sender subjects' choices, in both the deception and the dictator games.[c]

## 3.1 Lie aversion

The choices made by all 96 senders in deception and dictator games for all six CE sessions are summarized in Table 3.

First, following Gneezy (2005), we report on the proportions of senders who chose to lie in the deception game and on those of players who chose to allocate B payoffs in the dictator game. Recall that the same payoff pair combinations

b. For detailed experiment instructions, see Appendix.

c. Although we examine only senders' data, we needed the receivers in our experiment, too. This is because monetary payments to participants depended both on senders' messages and on receivers' reports (in the deception game).

**TABLE 2** Experiment Session Details

| CE (control) | | | | | | | |
|---|---|---|---|---|---|---|---|
| | | Session 1 (Jun 2014) | Session 2 (Jun 2014) | Session 3 (Nov 2014) | Session 4 (Nov 2014) | Session 5 (Nov 2014) | Session 6 (Nov 2014) |
| Number of subjects | | 20 | 18 | 36 | 38 | 42 | 38 |
| Order of games | Game 1 | Deception | Dictator | Deception | Dictator | Deception | Dictator |
| | Game 2 | Dictator | Deception | Dictator | Deception | Dictator | Deception |

| TE (Treatments) | | | | | | | |
|---|---|---|---|---|---|---|---|
| | | Session 7 (Nov 2015) | Session 8 (Nov 2015) | Session 9 (Nov 2015) | Session 10 (Dec 2015) | Session 11 (Dec 2015) | Session 12 (Dec 2015) |
| Number of subjects | | 38 | 26 | 40 | 38 | 28 | 32 |
| TE1/TE2 | | TE1 | TE1 | TE2 | TE2 | TE2 | TE2 |
| Majority of peers in | The deception game | Lied | Lied | Told the truth | Told the truth | Told the truth | Told the truth |
| | The dictator game | Chose B | Chose B | Chose A | Chose A | Chose A | Chose A |
| Order of games | Game 1 | Deception | Dictator | Deception | Dictator | Deception | Deception |
| | Game 2 | Dictator | Deception | Dictator | Deception | Dictator | Dictator |

**TABLE 3** Results—The Control Experiment (CE)

| Payoff number | Deception game | | | Dictator game | | | McNemar's test | Subjects who | | | |
|---|---|---|---|---|---|---|---|---|---|---|---|
| | A (truth) | B (lie) | % of lie | A | B | % of B | | Told truth in the deception game and chose A in the dictator game | Told truth in the deception game and chose B in dictator game | Told lie in the deception game and chose A in the dictator game | Told lie in the deception game and chose B in the dictator game |
| 1 (Altruistic) | 53 | 43 | 44.79% | 53 | 43 | 44.79% | $\chi^2(1)=0.00$, $p=1.000$ | 36 (37.50%) | 17 (17.71%) | 17 (17.71%) | 26 (27.08%) |
| 2 (Spiteful) | 63 | 33 | 34.38% | 74 | 22 | 22.92% | $\chi^2(1)=3.67$, $p=0.0555$ | 52 (54.17%) | 11 (11.46%) | 22 (22.92%) | 11 (11.46%) |
| 3 (Selfish 1) | 39 | 57 | 59.38% | 24 | 72 | 75.00% | $\chi^2(1)6.82$, $p=0.0090$ | 15 (15.63%) | 24 (25.00%) | 9 (9.38%) | 48 (50.00%) |
| 4 (Selfish 2) | 31 | 65 | 67.71% | 32 | 64 | 66.67% | $\chi^2(1)=0.04$, $p=0.8348$ | 20 (20.83%) | 11 (11.46%) | 12 (12.50%) | 53 (55.21%) |
| 5 (Selfish 3) | 35 | 61 | 63.54% | 35 | 61 | 63.54% | $\chi^2(1)=0.00$, $p=1.000$ | 21 (21.88%) | 14 (14.58%) | 14 (14.58%) | 47 (48.96%) |

were used in both the deception and the dictator games, and that the same subjects played both games (albeit pairs were randomly shuffled between rounds).

If we find the proportion of subjects who lied in the deception game to be statistically equivalent to the corresponding proportion of subjects who allocated B payoffs in the dictator game for a particular payoff number, we should conclude that the subjects were, on average, indifferent between lying and choosing the B payoffs. If, however, the proportion of subjects who lied in the deception game is smaller than the corresponding proportion of subjects who chose B payoffs in the dictator game for a particular payoff number, we should conclude that the subjects were, on average, lie-averse.

Respective proportions of subjects who lied in the deception game and of those who allocated B payoffs in the dictator game, for all payoff pair combinations, are reported in the fourth and the seventh columns of Table 3. In addition, from 9th column to 12th column of Table 3 provide the numbers (proportions) of all combinations of subjects' behaviors in the deception and the dictator game.

From the fourth and the seventh columns of Table 3, we observe that the proportions of subjects who lied is larger than that of subjects who allocated B payoffs for payoff numbers 2 and 4, but it is smaller for payoff number 3. However, McNemar's tests for the equality of the paired proportion indicate that the difference in the proportion of subjects who lied and that of subjects who chose B payoff is significant only for payoff number 3. We summarize these results in the following:

> Result 1. The proportions of subjects who told lies are not significantly different from the proportions of subjects who chose B payoffs for the payoff numbers 1, 2, 4, and 5.
> Result 2. Subjects were, on average, more likely to choose a selfish payoff allocation in the dictator game than to lie selfishly in the deception game, but only when the payoff difference between senders and receivers is relatively small.

For Result 1, subjects were, on average, indifferent between lying and choosing B payoffs for the payoff numbers 1, 2, 4, and 5. Result 2, in turn, implies that subjects were lie-averse for the weakest one of the three selfish conditions of the experiment, in which the relative payoff difference between senders and receivers is smallest. These results are summarized in Table 4(a). Interestingly, the latter result is not consistent with Gneezy's (2005) findings. In his study, proportions of selfish lies were always significantly smaller than those of selfish dictator payoff allocations.

## 3.2 Conformity in deception

To examine potential conformity effects in deceptive communication, we directly compare senders' choices in the treatment experiments TE to those in the control experiment CE. Recall that senders in the CE did not have any information whatsoever about their peers' choices—their decision environment was fully isolated from any outside influence. Accordingly, if we find the proportions of senders'

**TABLE 4** Summary of the Result

| Hypothesis | | Results | Is the result consistent with the hypothesis? |
|---|---|---|---|
| (a) Hypothesis 1 | Subjects are averse to lying | Subjects are not lie-averse for payoff numbers 1, 2, 4, and 5 (Result 1) | Not consistent |
| | | Subjects are lie-averse for payoff number 3 (Result 2) | Consistent |
| (b) Hypothesis 2 | Subjects tend to conform to others' behaviors | Subjects conform to others' selfish lies, but not to truthful messages in deception game (Result 3) | Partially consistent |
| | | Subjects conform to others' selfish payoff allocations, but not to equal payoff allocations in dictator game (Result 4) | Partially consistent |
| | | Subjects conform to others' truthful messages, but not to altruistic lies in deception game<br>Knowledge of others' behaviors does not affect subjects' choices in dictator game (Result 5) | Partially consistent |
| | | Subjects conform to others' truthful messages, but not to spiteful lies in deception game<br>Knowledge of others' behaviors does not affect subjects' choices in dictator game (Result 6) | Partially consistent |

choices in TEs to be different from those of senders' choices in CE, we should conclude that senders' choices in TEs were influenced by peer information contained in the reference rounds (RR) data graphically summarized and made available for easy reference to senders in TEs.

Specifically, if the proportion of lies messaged in the deception game or the proportion of B payoffs allocated in the dictator game in TEs move toward those in RRs, we should conclude that subjects exhibited *conformist* tendencies with respect to peer behaviors. Should our findings point toward conformist tendency, we will conclude that peer information significantly affects subjects' strategic choices in the deception and dictator games.

Seventh columns in Tables 5 (6) and 7 (8) report on the respective proportions of subjects who lied (chose B payoffs) in the deception game (dictator game) in the TEs. Eighth columns in these same tables report on the proportions of subjects who had lied (had chosen B payoffs) in the RRs of the deception game (dictator game) in CE.

First, let us examine subjects' choices in TE1, wherein peer information revealed that majority of subjects lied in the deception game RRs of previous sessions of the experiment (Table 5[d]). One-tailed tests for the equality of the proportion indicate that the proportion of subjects who lied in TE1 was significantly larger than the corresponding proportion in CE at the 0.05 level for payoff numbers 3 and 4 (two of the "selfish" conditions),

When TE1 subjects were given information pointing to a majority of RR subjects having chosen B payoffs in the dictator game, the proportion of sender subjects who chose B payoffs in TE1 was significantly larger than that in CE for all three "selfish" conditions, i.e., for payoff numbers 3, 4, and 5 (as reported in Table 6) at the 0.05 level.

Next, we examine the results of TE2, wherein peer information from RR data pointed to a majority of sender subjects having been truthful in the CE deception games (Table 7). One-tailed tests for the equality of the proportion indicate that for payoff numbers 1 (the "altruistic" condition) and 2 (the "spiteful" condition), the proportions of subjects who were truthful in TE2 was significantly larger than that in CE at the 0.05 level.

When TE2 sender subjects knew that a large proportion of RR peer subjects had chosen A payoffs in the dictator game, the proportion of subjects who chose A payoffs in TE2 was not significantly different from that in CE for all payoff numbers at the 0.05 level (as reported in Table 8).

In Tables 9 and 10 we summarize all the results on conformist tendencies reported above.

From the results for payoff numbers 3 and 4 in Table 9, we observe that subjects conformed to selfish lies in (a), i.e., in the "unequal" treatment TE1, but did not conform to truthful choices in (b), i.e., in the "equal" treatment TE2. This observation leads to the following result.

Result 3. Sender subjects in the deception game in our treatment experiments exhibited an overall tendency to conform to selfish lies, but not to truthful messages.

---

d. As can be confirmed from Table 2, there were 32 sender subjects in Sessions 7 and 8, and 69 sender subjects in Sessions 9–12. However, total numbers of decisions reported in Tables 5 and 6 for several payoff numbers are less than 32, as are those in Tables 7 and 8 less than 69 for all payoff numbers. This is due to a sudden malfunction of the computer software used in the experiment, which rendered some of sender subjects unable to continue playing the deception/dictator games through all five payoff number conditions. Consequently, we report only results for which data is available for all five payoff number conditions.

**TABLE 5** Conformity in the Deception Game in TE1 (Peer Majority of Senders in RR Lied)

| Payoff number | Deception game (CE) | | | Deception game (TE1) | | | Deception game (RR) | Test for equality of proportions between CE and TE1 |
|---|---|---|---|---|---|---|---|---|
| | A (truth) | B (lie) | % of lie | A (truth) | B (lie) | % of lie | % of lie | |
| 1 (Altruistic) | 53 | 43 | 44.79% | 16 | 16 | 50.00% | 67% | $z=-0.5119$ $p=0.3044$ |
| 2 (Spiteful) | 63 | 33 | 34.38% | 25 | 7 | 21.88% | 52% | $z=1.3212$ $p=0.9068$ |
| 3 (Selfish 1) | 39 | 57 | 59.38% | 7 | 25 | 78.13% | 78% | $z=-1.9144$ $p=0.0278$ |
| 4 (Selfish 2) | 31 | 65 | 67.71% | 3 | 29 | 90.63% | 89% | $z=-2.5419$ $p=0.0055$ |
| 5 (Selfish 3) | 35 | 61 | 63.54% | 8 | 24 | 75.00% | 78% | $z=-1.1885$ $p=0.1173$ |

**TABLE 6** Conformity in the Dictator Game in TE1 (Peer Majority of Dictators in RR Allocated B Payoffs)

| | Dictator game (CE) | | | Dictator game (TE1) | | | Dictator game (RR) | Test for equality of proportions between CE and TE1 |
|---|---|---|---|---|---|---|---|---|
| **Payoff number** | **A** | **B** | **% of B** | **A** | **B** | **% of B** | **% of B** | |
| 1 (Altruistic) | 53 | 43 | 44.79% | 13 | 17 | 56.67% | 53% | $z=-1.1368$ $p=0.1278$ |
| 2 (Spiteful) | 74 | 22 | 22.92% | 25 | 7 | 21.88% | 38% | $z=0.1219$ $p=0.5485$ |
| 3 (Selfish 1) | 24 | 72 | 75.00% | 3 | 28 | 90.32% | 90% | $z=-1.8129$ $p=0.0349$ |
| 4 (Selfish 2) | 32 | 64 | 66.67% | 3 | 27 | 90.00% | 90% | $z=-2.4906$ $p=0.0064$ |
| 5 (Selfish 3) | 35 | 61 | 63.54% | 3 | 27 | 90.00% | 80% | $z=-2.7562$ $p=0.0029$ |

**TABLE 7** Conformity in the Deception Game in TE2 (Peer Majority of Senders in RR Were Truthful)

| Payoff number | Deception game (CE) | | | Deception game (TE2) | | | Deception game (RR) | Test for equality of proportions between CE and TE2 |
|---|---|---|---|---|---|---|---|---|
| | A (truth) | B (lie) | % of lie | A (truth) | B (lie) | % of lie | % of lie | |
| 1 (Altruistic) | 53 | 43 | 44.79% | 45 | 20 | 30.77% | 33% | $z=1.7887$ $p=0.0368$ |
| 2 (Spiteful) | 63 | 33 | 34.38% | 53 | 14 | 20.90% | 11% | $z=1.8692$ $p=0.0308$ |
| 3 (Selfish 1) | 39 | 57 | 59.38% | 25 | 41 | 62.12% | 42% | $z=-0.3513$ $p=0.6373$ |
| 4 (Selfish 2) | 31 | 65 | 67.71% | 22 | 44 | 66.67% | 42% | $z=0.1388$ $p=0.4448$ |
| 5 (Selfish 3) | 35 | 61 | 63.54% | 23 | 44 | 65.67% | 42% | $z=-0.2795$ $p=0.6101$ |

**TABLE 8** Conformity in the Dictator Game in TE2 (Peer Majority of Dictators in RR Allocated A Payoffs)

| | Dictator game (CE) | | | Dictator game (TE2) | | | Dictator game (RR) | Test for equality of proportions between CE and TE2 |
|---|---|---|---|---|---|---|---|---|
| Payoff number | A | B | % of B | A | B | % of B | % of B | |
| 1 (Altruistic) | 53 | 43 | 44.79% | 31 | 26 | 45.61% | 33% | $z=-0.0988$ $p=0.5394$ |
| 2 (Spiteful) | 74 | 22 | 22.92% | 41 | 13 | 23.21% | 17% | $z=-0.0420$ $p=0.5168$ |
| 3 (Selfish 1) | 24 | 72 | 75.00% | 19 | 39 | 67.24% | 67% | $z=1.0399$ $p=0.1492$ |
| 4 (Selfish 2) | 32 | 64 | 66.67% | 26 | 30 | 53.57% | 37% | $z=1.6038$ $p=0.0544$ |
| 5 (Selfish 3) | 35 | 61 | 0.6354 | 19 | 39 | 67.24% | 42% | $z=-0.4662$ $p=0.6795$ |

**TABLE 9 Summary of Treatments: The Deception Game**

| | | Payoff number | Subjects in TE |
|---|---|---|---|
| Peer majority of senders in RR were | (a) liars (Table 5) | 1 (Altruistic) | — |
| | | 2 (Spiteful) | — |
| | | 3 (Selfish 1) | Conformist |
| | | 4 (Selfish 2) | Conformist |
| | | 5 (Selfish 3) | — |
| | (b) truth-tellers (Table 7) | 1 (Altruistic) | Conformist |
| | | 2 (Spiteful) | Conformist |
| | | 3 (Selfish 1) | — |
| | | 4 (Selfish 2) | — |
| | | 5 (Selfish 3) | — |

**TABLE 10 Summary of Treatments: The Dictator Game**

| | | Payoff number | Subjects in TE |
|---|---|---|---|
| Peer majority of dictators in RR allocated | (a) B payoffs (Table 6) | 1 (Altruistic) | — |
| | | 2 (Spiteful) | — |
| | | 3 (Selfish 1) | Conformist |
| | | 4 (Selfish 2) | Conformist |
| | | 5 (Selfish 3) | Conformist |
| | (b) A payoffs (Table 8) | 1 (Altruistic) | — |
| | | 2 (Spiteful) | — |
| | | 3 (Selfish 1) | — |
| | | 4 (Selfish 2) | — |
| | | 5 (Selfish 3) | — |

Result 3 is consistent with Innes and Mitra (2013), in that in their study senders also tended to selfishly lie to receivers whenever the former observed that a large number of other senders had also told selfish lies. Relatedly, conformity in deceptive communication has also been found in Fosgaard et al. (2013), where subjects were more likely to self-interestedly misreport a coin flip result in order to gain more profits whenever they believed that other subjects had also engaged in self-interested misreporting.

For the three "selfish" conditions, i.e., for payoff numbers 3, 4, and 5 in Table 10(a), we verify that subjects conformed to selfish dictator allocations, and that they did not conform to fair allocations for the same payoff numbers in Table 10(b). We summarize these findings in the following.

Result 4. Dictator subjects exhibited, overall, conformist tendencies for selfish payoff allocations, but not for equal payoff allocations.

This observation is consistent with previous experimental studies which focused on the influence of social learning on prosocial behaviors, as for instance in Croson and Shang (2008), Krupka and Weber (2009), Sasaki (2017), Thöni and Gächter (2015), and Zafar (2011). These studies have shown that experimental subjects are, in general, more likely to behave selfishly whenever they can know that their peers had behaved selfishly in similar or identical circumstances.

Results 3 and 4 are summarized in Table 4(b). These results suggest that selfish lies and, more generally, selfish behaviors are contagious. Are then altruistic and spiteful lies and behaviors also contagious?

For the "altruistic" payoff number 1 condition of our treatment experiments, subjects exhibited conformist tendencies for truthful choices, as reported in Table 9(b), but not for altruistic lies, as reported in Table 9(a). In addition, information that the majority of others had allocated payoffs altruistically or not did not influence subjects' behaviors as in payoff number 1 in Table 10(a) and (b). Thus, we obtain the following result.

Result 5. When subjects can know that a peer majority had been honest, they exhibited an overall tendency to conform to truthful choices. However, sender subjects in the deception game, overall, did not conform to altruistic lies when given the information on peer majority having altruistically lied. Moreover, knowing whether others had allocated payoffs altruistically or not did not affect dictators' own allocation choices.

For the "spiteful" payoff number 2 condition in our study, subjects appeared to exhibit overall conformist tendencies toward truthful peer behaviors, as reported in Table 9(b). However, information that the majority of others had allocated payoffs spitefully or not did not influence subjects' behaviors as in Table 10(a) and (b). Thus, we obtain the next result.

Result 6. Sender subjects in the deception game became, on average, less likely to tell spiteful lies when they knew that a peer majority had not told spiteful lies. However, knowing whether or not peers had allocated payoffs spitefully did not influence dictators' own allocation choices.

Results 5 and 6 are summarized in Table 4(b). These results suggest that honest behaviors are contagious in a situation where subjects can tell altruistic/spiteful lies.

For Result 5, it is not consistent with previous studies (Cason and Mui, 1998; Fischbacher et al., 2001; Frey and Meier, 2004; Shang and Croson, 2009), in which the reported consensus was that knowledge of altruistic peer behaviors had an overall amplifying effect on experimental subjects' own altruistic behaviors.

For Result 6, why dis sender subjects conform to others who had not told spiteful lies? A possible explanation lies in a social norm focusing effect, according to which the sheer recognition of other people's spiteful behaviors raises an awareness of the nonspitefulness social norm. As a matter of fact, Cialdini et al. (1990) looked into the influence of social learning on littering in an experimental study and confirmed the existence of a focusing effect, in which observation of others' littering behavior reminded subjects of the nonlittering social norm, whereas the absence of litter in the environment did not. Similarly, Krupka and Weber (2009) found that when subjects knew about the proportion of other subjects who had behaved prosocially in previous experiments, they themselves also became more likely to behave prosocially.

We consider it likely that a similar focusing effect was at work in our experiment. That is, when subjects observed information about others' having behaved nonspitefully in earlier sessions of the experiment, that information might have triggered their attention to focus on the existence of a social norm of not being spiteful toward others. Once subjects became conscious of the norm, they would turn reluctant to be spiteful toward others and come to eschew making spiteful choices themselves.

## 3.3 Inequality aversion

Our results point to the existence of conformist tendencies in various strategic situations. To investigate how the knowledge of others' behaviors affects subjects' own behaviors, we need to take a closer look at the relationship between social peer information and subjects' allocational preferences, in both the deception game and the dictator game. As lying in the deception game (allocating B payoffs in the dictator game) engenders payoff inequality between the senders and the receivers, whereas being truthful in the deception game (allocating A payoffs in the dictator game) does not, we conjecture that having access to information on peers' choices might have influenced subjects' preferences for payoff inequalities.

Before investigating these possibilities, we look at how subjects might have evaluated payoff inequalities when they did not know anything about their peers' choices.

### *3.3.1 Inequality aversion in the control experiment*

To examine how subjects might have valued payoff inequalities in CE, we consider Fehr and Schmidt's (1999) inequality aversion model. The Fehr and Schmidt (1999) model assumes that people dislike differences in monetary rewards between an individual and their counterpart. Their simple model is capable of accounting for a wide body of experimental results, in particular those concerning ultimatum games and dictator games.[e] Sender subjects in those games tend to allocate positive payoff amounts to the receiver subjects, even though standard economic models cannot explain those results. Many other experimental studies also have reported that subjects tend to dislike both disadvantageous (to themselves) payoff inequalities (Casal et al., 2012; Eisenkopf and Teyssier, 2013; Zizzo and Oswald, 2001) and advantageous payoff inequalities (Yang et al., 2016).

These results imply that Fehr and Schmidt's (1999) model might explain a variety of experimental results involving payoff inequalities. Can the Fehr and Schmidt's (1999) model also explain our subjects' strategic choices in CE? We now turn to a straightforward examination of this postulate, in which we use a two-player version of their inequality aversion model.

Let $x_S$, and $x_R$ denote the payoff amounts for the sender and receiver, respectively. Then, a utility function of an inequality-averse sender can be written as

$$u(x_S, x_R) = x_S - \alpha \max\{x_R - x_S, 0\} - \beta \max\{x_S - x_R, 0\} \quad (1)$$

where $\alpha > 0$ and $1 \geq \beta > 0$ are parameters which capture the magnitude of disutility experienced from a payoff inequality disadvantageous to the sender (envy) and from a payoff inequality advantageous to the sender (guilt), respectively.[f]

In order to examine whether CE subjects were in fact averse to the payoff inequality, we need to check whether the utility function in (1) can explain the experimental results obtained in CE.

For payoff pair combination number 1, if senders were truthful in the deception game (choose A payoffs in the dictator game), then their payoffs amounted to JPY 1200. On the other hand, if they lied (chose B), then their resultant payoffs were $u(x_S, x_R) = 1200 - 400\alpha$. As reported in Tables 3, majority of subjects were in fact truthful (chose A payoffs). Presumably, they evaluated $1200 > 1200 - 400\alpha$, which suggests $\alpha > 0$. This result is consistent with Fehr and Schmidt's (1999) model.

For the payoff pair combination number 2 in CE, majority of subjects were again truthful (chose A payoffs). Presumably, they evaluated $1200 > 1200 - 400\beta$, suggesting $\beta > 0$. This is also consistent with Fehr and Schmidt (1999).

For payoff pair combinations 3, 4, and 5, majority of subjects lied (chose B payoffs) in CE. They presumably evaluated $1200 < 1600 - 800\beta$ and thus $\beta < 1/2$ for payoff number 3, $1200 < 1800 - 1400\beta$ and thus $\beta < 3/7$ for payoff number 4, and $1200 < 2000 - 2000\beta$ and thus $\beta < 2/5$ for payoff number 5. These results are again consistent with Fehr and Schmidt (1999). The discussions above are summarized in the following result.

e. For example, Fehr and Schmidt's (1999) model is capable of explaining ultimatum game experimental results in Roth et al. (1991) and the dictator game results in Forsythe et al. (1994).

f. Similarly to Goeree and Holt (2000), we use the term 'guilt' to mean disutility from receiving a payoff larger than others. Note that we do not use this term to mean disutility from failing to meet others' expectations (e.g., Charness and Dufwenberg, 2006).

Result 7. Choices made by the majority of subjects in the control experiment were consistent with the model of inequality aversion.

### 3.3.2 *Inequality aversion in the treatment experiments*

Sender subjects/dictators in TE1 had information about the percentages of their peers who had lied in the deception game (chose unequal B payoffs in the dictator game). Opportunity to know the actual proportions of unequal payoff allocations chosen under identical circumstances by others might have influenced how payoff inequalities between the senders and the receivers were experienced in subjects' latent utility functions. Accordingly, we introduce additional parameters $\gamma$ and $\delta$ to capture potential effects peer information might have exerted on subjects' inequality aversion. We rewrite the utility function in (1) as.

$$\mathrm{u}(x_S, x_R) = x_S - (\alpha + \gamma)\max\{x_R - x_S, 0\} - (\beta + \delta)\max\{x_S - x_R, 0\} \quad (1')$$

where $\gamma$ and δ represent the effects of peer information on envy and guilt, respectively, and analyze subjects' choices under the assumption that they had the utility function in (1′).

In Table 5 (6), we reported that majority of subjects in TE1 communicated selfish lies (chose B payoffs) for payoff pair combinations 3, 4, and 5. This implies that subjects evaluated $1200 < 1600 - 800(\beta + \delta)$ and thus $\delta + \beta < \frac{1}{2}$ for payoff number 3, $1200 < 1800 - 1400(\beta + \delta)$ and thus $\delta + \beta < \frac{3}{7}$ for payoff number 4, and $1200 < 2000 - 2000(\beta + \delta)$ and thus $\delta + \beta < \frac{2}{5}$ for payoff number 5. On the other hand, we have also found that subjects' "guilt" parameters in CE were $\beta < \frac{1}{2}$, $\beta < \frac{3}{7}$, and $\beta < \frac{2}{5}$ in Result 7. Note also that the proportions of lie messages (B payoffs) in TE1 tended to be greater than the respective proportions in CE, whenever subjects knew their peers in RRs lied (chose B payoffs) as seen in Results 3 and 4. These results reflect the fact that subjects were relatively more likely to lie (choose B payoffs) in TE1 than in CE, as the value of $\beta + \delta$ in TE1 is necessarily smaller than that of $\beta$ in CE (under the implicit assumption that the $\beta$ values for subjects in TE1 are equal or nearly equal to CE subjects' $\beta$ values). This reasoning leads to $\delta + \beta < \beta < \frac{1}{2}$, $\delta + \beta < \beta < \frac{3}{7}$, and to $\delta + \beta < \beta < \frac{2}{5}$. Thus, we interpret Results 3 and 4 as implying that knowledge of peer majority having selfishly lied (having chosen B payoffs) for payoff pair combination numbers 3, 4, and 5 reduced subjects' guilt.

We now turn to the "equal" treatment TE2. Proportion of dictators who chose A payoffs in TE2 was not different from the proportion who chose A in CE, as seen above in Result 4. Thus, the $\beta + \delta$ value in TE2 had to be the same as that of $\beta$ in CE, even when subjects knew that majority of others had been truthful (chose A payoffs) for payoff combinations 3, 4, and 5. Hence, we obtain the following result.

Result 8. Knowing that a peer majority had selfishly lied (had chosen selfish payoff allocations) tended to reduce subjects' guilt.

From Table 7, we readily confirm that majority of TE2 subjects were truthful for the altruistic payoff combination number 1. This implies that subjects evaluated $1200 > 1200 - 400(\alpha + \gamma)$ and thus $\alpha + \gamma > 0$. On the other hand, we have also seen that the "envy" parameter in subjects' utility functions in CE was $\alpha > 0$. We also saw that the proportion of truthful messages in TE2 was greater than that in CE whenever sender subjects knew that a large number of senders in RR sent truthful messages, as seen in Result 5. This presumably reflects the fact that subjects were more likely to behave truthfully in TE2 as opposed to CE because the value of $\alpha + \gamma$ in TE was greater than that of $\alpha$ in CE, which implies that $\alpha + \gamma > \alpha > 0$. We thus interpret Result 5 as pointing to subjects' growing envy whenever they knew that majority of their peers did not lie altruistically.

The proportion of sender subjects who lied altruistically in TE1, on the other hand, was not significantly larger than that in CE, as reported in Result 5. Thus, $\alpha + \gamma$ in TE1 does not differ from $\alpha$ in CE, even when subjects knew that majority of their peer sender subjects had sent deceptive altruistic messages.

Additionally, the proportion of dictators who chose B payoffs in TE was not significantly different from that in CE, as seen in Result 5. Thus, the $\alpha + \gamma$ value in TE has to be the same as that of $\alpha$ in CE for payoff pair combination number 1, in the dictator game. Hence, we obtain the following result.

Result 9. Knowing that a peer majority had not told altruistic lies raises subjects' envy.

From Table 7, we have seen that majority of subjects in TE2 were truthful for the "spiteful" payoff combination number 2. This implies that subjects evaluated $1200 > 1200 - 400(\beta + \delta)$ and thus $\beta + \delta > 0$. On the other hand, we have also seen that subjects' "guilt" parameter in CE was $\beta > 0$. We also have seen that the proportions of senders who were truthful in TE2 were greater than that in CE when senders knew that their peers in RR had not lied spitefully, as seen in Result 6. This result, presumably, reflects the fact that subjects were more likely to be honest in TE2 compared to CE, as the value of $\beta + \delta$ in TE2 is always greater than that of $\beta$ in CE. This, in turn, implies $\beta + \delta > \beta > 0$. We therefore interpret Result 6 as implying that when subjects knew that majority of others had not told spiteful lies, their guilt grew larger.

On the other hand, the proportions of dictator subjects who chose B payoffs in TE1 and in TE2 were not significantly different from those in CE, as we have gathered in Result 6. Thus, the value of $\beta + \delta$ in TE is equal to that of $\beta$ in CE for payoff pair combination number 2 in the dictator game. Hence, we obtain the following result.

Result 10. Knowing that a peer majority had not told spiteful lies raises subjects' guilt.

Result 10 implies that at least for some subjects, feelings of guilt were amplified once they knew that others had not told spiteful lies in the deception game. We conjecture that this is due to it being rather difficult for subjects to recognize that spiteful lies induce payoff inequality without knowing that some others had in fact lied spitefully. Conversely, we have seen that subjects' guilt did not differ between TE and CE in the dictator game. This could be attributed to the fact that it was rather easy to find out that choosing to allocate B payoffs would induce payoff inequality in the dictator game.

In Section 3.2, we pointed out the possibility that a focusing effect could be at work in the deception game for the "spiteful" payoff combination number 2 condition. We point out here that the same focusing effect is consistent with Result 10 as well. For subjects who could not easily recognize that spiteful lying induced payoff inequality unless they knew of their peers' spiteful lies, their guilt increased from $\beta$ to $\beta+\delta$ when they knew that their peers had not told spiteful lies in the TE deception game. Once guilt has grown to $\beta+\delta$, it could trigger the focusing effect on the social norm of nonspitefulness, so that subject then chose to be truthful in the payoff combination number 2 "spiteful" condition.

## 4. Conclusions

Through straightforward comparisons of subjects' strategic communication and dictator choices in a control experiment (CE) and in two treatment experiments (TE1 and TE2), this study examined whether and how social information on peer choices influenced subjects' own strategic choices.

In the control experiment, we have found that subjects exhibited lie-aversion for selfish lies only when the relative payoff difference between sender and receiver subjects was small. In our treatments, we have found that subjects exhibited conformist tendencies for selfish lies in the deception game as well as for selfish payoff allocations in the dictator game. In addition, we observe that subjects tended to be truthful when they saw that their peer majority had been truthful in apparent reluctance to altruistically lie. We have also found that subjects tended to be truthful when they knew that the peer majority had not told spiteful lies.

These results imply that information about one's peers' strategic choices might influence subjects' deceptive communication and dictator behaviors in various ways. Using the inequality aversion model of Fehr and Schmidt (1999), we interpret these experimental results as implying that having access to information about one's peer having behaved selfishly might reduce subjects' feelings of guilt, and conversely, knowing that one's peers did not altruistically lie to benefit others might increase subjects' feelings of envy. Additionally, knowing that others had not told spiteful lies also appears to potentially increase one's own feelings of guilt.

The present study does not come without limitations, in that we cannot claim to be able to explain why it is that knowledge of spiteful lying on the part of one's peers appears to amplify one's guilt feelings, whereas knowledge of peer's selfish lying appears to appease guilt. These questions present an important research avenue for future experiments, in which the mechanisms that relate conformist tendencies in strategic interactions to social preferences should be examined in more detail.

# Appendix Experiment instructions (translated from Japanese)

## Instructions for Experiment 1[g]

In Experiment 1, first you will be randomly paired with another subject by the computer. Then, you will be randomly assigned a role—either "sender" or "receiver."

The sender's task will be to privately observe a payoff number on the computer screen, and then to send a message about the observed payoff number to the receiver. The receiver cannot observe the actual payoff number. They can only observe the message received from the sender. The receiver will then be asked to report the payoff number conveyed in the sender's message.

The money payoffs to be paid to the sender and to the receiver will depend on *whether or not the payoff number reported by the receiver matches the actual payoff number privately observed by the sender.*

## Your role

Before the first round of the experiment starts, you will be randomly assigned a role—either a sender or a receiver—and randomly paired with another subject to form a sender–receiver pair. Your assigned role will be communicated to you on the computer screen. You will not know the identity of the person with whom you are paired, neither during nor after the experiment.

Your task will be to make decisions as per your assigned role for five rounds. During these five rounds, your role (sender or receiver) will not change, but the subjects with whom you will be paired will randomly change in each round.

## [Instruction to the sender] Payoff number, payoff combination, and message

The sender will be communicated a payoff number. There will be five payoff numbers, from 1 through 5. The sender will observe one number in each of the five rounds of Experiment 1. Each payoff number corresponds to a different combination of sender's and receiver's payoffs. The sender will be informed of these payoff combinations. If you are assigned a sender role, make sure to check the following information:

- The sender's and the receiver's payoffs in case the receiver's report matches the actual payoff number you observe on the computer screen;
- The sender's and the receiver's payoffs in case the receiver's report does not match the actual payoff number you observe on the computer screen.

After checking the above information, you will be asked to choose a message which will be sent to the receiver.

g. In these instructions, we refer the deception game as "Experiment 1", and to the dictator game as "Experiment 2".

*Note*: The sender's and receiver's payoff combination varies with the payoff number. However, the receiver cannot observe the payoff numbers, nor can they observe the corresponding payoff combinations.

Your payoff number is: 1

You should now choose a message about the above number to be sent to the receiver.

If the receiver's report matches the above number,
you will be paid ¥1200, and the receiver will be paid ¥1200.
If the receiver's report does not match the above number,
you will be paid ¥1400, and the receiver will be paid ¥1800.

Please choose the message to be sent to the receiver.
○ The number I had observed was 1.
○ The number I had observed was 2.
○ The number I had observed was 3.
○ The number I had observed was 4.
○ The number I had observed was 5.
[Send]

(A sample computer screen displayed to the sender. The payoff combinations in this sample will not be actually used in the experiment.)

## [Instructions for the receiver] checking the sender's message and reporting the number

The message chosen by the sender will appear on the receiver's computer screen. If you are assigned a receiver role, your task will be to check the sender's message and to submit a report, as in the sample screen below.

Message from the sender:
"The number I observed in this round was 2."

Please choose the report to submit in this round:
○ The number the sender had observed was 1.
○ The number the sender had observed was 2.
○ The number the sender had observed was 3.
○ The number the sender had observed was 4.
○ The number the sender had observed was 5.
[Send]

## [Instructions to both the sender and to the receiver] payoff allocations

Your payoffs will depend on the number privately observed by the sender and on the number reported by the receiver.

The payoff number observed by the sender, the number conveyed in the sender's message, the number reported by the receiver, as well as sender's and receiver's payoffs will be displayed on the sender's computer screen, as in the sample below.

Results – Round 1

| Payoff number | Sender's message | Receiver's report | Sender's payoff | Receiver's payoff |
|---|---|---|---|---|
| 1 | 2 | 2 | 1400 | 1800 |

Continue to the next round

On the receiver's computer screen, only the sender's and receiver's payoffs will be displayed, as illustrated below.

Results – Round 1

| Sender's payoff | Receiver's payoff |
|---|---|
| 1400 | 1800 |

Continue to the next round

This will conclude each round of Experiment 1. The above procedures will be repeated five times, from Round 1 through to Round 5. During these five rounds, your role (either sender or receiver) will not change, but the subjects with whom you will be paired will be randomly shuffled in each round.

*Note*: The receiver cannot observe the payoff numbers, nor can they observe the payoff combinations. However, the final payoffs to both the sender and to the receiver are determined by the content of the receiver's report.

## Instruction for Experiment 2

In Experiment 2, you will again be randomly paired with another subject by the computer. Then, you will be randomly assigned a role—either "sender" or "receiver."

The sender's task is to observe a payoff combination and allocate the payoffs between the sender and the receiver. The receiver's sole task is to endorse the sender's allocation decision.

## Your role

Before the first round of the experiment starts, you will be randomly assigned a role—either a sender or a receiver—and randomly paired with another subject to form a sender–receiver pair. Your assigned role will be communicated to you on the computer screen. You will not know the identity of the person with whom you are paired, neither during nor after the experiment.

Your task will be to make decisions as per your assigned role for five rounds. During these five rounds, your role (sender or receiver) will not change, but the subjects with whom you will be paired will randomly change in each round.

## [Instructions to the sender] allocating payoffs

If you are assigned a sender role, you will be communicated two pairs of payoff combinations, as in the sample screen below. The receiver cannot observe those payoff combinations. Senders should make sure to check the following information:

– The payoffs to the sender and the receiver.

After checking the above information, you will be asked to select one of the payoff combinations, as in the sample screen below.

Please choose one of the following payoff combinations:

O The sender's payoff: ¥1200, The receiver's payoff: ¥1200

O The sender's payoff: ¥1400, The receiver's payoff: ¥1800

Send

## [Instructions for the receiver] endorsing sender's allocation decision

If you are assigned a receiver role, the payoff combination selected by the sender will be communicated to you, as in the sample screen below. You task is to simply check the payoff amounts and click the OK button.

Please confirm the following payoffs:

The sender's payoff: ¥1400, The receiver's payoff: ¥1800

OK

## [Instructions to both the sender and to the receiver] payoff allocations

Check the final payoffs for this round and click "Continue to the next round."

Results – Round 1

| Sender's payoff | Receiver's payoff |
|---|---|
| 1400 | 1800 |

Continue to the next round

This will conclude each round of Experiment 2. The above procedures will be repeated five times, from Round 1 through to Round 5. During these five rounds, your role (either sender or receiver) will not change, but the subjects with whom you will be paired will be randomly shuffled in each round.

*Note*: The payoffs to both the sender and the receiver are determined entirely by the sender's choice. The receiver cannot observe the payoff combinations other than the final payoffs.

## Acknowledgement

This study is supported by JSPS KAKENHI Grant Number 50423158.

## References

Casal, S., Güth, W., Jia, M., Ploner, M., 2012. Would you mind if I get more? An experimental study of the envy game. J. Econ. Behav. Organ. 84 (3), 857–865.

Cason, T.N., Mui, V.L., 1998. Social influence in the sequential dictator game. J. Math. Psychol. 42, 248–265.

Charness, G., Dufwenberg, M., 2006. Promises and partnership. Econometrica 74 (6), 1579–1601.

Childs, J., 2012. Gender differences in lying. Econ. Lett. 114, 147–149.

Cialdini, R., Reno, R., Kallgren, C.A., 1990. A focus theory of normative conduct: recycling the concept of norms to reduce littering in public places. J. Pers. Soc. Psychol. 58, 1015–1026.

Croson, R., Shang, J., 2008. The impact of downward social information on contribution decisions. Exp. Econ. 11, 221–233.

Dreber, A., Johannesson, M., 2008. Gender differences in deception. Econ. Lett. 99, 197–199.

Eisenkopf, G., Teyssier, S., 2013. Envy and loss aversion in tournaments. J. Econ. Psychol. 34, 240–255.

Erat, S., Gneezy, U., 2012. White lies. Manag. Sci. 58 (4), 723–733.

Fehr, E., Schmidt, K.M., 1999. A theory of fairness, competition, and cooperation. Q. J. Econ. 114 (3), 817–868.

Fischbacher, U., Gächter, S., Fehr, E., 2001. Are people conditionally cooperative? Evidence from a public goods experiment. Econ. Lett. 71, 397–404.

Forsythe, R., Horowitz, N.E., Savin, L.H., Sefton, M., 1994. Fairness in simple bargaining games. Games Econ. Behav., 347–369.

Fosgaard, T.R., Hansen, L.G., Piovesan, M., 2013. Separating will from grace: an experiment on conformity and awareness in cheating. J. Econ. Behav. Organ. 93, 279–284.

Frey, B., Meier, S., 2004. Social comparisons and pro-social behaviour: testing "conditional cooperation" in a field experiment. Am. Econ. Rev. 94, 1717–1722.

Gneezy, U., 2005. Deception: the role of consequences. Am. Econ. Rev. 95, 384–394.

Goeree, J., Holt, C.A., 2000. Asymmetric inequality aversion and noisy behavior in alternating-offer bargaining games. Eur. Econ. Rev. 44, 1079–1089.

Gylfason, H.F., Arnardottir, A.A., Kristinsson, K., 2013. More on gender difference on lying. Econ. Lett. 119, 94–96.

Innes, R., Mitra, A., 2013. Is dishonesty contagious? Econ. Inq. 51 (1), 722–734.

Krupka, E., Weber, R.A., 2009. The focusing and informational effects of norms on pro-social behavior. J. Econ. Psychol. 30, 107–320.

López-Pérez, R., Spiegelman, E., 2012. Do economists lie more?. Working papers in economic theory in Universidad Autónoma de Madrid, Department of Economic Analysis (Economic Theory and Economic History).

Lundquist, T., Ellingsen, T., Gribbe, E., Johannesson, M., 2009. The aversion to lying. J. Econ. Behav. Organ. 70 (1–2), 81–92.

Roth, A.E., Prasnikar, V., Okuno-Fujiwara, M., Zamir, S., 1991. Bargaining and market behavior in Jerusalem, Ljubljana, Pittsburgh, and Tokyo: an experimental study. Am. Econ. Rev., 81 (5), 1068–1095.

Sasaki, S., 2017. Observing descriptive social norm and conformity: experimental evidence. J. Behav. Econ. Financ. 10, 81–94.

Shang, J., Croson, R., 2009. A field experiment in charitable contribution: the impact of social information on the voluntary provision of public goods. Econ. J. 119, 1422–1438.

Sutter, M., 2009. Deception through telling the truth?! Experimental evidence from individuals and teams. Econ. J. 119, 47–60.

Thöni, C., Gächter, S., 2015. Peer effects and social preference in voluntary cooperation: a theoretical and experimental analysis. J. Econ. Psychol. 48, 72–88.

Yang, Y., Onderstal, S., Schram, A., 2016. Inequality aversion revisited. J. Econ. Psychol. 54, 1–16.

Zafar, B., 2011. An experimental investigation of why individuals conform. Eur. Econ. Rev. 55, 774–798.

Zizzo, D.J., Oswald, A., 2001. Are people willing to pay to reduce others' incomes? Ann. Econ. Stat. (63–64), 39–65.

Section 4

# Dishonesty in daily life

Chapter 4.1

# Fare-dodging in the lab and the moral cost of dishonesty

Zhixin Dai[a,b], Fabio Galeotti[b], Marie Claire Villeval[b,c]

[a]*China Financial Policy Research Center, School of Finance, Renmin University of China, Beijing, China,* [b]*Univ Lyon, CNRS, GATE, UMR5824, Ecully, France,* [c]*IZA, Bonn, Germany*

**Chapter Outline**



**JEL Classification:** C91, D83, K42

## 1. Introduction

Dishonesty is a worldwide problem and examples abound in every sector, including corruption of the political class, embezzlement of international aid, doping in sports, cheating at exams, or tax evasion. Although much less spectacular, the everyday lies and deceits of ordinary people are also particularly pervasive and detrimental for the society, even if they seem innocuous at first sight. Fare-dodging in public transport illustrates such ordinary dishonesty. Many people consider that not paying their fare in a bus or a tram does not constitute a serious offense; however, this misconduct results in huge losses every year for public transport companies in many countries (e.g., Cour des Comptes, 2016; Donohue, 2010; Fürst, 2012). It is thus important from an economic perspective to understand better the monetary and non-monetary factors that determine an individual's willingness to pay or not his/her fare. In this chapter we report the results of a framed laboratory experiment that was designed to measure the moral costs of fare-dodging with respect to the size of fraud and the impact of deterrent incentives, such as the probability of an inspection and the level of fines, on the individuals' decision to evade fares.

**Dishonesty in Behavioral Economics. https://doi.org/10.1016/B978-0-12-815857-9.00004-2**

Using experimental methods to study ordinary dishonesty such as fare-dodging is promising. Indeed, although fraud in daily life is widespread, it is very difficult in this domain to study the determinants of individuals' behavior using observational data. People are usually afraid or uncomfortable to reveal their misdeeds and dishonest actions in surveys. On the other hand, official statistics based on petty crimes detected by an enforcement authority suffer from selection biases and many unobservable factors are beyond the control of the researcher. Experimental methods offer a powerful tool for identifying causal relationships between some factors and observed dishonesty in a controlled environment. This explains why studies on dishonesty have boomed in social sciences. Important contributions have been made to understand which contextual and social factors promote or hamper dishonesty (e.g., Ayal et al., 2016), and which economic and psychological mechanisms explain dishonest behavior in the lab (e.g., Abeler et al., 2019; Gneezy et al., 2018; Mazar et al., 2008; for surveys, see, e.g., Dhami, 2017; Irlenbusch and Villeval, 2015; Jacobsen et al., 2018; Rosenbaum et al., 2014).

However, a general critique related to laboratory experiments is their artificiality, which might limit the generalizability of the results to real world settings. The significance of this criticism is still debated in the profession (see, e.g., Falk and Heckman, 2009; Fréchette and Schotter, 2015; Levitt and List, 2007) even if more and more evidence from lab-field comparisons seems to support the generalizability of the lab results to the field, at least in terms of directional effects (see Camerer, 2015). This critique is of particular concern when studying cheating for several reasons. First, in the lab subjects may feel scrutinized and this might discourage their willingness to cheat if they want to maintain a positive social image. Second, contextual factors are different inside and outside the lab, and they might trigger dissimilar responses to cheating incentives. Third, lab experiments are conducted with volunteers (usually students) who might have higher prosocial concerns than non-volunteers, and therefore, be less willing to cheat. From a policy perspective, it is thus important to investigate the extent to which the results obtained in the lab can be used to understand fare evasion in the field.

In this chapter, we introduce a public transportation game and experimental procedures that allow us to explore whether fraudulent behavior in the lab is related to fare-dodging in real life, thus testing the external validity of lab findings on small-scale dishonesty. We invited passengers of the public transport service in Lyon (France) with diverse socio-demographic characteristics to participate. Our design enables us to identify, among these participants, those who fare-dodge in real life and those who do not, and link this information with their behavior in the game. This protocol allows us to study the dishonesty of ordinary people at the individual level in a context in which the level of stakes is comparable between the lab and real-world settings.

This chapter provides several contributions. First, we add to the debate about the generalizability of lab findings on dishonesty to the field. Recent contributions in this direction have been made by scholars using specific populations (e.g., open air sellers in List (2009); graders in Armantier and Boly (2013);

bankers in Cohn et al. (2014); prisoners in Cohn et al. (2015); milkmen in Kröll and Rustagi (2016); university students in Potters and Stoop (2016); nurses in Hanna and Wang (2017); pupils in Cohn and Maréchal (2018)). An exception is Dai et al. (2018) who enrolled passengers of public transport that represent a diversified sample of individuals from the general population. All these studies find a positive correlation between cheating in the lab and in the field. In this chapter we provide additional results obtained within the context of the same lab-in-the-field experiment reported in Dai et al. (2018) but which were not included in the original publication. We here focus on behavior in a contextualized task—the public transportation game—where subjects decide to buy or not a ticket for various distances covered by a fictional bus. While Dai et al. (2018) only considered the first round of this game where there was no probability of being inspected, we here analyze also the results of the subsequent rounds where we introduced various probabilities of being controlled and fines.

The second contribution of this chapter is investigating, both for fraudsters and non-fraudsters in real life, how the intrinsic cost of cheating in the game varies with the size of fraud. In our framed experiment, the size of fraud is represented by the distance traveled without a ticket. It is measured in two alternative ways.[a] One measure concerns the payoff dimension, and it is captured by the fact that the monetary benefit of using the bus increases with the distance traveled (which decreases the relative gain of fraud). According to the payoff dimension, not buying the ticket when the benefit of using the bus is bigger is a more dishonest act than when the benefit is smaller because the relative gain of cheating is smaller. A second measure concerns the outcome dimension. It is captured by the distance between the departure point and the final destination, irrespective of the monetary incentives associated to the distance traveled. If the intrinsic cost of cheating is connected to the outcome dimension, we should expect participants to behave more dishonestly for short journeys. This is because the final destination is closer to the departure point and, therefore, not buying the ticket can be seen as a smaller fraud. To isolate the outcome dimension from the payoff dimension we ran two treatments. In the Variable treatment, the benefit increases in the distance traveled. Hence, both the payoff and outcome dimensions are relevant. In the Constant treatment, the benefit is held constant across distances and thus, only the outcome dimension matters. We are aware of only one experimental study (i.e., Gneezy et al., 2018) that compares the payoff and the outcome dimensions of dishonesty.[b] Differently from us, they vary the

a. Gneezy et al. (2018) identify three measures of the size of a lie: the payoff dimension, the outcome dimension, and the likelihood dimension. Here, the likelihood dimension does not apply since the game is not strategic (there is no uncertainty regarding whether a subject behaves honestly or not).

b. Lundquist et al. (2009) investigated in a sender–receiver game whether lying aversion depends on the outcome dimension of the size of the lie (measured as the distance between a lie and the truth) but they ignore the payoff dimension. Using a dice game in which only one target number triggers payoff, Hilbig and Hessler (2013) showed that the likelihood of lying is a decreasing function of the distance between the truth and the lie. They do not manipulate the payoff dimension either.

outcome dimension across treatments but not the payoff dimension. We do the opposite: we vary the payoff dimension (i.e., whether the payoffs are increasing or constant in the distance traveled) and keep constant the outcome dimension.

Finally, our third contribution is to study whether and how real fraudsters and non-fraudsters react to a series of deterrence policies where we vary the probability of being inspected and the amount of the fine. This enables us to test Becker's (1968) deterrence hypothesis according to which dishonest behavior can be decreased with appropriate incentives. By running our experiment with a diversified pool of passengers of the public transport for which deterrence policies are directly relevant, we offer a new perspective to the experimental literature on deterrence which is mainly based on experiments conducted with university students (for an exception with prison inmates, see Khadjavi, 2018).

Our results show that dishonesty in the laboratory correlates with fare evasion in real life, i.e., actual fare-dodgers cheat significantly more in all the experimental conditions compared to non-fare-dodgers. We also find that individuals have a moral cost of cheating that depends on the distance traveled independently of the relative monetary benefit of the fraud and of the monetary cost of its detection. In other words, in the context of our game the size of a fraud increases the moral cost of acting dishonestly in terms of outcome but not in terms of payoffs. Finally, we find clear evidence that deterrence works for ordinary people: both fraudsters and non-fraudsters in real life respond to changes in the detection probability, uncertainty, and severity of the punishment in the game, and this effect is stronger among real fare-dodgers.

In the remainder of this chapter, Section 2 describes the experimental design and the procedures, and presents our conjectures. Section 3 reports the experimental results while Section 4 concludes.

## 2. Experimental design, procedures, and predictions

We first introduce our experimental design and our behavioral conjectures. Then, we present the procedures and finally, our method for identifying fraudsters in real life.

### 2.1 Experimental design

The experiment is divided in several parts. Part 1 consists of some standard experimental procedures to elicit risk and ambiguity attitudes in both gains and losses domains.[c] Part 2 is a die-under-cup task to elicit subjects' proneness to lying (Fischbacher and Föllmi-Heusi, 2013; Shalvi et al., 2011). Part 3 consists

c. We adopted the method developed by Eckel and Grossman (2008) and extended in Eckel et al. (2012). Subjects make four consecutive lottery choices among six gambles in each lottery. Each gamble is a 50–50 chances to win (lose) €$X$ or €$Y$. The six gambles increase in both expected return and risk. The first (second) lottery choice involves gambles in the gain (loss) domain. In the third and fourth lottery, we introduce ambiguity both in the gain and loss domain, respectively. See Dai et al. (2018) for details.

of a public transportation game that we describe below. In Part 4, subjects play a dynamic public transportation game in which we manipulate the concentration vs randomization of inspections. Before being paid, participants also completed a socio-demographic questionnaire including questions on age, gender, income category, status, residence. For the purpose of this chapter, we only consider Part 3. The results of the other parts are reported in two companion studies (Dai et al., 2017, 2018).

We now describe the public transportation game. This game was described to the participants as the choice of buying or not a ticket to use a fictional bus in order to reach one of seven possible destinations on the same line. Introducing context aimed at maximizing the ecological validity of the task (Fréchette, 2015), but also at facilitating the comprehension of the instructions (recall that our participants have very diverse socio-economic and educational backgrounds). Each destination corresponds to a subsequent stop of the bus. This means that to reach a certain destination, the bus goes through all the preceding stops. Participants played five rounds of the public transportation game under different deterrent incentives. Before beginning the first round, participants were endowed with €8 to cover potential losses. This endowment was attributed only at the beginning of the stage and not for each round. For the payment, only one round, chosen at random, was relevant.

The transportation game was played under the strategy method. In each round, every participant made the decision to buy or not a ticket for each of the seven possible destinations (stops 1–7), knowing that only one round may count for determining the subjects' earnings. The cost of a ticket was €1.70, regardless of the destination (equivalent to the actual price of a ticket in Lyon at the time the experiment was run). Participants were told that there are benefits from using the bus (we explained them in terms of time saved) and these were paid in euros to the subjects at the end of the experiment. Between subjects, we varied the payment scheme in two treatments. In the Variable treatment, the benefit increased by €2 for each destination, starting at €2 for stop 1 up to €14 for stop 7. In the Constant treatment, the benefit was held constant across distances and was equal to €8. The expected benefit was the same in the two treatments. Fig. 1 reproduces the decision screen faced by a subject in the Variable treatment.

Within subjects, we varied the conditions of inspection in each of the five rounds, always played in the same order. In the first round of the game—No-Inspection (NI) condition—participants were informed that there was no inspection on the line. So, they could cheat without fearing a punishment. In the following rounds, we introduced random inspections and fines. In round 2 (condition P20), there was a probability of 20% that an inspection takes place. The inspection could occur at any stop but it was made common knowledge that participants could not be inspected more than once on the line. This means that *ex ante* the probability of being inspected increases with the distance traveled (recall that the bus stops at each destination). If an inspection took place and the participant was inspected and found without a ticket, her/his endowment was

| Your final destination | Euros gained thanks to the saved time | Your decision | |
|---|---|---|---|
| 1 | €2 | Ticket €1.7 | No ticket |
| 2 | €4 | Ticket €1.7 | No ticket |
| 3 | €6 | Ticket €1.7 | No ticket |
| 4 | €8 | Ticket €1.7 | No ticket |
| 5 | €10 | Ticket €1.7 | No ticket |
| 6 | €12 | Ticket €1.7 | No ticket |
| 7 | €14 | Ticket €1.7 | No ticket |

Journey

**FIG. 1** Decision screen in the Variable treatment.

reduced by the price of the ticket and a fine of €4.[d] In round 3 (condition P50), the probability of inspection was raised to 50%. In round 4 (condition P20P50), we tested how participants react to uncertainty by telling them that the probability of inspection was either 20% or 50% (the actual probability was determined by the program based on a 50–50 random draw). The last round (condition H_P20P50) was identical to the previous one, except that the amount of the fine was doubled (€8). Table 1 summarizes the main features of each round.

**TABLE 1** Timeline of the Transportation Game

| Round | Condition | Probability of inspection | Fine |
|---|---|---|---|
| 1 | NI | 0 | €0 |
| 2 | P20 | 20% | €4 |
| 3 | P50 | 50% | €4 |
| 4 | P20P50 | 20% or 50% | €4 |
| 5 | H_P20P50 | 20% or 50% | €8 |

*Notes:* NI for No-Inspection, P20 for the condition with a 20% probability of inspection; P50 for the condition with a 50% probability; P20P50 for the condition with a probability of either 20% or 50%; H_P20P50 for the condition with a probability of either 20% or 50% and with a high level of fine.

d. At the time of the experiment, the real fine was €50 in Lyon. To keep the incentives comparable between the lab and the field, we chose a much lower fine for the experiment. This is because the probability of being inspected is much lower in the field compared to our lab setting.

Participants received feedback on inspections only at the end of the experiment. At the end of the experiment, they were paid based on Parts 1 and 2, and either Part 3 or 4 of the experiment. If Part 3 was relevant for payment, one round and one decision in that round were randomly selected to determine the participant's payoff (recall that we employed a strategy method). Subjects could not make losses in Part 3. In the worst case scenario (i.e., Variable treatment, condition H_P20P50 and payment based on decision in stop 1), if subjects chose not to buy a ticket and were inspected, they would earn €8 (endowment) + €2 (benefit of traveling until stop 1) – €8 (fine) – €1.70 (price of the ticket) = €0.30.

## 2.2 Conjectures

The theoretical predictions are straightforward. If participants are risk-neutral, rational, and profit-maximizing, they should never buy the ticket, except when the probability of inspection is 50% and the final destination is stop 5, 6, or 7, regardless of the treatment. This should be observed for both fraudsters and non-fraudsters in real life.

Alternatively, we may anticipate that behavioral dimensions play a role. In particular, buying a ticket for a shorter distance or with a lower probability of inspection indicates either a very high degree of risk aversion or the presence of moral costs of cheating. Since in the No-Inspection condition, subjects know that there is no risk of control, buying a ticket in this condition indicates the importance of moral concerns in our population.

Our behavioral conjectures are the following:

Conjecture 1Fraudsters in real life are more likely to cheat in our game than non-fraudsters.

Conjecture 2If they suffer from a moral cost of cheating, participants may comply even when there is no risk of inspection.

Conjecture 3If the outcome dimension of fraud is positive, participants who suffer a moral cost of cheating are more likely to comply when the distance is longer than when it is shorter, even when there is no risk of inspection.

Conjecture 4If the payoff dimension of fraud is positive, participants are more likely to cheat in the Variable treatment than in the Constant treatment when the distance is short. This is because the *relative gain* from fraud is higher in the Variable treatment (for example, at stop 1 it is 6.67 in the Variable treatment and 1.27 in the Constant treatment).[e]

Conjecture 5Participants respond to the size of the risk of inspection and to the size of the fine.

e. The relative gain is computed as the increment in earnings if a person cheats relative to the increment in earnings if a person does not cheat. For stop 1, this is equal to €2/(€2 – €1.70) = 6.67 in the Variable treatment, and €8/(€8 – €1.70) = 1.27 in the Constant treatment.

## 2.3 Experimental procedures

We recruited 244 passengers of the public transport (excluding those with a monthly pass) at the exit of buses or trams near the main railway station of Lyon between 11:00am and 7:00pm. The recruitment was conducted by a team of recruiters wearing no uniform in order not to be confused with ticket inspectors. Recruiters were not aware of the content of the experiment and this is what they were instructed to say to participants who asked for more information. The passengers were invited to take part in a study organized by researchers from the University of Lyon. The recruiters informed passengers that the study would last about 45 min, they could earn at least €25 paid immediately at the end of the study in gift vouchers (these vouchers could be exchanged for goods and services in almost 50,000 shops). Participants were also told that participating did not require any special knowledge. If a passenger agreed to participate, she/he was told to keep her/his travel ticket if she/he had one because it would be exchanged by the researchers against a new one. The reason was that the previous ticket would not be valid any longer at the end of the study (in Lyon a ticket is valid only for 1 h from its first validation). We also recruited 35 participants at their exit of the Fine Collection Office (FCO). These were passengers who had been caught traveling without a ticket in the past and went to pay their fine at the FCO because they did not pay it on the spot. Thus, in total 279 persons played our game.

Any person who agreed to participate was escorted to a near building where we had reconstituted an experimental laboratory which fitted a maximum of nine participants at a time. The experiment was conducted with tactile tablets to facilitate the entry decisions of the participants. Upon arrival, a participant was assigned to a desk after signing a consent form and could immediately start the experiment. The instructions were displayed on the tablet, and the participant was informed that questions were allowed at any time during the experiment and that they would be answered in private. All decisions were individual and participants arrived and completed the experiment at different moments in time.

Once a participant completed the experiment, she/he was escorted to another room to receive her/his payment in private and to exchange her/his validated ticket (if any) against a free daily pass. Subjects earned on average €60 for the whole experiment (min: €25; max: €110) (in addition to the daily pass if they had a validated ticket to exchange).

## 2.4 Identification of fraudsters

One crucial dimension of our study is the clear identification of fare-dodgers in real life to be able to directly compare how real fraudsters behave in the lab compared to non-fraudsters, and how the two groups respond to the various deterrence incentives.

We identified fraudsters in three complementary ways. First, we classified as fraudsters those participants who were recruited at the FCO. Second, we labeled as fraudsters all participants who were not able to present a validated ticket at the end of the experiment. As participants were recruited at the exit of buses or trams, they were supposed to carry a validated ticket, and they were reminded to keep their ticket in order to get a new one at the end of the experiment. The procedure was incentive-compatible: any participant holding a validated ticket for her/his trip should be willing to exchange this ticket since the monetary value of the daily pass was €5.60. The subjects who did not exchange their ticket at the end of the experiment can thus be classified, with confidence, as fraudsters. Finally, we categorized as fraudsters all those participants who, in the final questionnaire, self-reported to travel without a valid ticket at least once out of 10 trips. We defined as non-fraudster any participant who does not fall in any of the above categories.

We do not deny that this classification has some limitations. In particular, it may underestimate the number of real fraudsters. For example, certain participants who do not cheat all the time may have bought the ticket on the day of the experiment and self-reported that they never cheat despite they are occasional fare-dodgers. This, however, can only make our results stronger if we find significant differences in behavior between fraudsters and non-fraudsters.

To provide some numbers, excluding subjects from the FCO, we found that 41.80% of the participants did not display a ticket at the end of the experiment, while 54.92% self-admitted to be fraudsters sometimes; participants who both self-reported their fare-dodging behavior and did not display a ticket are 28.28%; finally, participants who are at least one of the above total up to 68.44% (excluding participants from the FCO). The public transport operator confirmed that these numbers are consistent with their measures of fraud on these lines (excluding people with a monthly pass). This suggests that our study was not plagued by serious self-selection biases since both fraudsters and non-fraudsters participated. Also, participants were not aware of the content of the experiment when they were recruited, which alleviates the potential self-selection issue.

## 3. Experimental results

In analyzing the results, we first focus on whether actual fraudsters cheated more than non-fraudsters in the lab. We then focus on the moral cost of cheating and test whether cheating behavior decreased over the distance traveled (which captures the size of fraud). We analyze to what extent the moral cost of cheating was sensitive to the payoff vs the outcome dimension of fraud. Finally, we investigate how participants reacted to various policy interventions. All our tests are two-tailed.

We introduce our first result that supports our first conjecture:

> **Result 1**. The fraud rate is always higher for actual fraudsters than non-fraudsters.
>
> *Support for Result 1:* Table 2 reports the main summary statistics about the fraud rates for each possible destination. Aggregating all destinations, Fig. 2A and B displays the fraud rates by condition and by treatment, for fraudsters and non-fraudsters in real life, respectively.

**TABLE 2** Fraud Rates for Different Destinations, by Condition and Treatment

| Stop | Constant treatment | | | | | Variable treatment | | | | |
|---|---|---|---|---|---|---|---|---|---|---|
| | NI | P20 | P50 | P20P50 | H_P20P50 | NI | P20 | P50 | P20P50 | H_P20P50 |
| ***Fraudsters*** | | | | | | | | | | |
| 1 | 0.57 | 0.55 | 0.5 | 0.47 | 0.48 | 0.6 | 0.56 | 0.41 | 0.42 | 0.28 |
| 2 | 0.61 | 0.46 | 0.36 | 0.4 | 0.35 | 0.51 | 0.47 | 0.29 | 0.34 | 0.27 |
| 3 | 0.55 | 0.46 | 0.31 | 0.39 | 0.29 | 0.43 | 0.31 | 0.13 | 0.26 | 0.17 |
| 4 | 0.47 | 0.3 | 0.22 | 0.31 | 0.24 | 0.38 | 0.21 | 0.12 | 0.17 | 0.18 |
| 5 | 0.45 | 0.27 | 0.16 | 0.26 | 0.21 | 0.29 | 0.19 | 0.14 | 0.17 | 0.15 |
| 6 | 0.44 | 0.32 | 0.26 | 0.23 | 0.2 | 0.27 | 0.15 | 0.12 | 0.17 | 0.17 |
| 7 | 0.32 | 0.26 | 0.2 | 0.21 | 0.19 | 0.26 | 0.21 | 0.17 | 0.22 | 0.16 |
| Total | 0.49 | 0.37 | 0.29 | 0.32 | 0.28 | 0.39 | 0.3 | 0.2 | 0.25 | 0.2 |
| ***Non-fraudsters*** | | | | | | | | | | |
| 1 | 0.14 | 0.29 | 0.23 | 0.17 | 0.11 | 0.24 | 0.24 | 0.17 | 0.19 | 0.07 |
| 2 | 0.2 | 0.17 | 0.14 | 0.14 | 0.14 | 0.26 | 0.24 | 0.1 | 0.12 | 0 |
| 3 | 0.14 | 0.17 | 0.11 | 0.09 | 0.09 | 0.14 | 0.17 | 0.05 | 0.02 | 0.02 |
| 4 | 0.17 | 0.09 | 0.11 | 0.11 | 0.06 | 0.12 | 0.02 | 0.05 | 0.05 | 0.02 |
| 5 | 0.09 | 0 | 0.06 | 0.06 | 0.06 | 0.14 | 0.1 | 0 | 0.02 | 0.02 |
| 6 | 0.14 | 0.09 | 0.06 | 0.09 | 0.03 | 0.17 | 0.1 | 0.07 | 0.1 | 0.02 |
| 7 | 0.06 | 0.03 | 0.03 | 0.03 | 0 | 0.12 | 0.05 | 0.07 | 0.05 | 0.02 |
| Total | 0.13 | 0.12 | 0.11 | 0.1 | 0.07 | 0.17 | 0.13 | 0.07 | 0.08 | 0.03 |

*Notes*: Standard errors of the mean are between 0.032 and 0.050 for fraudsters, and between 0 and 0.077 for non-fraudsters. NI for No-Inspection; P20 for the condition with a 20% probability of inspection; P50 for the condition with a 50% probability; P20P50 for the condition with a probability of either 20% or 50%; H_P20P50 for the condition with a probability of either 20% or 50% and with a high level of fine.

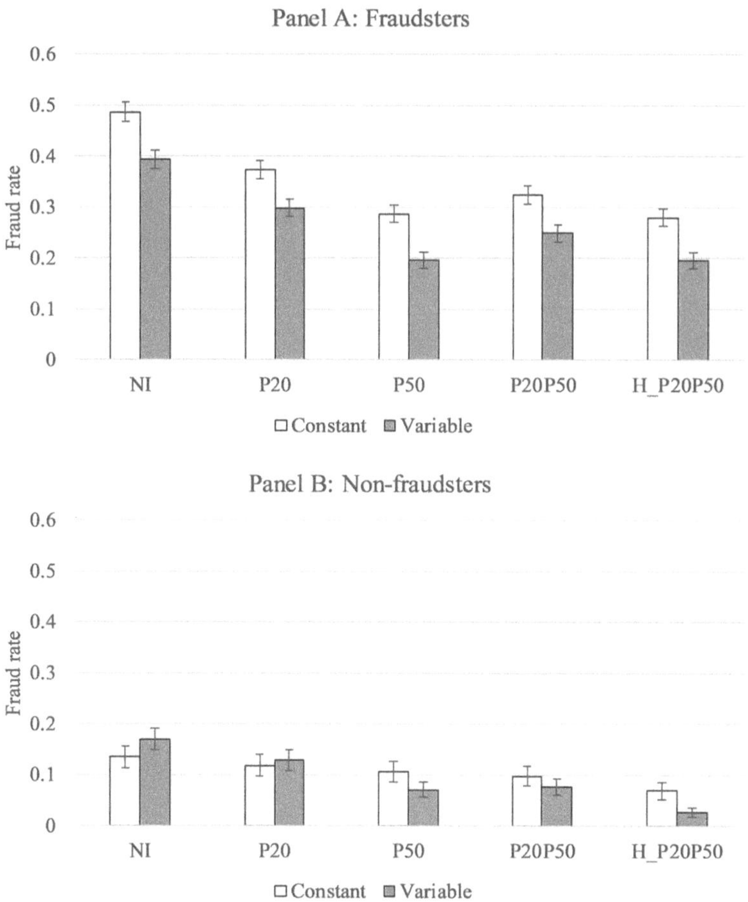


**FIG. 2** Fraud rates in the game of fraudsters and non-fraudsters. *Note*: Error bars represent standard errors of the mean. NI for No-Inspection, P20 for the condition with a 20% probability of inspection; P50 for the condition with a 50% probability; P20P50 for the condition with a probability of either 20% or 50%; H_P20P50 for the condition with a probability of either 20% or 50% and with a high level of fine.

As visible in Table 2 and in Fig. 2, fraudsters cheated significantly more in the game than non-fraudsters. The difference is significant according to Mann–Whitney tests ($P<0.01$ for all possible pairwise comparisons in Fig. 2). In particular, on average fraudsters cheated between 2.3 and 7.2 times more than non-fraudsters, depending on the condition. This confirms that cheating in the lab strongly relates to dishonesty in real life, and it provides additional evidence of the external validity of the laboratory setting for the study of dishonesty.

The second result supports our second conjecture:

**Result 2**. There is evidence of a moral cost of cheating for both fraudsters and non-fraudsters.

*Support for Result 2:* As visible in Fig. 2, all fraud rates in the game remain below 50% even in the No-Inspection and in the P20 conditions, suggesting that both fraudsters and non-fraudsters have a moral cost of cheating.[f] Fig. 2B shows that non-fraudsters displayed small but still positive fraud rates in all conditions (up to 17.01% in the No-Inspection condition, and with a minimum of 2.72% in the H_P20P50 condition). This suggests that even non-fraudsters faced the temptation to cheat in our lab setting. However, their dishonesty was very tiny compared to that of fraudsters who displayed average fraud rates ranging from 19.61% (in H_P20P50) to 48.71% (in the No-Inspection condition).

The third result supports more our third than our fourth conjecture:

**Result 3**. The moral cost of cheating depends on the outcome dimension of the size of fraud but not on its payoff dimension.

*Support for Result 3:* We analyze the payoff and outcome dimensions of the size of fraud by examining how behavior adjusted to the distance traveled. To explore these two dimensions we now focus exclusively on the No-Inspection condition in both treatments where there was no risk of punishment and thus, no possible influence of the individual degree of risk aversion on behavior (note that analogous patterns were observed for the other conditions, but with more noise). In the Variable treatment, dishonesty may decrease with the distance traveled for two reasons. First, participants may be less willing to fraud for longer distances because, compared to short distances, they gain less from being dishonest relative to being honest (the relative gain is 6.67 for stop 1 and 1.17 for stop 7): this captures the payoff dimension of the size of fraud. Second, they may be less willing to fraud for longer distances because this would represent a bigger deception: this captures the outcome dimension of the size of fraud. In the Constant treatment, only the outcome dimension may matter since payoffs were the same across distances. By comparing the drop in fraud across the distance traveled between the Control treatment and the Variable treatment, we can test to which extent the moral cost of dishonesty depends on the payoff and outcome dimensions, respectively.

Fig. 3 shows how cheating behavior in the game evolved over the distance traveled for fraudsters and non-fraudsters in real life, in the No-Inspection condition of the Variable and Constant treatments, respectively.

f. We acknowledge that this moral cost may in part be the result of a possible feeling of scrutiny of our lab environment. Indeed, the experimenter can, ex-post, verify the decisions of the participants even if they remain anonymous. Previous studies generally find a small effect of having the experimenter or another subject observing behavior (e.g., Bäker and Mechtel, 2015; Gneezy et al., 2018; Houser et al., 2016), but others find no effect (e.g., Van de Ven and Villeval, 2015). The advantage of using a "full information" setup is that we can measure dishonesty at the individual level. There are many studies that use a similar setup, e.g., Maggian and Villeval (2016), Galeotti et al. (2017), Abeler et al. (2019), Gneezy et al. (2018), Kocher et al. (2018), and almost all the controlled experiments on tax evasion.

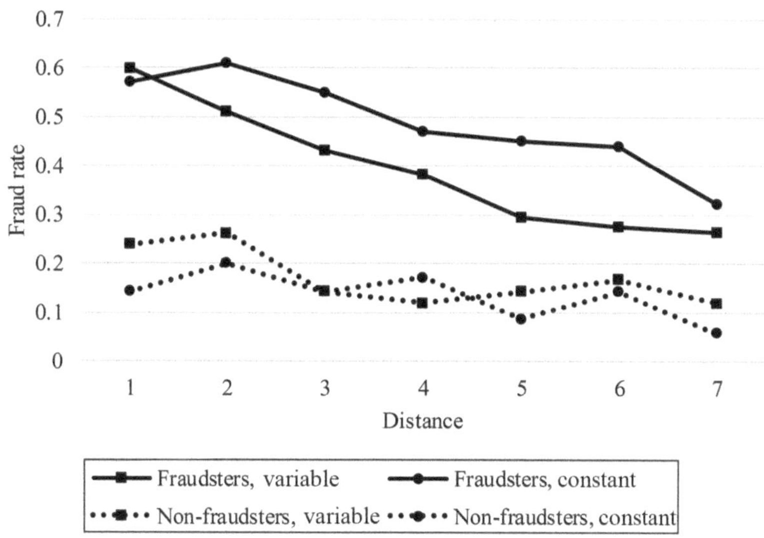


**FIG. 3** Fraud rate of fraudsters and non-fraudsters in real life over distance traveled in the No-Inspection condition, by treatment.

Fig. 3 shows that fraud dropped as the distance increased (at least for fraudsters in real life) but there seems to be no difference in the rate of decay between the Variable and Constant treatments. If anything, fraud was, for fraudsters, slightly lower in the Variable treatment for all stops except the first one.[g] Also, in stop 1 fraud was roughly the same across treatments. If the payoff dimension had mattered, we should have observed, for stop 1, a higher fraud rate in the Variable treatment since for stop 1, the relative gain from cheating is 6.67 in the Variable treatment but only 1.27 in the Constant treatment. Fig. 3 contradicts this hypothesis. This suggests that the moral cost of dishonesty is sensitive to the outcome dimension of fraud but not to the payoff dimension. It is as if participants considered that it is more morally reprehensible to travel on a longer distance without a ticket, regardless of the relative monetary benefit associated with a longer distance.

Formal tests based on logit regressions confirm this evidence. The dependent variable is whether a participant bought or not a ticket for each distance of the No-Inspection condition. Independent variables are the distance (the number of stops), a treatment dummy for the Variable treatment, and an interaction term between the distance and the Variable treatment dummy.

g. When we pool the observations from all conditions together, we find that real fraudsters cheat overall less in the Variable condition but this equally occurs in all distances. A possible explanation is that they perceive the Variable (Constant) treatment as more just (unjust) since the earnings are (not) proportional to the distance traveled. This would be consistent with previous literature showing that people cheat more when the environment is more unjust (see Galeotti et al., 2017).

We also control for individuals characteristics (being a male, age, having a monthly income less than €1000, being a student, being employed, having a high school education or lower, having children, and attitudes toward risk in the gain and the loss domains with and without uncertainty, as measured in the first part of the experiment). We ran separate regressions for fraudsters and non-fraudsters in real life, and we clustered standard errors at the individual level since we have multiple observations for each participant. The full results are available from the authors upon request.

We found that, for fraudsters, fraud decreases over distance ($P<0.001$) and at the same rate in the Variable and the Constant treatments: the marginal effects are −5.58% and −4.24%, respectively, and they do not differ significantly ($P=0.302$). Also for non-fraudsters, fraud slightly decreases over distance but not significantly so ($P=0.130$), and there is no significant difference in decay between the Variable and the Constant treatments: the marginal effects are −1.84% and −1.66%, respectively ($P=0.893$). Similar results are obtained if we consider the other conditions where we introduce a risk of inspection and penalties, or if we pool all the observations from the different conditions together (see later results from additional regression analysis). These findings confirm that participants suffer a moral cost of frauding that is increasing in the outcome dimension of dishonesty (i.e., the distance traveled) but not in its payoff dimension (i.e., the relative amount of payoff gained from not buying a ticket).

This result contrasts with those of Gneezy et al. (2018) who, in a variation of a cheating game, find quite the opposite. However, it is in line with the results of Lundquist et al. (2009) who find a significant positive effect of the outcome dimension on the aversion to lie and with Abeler et al. (2019) who do not find that the payoff dimension influences the lying rate in a meta-analysis of lying games involving random devices. One can offer different explanations of why our results differ from the findings of Gneezy et al. (2018). First, the way we represent the outcome dimension is slightly different (although conceptually identical). In Gneezy et al. (2018), the outcome dimension of the size of a lie is defined as the difference between the potential lie and the truth. In our setting, it is the number of consecutive stops for which a subject can fraud given a certain destination. This different framing may be linked to different behavioral responses. This explanation, however, does not seem very convincing. Indeed, our result is consistent with Lundquist et al. (2009) who use the same representation of the outcome dimension as Gneezy et al. (2018) and find a significant effect of the size of the lie on this dimension. Second, our game is presented in a typical public transportation context while the experiment of Gneezy et al. (2018) is context-free. The in-context presentation of our task might have induced the participants to behave as if they were in the field (where the payoff dimension might always be relevant), irrespectively of the different payoff structure of our treatments. Again, this does not seem very convincing since the experiment of Lundquist et al. (2009) is also context-free. A more likely explanation is that the impact of the size of dishonesty and of its nature depends on the game being played and it might be different if the task is a cheating game (like in Gneezy et al., 2018), a sender–receiver game (like in Lundquist et al., 2009) or a public transportation game (like in our case). Future studies should be devoted to investigate this.

The last result supports our fifth conjecture:

**Result 4**. Both fraudsters and non-fraudsters in real life responded to changes in the detection probability, the uncertainty, and the severity of punishment.

*Support for Result 4:* The two panels of Fig. 2 (as well as Table 2) show that the average fraud rate dropped for both fraudsters and non-fraudsters as soon as we introduced deterrence incentives. The effect is stronger for fraudsters. They cheated significantly less when there was a positive probability of being detected (Wilcoxon signed rank tests, $P<0.001$ for all pairwise comparisons with the No-Inspection condition, and for both treatments). This effect is more pronounced for a higher probability of detection ($P<0.001$, P20 vs P50). Under ambiguity on the probability of inspection (P20P50 condition), the fraudsters' fraud rate in the game lies between the one observed for conditions P20 and P50 ($P<0.05$, for P20P50 vs P20 and P20P50 vs P50), as if they expected the probability to be between 20% and 50%. Finally, doubling the fine reduced their cheating behavior by 5% ($P<0.01$, P20P50 vs H_P20P50).

Non-fraudsters in real life display similar but less pronounced patterns of behavior. In fact, the only significant comparisons (at 5% level) are between H_P20P50 and any of the other conditions ($P<0.01$) in the Variable treatment. This is because non-fraudsters were already characterized by very low fraud rates when there was a null inspection probability, and, therefore, there is less scope for any policy to improve their behavior.

To test the robustness of all our results, we now report the results of an econometric analysis. We estimated three logit regressions, one for all participants pooled together (model (1)), one only for non-fraudsters in real life (model (2)), and one only for fraudsters (model (3)). Standard errors are clustered at the individual level, as there are multiple observations for each participant. The dependent variable is whether a participant frauds by not buying a ticket for a given destination. The explanatory variables include a dummy variable which identifies fraudsters in real life (only in model (1)), the distance traveled, a dummy for the Variable treatment, an interaction term between the treatment and the distance traveled, and a dummy for each policy intervention (P20, P50, P20P50, H_P20P50). We control for individuals characteristics (being a male, age, having a monthly income of less than €1000, being a student, being employed, having a high school education or lower, and attitudes toward risk in the gain and the loss domains with and without uncertainty, as measured in the first part of the experiment). Table 3 reports the average marginal effects, while Fig. 4 shows how the distance traveled affects

**TABLE 3** Determinants of the Decision to Fraud in the Game

| | All participants (1) | | Non-fraudsters (2) | | Fraudsters (3) | |
|---|---|---|---|---|---|---|
| | dy/dx | se | dy/dx | se | dy/dx | se |
| Fraudster | 0.217*** | 0.035 | – | – | – | – |
| Distance traveled | −0.038*** | 0.004 | −0.021*** | 0.005 | −0.044*** | 0.005 |
| Variable treatment | −0.082** | 0.029 | −0.038 | 0.029 | −0.102** | 0.039 |
| Condition (*Ref.* = *No Inspection)* | | | | | | |
| P20 | −0.072*** | 0.014 | −0.022 | 0.024 | −0.092*** | 0.017 |
| P50 | −0.152*** | 0.017 | −0.057* | 0.025 | −0.188*** | 0.021 |
| P20P50 | −0.117*** | 0.016 | −0.057* | 0.024 | −0.140*** | 0.02 |
| H_P20P50 | −0.168*** | 0.018 | −0.115*** | 0.035 | −0.192*** | 0.021 |
| Individual characteristics | *Yes* | | *Yes* | | *Yes* | |
| Obs. | 9765 | | 2695 | | 7070 | |

*Notes*: Marginal effects from logit regressions are reported. Standard errors are clustered at the individual level. P20 for the condition with a 20% probability of inspection; P50 for the condition with a 50% probability; P20P50 for the condition with a probability of either 20% or 50%; H_P20P50 for the condition with a probability of either 20% or 50% and with a high level of fine. Controls for individual characteristics include: risk index in the gain domain and in the loss domain (with and without uncertainty), age categories, dummy variables for gender, income lower than €1000, student status, employed status, education lower than Baccalaureat, and having children. *$P<0.10$, **$P<0.05$, ***$P<0.01$.

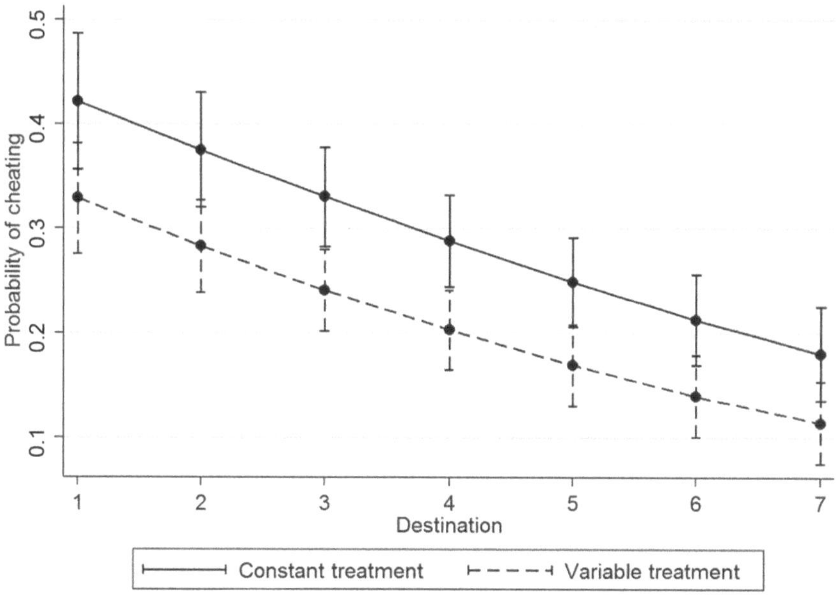


**FIG. 4** Effect of the distance traveled on predicted cheating probabilities, by treatment. *Note:* Calculations are based on model (1) of Table 3.

the marginal predicted probability of fraud in the Constant and the Variable treatments, respectively (calculations are based on model (1)).

The results of the regression analysis confirm our previous findings. The probability of fraud was higher for fraudsters than non-fraudsters (+21.7%), it decreased by 3.8% at each reached destination, and this drop is the same in both Variable and Constant treatments (see patterns in Fig. 4). Participants were overall less likely to cheat in the Variable treatment (−8.2%), and this is mainly driven by fraudsters (−10.2%). Moreover, individuals, and especially fraudsters, were sensitive to deterrence incentives. In particular, the probability to cheat of fraudsters dropped by 9.2% in P20, 18.8% in P50, 14% in P20P50, and 19.2% in H_P20P50. The probability to cheat of non-fraudsters decreased by 5.7% in both P50 and P20P50 (but these effects are significant only at 10%), and by 11.5% in H_P20P50. Finally, none of the individual characteristics influenced the participants' decisions at conventional levels of significance, except that participants with children were marginally less likely to fraud (models (1, 3)) and participants with a lower level of risk aversion in the gain domain were marginally more likely to fraud (model (1)).

## 4. Discussion and conclusion

Fare-dodging in public transport is one the many examples of everyday life dishonesty by ordinary people. Identifying the factors that make an individual indifferent between the honest action and the dishonest one is particularly important to be able to design effective policy interventions. Inspection and sanctions are natural deterrence instruments, but they are costly to implement and they cannot be systematic for several reasons. It is therefore useful to characterize also the intrinsic motivations that can prevent an individual to fraud. This chapter has reported on a framed experiment with a diversified sample of passengers in the context of public transport in which we examined how the size of a fraud influences moral behavior, with and without a risk of punishment, and for what reasons.

A first important result is a confirmation that cheating in this novel laboratory game correlates with dishonesty in the field in a similar context. This result should increase the confidence on the use of controlled experimental methods to study dishonesty and contributes to the debate about the external validity of lab findings. The laboratory offers the great opportunity of introducing manipulations that allow us to identify the moral costs of dishonesty. In particular, we have shown that both fraudsters and non-fraudsters in real life bear a moral cost of cheating in the game and this cost increases in the outcome dimension of the size of fraud, but not in its payoff dimension.

Indeed, independently of the monetary benefit of the fraud and of the cost of its detection, people do not like to fraud the further their dishonest action deviates from a reference point (which, in our experiment, is the distance traveled with a regular ticket). This is consistent with the results of Lundquist et al. (2009) in the context of sender–receiver games and with those of Hilbig and Hessler (2013) in a modified dice game. In contrast, in our game the moral cost of a fraud does not depend on the payoff dimension of the size of this fraud. People do not fraud more if the relative gain from behaving dishonestly increases. This is in line with the conclusion of the meta-analysis of Abeler et al. (2019). In other words, in the context of public transport, people can always find a justification for not buying a ticket when they make a short trip, but they find less and less justifiable in their own eyes to travel without a ticket when the trip gets longer. This is independent from the fact that an inspection is more likely the longer one stays onboard (as shown by the comparison between our No-Inspection condition and the other conditions), and also from the fact that one benefits from a bigger service from the transport company (as shown by the comparison between our two treatments).

Showing that behavior reacts to the outcome dimension of the size of fraud but not to its payoff dimension contrasts with Gneezy et al. (2018)'s findings about a positive effect of the payoff dimension of lying on dishonest behavior. In the previous section, we offered different explanations for this discrepancy. The most convincing one is that the relationship between cheating behavior and the size of fraud is context-dependent, and it is sensitive to the game being played (e.g., sender–receiver game, cheating game, or public transportation game). We leave this for investigation in future research.

Finally, we found that both fare-dodgers and non-fare-dodgers in real life responded to changes in the detection probability, the uncertainty, and the severity of punishment, which confirms the usefulness of deterrence policies. This result is very important from a policy-making perspective because it suggests that people, and especially fare-dodgers, react to incentives in the desired direction. It also relevant from a theoretical point of view since it confirms Becker's deterrence hypothesis that undesirable behavior can be curbed with appropriate deterrence incentives.

Altogether these results show that laboratory experiments are useful to study dishonest behavior and to inform policy-makers how to design more effective policy interventions. They suggest that both moral appeals to certain reference points and standard deterrence policies should be used as complements to discourage dishonest behavior and enhance ethical standards in the context of public transport.

## Acknowledgments

We are grateful to P. Jacquesson, R. Sauter, and F. German from Keolis and to D. Aubaret and L. Clerc-Gagnoux from Kisio for enabling the realization of this experiment with passengers of the public transport company. We thank Q. Thevenet for programming the experiment. This research has been supported by a grant from Keolis, a grant from the French National Research Agency (ANR, FELIS Grant, ANR-14-CE28- 0010-01), and funding from the European Union's Horizon 2020 research and innovation program under the Marie Sklodowska-Curie grant agreement (661645–IDEA–MSCA-IF-EF-ST). It was performed within the framework of the LABEX CORTEX (ANR-11-LABX-0042) of Université de Lyon, within the program Investissements d'Avenir (ANR-11-IDEX-007) operated by the French National Research Agency (ANR).

## References

Abeler, J., Nosenzo, D., Raymond, D., 2019. Preferences for truth-telling. Econometrica . forthcoming.

Armantier, O., Boly, A., 2013. Comparing corruption in the laboratory and in the field in Burkina Faso and in Canada. Econ. J. 123, 1168–1187.

Ayal, S., Hochman, G., Ariely, D., 2016. Dishonest behavior, from theory to practice. Front. Psychol. 7, https://doi.org/10.3389/fpsyg.2016.01521.

Bäker, A., Mechtel, M., 2015. Peer settings induce cheating on task performance. In: IAAEU Discussion Paper Series in Economics No. 06/2015.

Becker, G.S., 1968. Crime and punishment: an economic approach. J. Polit. Econ. 76, 169–217.

Camerer, C.F., 2015. The promise and success of lab-field generalizability in experimental economics: a critical reply to Levitt and List. In: Frechette, G.R., Schotter, A. (Eds.), Handbook of Experimental Economic Methodology. Oxford University Press, Oxford, pp. 249–295.

Cohn, A., Maréchal, M.A., 2018. Laboratory measures of cheating predict misbehavior at school. Econ. J. 128 (615), 2743–2754.

Cohn, A., Fehr, E., Maréchal, M.A., 2014. Business culture and dishonesty in the banking industry. Nature 516, 86–89.

Cohn, A., Maréchal, M.A., Noll, T., 2015. Bad boys: how criminal identity salience affects rule violation. Rev. Econ. Stud. 82 (4), 1289–1308.

Cour des Comptes, 2016. La Lutte Contre la Fraude Dans les Transports Urbains En Île-De-France: Un Échec Collectif. Rapport Public Annuel 2016, pp. 537–577.

Dai, Z., Galeotti, F., Villeval, M.C., 2017. The efficiency of crackdowns: a lab-in-the-field experiment in public transportations. Theor. Decis. 82 (2), 249–271.

Dai, Z., Galeotti, F., Villeval, M.C., 2018. Cheating in the lab predicts fraud in the field: an experiment in public transportation. Manage. Sci. 64 (3), 1081–1100.

Dhami, S., 2017. Human Ethics and Virtues: Rethinking the Homo-Oeconomicus Model. CESifo Working Paper 6836.

Donohue, P., 2010. Millions of Fare-Beaters Take MTA for an $8 Million Bus Ride. Daily News, 17 March. http://www.nydailynews.com/news/crime/millions-fare-beaters-mta-8-million-bus-ride-article-1.175537. [(Accessed January 22, 2018)].

Eckel, C.C., Grossman, P.J., 2008. Forecasting risk attitudes: an experimental study using actual and forecast gamble choices. J. Econ. Behav. Organ. 68 (1), 1–17.

Eckel, C.C., Grossman, P.J., Johnson, C.A., de Oliveira, A.C., Rojas, C., Wilson, R.K., 2012. School environment and risk preferences: experimental evidence. J. Risk Uncertain. 45 (3), 265–292.

Falk, A., Heckman, J., 2009. Lab experiments are a major source of knowledge in the social sciences. Science 326 (5952), 535–538.

Fischbacher, U., Föllmi-Heusi, F., 2013. Lies in disguise: an experimental study on cheating. J. Eur. Econ. Assoc. 11 (3), 525–547.

Fréchette, G.R., 2015. Laboratory experiments: professionals versus students. In: Fréchette, G.R., Schotter, A. (Eds.), Handbook of Experimental Economic Methodology. Oxford University Press, Oxford, pp. 360–390.

Fréchette, G.R., Schotter, A., 2015. Handbook of Experimental Economic Methodology. Oxford University Press, Oxford.

Fürst, E., 2012. Free Riders and Ticket Fraud in Public Transport: A Delphi Analysis. Association for European Transport Papers Repository.

Galeotti, F., Kline, R., Orsini, R., 2017. When foul play seems fair: exploring the link between just deserts and honesty. J. Econ. Behav. Organ. 142, 451–467.

Gneezy, U., Kajackaite, A., Sobel, J., 2018. Lying aversion and the size of the lie. Am. Econ. Rev. 108 (2), 419–453.

Hanna, R., Wang, S.Y., 2017. Dishonesty and selection into public service: evidence from India. Am. Econ. J. Econ. Pol. 9 (3), 262–290.

Hilbig, B.E., Hessler, C.M., 2013. What lies beneath: how the distance between truth and lie drives dishonesty. J. Econ. Psychol. 49 (2), 263–266.

Houser, D., List, J.A., Piovesan, M., Samek, A., Winter, J., 2016. Dishonesty: from parents to children. Eur. Econ. Rev. 82, 242–254.

Irlenbusch, B., Villeval, M.C., 2015. Behavioral ethics: how psychology influenced economics and how economics might inform psychology? Curr. Opin. Psychol. 6, 87–92.

Jacobsen, C., Fosgaard, T.R., Pascual-Ezama, D., 2018. Why do we lie? A practical guide to the dishonesty literature. J. Econ. Surv. 32 (2), 357–387. https://doi.org/10.1111/joes.12204.

Khadjavi, M., 2018. Deterrence works for criminals. Eur. J. Law Econ. 46 (1), 165–178.

Kocher, M.G., Schudy, S., Spantig, L., 2018. I lie? We lie! Why? Experimental evidence on a dishonesty shift in groups. Manage. Sci. 64 (9), 3995–4008.

Kröll, M., Rustagi, D., 2016. Shades of Dishonesty and Cheating in Informal Milk Markets in India. SAFE Working Paper, vol. 134, Goethe University, Frankfurt.

Levitt, S., List, J.A., 2007. What do laboratory experiments social preferences reveal about the real world. J. Econ. Perspect. 21 (2), 153–174.

List, J.A., 2009. The Economics of Open Air Markets. NBER Working Paper 15420.

Lundquist, T., Ellingsen, T., Gribbe, E., Johannesson, M., 2009. The aversion to lying. J. Econ. Behav. Organ. 70 (1–2), 81–92.

Maggian, V., Villeval, M.C., 2016. Social preferences and lying aversion in children. Exerimental. Econ. 19 (3), 663–685.

Mazar, N., Amir, O., Ariely, D., 2008. The dishonesty of honest people: a theory of self-concept maintenance. J. Market. Res. 45, 633–644.

Potters, J., Stoop, J., 2016. Do cheaters in the lab also cheat in the field? Eur. Econ. Rev. 87, 26–33.

Rosenbaum, S.M., Billinger, S., Stieglitz, N., 2014. Let's be honest: a review of experimental evidence of honesty and truth-telling. J. Econ. Psychol. 45, 181–196.

Shalvi, S., Dana, J., Handgraaf, M.J.J., De Dreu, C.K.W., 2011. Justified ethicality: observing desired counterfactuals modifies ethical perceptions and behavior. Organ. Behav. Hum. Decis. Process. 115, 181–190.

Van de Ven, J., Villeval, M.C., 2015. Dishonesty under scrutiny. J. Econ. Sci. Assoc. 1 (1), 86–99.

Chapter 4.2

# The cost of being honest: Excessive change at the restaurant

Ofer H. Azar[1,2], Shira Yosef[1], Michael Bar-Eli[1,3]
[1]*Ben-Gurion University of the Negev, Beersheba, Israel,* [2]*Laboratory of Economic Behavior of the Center of Psycho-Economic Research, Povolzhsky Institute of Administration named after P.A. Stolypin—Branch of RANEPA, Saratov, Russia,* [3]*The Academic College at Wingate, Wingate Institute, Netanya, Israel*

**Chapter Outline**



**JEL Classification:** C93, D03, D12

## 1. Introduction

Dishonesty and cheating are prevalent behaviors, which affect various economic activities (Mazar and Ariely, 2006). The losses that result from such behaviors are large. For example, theft and cheating in the workplace are estimated to reach 600 billion dollars every year (Mazar et al., 2008). Insurance companies report that their customers add annually 24 billion dollars fraudulently to claims of property loss. Retailers lose 16 billion dollars in a year due to customers who buy clothes, wear them, and return the used clothes for a full refund (Ariely, 2008).

While cheating can result in various rewards, it also has its costs, which can be divided into two main categories. One is external punishment, which often bears negative economic consequences. For example, if one cheats on his taxes and gets caught, he can be fined and may also go to prison. The second cost is psychological. Cheating may lead the cheating person to experience negative feelings, such as shame (Wirtz and Kum, 2004) and weakening

**Dishonesty in Behavioral Economics. https://doi.org/10.1016/B978-0-12-815857-9.00015-7**

of the self-perception as a moral person (Mazar et al., 2008). People feel good when they obey social norms and act according to the values of the society in which they live (De Quervain et al., 2004). People usually value honesty, hold strong beliefs about their morality, and want to preserve this aspect of their self-perception (Greenwald, 1980; Sanitioso et al., 1990). Cheating obviously hurts one's self image as an honest person. Cheating also hurts the trust relationship between the cheater and the cheated (Wirtz and Kum, 2004).

In situations where external punishment for cheaters does not exist or is extremely unlikely to happen, a traditional economic agent, one that is selfish and does not have any psychological motivations but rather only wants to maximize his utility by increasing consumption, should cheat whenever it provides him financial gains, regardless of the implications of cheating for other people. However, research shows that people often do have psychological motivations. Not only they usually behave honestly, but also they care about fairness and reciprocate (Fehr and Gachter, 2000) and dislike inequality (Bolton and Ockenfels, 2000). Various experiments show that people contribute to public goods, offer significant shares of the pie in the ultimatum game, reject offers they perceive as unfair in that game, and give to others in the dictator game. People also tip where this is the social norm even if they do not expect to return to the same place. We can therefore see that on one hand there is evidence for fair and prosocial behavior, and on the other hand also ample evidence for cheating and dishonesty. This raises the question "what are the conditions and factors that influence one's decision whether to behave in a fair manner or in a dishonest and selfish manner?". The literature discussed above and other research in this area provide some insights about this question, mostly using lab experiments.

We decided to contribute to this literature using the methodology of a field experiment (see Harrison and List, 2004 for a literature review on field experiments), which offers certain advantages over lab experiments, such as a real context and a stronger external validity. We also obtained a diverse subject pool, which is often absent in experiments done with students. We set up to examine the question what affects dishonest behavior in a field experiment conducted in a restaurant, in which customers who paid with cash received excessive change (we use the expressions "excessive change" and "extra change" interchangeably; both mean the same thing). We assumed that in such a situation people generally perceive the honest action as being to inform the waiter that too much change has been returned, and not keep the extra money that the customer believes was returned by mistake. On the other hand, it is clear that keeping the excessive change provides a financial gain and therefore some customers might be tempted not to return the excessive change. We examined whether the customers returned the excessive change and how this depends on various factors. Our main results were first reported in Azar et al. (2013). This chapter extends that previous article in several ways. First, the literature review and the basis for our hypotheses are discussed here in more detail. Second, we consider in the analysis additional control variables (age and oriental origin). Third, we elaborate much more in the discussion of the results. In contrast, Azar et al. (2013) also focused in their discussion on gender differences, which here we omit to a large extent.

Gneezy (2005) shows that the stakes on both sides—of the cheater and the cheated—can affect the decision whether to cheat. In his experiment, the sender of a message can deceive the receiver, which increases the payoff of the sender but decreases the payoff of the receiver. When the sender's gain and the receiver's loss from deception were both \$1, Gneezy documented deception in 36% of the cases. When the gain and loss were \$10, deception happened in 52% of the cases. When the receiver's loss was \$10 but the sender's gain only \$1, only 17% deception was documented. These results suggest that when deciding whether to cheat, people are affected not only by their possible gain but also by the others' loss.

In our experiment one of the variables we controlled was the level of excessive change given to the customer, with two levels, either 10 Shekels or 40 Shekels (about \$3 or \$12). The gain to the customer from not returning the excessive change is therefore the same as the loss to the other side. The actual loss is to the experimenter, but the customers did not know that. Presumably they thought that the extra change is given by mistake, at the expense of either the restaurant's owner or the waiter. In Gneezy's experiment there was more deception when the stakes were higher for both the cheater and the cheated, and similarly we hypothesized that we will observe less returning of the extra change in the 40-shekels treatment in our experiment.

Earlier literature suggests that gender differences exist in cheating behavior. Ward and Beck (1990) found that men are more dishonest than women. In addition, the ability to give excuses for behaving dishonestly did not affect men but did increase dishonesty of women. Tibbetts (1999) found that men have more cheating intentions than women on exams. Tibbetts argued that women have a stronger tendency to feel shame from actions that deviate from the norm and are more influenced by moral limitations and beliefs, whereas men have less self-control, leading them to disobey rules more frequently. Jackson et al. (2002), dealing with university cheating, reported that men were more likely to cheat than women. Erat and Gneezy (2012) showed that men are more likely than women to tell lies that are selfish, and to tell lies that benefit both the cheater and the other person. Women, on the other hand, are more likely to tell lies that hurt them but benefit the other person. Bucciol et al. (2013), in a study of bus passengers in Italy, find that men are more likely to travel without a ticket. Azar and Applebaum (2017) use data from a national mathematics contest in Israel that involved two stages with equal difficulty levels: a first unmonitored online stage at home and a second monitored stage in class. The performance deterioration from the first stage to the second stage allows estimating the dishonesty in the unmonitored first stage. Dishonesty is also analyzed using a set of three–four problems that appeared in both tests. Contrary to much of the literature on gender effects in dishonesty, girls were not more honest than boys.

To examine gender differences in our study, we recorded the gender of the diners and limited our sample to tables with one or two diners. We hypothesized that female tables would return the excessive change more often than male tables.

Depaulo and Kashy (1998) examined everyday lies and report that people lie less to those who are closer to them, to those whom they meet more frequently, and to those that they know for a longer period. The explanation is that lies hurt the nature of close relationships, which are characterized by trust. Research on academic cheating also showed that the nature of the relationship affects the tendency to cheat, with less cheating when the students perceived their lecturer and their relationship with him as more positive (Genereux and McLeod, 1995; Stearns, 2001). Repeated customers have a tendency to cheat less than one-time customers due to the development of trust relationship between the customer and the organization or service provider. The customer has an incentive to retain the good relationship to ensure high service quality in the future (Wirtz and Kum, 2004). To examine the issue of closeness in our experiment, we recorded for every customer whether he or she is a repeated customer or not, and whether he or she has the restaurant's membership card. A repeated customer knows the waiters and is closer to them, and is also more likely to return to the restaurant compared to one-time customers. Therefore, we hypothesized that repeated customers and restaurant members will return the excessive change more often than others.

When people disobey social moral norms they feel bad and ashamed (Wirtz and Kum, 2004). An audience who can detect and punish immoral behavior may deter such behavior. Moreover, because people care about how others perceive them, they behave in certain ways to improve their social image (Leary and Kowalski, 1990). Leary and Kowalski also suggest that affecting how others perceive a person is important to him for various reasons. It can help to get accepted, to create social ties, to get help, obtain power, etc. The responses of others also affect one's self image, e.g., by receiving compliments and empathy (or criticism and rejection on the negative side). The impression one creates on others also affects his identity creation. Therefore people often adopt, when in public, behaviors that correspond to the impression they want to create. Assuming that honesty is a valuable trait, we hypothesized that people would have more incentive to behave honestly and return the extra change given to them when they dine with someone else compared to the case that they dine alone.

## 2. Method

To explore the conditions that affect the decision whether to behave honestly in a real-life situation and under natural conditions of a field experiment (with subjects not being aware that this is part of an experiment), we obtained the approval of the owners and management of a restaurant in the center of Israel to conduct the experiment at the restaurant. Over a period of about half a year, waiters were asked to report to one of the authors (who worked at that time as a manager in the restaurant) about cases of a table with one or two adult customers who paid the bill in cash. In these cases, the change that was returned to the table was higher than the correct amount. In one treatment 10 extra Shekels (about €2) were returned, and in the other treatment 40 extra Shekels were returned. In total, 192 tables received too much change.

The research was conducted during all week days and all operating hours of the restaurant, from lunch until late night. As part of the regular procedures in the restaurant, waiters stay not far from a table that received the bill so that customers who want to leave are not delayed. This allowed the waiters to observe whether the diners share the bill, a variable that was collected for the data analysis. It also allowed customers who wanted to return the excessive change to do so easily.

After the customers left the restaurant, the waiters reported the outcomes of several variables to one of the authors. This occurred in a separate room that is not visible to the restaurant's customers. These variables included the customers' satisfaction from the meal (asking them about it is part of the regular procedure in the restaurant), who paid and whether the bill was divided between the customers, the tip left by the customers, and whether the customers returned the excessive change.

In addition, some more data were collected. The author who served as a manager in the restaurant knew about incidents related to the meal, such as dishes that were delayed, dissatisfaction of the customers from the service, and appraisal from the customers. This together with the feedback collected from the waiters was combined to create a variable of customer satisfaction on a 1–3 scale (3 being high satisfaction). The level of occupancy of the restaurant was also ranked on a 1–3 scale (3 being high occupancy). Based on the customers' appearance, their age was estimated (the average age in case of two diners). Also based on appearance, it was estimated whether the customers are Ashkenazi (European ethnic origin, especially from Eastern or Central Europe) or Sephardic (oriental ethnic origin, such as from North Africa or the Middle East). This resulted in a variable denoted as Oriental that equals 1 for Sephardic customers, 0 for Ashkenazi customers, and 0.5 for tables of two diners with one Sephardic and one Ashkenazi.

The receipts were used to record additional information: whether the customers have the restaurant's membership card, the time when the order was made, which meal was ordered and whether it included alcoholic beverages, and the amount of the bill. We are interested in the bill as a potential proxy for the customer's income. Two diners, however, usually have a larger bill than one diner simply because they consume more food. Moreover, the number of diners appears elsewhere in the analysis. Therefore we used in the analysis not the total bill but rather the bill per person (i.e., in tables of two diners the bill was divided by two). In addition, we documented the date and day of the week, the time of the customers' exit from the restaurant (which was then used with the time when the order was made to compute the duration of the customers' visit), and the gender of the main server that provided service to the table.

The customers were divided to repeated and one-time customers based on several parameters. First, the waiters reported to what extent they are familiar with the customer. Second, one of the authors had worked in the restaurant for 3 years and knew many of the customers. Third, the regular procedure in the restaurant involved asking the customers whether they know the restaurant and/or the menu and if they dined in it previously. Finally, we knew whether the customer holds a membership card of the restaurant. Such card can be purchased and then provides certain discounts and benefits, so the waiters are regularly obliged to ask the customers if they have this membership so that they can give them the relevant benefits. In tables of two diners, if one was a repeated customer the table was classified as having a repeated customer. The same applies to holding a membership card.

The sample was chosen to create a balanced sample between the main variables of interest (amount of excessive change—10 or 40 Shekels, repeated vs one-time customers, one vs two diners, gender). The 97 observations of two-diners tables are divided roughly equally between two women, two men, and a woman with a man.

## 3. Analysis and Results

Table 1 presents the summary statistics and the explanations of the main variables. About 69% of the tables were served by waitresses and the rest by waiters. 19% of the tables were collected over the weekend. Average visit lasted 49 min. In 61% of the cases one of the business meals, which are discounted, was ordered. Only 12% of the tables consumed alcohol. Satisfaction was high in most cases (89%), and in the other cases the complaints were handled by the servers or the management. The bill per person ranged between 7 and 127 Shekels (with an average of 64). The tip average was 13.3%. The bill was paid by a woman in 29% of the tables, and by a man in 37% of the tables. In 34% of the tables the bill was shared between two diners (13% two women; 15% two men; 6% a woman and a man). In the 32 tables with a woman and a man, both shared the bill in 11 tables, the man paid in 19 tables, and the woman paid in 2 tables. The results show that most customers did not return the excessive change they received; only 64 out of 192 tables (33%) did so.

The dependent variable we are interested in is the binary variable Return, i.e., whether the customer returned the extra change that was received. Before turning to the more complex regressions, it may be helpful to get an overview of the main results by considering the average level of returning the excessive change in different groups. Table 2 presents these results, using the Fisher exact test (two-sided) to test whether the difference in each case is statistically significant.

**TABLE 1 Summary Statistics and Explanations of the Main Variables**

| Variable | Explanation | Mean | STD |
|---|---|---|---|
| Return | 1 if excessive change was returned, 0 otherwise | 0.33 | 0.47 |
| High-change | 1 if 40 Shekels extra change, 0 if 10 Shekels | 0.50 | 0.50 |
| Repeated | 1 if a repeated customer, 0 otherwise | 0.51 | 0.50 |
| Member | 1 if the customer is a restaurant club member, 0 otherwise | 0.06 | 0.23 |
| Age | Approximate age evaluated by appearance (average for tables of two diners) | 36.67 | 9.36 |
| Oriental | Equal to 1 if all diners appear oriental (Sephardic), 0 if all diners appear Ashkenazi, 0.5 if one oriental and one Ashkenazi | 0.27 | 0.43 |
| Weekend | 1 if weekend, 0 otherwise | 0.19 | 0.39 |
| Summer | 1 if July–August, 0 otherwise | 0.53 | 0.50 |
| Occupancy | Restaurant occupancy on a 1–3 scale (3 = high) | 1.87 | 0.75 |
| Booth | 1 if a booth table, 0 otherwise | 0.38 | 0.49 |
| Lunch | 1 if the order is made between 12:00 and 16:59, 0 otherwise | 0.40 | 0.49 |
| Evening | 1 if the order is made between 17:00 and 21:59, 0 otherwise | 0.26 | 0.44 |
| Night | 1 if the order is made between 22:00 and 03:00, 0 otherwise | 0.34 | 0.48 |
| Minutes | Duration of stay in the restaurant (in minutes) | 48.69 | 13.78 |
| Male waiter | 1 if the server is male, 0 otherwise | 0.31 | 0.46 |
| Business | 1 if the customer had a business meal, 0 otherwise | 0.61 | 0.49 |
| Alcohol | 1 if the customer consumed alcohol, 0 otherwise | 0.11 | 0.32 |
| Bill-per-person | Bill in Shekels divided by the number of diners | 64.25 | 20.5 |
| Woman-payer | 1 if the bill was paid by a woman, 0 otherwise | 0.29 | 0.46 |

*(Continued)*

**TABLE 1** Summary Statistics and Explanations of the Main Variables—cont'd

| Variable | Explanation | Mean | STD |
|---|---|---|---|
| Man-payer | 1 if the bill was paid by a man, 0 otherwise | 0.37 | 0.48 |
| Sharing | 1 if the bill was paid by more than one person, 0 otherwise | 0.34 | 0.47 |
| Women-payers | 1 if the bill was paid by two women, 0 otherwise | 0.13 | 0.34 |
| Men-payers | 1 if the bill was paid by two men, 0 otherwise | 0.15 | 0.36 |
| Mixed-payers | 1 if the bill was paid by a man and a woman, 0 otherwise | 0.06 | 0.23 |
| Satisfaction | Satisfaction level on a 1–3 scale (3 = high) | 2.84 | 0.48 |
| Tip-percent | Tip in percentage of the bill | 13.34 | 9.87 |

**TABLE 2** Probability of Returning the Excessive Change

| Group | Probability of returning the excessive change | Number of observations | p-Value of Fisher exact test (2-sided) |
|---|---|---|---|
| One-time customers<br>Repeated customers | 13.7%<br>52.6% | 95<br>97 | 0.000 |
| Non-member diners<br>Member diners | 31.5%<br>63.6% | 181<br>11 | 0.044 |
| One-diner tables<br>Two-diner tables | 31.6%<br>35.1% | 95<br>97 | 0.648 |
| One female diner<br>Two female diners<br>One male diner<br>Two male diners<br>A female and a male diners | 44.7%<br>53.1%<br>18.8%<br>24.2%<br>28.1% | 47<br>32<br>48<br>33<br>32 | 0.006 |
| 10-Shekels extra change<br>40-Shekels extra change | 15.6%<br>51.0% | 96<br>96 | 0.000 |

We found, in line with our hypothesis, that repeated customers return the extra change much more often than one-time customers (52.6% vs 13.7%, $p$-value=0.000). Similarly, diners who have the restaurant club membership return much more often than nonmembers (63.6% vs 31.5%). Despite the small number of member diners in the sample (11 out of 192 tables), this difference is statistically significant at the 5% level ($p$-value=0.044). The number of diners in the table does not appear to affect the probability of returning the excessive change (35.1% vs 31.6%, $p$-value=0.648), despite the rationale that led us to hypothesize that tables with two diners will behave honestly more often. Finally, we see that the gender composition of tables has an important effect, with female tables returning the extra change much more often than male tables (44.7% and 53.1% for one and two female diners, 18.8% and 24.2% for one and two male diners). Interestingly, the behavior of mixed tables is much closer to male than to female tables, with 28.1%. The five possibilities of table composition in terms of the number of diners and their gender (M, F, MM, FF, FM) have a statistically significant different in their behavior ($p$-value=0.006).

The last part of the table shows a striking difference between the two levels of extra change. While we hypothesized that a larger financial gain will cause more people to behave dishonestly, we see that only 15.6% of the people who got 10 extra Shekels returned it, whereas 51% of those who received 40 extra Shekels returned it ($p$-value=0.000). This finding was surprising, as it was opposite to previous results (Gneezy, 2005), to our hypothesis, and to economic reasoning. If the psychological cost of behaving dishonestly and not returning the excessive change is something that does not depend on the amount of excessive change, and even if it depends on the amount but increases less than linearly (i.e., when not returning 40 Shekels the psychological cost of behaving dishonestly is less than four times the cost when not returning 10 Shekels), then we should see the opposite pattern, of less returning in the 40 Shekels condition. The strong positive effect of the higher amount on returning it suggests that the psychological cost of not returning the 40 Shekels is in fact much higher than four times the psychological cost of not returning 10 Shekels. Then the cost-benefit analysis between the financial gain from keeping the money and the psychological cost from behaving dishonestly may result in more returning of the excessive change in the 40-Shekels condition. In other words, when the amounts involved are relatively low (10 Shekels), the dishonest act of not returning the excessive change is possibly not perceived as being significantly dishonest by many people. They may justify to themselves why not returning the change is therefore fine and does not mean they behave dishonestly (e.g., it is a small amount and it is not worth the trouble to return it). With the larger amount (40 Shekels), it is clearer that not returning it is dishonest, finding excuses not to return the change that retain the self-image as being honest is more challenging, and consequently the psychological cost of being dishonest becomes much higher. This finding is consistent with Mazar et al. (2008), who find that people behave dishonestly to some degree but not too much, thus gaining monetarily but still without spoiling their positive self-view.

One other alternative explanation we could think of was that maybe when the excessive change was 10 Shekels not many people noticed it and therefore they did not return it, but when it was 40 Shekels everyone noticed. However, it seems reasonable that people who pay cash know how much change to expect. They have a lot of time to compute this. It takes a few minutes for the process of receiving the bill and looking at it, taking out money for payment, calling the waiter or waiting for him to come, and waiting for the waiter to come back with the change (the waiters go back to bring the change from the cashier). A few minutes seem like a sufficient time to compute the expected change (e.g., if a 100-Shekels note was used to pay a 63-Shekels bill, to compute 100–63 =?). Therefore customers should observe the excessive change also in the 10-Shekels condition. Nevertheless, we were interested to know if there is a way to rule out this alternative explanation. Fortunately, the experimental design offers a way. We analyzed the difference between the 10-Shekels and 40-Shekels treatments in the group of repeated customers in comparison to the one-time customers. If fewer people return the excessive change in the 10-Shekels condition simply because they do not notice the mistaken change, this should be similar for one-time and repeated customers. The results are striking and clearly refute this alternative explanation. For one-time customers, the difference in returning is less than 20% (23.4% returning in the 40-Shekels condition vs 4.2% in the 10-Shekels condition). For repeated customers, the difference is over 50% (77.6% in the 40-Shekels condition vs 27.1% in the 10-Shekels condition). To further verify that this huge difference is statistically significant even when controlling for other variables, we included an interaction term between High-change and Repeated in regression (1) reported in Table 3.[a] The finding that this interaction term is positive, very large, and statistically significant refutes the alternative explanation of customers not noticing 10 extra Shekels but noticing 40 extra Shekels.

The results about the effects of the level of extra change, repeated vs one-time customers, and gender are sufficiently strong that they are unlikely to change using a different analysis. Nevertheless, it is still helpful to proceed to a more extensive analysis that takes into account more variables. First, because it serves as a robustness check. Second, it is interesting to know how additional variables affect the decision whether to behave honestly, and also controlling for other variables helps to measure the main effects discussed above more accurately. Third, it may show whether results that were not significant, such as the effect of the number of diners, become significant under a more careful analysis.

---

a. We use LPM (linear probability model) regressions rather than logistic regressions because several important effects in our analysis are related to interaction terms, which are problematic in logit and probit models (Ai and Norton, 2003)

**TABLE 3** Determinants of the Decision to Return the Extra Change—Full Sample and Composition of Diners

| Regression | (1) |
|---|---|
| **Variable** | **Coefficient (Robust Standard Error)** |
| **High-change** | **0.1759**** **(0.0743)** |
| **Repeated** | **0.2305***** **(0.0777)** |
| **High-change × Repeated** | **0.3315***** **(0.1162)** |
| Member | 0.1464 (0.1522) |
| Age | 0.0014 (0.0035) |
| Oriental | 0.0434 (0.0676) |
| Weekend | 0.1067 (0.0808) |
| Summer | 0.0132 (0.0667) |
| Occupancy | 0.0198 (0.0386) |
| Booth | −0.0290 (0.0612) |
| Evening | 0.0361 (0.0919) |
| Night | 0.0016 (0.0934) |
| Minutes | −0.0030 (0.0022) |
| Male waiter | −0.0696 (0.0620) |
| Business | −0.0071 (0.0796) |
| Alcohol | −0.0200 (0.0865) |
| Bill-per-person | 0.0020 (0.0014) |

*(Continued)*

**TABLE 3 Determinants of the Decision to Return the Extra Change—Full Sample and Composition of Diners—cont'd**

| Regression | (1) |
|---|---|
| Satisfaction | −0.0858<br>(0.0597) |
| Tip-percent | −0.0010<br>(0.0019) |
| **Woman-diner** | **0.2932*****<br>**(0.0900)** |
| **Women-diners** | **0.4027*****<br>**(0.0922)** |
| Men-diners | 0.0453<br>(0.1045) |
| Mixed-diners | 0.1174<br>(0.0938) |
| Constant | 0.0431<br>(0.2968) |
| $R^2$ | 0.4487 |
| N | 192 |

Comments: The regression uses the linear probability model (OLS) and *p*-values are computed using robust standard errors. The dependent variable is Return, which equals 1 if the customer returned the excessive change and 0 otherwise. Variables that are statistically significant at the 5% or 1% level are in *bold*. *, **, and *** denote statistically significant at the 10%, 5%, and 1%, respectively. Robust standard errors are presented in *parentheses* below the coefficients.

Regression (1) in Table 3 includes in addition to the variables that are common to all regressions the gender composition of the diners. The benchmark is a sole male diner, and four dummy variables capture the other alternatives: Woman-diner (sole female diner), Men-diners (two male diners), Women-diners (two female diners), and Mixed-diners (a woman and a man). As in the more simplistic analysis of Table 2, we see again the large and statistically significant effect of the extra change amount: customers who received 40 extra Shekels have a probability higher by 17.6% (one-time customers) or 50.7% (repeated customers) to return it than customers who received 10 extra Shekels. The number 50.7% is obtained by adding to 17.6% the coefficient of the interaction term High-change X Repeated. Notice that these percentages are absolute differences in probability: a 50.7% increased probability means for example 10% vs 60.7%, not 10% vs 15.07%.

Our hypothesis that repeated customers will behave more honestly is strongly supported by the data. A repeated customer returns the excessive change with a probability higher by 23.1% (in the 10-Shekels treatment) or 56.2%

(in the 40-Shekels treatment), results that are also highly statistically significant. The impact of restaurant club membership is large and in the predicted direction—members return the excessive change 14.6% more often—but this is not statistically significant, due to the small number of tables with member diners (only 11 tables).

We can see that tables with two men or mixed tables with a woman and a man return on average the excessive change more often than the benchmark of a single male diner, but the difference is not statistically significant. However, a table with one woman is more likely to return the excessive change by 29.3% and with two women by 40.3% compared to a single man, both results being statistically significant at the 1% level.

The regression includes also many control variables that could potentially affect the returning decision. Age and Oriental have a coefficient that is small and not statistically significant. Dining over the weekend, or during the evening or night (as opposed to the benchmark, which is lunch) could possibly be associated with more leisurely dining experience than a midweek lunch, and thus could affect the customer's mood and possibly his behavior as well. The weekend coefficient is indeed positive and relatively large (0.1067), but neither it nor the evening and night variables are statistically significant.

We thought that choosing a discounted business meal could signal caring more about one's money and be associated with lower returning of the excessive change, but did not find any such correlation. A higher occupancy of the restaurant, a booth table, and a shorter visit (a lower value in the variable Minutes), we thought, might result in less contact between the waiter and the customer and therefore result in less established closeness between them and consequently less returning of the excessive change. Only the coefficient of Booth is in the predicted direction, and all three are not statistically significant.

The variable Male waiter has a negative coefficient, meaning that on average male waiters received the excessive change less often than female waitresses, but the difference is not statistically significant. The consumption of alcohol could on one hand signal higher income or better mood (encouraging more returning of the excessive change). On the other hand, it could imply a weakening of one's self-control and thus less returning due to less ability to overcome the temptation to keep the extra change. It may also result in a reduced cognitive ability and less detection of the excessive change (and therefore less returning). The results show no significant effect of alcohol consumption on returning, which can mean either that none of the effects mentioned above is present, or that they cancel each other.

The bill-per-person amount presumably is associated with the customer's income, and if people with a higher income have a lower marginal utility from money (which is reasonable with a concave utility function), this could mean that a higher bill per person should be associated with more returning. While the coefficient of Bill-per-person is indeed positive, it is not statistically significant, however.

We hypothesized that a higher customer satisfaction will be associated with more honest behavior; this is what one might expect if people reciprocate—if they are happy with the service they may be more inclined to behave nicely and return excessive change they believe they received by mistake. Surprisingly, the coefficient of Satisfaction is negative (−0.0858) rather than positive, although it is not statistically significant. We should emphasize that the different factors that affected the satisfaction score (and were explained in the previous section) were taken before the change was given to the table. Therefore the provision of excessive change could not affect the satisfaction score.

Because the tip is given after the change is received, we thought that maybe customers who did not return the excessive change will be in a good mood and grateful for the unexpected financial gain and will consequently leave larger tips. On the other hand, possibly those for whom not spending money unnecessarily is more important will not return the excessive change and leave smaller tips. The coefficient of Tip-percent is very small, suggesting that either the two effects cancel out each other, or that none of them is significant.

To further examine the robustness of our results we also ran a regression where instead of considering the composition of the diners, we considered the composition of those who paid the bill. Because of the high correlation between the two we cannot put both in the same regression. The difference between diners and payers obviously may exist only in tables of two diners. In some cases customers who dine but let the second person pay still check the change (or are informed by the other person that the change is higher than it should be) and can affect the decision whether to return the extra change. If this is the common behavior then the better option is to consider the composition of the diners, as we did in regression (1). However, it is also possible that only those who actually pay the bill check the change and decide whether to return the excessive change, and if this is the usual case then it seems better to consider the composition of the payers. To be on the safe side we therefore ran both types of regressions.

Regression (2) in Table 4 presents the results in this alternative regression. The variables that are common to both regressions have similar coefficients and statistical significance in both regressions, showing that the results discussed above are robust to this alternative specification. With respect to the gender composition, which is treated differently in the two regressions, we can see small differences. In regression (2) we have a benchmark of a single man paying the bill, with four dummy variables that capture the other possibilities (Woman-payer, Men-payers, Women-payers, and Mixed-payers). The coefficients of Men-payers and Mixed-payers are close to zero and not statistically significant. The coefficient of Woman-payer is similar to Woman-diner in regression (1) and again statistically significant at the 1% level. The coefficient of Women-payers (two women sharing the bill) is smaller than that of Women-diners in regression (1), 0.2815 vs 0.4027.

To isolate the effects of gender and of the presence of others, two additional regressions were run, reported in Table 5. To be able to make a clear distinction

**TABLE 4 Determinants of the Decision to Return the Extra Change—Full Sample and Composition of Payers**

| Regression | (2) |
|---|---|
| Variable | Coefficient (Robust Standard Error) |
| **High-change** | **0.1705**** **(0.0774)** |
| **Repeated** | **0.2363***** **(0.0779)** |
| **High-change × Repeated** | **0.3279***** **(0.1174)** |
| Member | 0.1308 (0.1447) |
| Age | −0.0001 (0.0035) |
| Oriental | 0.05244 (0.0669) |
| Weekend | 0.1006 (0.0808) |
| Summer | 0.0150 (0.0627) |
| Occupancy | 0.0177 (0.0379) |
| Booth | −0.0201 (0.0631) |
| Evening | 0.0397 (0.0900) |
| Night | −0.0010 (0.0974) |
| Minutes | −0.0018 (0.0021) |
| Male waiter | −0.0730 (0.0624) |
| Business | −0.0078 (0.0771) |
| Alcohol | −0.0192 (0.0897) |
| Bill-per-person | 0.0019 (0.0015) |

*(Continued)*

**TABLE 4** Determinants of the Decision to Return the Extra Change—Full Sample and Composition of Payers—cont'd

| Regression | (2) |
|---|---|
| Satisfaction | −0.0854<br>(0.0598) |
| Tip-percent | −0.0014<br>(0.0020) |
| **Woman-payer** | **0.2734*****<br>**(0.0756)** |
| **Women-payers** | **0.2815*****<br>**(0.0941)** |
| Men-payers | −0.0271<br>(0.0999) |
| Mixed-payers | 0.0005<br>(0.0833) |
| Constant | 0.1067<br>(0.3058) |
| $R^2$ | 0.4386 |
| N | 192 |

Comments: The regression uses the linear probability model (OLS) and *p*-values are computed using robust standard errors. The dependent variable is Return, which equals 1 if the customer returned the excessive change and 0 otherwise. Variables that are statistically significant at the 5% or 1% level are in *bold*. *, **, and *** denote statistically significant at the 10%, 5%, and 1%, respectively. Robust standard errors are presented in *parentheses* below the coefficients.

between male and female tables, we exclude the observations of mixed tables for this analysis, resulting in a sample of 160 tables. The coefficient of Male-table in regression (3) in Table 5 shows that tables of one man or two men are 33.5% less likely to return the excessive change than tables of one woman or two women (*p*-value = 0.000). The coefficient of Two-diners is positive but not statistically significant, so the hypothesis that tables of two will return the extra change more often than tables with one diner is not supported by the data in a significant manner. We observe once again that returning the extra change is positively affected by the higher level of excessive change, repeated customers, and their interaction.

The data show that in all those cases (20 in total) in which all the three main factors that affect returning are in the negative side—that is, when a male table (with either one or two male diners) received 10 Shekels of extra change and did not include repeated customers—the excessive change was not returned. On the other hand, in all cases (also 20 in total) in which all the three main factors that

**TABLE 5 Determinants of the Decision to Return the Extra Change—Excluding Mixed Tables**

| **Regression** | **(3)** | **(4)** |
|---|---|---|
| **Variable** | **Coefficient (Robust Standard Error)** | **Coefficient (Robust Standard Error)** |
| **High-change** | **0.1873**** (0.0856) | 0.2283* (0.1190) |
| **Repeated** | **0.245***** (0.0899) | **0.3787***** (0.1218) |
| **High-change × Repeated** | **0.2784**** (0.1330) | **0.2960**** (0.1309) |
| Member | 0.2267 (0.1622) | 0.2676 (0.1674) |
| Age | 0.0027 (0.0048) | 0.0024 (0.0049) |
| Oriental | 0.0503 (0.0738) | 0.0566 (0.0762) |
| Weekend | 0.0549 (0.0774) | 0.0205 (0.0746) |
| Summer | 0.0522 (0.0728) | 0.0141 (0.0755) |
| Occupancy | 0.0141 (0.0449) | 0.0089 (0.0443) |
| Booth | −0.0537 (0.0699) | −0.0763 (0.0694) |
| Evening | 0.0421 (0.1113) | 0.0317 (0.1134) |
| Night | 0.0249 (0.1031) | 0.0204 (0.1027) |
| Minutes | −0.0032 (0.0025) | −0.0035 (0.0025) |
| Male waiter | −0.1041 (0.0662) | −0.1306 (0.0983) |
| Business | −0.0119 (0.0887) | −0.0375 (0.0894) |
| Alcohol | −0.0391 (0.0932) | −0.0200 (0.0980) |
| Bill-per-person | 0.0026 (0.0015) | 0.0022 (0.0016) |

*(Continued)*

**TABLE 5 Determinants of the Decision to Return the Extra Change—Excluding Mixed Tables—cont'd**

| Regression | (3) | (4) |
|---|---|---|
| Satisfaction | −0.1003<br>(0.0738) | −0.1163<br>(0.0750) |
| Tip-percent | −0.0014<br>(0.0020) | −0.0026<br>(0.0018) |
| **Male-table** | **−0.3345*****<br>(0.0721) | −0.1157<br>(0.1387) |
| Two-diners | 0.0753<br>(0.0760) | 0.1367<br>(0.0976) |
| Two-diners × Male-table | | −0.1010<br>(0.1421) |
| Male waiter × Male-table | | 0.0916<br>(0.1331) |
| **Repeated × Male-table** | | **−0.3017****<br>(0.1263) |
| High-change × Male-table | | −0.0956<br>(0.1248) |
| Constant | 0.3407<br>(0.3755) | 0.4018<br>(0.3805) |
| $R^2$ | 0.4339 | 0.4631 |
| N | 160 | 160 |

Comments: The two regressions use the linear probability model (OLS) and *p*-values are computed using robust standard errors. The dependent variable is Return, which equals 1 if the customer returned the excessive change and 0 otherwise. Variables that are statistically significant at the 5% or 1% level are in *bold*. *, **, and *** denote statistically significant at the 10%, 5%, and 1%, respectively. Robust standard errors are presented in *parentheses* below the coefficients.

affect returning are in the positive side—that is, when a female table (with either one or two female diners) received 40 Shekels of extra change and included repeated customers—the excessive change was returned.

In regression (4) we attempted to gain more insights about gender differences by including also some interactions between Male-table and other variables. In particular, we were interested to know if one of the main effects (repeated customers and high excessive change) has an interesting interaction with gender, and whether the gender of the server and the presence of others do. The results provided some surprises. The coefficient of High-change remained large and positive but its *p*-value now increased to 0.057. The coefficient of Repeated and its interaction with High-change remained large, positive and statistically significant, and variables that were not statistically significant before remained so. However, we were surprised to see that much of the large impact of female diners on returning the extra change disappeared from the coefficient of Male-table. This variable is no longer statistically significant; its coefficient changed from −0.3345 to −0.1157 and the $p$-value changed from 0.000 to 0.406. The interaction of Male-Table with Repeated now captures most of the gender difference, with a coefficient of −0.3017 and $p$-value of 0.018. This suggests that the gender difference in returning the excessive change is not large for one-time customers. However, the positive effect of being a repeated customer on the willingness to return the excessive change is much higher for women than for men, so in the entire sample (of which half is repeated customers) we see a very large gender difference.

The data show that among one-time customers, female tables returned the extra change in 9 out of 40 tables (22.5%) whereas male tables did so in 3 out of 39 tables (7.7%). In all the cases when a man dined alone and was a one-time customer (there were 23 such cases), he did not return the excessive change. Among repeated customers, female tables returned the extra change in 29 out of 39 tables (74.4%) whereas male tables did so in 14 out of 42 tables (33.3%). The absolute difference between male and female tables therefore grows from 14.8% for one-time customers to 41.1% for repeated customers, leading to the statistically significant interaction that we found in regression (4). The other interactions we examined for Male-table, with Two-diners, Male waiter, and High-change, are not statistically significant.

## 4. Conclusion

We used a field experiment to study dishonest behavior in a natural setting. Customers in a restaurant who paid with cash received excessive change and we analyzed the different factors that affect whether the customers decided to return the excessive change or to keep it to themselves. Most customers (128 out of 192) did not return the excessive change. Several factors appeared to have a large effect on the decision whether to return the excessive change.

Consistent with our hypothesis, women were much more likely to return the extra change than men. However, we found that for one-time customers the gender difference is not large; it becomes significant only for repeated customers. It seems that women feel more need than men to behave honestly when they know the server or expect to see him again in the future, but not so much otherwise.

Interestingly, a mixed table (with a woman and a man) behaves much more similar to two men (or one man) than to two women (or one woman). This is true both if we consider the diners' gender or the payers' gender. The difference between a mixed table and a table with one man is not statistically significant, whereas one or two women return the extra change significantly more often than a man. This seems to suggest that in mixed tables not only the man affects the decision whether to return the extra change more than the woman, but also that the man does not try to impress the woman by behaving honestly. Instead, he acts in the same way that he would if he were alone or with another man.

In line with our hypothesis, repeated customers returned the excessive change much more often than one-time customers. One possible reason is that repeated customers are much more likely to visit the restaurant in the future than first-time customers. The possibility that the waiter will find out that he gave too much change and will be upset with them and even remember it on their next visit is a possible motivation to behave more honestly. Another possible reason for more honesty of repeated customers is that they already know some of the restaurant's staff and may feel worse than one-time customers to keep to themselves the extra change at the cost of the waiter or the restaurant.

Some results contradicted our initial hypotheses. We hypothesized that in tables of two diners there will be social pressure to behave honestly and the excessive change will be returned more often than in tables with one diner. The analysis shows no statistically significant effect of the number of diners. A possible reason is that those who do not feel internally the need to behave honestly and return the excessive change also do not think that others believe that this is the appropriate behavior and therefore they do not try to impress others by behaving honestly and returning the extra change.

Even more surprising was the comparison between customers who received 40 extra Shekels to those who received 10 extra Shekels. We thought, in line with earlier findings (Gneezy, 2005), that more people will report the extra change when it is smaller, because the financial loss from returning 10 Shekels is only 25% of the loss from returning 40 Shekels. However, we found a strong and statistically significant pattern in the opposite direction: returning the excessive change was much more common when 40 extra Shekels were given to the customer. Because the financial gain is four times higher in the 40-Shekels treatment, this suggests that the psychological cost of behaving dishonestly and keeping the extra change is more than four times higher in the 40-Shekels condition than in the 10-Shekels condition. It seems that for the smaller amount of 10 Shekels, many people did not consider it as seriously dishonest to keep the extra change to themselves (i.e., the psychological cost of being dishonest was minimal). With the larger amount of 40 Shekels, however, the psychological cost of dishonesty became much more pronounced.

The finding that the psychological cost of dishonest behavior is higher when the negative impact on others (the waiter or the restaurant) is higher is not surprising, and is in line with the findings of Gneezy (2005). But the observation that the psychological cost increases more than the amount involved, and that higher stakes when one's financial gain is the other's loss lead to less dishonesty, is surprising. It is also contrary to Gneezy's results, where increasing the stakes from $1 to $10 resulted in more deception. Thus, our results support the conclusion of Gneezy that the consequences of dishonesty affect the willingness to behave honestly, but they also stress that the exact pattern in which higher stakes affect dishonesty is subtle and may change between different contexts.

We also found a large and statistically significant interaction effect between the High-change and Repeated variables. In other words, the difference in behavior between the 10-Shekels and 40-Shekels treatments is much more pronounced for repeated customers.

## Acknowledgments

We are grateful to Shai Danziger and Simone Moran for helpful comments. We also thank for their insights and comments participants in the Deception, Incentives and Behavior conference in the Rady School of Management, UC San Diego, US; the 2nd International Research-to-Practice Conference "Economic psychology: Past, Present, Future" in Saratov, the Russian Federation; the Herbert Simon Lecture, National Chengchi University, Taiwan; and the SABE-IAREP-ICABEEP 2013 conference, Atlanta, US. We are further grateful for helpful comments made by seminar participants in the Max Planck Institute of Economics in Jena, Germany; University Paris 13, France; University of Granada, Spain; Ben-Gurion University of the Negev, Israel; and the RWTH Aachen University, Germany. We also thank the staff of the restaurant for their cooperation and help in conducting the research and to the management for allowing us to run the experiment in the restaurant.

## References

Ai, C., Norton, E.C., 2003. Interaction terms in logit and probit models. Econ. Lett. 80, 123–129.

Ariely, D., 2008. Predictably Irrational: The Hidden Forces That Shape Our Decisions. HarperCollins.

Azar, O.H., Applebaum, M., 2017. Do Children Cheat to Be Honored? A Natural Experiment on Dishonesty in a Math Competition. (Working paper).

Azar, O.H., Yosef, S., Bar-Eli, M., 2013. Do customers return excessive change in a restaurant? A field experiment on dishonesty. J. Econ. Behav. Organ. 93, 219–226.

Bolton, G.E., Ockenfels, A., 2000. ERC: a theory of equity, reciprocity, and competition. Am. Econ. Rev. 90, 166–193.

Bucciol, A., Landini, F., Piovesan, M., 2013. Unethical behavior in the field: demographic characteristics and beliefs of the cheater. J. Econ. Behav. Organ. 93, 248–257.

De Quervain, D.J.–.F., Fischbacher, U., Treyer, V., Schellhammer, M., Schnyder, U., Buck, A., Fehr, E., 2004. The neural basis of altruistic punishment. Science 305, 1254–1258.

DePaulo, B.M., Kashy, D.A., 1998. Everyday lies in close and casual relationships. J. Pers. Soc. Psychol. 74, 63–79.

Erat, S., Gneezy, U., 2012. White lies. Manag. Sci. 58, 723–733.

Fehr, E., Gachter, S., 2000. Fairness and retaliation: the economics of reciprocity. J. Econ. Perspect. 14, 159–181.

Genereux, R.L., McLeod, B.A., 1995. Circumstances surrounding cheating: a questionnaire study of college students. Res. High. Educ. 36, 687–704.

Gneezy, U., 2005. Deception: the role of consequences. Am. Econ. Rev. 95, 384–394.

Greenwald, A.G., 1980. The totalitarian ego: fabrication and revision of personal history. Am. Psychol. 35, 603–618.

Harrison, G.W., List, J.A., 2004. Field experiments. J. Econ. Lit. XLII, 1009–1055.

Jackson, C.J., Levine, S.Z., Furnham, A., Burr, N., 2002. Predictors of cheating behavior at a university: a lesson from the psychology of work. J. Appl. Soc. Psychol. 32, 1031–1046.

Leary, M.R., Kowalski, R.M., 1990. Impression management: a literature review and two-component model. Psychol. Bull. 107, 34–47.

Mazar, N., Ariely, D., 2006. Dishonesty in everyday life and its policy implications. J. Public Policy Mark. 25, 117–126.

Mazar, N., Amir, O., Ariely, D., 2008. The dishonesty of honest people: a theory of self-concept maintenance. J. Market. Res. 45, 633–644.

Sanitioso, R., Kunda, Z., Fong, G.T., 1990. Motivated recruitment of autobiographical memories. J. Pers. Soc. Psychol. 59, 229–241.

Stearns, S.A., 2001. The student-instructor relationship's effect on academic integrity. Ethics Behav. 11, 275–285.

Tibbetts, S.G., 1999. Differences between women and men regarding decisions to commit test cheating. Res. High. Educ. 40, 323–342.

Ward, D.A., Beck, W.L., 1990. Gender and dishonesty. J. Soc. Psychol. 130, 333–339.

Wirtz, J., Kum, D., 2004. Consumer cheating on service guarantees. J. Acad. Mark. Sci. 32, 159–175.

# Chapter 4.3

# Prosociality and fiscal honesty: Tax evasion in Italy, United Kingdom, and Sweden

Ferruccio Ponzano[1], Stefania Ottone[2]
[1]*DIGSPES—University of Eastern Piedmont, Vercelli, Italy,* [2]*DEMS e CISEPS—University of Milano Bicocca, Milano, Italy*

**Chapter Outline**



**JEL Classification:** C9, D31, H26

## 1. Introduction

Tax evasion is currently a relevant topic for economic, political, and social reasons. In the domestic context, tax evasion is responsible for budgetary problems, causes inefficiencies in the provision of public goods and services, and undermines redistributive policies. In the European context, the fact that the level of tax evasion varies across countries makes political relationships difficult. More specifically, virtuous countries are skeptical that countries where tax evasion levels are high will be able to respect the Maastricht parameters. Consequently, the reticence of virtuous countries that do not want to be burdened by the budgetary problems of vicious countries has slowed down the formation of a stronger European political union.

**Dishonesty in Behavioral Economics. https://doi.org/10.1016/B978-0-12-815857-9.00016-9**

Cross-country studies play a relevant role as they collect information on factors that could influence subjects' fiscal honesty/dishonesty. Broadly, these studies are based on information collected through wide-ranging surveys (the International Social Survey Programme, World Values Survey, and the European Values Survey). The output is twofold: the assignment of a synthetic measure of tax morale[a] to each country—whose value positively correlates to the national tax compliance level—and identification of sociodemographic, personal, and institutional factors that affect people's fiscal honesty (for a mostly exhaustive survey, see Lago-Peñas and Lago-Peñas, 2010). Despite the rich set of cross-country studies focusing on the determinants of tax morale, no analysis is devoted to the possible relationship between prosociality—intended as subjects' concern for other people's payoffs—and fiscal honesty.[b]

Tax evasion may be considered a selfish black lie.[c] Grosch and Rau (2017) found (through a laboratory experiment) that prosocial people are more likely to be honest in a context where dishonest behavior represents a selfish black lie. A simple explanation is that prosocial people, who care about others' payoffs, are less likely to cheat and negatively affect other people's utility. Broadly, prosocial subjects seem to be more sensitive to social norms and encounter social dilemmas in terms of morality (Baillet et al., 2009).

In this chapter, we present the results from a cross-country experimental study[d] where we identify whether prosociality positively correlates to fiscal honesty in the laboratory setting. Subjects from three European countries (Italy, Sweden, and the United Kingdom)[e] participated in several tax games where they

a. Tax morale is measured on the basis of the score obtained through the following question: "Please tell me whether you think that the following statement can always be justified, never be justified, or justified to some extent: Cheating on tax if you have the chance." The answer is organized on a 10-scale index where the extreme points are labeled as "never justified" and "always justified."

b. To our knowledge, Trivedi et al. (2003) is the only scholar who studied whether the attitude towards others affects tax compliance. However, his study is based on a small sample of only 98 Canadian university students.

c. Erat and Gneezy (2012) identify three categories of dishonest behavior: altruistic white lies (dishonesty advantages to other people but not the liar), Pareto white lies (dishonesty advantages to all the parties) and selfish black lies (dishonesty advantages to the liar at the detriment of others). Rational *Homo economicus* is expected to use selfish black lies.

d. See Alm et al. (1992), Torgler (2002), and Pickhardt and Prinz (2014) for in-depth analysis of the relevance of experiments for studying political and economic issues such as tax evasion. See also Poteete et al. (2010) for a discussion on the advantages of implementing a cross-methodological approach to study a phenomenon.

e. We selected these three countries because they belong to three different types of a welfare state, according to the classification by Esping-Andersen (1990): corporatist-statist, social democratic, and liberal, respectively. Moreover, Sweden and Italy have higher tax burden and larger public sectors, while in the United Kingdom the presence of the State in everyday life is limited (see Taxation trends in the European Union: 2017 edition, where the tax burden is measured as the percentage of total taxes with respect to GDP in 2015). On the other hand, Sweden and the United Kingdom are characterized by efficient public services while Italy is famous for public inefficiency and corruption (see Transparency International 2015 and World Bank Governance Indicators).

decided the amount of their experimental gross income to report for fiscal purposes. Each tax game is set in a different institutional context,[f] while the auditing procedure and the sanction are fixed across the scenarios. Sociodemographic and personal characteristics (including prosociality) identified in the literature as determinants of tax morale are controlled at the end of the experiment. This experimental design allows understanding if prosocial people are more honest in fiscal contexts and if this honesty is independent of the institutional characteristics. Our experimental evidence may provide some inputs to enhance understanding on the origin of the different levels of tax evasion among European countries and the role played by governments. In Section 2, we present the social value orientation (SVO) survey, which is the method we used to measure concern people have for others, and a new ordinal categorization of the most idealized form of social orientation (competitive, individualistic, prosocial, and altruist), with the aim to identify and isolate coherent people. In Section 3, we deal with the experimental design and procedure. Section 4 is devoted to statistical and econometric analysis. Section 5 concludes reflecting on the role of cross-country institutional differences in enhancing prosociality and honest behavior in view of a few hypotheses on the nature of prosociality. Further research on this issue to understand the extent to which social-dynamic-dependent rather than inborn prosocial attitudes are responsible for fiscal honesty is strongly recommended.

## 2. SVO survey: A new interpretation of the ordinal categories

Psychologists measure people's attitude toward others through an instrument called SVO. This categorization is based on people's own choices in a series of mini dictator games (DG), where the Dictator chooses how to allocate a certain sum of money between herself and a Receiver who cannot react. Further, the Receiver does not affect the decision maker in any way. Thus, this is not a strategic decision but a one-shot individual decision. However, this task has a social dimension, as the choices made by the Dictator will affect the other person and the decision maker is aware of this. For this reason, choices made in this context reveal important information about decision makers' social preferences. In this study, we use the Slider measure as it is a most reliable SVO measure (for more details, see Murphy et al., 2011).[g]

The Slider measure consists of six primary items. In each item, a subject has to choose an outcome allocation between herself and another player out of the nine options. The *SVO angle* can be computed based on a subject's preferred option in the items (see Fig. 1). The *SVO angle* is a continuous measure of

f. Our work focuses on three relevant characteristics of a tax system: efficiency, tax rate, and support for people in need. For an in-depth discussion of the effect of different institutional settings on tax evasion across countries, see Ottone et al. (2018).

g. The other two SVO measures are the Triple-Dominance measure and the Ring measure. We do not implement them in this study.

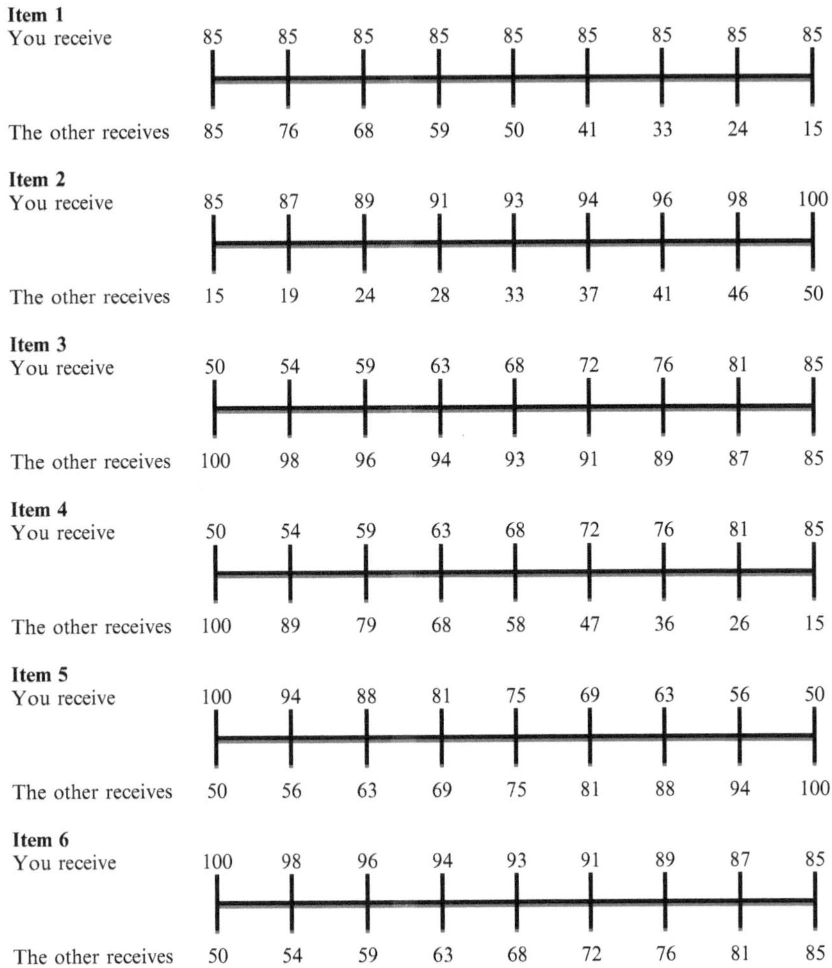


**FIG. 1** Six primary items.

people's SVO, starting from a perfectly competitive position and ending with perfectly altruistic behavior. Starting from the SVO angle, Murphy et al. (2011) identify four categories: altruistic, prosocial, individualistic, and competitive. However, we believe that this ordinal classification has problems that possibly prevent disentangling people's real behavior. Specifically, the same result can be obtained by making different choices. We discuss the results in detail in Appendix A.1, highlighting the problems of this classification and how our new method solves them.

Our redefinition of the four categories, using the Slider measure as a tool, is based on the following utility function:

$$U_i = x_i + ax_j$$

where $U_i$ represents the level of utility of subject *i*, $x_i$ is the pay-off of subject *i*, $x_j$ the pay-off of subject *j* (the other), and *a* is a parameter. The value of parameter *a* is crucial to define the categories. In particular, if *a* is lower than 0, you are categorized as competitive; if *a* is equal to 0, you are individualist; if *a* is higher than 0 and lower or equal to 1, you are prosocial. If *a* is higher than 1, you are categorized as altruist. Thus, it is possible to predict behavior in the mini-DGs starting from this utility function.

If a subject is *competitive*, she will never choose to maximize the other's pay-off even if it does not imply a monetary cost. An *individualist* will always maximize her own pay-off. A *prosocial* will sacrifice a part of her pay-off to give something to the other. If a subject is *altruistic*, she will always choose an option where her own pay-off is lower than the pay-off of the other player.

Each of the six items in the Slider measure has a particular function. The first two items indicate the propensity of a subject to decrease the pay-off of another subject without bearing a cost on the first item and by spending money on the second one. The other four items show the propensity of a subject to spend money to raise the pay-off for the other subject. Thus, if the first two items are seen as a measure to elicit nastiness, the other four items are useful to elicit information on the subject's inclination toward others. Consequently, starting from the observation of the subject's behavior in each mini-DG, it is possible to redefine the four categories developed by Murphy et al. (2011), namely competitive, individualistic, prosocial, and altruist.

In terms of choices in the six items, this classification provides the following regularities:

**(1)** A *competitive* subject will not choose the 85–85 option and the 100–50 option in the first and the second mini-DG, respectively. At the same time, in the third she will choose the 85–85 option, in the fourth the 85–15 option, in the fifth the 100–50, and in the sixth the 100–50 option.

**(2)** An *individualist* will be satisfied with any option in the first item even if she shows a level of nastiness if she does not choose the 85–85 option. In the second mini-DG, she will choose the 100–50 option, in the third she will choose the 85–85 option, in the fourth the 85–15 option, in the fifth the 100–50, and in the sixth the 100–50 option.

**(3)** A *prosocial* will choose the 85–85 option in the first mini-DG, in the second she will choose the 100–50 option. Moreover, she will sacrifice a part of her pay-off to give something to the other subject in at least one of the remaining mini-DGs. Obviously, the sacrificial level can be different. In some cases, the subject prefers to limit the contribution to maintain a higher payoff with respect to the other. In other cases, her payoff can be lower than the pay-off of the other subject to maximize the joint pay-off or minimize inequity.

**(4)** An *altruist* will choose the 85–85 option in the first DG and the 100–50 in the second one. In the remaining mini-DGs, she will always choose an option where her own pay-off is always lower than the pay-off of the other.

**TABLE 1** SVO Angle and Types

| | Lower limit | Upper limit |
|---|---|---|
| Competitive | −16.26 | −8.76 |
| Individualistic | −7.82 | 7.82 |
| Prosocial | 8.76 | 52.91 |
| Altruist | 61.39 | 61.39 |

Any behavior that does not correspond to the previously mentioned actions cannot be classified.

The categories we generate are in line with the SVO-angle. In fact, there is never a cross in the SVO-angle among them. See Table 1 for details.

## 3. The experiment: Design and procedure

This is a lab experiment where the subjects are recruited through a web-based recruitment system (ORSEE, Greiner, 2004) and the experiment is programmed with the software z-Tree (Fischbacher, 2007). This indicates that subjects' choices are recorded through a computer and participants read the instructions on their computer screens while a researcher reads the instructions aloud.[h] We run the experiment in eight different locations (Milan, Bologna, and Rome in Italy; Oxford, Exeter, and London in the United Kingdom; Stockholm and Gothenburg in Sweden). Each session lasted about 90 min and the average earning was 15€.

In each session, the participants enter the laboratory and take a seat in front of a computer. They are asked to switch off their mobiles and to stop talking to coparticipants. First, instructions are read aloud, and the structure of the experiment is presented. Subjects are informed that they will be participating in different phases and will be required to perform tasks and make choices (experimenters gradually describe each phase to the participants). Participants are informed that they will receive payment for participating in the experiment. Based on their and other participants' choices and on chance during the entire experiment, they will earn experimental currency units (ECUs), which will be converted into real money at the end of the session. Moreover, participants are informed that the experiment is anonymous during all the phases and partners' identities are unknown even after the experiment is completed.

The experiment consists of five phases (see Fig. 2). In the first three phases, participants play the tax game for nine rounds (three for each phase).

h. In each location, instructions are presented in the vernacular (local) language and read by a mother-tongue reader. Instructions are available on request.

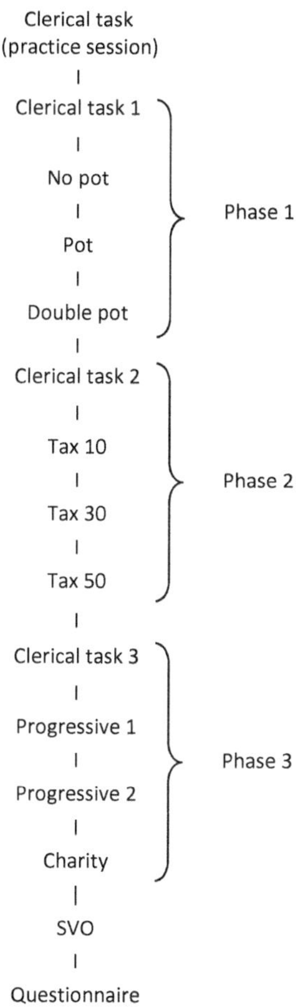


**FIG. 2** Experimental design and procedure.

The players are asked to report their (experimental) income for tax purposes in nine different scenarios where the institutional characteristics change. In the fourth phase, participants' attitude toward the other subjects is elicited through the SVO survey. In the fifth phase, all the participants complete a questionnaire focused on the sociodemographic characteristics that play a key role in determining people's tax morale (according to the literature). A more detailed description of the five phases is reported in the next three subsections.

## 3.1 First three phases: The tax game

Each phase has three rounds and focuses on a particular feature of the tax system—*efficiency*, *tax rate,* and *support for those in need,* respectively.

| Row | ID number | Last name | First name | Vote |
|---|---|---|---|---|
| 1 | 957302 | Iklmqy | Dglpqtwy | 0 |
| 2 | 023568 | Zsefgwt | Ipdbzycx | 6 |
| 3 | 469217 | Ginvxy | Zuexfkja | 8 |
| 4 | 528196 | Tmgczu | Zjpvwks | 9 |
| 5 | 816593 | Bcdhknoy | Klprswx | 9 |
| 6 | 125678 | Bhmoqsuy | Bcglnvwx | 1 |
| 7 | 012468 | Amnsux | Cfiloy | 0 |
| 8 | 912065 | Ysjzmucl | Cgiltvw | 7 |
| 9 | 432970 | Bdgnsx | Wbzaqv | 7 |
| 10 | 234567 | Vzbnjp | Zmfbgo | 6 |
| 11 | 391586 | Fijkln | Zwmvojn | 5 |

**FIG. 3** Example of information to be transcribed in the clerical task.

At the beginning of each phase, participants earn their gross income through an individual real-effort clerical task.[i] In this task, the participants have to copy information about fictitious students (enrolment number, name, surname, and marks) into a file for 5 min (see Fig. 3). For each correctly copied row, the participant earns 10 ECUs. This implies that subjects' gross income in each phase varies according to their ability to correctly type rows of text into predefined boxes on their computer screens; however, subjects do not know how much their earnings are compared to others in the session.

After completing the typing task, participants are asked to self-report their income for tax purposes, according to the specific characteristics of the tax system implemented in each round (see below for details). The participants are instructed round by round on the specific characteristics of the fiscal systems, and are provided some examples to define each scenario more clearly. In each round, participants can report any amount from 0% to 100% of their gross income and they are taxed only on the reported amount. In each round, however, there is a 5% possibility of being audited. At the end of the experiment, if a subject is audited and it is discovered that she has underreported her gross income, she will have to pay a penalty equal to twice the tax she would have paid on the income she did not report during that round.[j] Notice that subjects do not receive feedback on the auditing procedure until the end of the experiment to ensure that the eventual audit and penalties do not influence their choices.

---

i. Before starting the first phase, participants are involved in a practice session to familiarize them with the activity.

j. This implies that if, for example, a subject underreported her income in rounds two and four and she is audited in round three, no penalty is implemented.

The three different phases are designed as follows:

**PHASE 1: EFFICIENCY**. The fiscal system is based on proportional taxation and the tax rate is fixed at 30% for the three rounds, but the efficiency level of the virtual State changes.

Round 1—**No pot**: Tax revenue is not redistributed. This scenario represents a very inefficient State where the entire tax revenue is not used to produce public goods or services but is completely wasted.

Round 2—**Pot**: Tax revenue is divided equally among all the participants, irrespective of their individual contribution. In this case, the government does not waste public money but redistributes resources.

Round 3—**Double pot**: Tax revenue is doubled and divided among all the participants, irrespective of their individual contribution. This scenario represents a virtuous State where public resources are converted into efficient goods and services.

**PHASE 2: TAX RATE** The fiscal system is based on proportional taxation, but the tax rate changes. The level of efficiency is high and fixed (tax revenue is doubled and divided equally among all the participants, irrespective of their individual contribution).

Round 4—**Tax10**: participants pay a proportional tax of 10% of their reported income.

Round 5—**Tax30**: participants pay a proportional tax of 30% of their reported income.[k]

Round 6—**Tax50**: participants pay a proportional tax of 50% of their reported income.

**PHASE 3: SUPPORT FOR THOSE IN NEED**. Efficiency level is high and fixed (tax revenue is doubled), but redistribution favors different types of people based on their need (poor in the laboratory settings and in real life).

Round 7—**Progressive1**: participants pay a tax according to the following system. They are divided into three categories, based on the income reported for tax purposes. Participants are sorted according to the number of currency units reported for tax purposes in descending order (participant number 1 reported the highest number of currency units for tax purposes). The first 10% of the list will constitute Category 1. Category 3 will consist of the last 10%, whereas the remaining 80% will fall into Category 2. Subjects belonging to Category 1 will pay tax equal to 50% of their reported income; subjects belonging to Category 2 will pay tax equal to 30%, whereas subjects belonging to Category 3 will pay tax equal to 10%. Tax revenue is doubled and divided equally among all the participants, irrespective of their individual contribution.

k. Technically, round three and round five are equal.

Round 8—**Progressive2**: participants pay tax according to the following progressive system. The tax rate is equal to 10% and applies up to 50 currency units of the reported income, 30% on the reported income between 51 and 100 currency units, and 50% on the reported income above 100 currency units. Tax revenue is doubled and divided equally among all the participants, irrespective of their individual contribution.
Round 9—**Charity**: participants pay a proportional tax of 30% on the reported income. The tax revenue is doubled and donated to charity.

## 3.2 Fourth phase: Social value orientation survey

At the end of the third phase, subjects are randomly coupled, and they are invited to participate in the Social Value Orientation (SVO) Survey (six items) to measure their level of prosociality (see Murphy et al., 2011). Each subject is asked to play the role of a dictator and makes a series of decisions about allocating resources between herself and the other person. At the end of this phase, only one person in each pair will apply her decisions and these decisions will determine the ultimate pay out (in the form of ECUs) that both subjects receive at the end of this phase. Earnings from this phase (obtained by converting the ECUs into real money) are added to the earnings from the previous three stages of the experiment to determine the final income.

It is important to note here that the decision maker and the other person will remain mutually anonymous during and after making the choice.

## 3.3 Fifth phase: The questionnaire

At the end of the experiment, participants complete a questionnaire, which focuses on the variables identified in the literature as relevant for determining the level of tax morale (see Lago-Peñas and Lago-Peñas, 2010, for a detailed survey of the most relevant findings concerning the determinants of tax morale; see also Appendix A.2 for details concerning data collected through the questionnaire). Consequently, we collect data on:

*Age*, *Gender*, *Field of study*, *Risk aversion*, and *Belief that the other participants are honest.*

In addition, we asked a few questions dealing with the fact that some specific variables may affect the results obtained in a scenario implemented in the laboratory setting with the majority of participants as students. In particular:

*Employed* (we ask subjects if they have a job), *past participation in an experiment* (subjects have to declare whether they previously participated in a laboratory experiment).

Finally, we include some questions drawn from standard ISI international surveys with the aim to collect subjects' opinions both on the relation between the national level of tax evasion and institutional factors such as efficiency, corruption, tax burden, and on the ideal role played by the State in providing public services (see the next section for details and results).

# 4. Experimental results

## 4.1 The sample

Overall, 998 subjects participated in the experiment—311 in Italy, 327 in Sweden, and 360 in the United Kingdom (see Table 2 for details). They were either former or current university students recruited through a web-based recruitment system.

If we codify them according to our new classification, we find that a negligible percentage of subjects are competitive or altruistic, while a remarkable portion of our experimental subjects is labeled "indefinite" (20.9% in Italy, 17.2% in the United Kingdom, and 13.5% in Sweden; see Table 3 for more details). In all the three countries, most indefinite participants were considered individualistic subjects, according to the original classification. This is a relevant point: subjects

**TABLE 2** Number of Experimental Subjects by Location

| Location | Number of subjects |
|---|---|
| Milan (Italy) | 116 |
| Bologna (Italy) | 106 |
| Rome (Italy) | 89 |
| ***Italy*** | ***311*** |
| Stockholm (Sweden) | 227 |
| Gothenburg | 100 |
| ***Sweden*** | ***327*** |
| Oxford | 126 |
| Exeter | 120 |
| London | 114 |
| ***United Kingdom*** | ***360*** |

**TABLE 3** New Ordinal Classification of SVO Types by Country (%)

| | Competitive | Individualistic | Prosocial | Altruist | Indefinite |
|---|---|---|---|---|---|
| Italy | 1.9 | 36.7 | 40.2 | 0.3 | 20.9 |
| United Kingdom | 1.7 | 37.2 | 43.6 | 0.3 | 17.2 |
| Sweden | 0.6 | 19.6 | 66.3 | 0 | 13.5 |

who are supposed to be rational and selfish (the classical *Homo economicus* is included in this category) actually make their choices in a random way. To check if the confusing results obtained in the SVO survey corresponds to incoherent decisions in the tax game, we compare the choices of indefinite subjects with those made by the other participants in the first two rounds. More specifically, for each country, we begin with the original classification proposed by Murphy and identify the category to which "indefinite" subjects are assigned. We consider it as the "reference category." Further, indefinite participant's choices in the first two rounds are compared with those made by subjects in the "reference category," who are not indefinite according to the new classification. We focus on people's choices in the No Pot and Pot rounds since they switch from a highly inefficient scenario where money is wasted to an efficient situation where there is redistribution of the collected taxes. However, high contributions in the No Pot round and nonreaction to an increase in efficiency are dubious choices. From Table 4 it emerges that the choices made by indefinite subjects barely align with the preferences made by the other participants. Their level of compliance is relatively high and sticky over the two rounds.

Thus, for our cross-country analysis on the link between prosociality and honest tax attitudes, we only consider prosocial and individualistic people (according to the new classification). Our final sample of 811 subjects comprises 239 in Italy, 291 in the United Kingdom, and 281 in Sweden, with 43% being women students. Nearly 27% studied economics and 81% had previously participated in an experiment at least once. The average participant age was 25. Nearly 62% participants were prosocial. Table 5 reports the descriptive statistics of the sociodemographic characteristics of the sample.

Prior to analyzing the data, we check if the data obtained from different locations in the same country (Milan, Bologna, and Rome in Italy; Oxford, Exeter, and London in the United Kingdom; Stockholm and Gothenburg in Sweden) can be pooled. In other words, it is necessary to check if people's choices are homogeneous across locations in a country. Fig. 4 shows that no significant difference exists. The econometric analysis also confirms this result.[l] Accordingly, in our analysis we will pool data obtained from different locations of a country.[m]

## 4.2 First question: Are prosocial people more compliant?

As mentioned in the Section 1 of this chapter, taxpayers' value orientation can be expected to shape their tax behavior, since payment of taxes is a public good provision that also affects other taxpayers' wealth. An individualistic taxpayer

l. We run random-effects Tobit regressions for each phase in each country where the dependent variable is the subject's level of compliance and the list of regressors include dummies for location. See Tables 6, 7, and 8 for details.

m. Instead, a series of *t*-test confirm the visual evidence that participants in the United Kingdom comply less. We will discuss this point in details later.

**TABLE 4** Average Level of Compliance in Each Country in the First Two Rounds by SVO Types

| | Italy | | Sweden | | UK | |
|---|---|---|---|---|---|---|
| | *Individualistic (Murphy's definition)* | | | | | |
| | Definite | Indefinite | Definite | Indefinite | Definite | Indefinite |
| Nopot | 0.43 | 0.62 | 0.34 | 0.55 | 0.21 | 0.5 |
| Pot | 0.52 | 0.62 | 0.42 | 0.55 | 0.28 | 0.47 |
| | *Prosocial (Murphy's definition)* | | | | | |
| | Definite | Indefinite | Definite | Indefinite | Definite | Indefinite |
| Nopot | 0.61 | 0.51 | 0.59 | 0.73 | 0.51 | 0.51 |
| Pot | 0.74 | 0.63 | 0.76 | 0.78 | 0.66 | 0.63 |

Definite: A subject who is a definite type (competitive, individualistic, prosocial, or altruistic) according to the new classification.
Indefinite: A subject who is indefinite according to the new classification.

**TABLE 5** Participants' Characteristics

| | Italy | Sweden | UK | Δ(Italy−Sweden) | Δ(Italy−UK) | Δ(UK−Sweden) | Pooled sample |
|---|---|---|---|---|---|---|---|
| Age (mean) | 23.8 | 27.3 | 23.8 | *** | | *** | 24.7 |
| Male (%) | 53.8 | 59.1 | 57.8 | | | | 57.1 |
| Employed (%) | 21.5 | 44.5 | 27.6 | *** | | *** | 31.7 |
| Major econ (%) | 40.8 | 14.9 | 26.8 | *** | *** | *** | 26.8 |
| Past participation (%) | 85.6 | 74 | 83.3 | *** | | *** | 80.7 |
| Prosocial (%) | 52.3 | 77.2 | 53.9 | *** | | *** | 61.5 |
| Risk (mean) | 5.18 | 5.73 | 6.25 | *** | *** | *** | 5.6 |
| Other total compliance (%) | 5.9 | 21.3 | 10.5 | *** | * | *** | 12.9 |

For Age and Risk, we performed a series of t-tests. In all other cases, differences are detected through a series of chi2 tests.
***1% significance, **5% significance, *10% significance.

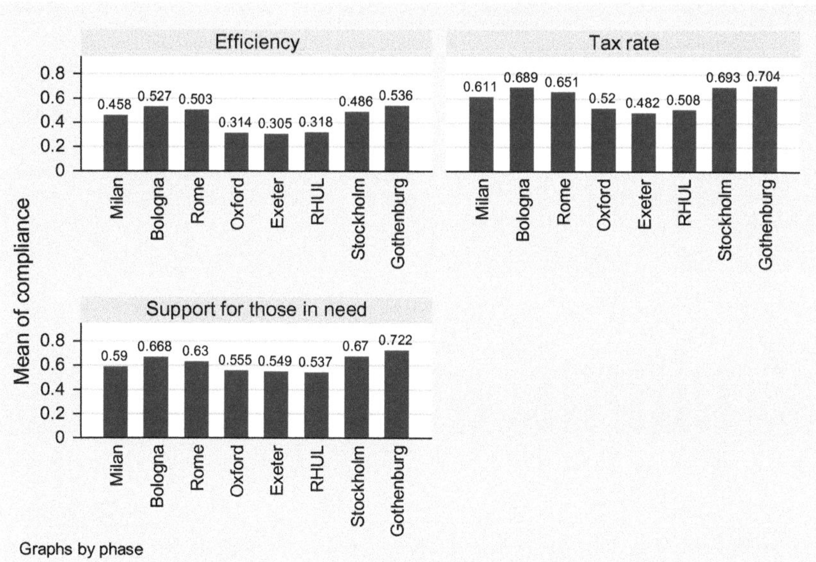


**FIG. 4** Average level of compliance in each phase across locations.

is more likely to evade taxes, regardless of the impact on others, while prosocial taxpayers are expected to take into account the negative effect of their tax evasion on others.

To answer the question, we identify prosocial and individualistic people and we analyze how they behave in each country, phase by phase. From Fig. 5 it emerges that in each round, prosocial people comply more, no matter the country. To confirm the graphical evidence, we run a series of random-effects Tobit regression where the dependent variable—TAX COMPLIANCE—ranges between 0 and 1, where 0 implies "total evasion" and 1 "total compliance." Regressors are a series of determinants of the tax morale identified in the literature, as mentioned in Section 3.3. More specifically, in each country, we run the following three regressions:

$$TAX\_COMPLIANCE_{it} = \alpha + \Sigma_l \beta_l EFFICIENCY_{it} + \Sigma_m \beta_m LOCATION_{it} + \Sigma_r \eta_r DEMOG_i + \Sigma_s \gamma_s PERSONAL\_CHARACTERISTICS_i + \varepsilon + \mu. \quad (R1)$$

$$TAX\_COMPLIANCE_{it} = \alpha + \Sigma_l \beta_l TAX\_RATE_{it} + \Sigma_m \beta_m LOCATION_{it} + \Sigma_r \eta_r DEMOG_i + \Sigma_s \gamma_s PERSONAL\_CHARACTERISTICS_i + \varepsilon + \mu. \quad (R2)$$

$$TAX\_COMPLIANCE_{it} = \alpha + \Sigma_l \beta_l NEED_{it} + \Sigma_m \beta_m LOCATION_{it} + \Sigma_r \eta_r DEMOG_i + \Sigma_s \gamma_s PERSONAL\_CHARACTERISTICS_i + \varepsilon + \mu. \quad (R3)$$

Regression R1 refers to the first phase where the institutional characteristic that changes in each round is the level of efficiency for public good.

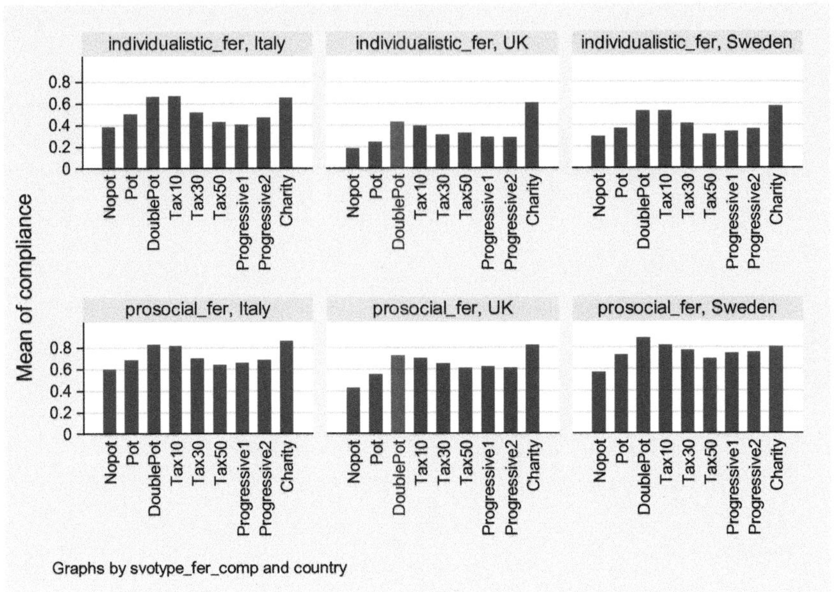


**FIG. 5** Average level of compliance in each phase by country and SVO types.

EFFICIENCY is represented by the two dummy variables *NoPot* and *DoublePot,* which are equal to 1 if the observation comes from the No Pot or the Double Pot round, respectively. The baseline is the Pot scenario. LOCATION dummies are *Rome* and *Bologna* for Italy (the baseline is Milan), *Oxford* and *London* for the United Kingdom (the baseline is Exeter), *Gothenburg* for Sweden (the baseline is Stockholm). Demographic variables (DEMOG) include age and dummy variables for participants who are *male*, *employed*, and studying (or studied) *economics* and *participated in a lab experiment* before. We also included the *income* earned in Phase 1 of the experiment.[n] PERSONAL_CHARACTERISTICS include participants' attitude toward *risk,* as measured by a the survey item that asks participants to rank themselves on a 10-point scale (1 refers to a person who "normally avoids taking risks" and 10 refers to someone who is "completely willing to take risks"), a dummy variable for participants who turn out to be *prosocial* in the SVO survey, and a dummy for participants who believe that most of the *other* experimental subjects *report their entire gross incomes*.

Regression R2 refers to the second phase, where the institutional characteristic that changes in each round is the tax rate. TAX_RATE is represented by the two dummy variables *Tax10* and *Tax50,* which are equal to 1 if the observation comes from the Tax10 or the Tax50 round, respectively. The baseline is the Tax30 scenario.

n. The higher the income, the higher the monetary advantage in case of evasion.

Finally, regression R3 refers to the third phase, where the institutional characteristic that changes in each round is the way different types of people in need are supported. NEED is represented by the two dummy variables *Prog1* and *Prog2*, which are equal to 1 if the observation comes from the Progressive1 or the Progressive2 round, respectively. The baseline is the Charity scenario.

The econometric analysis (see Tables 6, 7, and 8) confirms the graphical suggestion. Consequently, our first evidence is:

*Result 1. In all the phases—no matter the location—prosocial people comply more.*

In other words, prosocial people are more likely to comply with the rule and behave more honestly.

*From the first result, we move toward the second question: Do prosocial people behave unconditionally honestly, or do they respond to authorities' behavior?*

**TABLE 6 R1: Compliance Level in the First Phase by Country**

| | Italy | Sweden | UK |
|---|---|---|---|
| No Pot | −0.412*** | −0.794*** | −0.397*** |
| Double Pot | 0.608*** | 1.111*** | 0.784*** |
| Rome | −0.005 | | |
| Bologna | −0.025 | | |
| Gothenburg | | 0.128 | |
| Oxford | | | −0.30 |
| London | | | −0.303 |
| Prosocial | 0.37** | 1.522*** | 0.797*** |
| Sociodemographic controls | YES | YES | YES |
| Personal characteristic controls | YES | YES | YES |
| Left-censored obs | 177 | 233 | 379 |
| Uncensored obs | 179 | 125 | 185 |
| Right-censored obs | 319 | 470 | 270 |
| Subjects | 225 | 276 | 278 |

Random-effects Tobit model. Dependent variable: percentage of income declared in NOPOT, POT, and DOUBLEPOT rounds. Baseline: POT

*** 1% significance, ** 5% significance, * 10% significance.

Chow tests on regressions with rounds, sociodemographic controls, and personal characteristics as regressors report significant differences between the coefficients of the three countries ($p<0.04$).

**TABLE 7 R2: Compliance Level in the Second Phase by Country**

| | Italy | Sweden | UK |
|---|---|---|---|
| Tax10 | 0.528*** | 0.541*** | 0.343*** |
| Tax50 | −0.207** | −0.443*** | −0.073 |
| Rome | 0.117 | | |
| Bologna | −0.213 | | |
| Gothenburg | | 0.149 | |
| Oxford | | | 0.163 |
| London | | | −0.031 |
| Prosocial | 0.579*** | 1.683*** | 0.947*** |
| Sociodemographic controls | YES | YES | YES |
| Personal characteristics controls | YES | YES | YES |
| Left-censored obs | 163 | 253 | 317 |
| Uncensored obs | 180 | 168 | 175 |
| Right-censored obs | 332 | 542 | 342 |
| Subjects | 225 | 275 | 278 |

Random-effects Tobit model. Dependent variable: percentage of income declared in TAX10, TAX30, and TAX50 rounds. Baseline: TAX30.
*** 1% significance, ** 5% significance, * 10% significance.
Chow tests on regressions with rounds, sociodemographic controls, and personal characteristics as regressors report significant differences between the coefficients of Italy and United Kingdom ($p$=0.0003).

This question arises, as studies on prosocial behavior do not identify a univocal motivation behind people's kind attitude towards others. Van der Linden (2011) suggests that prosocial behavior is mainly due to internal moral norms rather than social norms. Batson (1987) suggests that prosociality emerges because of empathic concerns, which is an inborn characteristic. On the other hand, according to House (2018), prosociality is the result of social dynamics. In particular, social norms shape prosocial behavior. In other words, prosociality may be learnt, internalized, and depends on the social context. If fiscal honesty mostly depends on prosociality as a personal characteristic, we expect unconditional compliance. In contrast, if the context matters, prosocial people's honesty varies with the institutional scenario.

To answer this question, we focus on the first phase where there is no doubt that the Pot and Double Pot scenarios represent a better situation with respect

**TABLE 8** R3: Compliance Level in the Third Phase by Country

| | Italy | Sweden | United Kingdom |
|---|---|---|---|
| Prog1 | −0.761*** | −0.639*** | −0.965*** |
| Prog2 | −056*** | −0.546 *** | −1.005*** |
| Rome | −0.038 | | |
| Bologna | −0.057 | | |
| Gothenburg | | 0.277 | |
| Oxford | | | −0.148 |
| London | | | −0.205 |
| Prosocial | 0.57*** | | 0.717*** |
| Sociodemographic controls | YES | YES | YES |
| Personal characteristics controls | YES | YES | YES |
| Left-censored obs | 151 | 190 | 269 |
| Uncensored obs | 202 | 151 | 210 |
| Right-censored obs | 322 | 487 | 355 |
| N | | | |
| Subjects | 225 | 276 | 278 |

Random-effects Tobit model. Dependent variable: percentage of income declared in PROGRESSIVE1, PROGRESSIVE2, and CHARITY rounds. Baseline: CHARITY
*** 1% significance, ** 5% significance, * 10% significance.
Chow tests on regressions with rounds, sociodemographic controls, and personal characteristics as regressors report significant differences between the coefficients of United Kingdom and the remaining two countries ($P<0.03$).

to the No Pot round. This is because inefficiency is a negative feature of a government. It harms citizens and represents an unfair behavior toward taxpayers. Consequently, a scenario where the tax revenue is entirely wasted should elicit disappointment and negative reactions. Thus, if prosocial people do not behave differently in the first three rounds (switching from high inefficiency to high efficiency), we can conclude that they are not only more honest but also unconditionally more honest.

From Fig. 5 it emerges that even if prosocial people are more compliant versus individualistic people in all the three rounds of the first phase, they are not unresponsive to changes in efficiency. The econometric analysis confirms the graphical evidence. Again, we run a random-effects Tobit regression on the prosocial subsample for each country. The dependent variable is TAX COMPLIANCE and the specification is:

$$TAX\_COMPLIANCE_{it} = \alpha + \Sigma_l \beta_l EFFICIENCY_{it} + \Sigma_r \eta_r DEMOG_i + \Sigma_s \gamma_s PERSONAL\_CHARACTERISTICS_i + \varepsilon + \mu. \quad \text{(R4)}$$

Table 9 confirms that even prosocial people increase their level of compliance as efficiency increases.

*Result 2. Even if prosocial people are more honest than individualists, they are not unconditionally honest. In fact, they react to the efficiency/inefficiency of the virtual state and increase their level of compliance as far as efficiency increases.*

*The final questions refer to a cross-country comparison: What is the role of culture and institutions in determining the various levels of tax compliance across different countries? Do these factors explain a high level of tax evasion in Italy?*

Results from R1 to R3 show that institutions affect subjects' fiscal honesty in each country. In particular, tax evasion decreases as efficiency increases, tax rate decreases and tax revenue is allocated to those who are really in need. Moreover, we observe that prosocial people are more compliant, compared to

**TABLE 9** R4: Compliance Level of Prosocials in the First Phase by Country

| | Italy | Sweden | United Kingdom |
|---|---|---|---|
| No Pot | −0.298*** | −0.835*** | −0.39*** |
| Double Pot | 0.538*** | 1.048*** | 0.576*** |
| Sociodemographic controls | YES | YES | YES |
| Personal characteristics controls | YES | YES | YES |
| Left-censored obs | 57 | 130 | 133 |
| Uncensored obs | 109 | 103 | 132 |
| Right-censored obs | 188 | 406 | 188 |
| Subjects | 118 | 213 | 151 |

Random-effects Tobit model. Dependent variable: percentage of income declared in NOPOT, POT, and DOUBLEPOT rounds. Baseline: POT

*** 1% significance,** 5% significance,* 10% significance.

Chow tests on regressions with rounds, sociodemographic controls, and personal characteristics as regressors report significant differences between the coefficients of the United Kingdom and the remaining two countries ($P<0.08$).

individualistic people. Now, we wish to detect if these factors have an impact on different levels of fiscal honesty across countries.

In real life, Sweden is famous for low levels of tax evasion and high efficiency of goods and services provided by the State. At the same time, it turns out that Sweden has a higher percentage of prosocial people. If we assume that prosocial behavior is not necessarily innate but may be the result of social dynamics, we can assume that the two factors are correlated. If I live in a society where the State is fair and efficient, where the social dimension is relevant, and the social norm is to be honest and compliant, I am more likely to be prosocial and expect others to behave in the same way. In contrast, I may assume that in a country like Italy, where taxation is high and the government has the reputation of wasting money, people are more likely to cheat and expect others to do the same. In the presence of corruption and inefficiency, the higher the tax rate, the bigger is the amount of public money that is wasted by the State. In the final questionnaire, 69.3% Italian participants completely agree that people would more likely pay taxes if the government were more efficient (vs 34.8% and 32.4% in the United Kingdom and Sweden, respectively). Further, 55.6% would comply with their fiscal obligations if they had some control over how the tax money is spent (vs 30% and 25.7% in the United Kingdom and Sweden, respectively). About 14% said that most people in Italy evade their fiscal obligations because politicians are corrupt (vs 7.3% in the United Kingdom and 2.1% in Sweden), and 25.2% of Italian participants completely agree with the fact that most people are forced to evade because of the high tax rates (vs 14.3% and 10.7% in the United Kingdom and Sweden, respectively).

However, this does not mean that all the subjects will be individualistic. Perhaps, it may be the case that prosociality is acquired and cultivated in familiar or neighborhood contexts. However, since prosociality does not imply unconditional compliance, it is possible that even prosocial people evade taxes in the context where the res publica does not work.

The implication is that with the same ratio of prosocials and an efficient public sector, we can expect Italian people to be honest. In addition, even when the tax revenue is used in an efficient way, in scenarios where the tax rate is high and the public sector is large, we can expect the Italian and Swedish people to be more compliant than the United Kingdom participants. The reason is that the latter are used to low tax rates and a small role for the government. In fact, the Italian and Swedish public sector is large, implying that the State is likely to affect its citizens' lives more than in the United Kingdom. Moreover, the perception of the importance of public services is different between these countries: in our sample, Italians and Swedes, 47.9% and 54.5%, respectively, "completely agree on the fact that paying taxes is rational because it finances useful and important services." This percentage drops to 30.6% in the United Kingdom. When we asked subjects to rank themselves on a 0–10 point scale where 10 indicates complete agreement with the statement "Individuals should take more responsibility for providing for themselves," and 0 shows complete agreement with the statement, "The state should take more responsibility to ensure that everyone is provided for," subjects from Italy and Sweden scored 3.6 and 4.2, respectively, while the United Kingdom subjects scored 5.6. This implies that Italian and Swedish subjects are more likely to accept expanded government presence in everyday life.

We can analyze our data to check if, in the lab, there is any difference between fiscal honesty in the three countries once we control for institutional characteristics and prosociality.

We ran a series of random-effects Tobit regression on the pooled sample, where the dependent variable is TAX COMPLIANCE. Regressors are the same as in Regressions R1 to R3, with the inclusion of COUNTRY dummies and the exclusion of LOCATION dummies. More specifically:

$$TAX\_COMPLIANCE_{it} = \alpha + \Sigma_l \beta_l EFFICIENCY_{it} + \Sigma_m \beta_m COUNTRY_{it} + \Sigma_r \eta_r DEMOG_i + \Sigma_s \gamma_s PERSONAL\_CHARACTERISTICS_i + \varepsilon + \mu. \quad \text{(R5)}$$

$$TAX\_COMPLIANCE_{it} = \alpha + \Sigma_l \beta_l TAX\_RATE_{it} + \Sigma_m \beta_m COUNTRY_{it} + \Sigma_r \eta_r DEMOG_i + \Sigma_s \gamma_s PERSONAL\_CHARACTERISTICS_i + \varepsilon + \mu. \quad \text{(R6)}$$

$$TAX\_COMPLIANCE_{it} = \alpha + \Sigma_l \beta_l NEED_{it} + \Sigma_m \beta_m COUNTRY_{it} + \Sigma_r \eta_r DEMOG_i + \Sigma_s \gamma_s PERSONAL\_CHARACTERISTICS_i + \varepsilon + \mu. \quad \text{(R7)}$$

For each specification, we ran two regressions where the dummies for COUNTRY are *Italy* and *Sweden* (baseline the United Kingdom) and *Sweden* and the *United Kingdom* (baseline Italy), respectively.

Broadly, from our analysis it emerges that Sweden and Italy are characterized by the same level of fiscal honesty, while in the lab setting tax evasion is more common in the United Kingdom (see Table 10). If we split our sample between individualistic and prosocial participants, we find that there is no difference between Swedish and British individualistic people, while both Italian and Swedish prosocials are more honest compared to their United Kingdom counterparts, except in Phase 3 (see Tables 11 and 12).

To explain this evidence, different factors seem to play a role. First, institutional factors matter. What emerges from this experiment is that public sector inefficiency leads to a high level of fiscal dishonesty in all the countries; in the presence of efficiency, Italian subjects do not behave less honestly than participants from the other countries, even in scenarios where the tax rate is high.

Second, the difference in the nature of fiscal dishonesty in the three countries may affect this result. With respect to Sweden, as in previous works (Andrighetto et al., 2016; Ottone et al., 2018), Italians are more likely to "fudge" (i.e., evade slightly); consequently, Italian individualists totally evade paying tax less frequently than Swedish people (see Table 13). However, from the analysis of the pooled sample, it is observed that there are no major difference between Italy and Sweden because the higher number of prosocials (more prosocial than

**TABLE 10** R5–R6–R7: Compliance Level by Phase

| | Efficiency | Tax rate | Support for those in need |
|---|---|---|---|
| No Pot | −0.511*** | | |
| Double Pot | 0.798*** | | |
| Tax10 | | 0.463*** | |
| Tax50 | | −0.227*** | |
| Prog1 | | | −0.74*** |
| Prog2 | | | −0.81*** |
| Italy | 0.215 | 0.228 | 0.122 |
| United Kingdom | −0.473*** | −0.272* | −0.102 |
| Age | 0.007 | 0.009 | 0.004 |
| Male | −0.674*** | −0.631*** | −0.485*** |
| Employed | −0.023 | 0.142 | −0.016 |
| Econ major | −0.287** | −0.37*** | −0.277*** |
| Past participation | −0.562*** | −0.215 | −0.285** |
| Prosocial | 0.810*** | 0.964*** | 0.777*** |
| Risk | −0.137*** | −0.076*** | −0101*** |
| Others report: total compliance | 0.934*** | 1.021*** | 0.834*** |
| Income | −0.002 | −0.004** | −0.003*** |
| Constant | 1.906*** | 1.529*** | 2.412*** |
| Left-censored obs | 789 | 681 | 610 |
| Uncensored obs | 489 | 485 | 563 |
| Right-censored obs | 1059 | 1168 | 1164 |
| Subjects | 779 | 778 | 779 |

Random-effects Tobit model regression. Dependent variable: percentage of income declared. Reference country: Sweden
*** 1% significance, ** 5% significance, * 10% significance.

individualistic people) in Sweden counterbalances the fact that individualistic Italians are less dishonest.

Lower compliance in the United Kingdom at the aggregate level may depend both on the fact that individualistic people in the United Kingdom (proportionately the same as in Italy) totally evade more than Italians do (see Table 13), and prosocials

**TABLE 11** R5–R6–R7: Compliance Level of Individualistic People by Phase

| | Efficiency | Tax rate | Support for those in need |
|---|---|---|---|
| No Pot | −0.515*** | | |
| Double Pot | 1.050*** | | |
| Tax10 | | 0.614*** | |
| Tax50 | | −0.225* | |
| Prog1 | | | −1.213*** |
| Prog2 | | | −1.081*** |
| Italy | 0.941*** | 0.829** | 0.521** |
| United Kingdom | −0.308 | 0.061 | 0.085 |
| Sociodemographic controls | YES | YES | YES |
| Personal characteristics controls | YES | YES | YES |
| Left-censored obs | 469 | 423 | 396 |
| Uncensored obs | 145 | 164 | 190 |
| Right-censored obs | 277 | 304 | 305 |
| Subjects | 297 | 297 | 297 |

Random-effects Tobit model regression. Dependent variable: percentage of income declared. Reference country: Sweden.
*** 1% significance, ** 5% significance, * 10% significance.

are less compliant in Sweden and Italy in the first two phases (see Table 12). The fact that prosocials in the United Kingdom are less compliant in Phase 3 may be explained by the fact that fiscal systems in the first two phases (characterized by inefficiency, high tax rates, and proportional taxation) are far from their typical and probably preferred context (limited presence of the State, efficiency, and progressivity).

All these considerations lead to the third result.

*Result 3: Both institutional characteristics and cultural factors explain cross-country differences in tax evasion.*

## 5. Conclusions

In this cross-country experimental study, we focus on the relationship between prosociality and fiscal honesty in different institutional scenarios. Our main result is that prosociality plays a role in determining tax compliance in the different laboratories in Italy, the United Kingdom, and Sweden, even if prosocial people's

**TABLE 12 R5–R6–R7: Compliance Level of Prosocial People by Phase**

| | Efficiency | Tax rate | Support for those in need |
|---|---|---|---|
| No Pot | −0.502*** | | |
| Double Pot | 0.697*** | | |
| Tax10 | | 0.382*** | |
| Tax50 | | −0.227*** | |
| Prog1 | | | −0.590*** |
| Prog2 | | | −0.551*** |
| Italy | −0.075 | −0.045 | −0.033 |
| United Kingdom | −0.491*** | −0.352** | −0.169 |
| Sociodemographic controls | YES | YES | YES |
| Personal characteristics controls | YES | YES | YES |
| Left-censored obs | 320 | 258 | 214 |
| Uncensored obs | 344 | 321 | 373 |
| Right-censored obs | 782 | 864 | 859 |
| Subjects | 482 | 481 | 482 |

Random-effects Tobit model regression. Dependent variable: percentage of income declared. Reference country: Sweden.
*** 1% significance,** 5% significance,* 10% significance.

choices are not independent from the institutional context. Thus, even prosocials decrease their level of fiscal honesty when the State is inefficient.

Therefore, the take-home message for countries where tax evasion is widespread is to invest in efficient public goods and services. This may affect citizens' tax compliance levels both directly and indirectly. First, efficiency increases compliance since people are ready to pay taxes when the tax revenue is not wasted and their sacrifice is useless. Thus, if prosociality can be learnt, an efficient State may trigger a virtuous circle where the government itself shares the social norm of fair behavior and honesty, and general compliance in different social contexts can be expected (as in Sweden).

Future research should be devoted to a deeper analysis of the nature of prosociality to disentangle the innate essence and the socially dependent attitude. This will likely provide a better insight into the extent to which personal characteristics vs institutions affect people's fiscal honesty. Elucidating this issue may help to better understand the cross-country differences.

**TABLE 13** Multinomial Probit Model Regressions: Taxpayers' Behavior by Phase

| | *Pooled sample* | | | *Individualists* |
|---|---|---|---|---|
| | **Total compliance** | **Fudging** | **Total evasion** | **Total evasion** |
| Phase 1 | | | | |
| Sweden | 0.006 | −0.139*** | 0.133*** | 0.224*** |
| United Kingdom | −0.173*** | −0.04 | 0.211*** | 0.276*** |
| Phase 2 | | | | |
| Sweden | −0.007 | −0.11*** | 0.117*** | 0.199*** |
| United Kingdom | −0.095** | −0.04 | 0.139*** | 0.193*** |
| Phase 3 | | | | |
| Sweden | 0.01 | −0.115*** | 0.105*** | 0.198*** |
| United Kingdom | −0.048 | −0.036 | 0.085*** | 0.144*** |
| Sociodemographic controls | YES | YES | YES | YES |
| Personal characteristics controls | YES | YES | YES | YES |
| N | 2337 | 2337 | 2337 | 891 |
| Subjects | 779 | 779 | 779 | 297 |

Marginal effects. Cluster at the subject level.
*** 1% significance, ** 5% significance, * 10% significance.

# Appendix

## A.1 Advantages and Criticism of SVO Classification by Murphy et al. (2011)

The Slider measure provides a continuous measure of people's social value orientation (SVO), starting from a perfectly competitive position at −16.26°, and ending with perfectly altruistic behavior at 61.39°. Murphy et al. (2011) identify four different nominal categories: competitive (angle lower than −12.04), individualistic (angle between −12.04 and 22.45), prosocial (angle between 22.45 and 57.15) and altruistic (angle higher than 57.15).

This classification has some interesting properties. First, it provides a measure of the intensity of people's attitude towards others. Next, it is easy to administer. Finally, it is efficient, as it does not identify rarely represented pathological types such as sadomasochism. This allows asking people to choose six items only to provide a one-dimensional measure of SVO, which simplify data analyses.

However, despite all these positive relevant properties, the classification presents a twofold critical issue. First, it concerns the way nominal categories are drawn. For instance, the division between prosocial and individualistic is based on the average between the upper value of the pure individualist in the SVO angle (7.82) and the lower value of the pure prosocial (37.09). Thus, if an individual shows a value that is higher (lower) than 22.45, she is considered a prosocial (individualistic). Second, the SVO angle per se does not allow isolating incoherent people. In other words, an angle is assigned to everybody, no matter the coherence of the choices. Therefore, the presence of a large number of inconsistent people biases leads to the sample over representing either prosocial or individualistic subjects. We provide a couple of examples to explain this point. First, consider the case where a subject always chooses the median option (option 5 in each item). Her SVO angle will measure 22.93°. This pattern of choices does not belong to any coherent behavior. It is probably a rule of thumb result to save time. However, this subject is classified as prosocial. Second, consider a subject that always chooses the first option starting from the right. Her SVO angle measures 14.74 and she is classified as an individualist even if in item 5 she is ready to maximize the pay-off of the other subject reducing her own.

In our study, before checking whether a relationship between prosociality and fiscal honesty exists, we deal with these critical issues and we try to define new nominal categories whose classification is based on specific behavioral traits. This new classification has three main advantages. First, it provides a clear behavioral portrait of each type. Second, it allows excluding incoherent subjects. Finally, it is perfectly in line with the SVO angle measure. In fact, each category is characterized by a different level of intensity of either *proself* or *prosocial* attitude, which is correlated to the SVO angle. This allows using a discrete classification that keeps the same characteristics of the continuous measure.

## A.2 Details of The Questionnaire

In this section, we report both some findings concerning the variables the literature has identified as relevant to determining the level of tax morale (for a detailed survey, see Lago-Peñas and Lago-Peñas, 2010,) and the reasons why we included some questions focused on subjects' specific personal details in the questionnaire.

*Age*: Tax morale tends to be higher among older people.

*Gender*: The effect of gender on tax compliance is controversial. In most studies, women are more honest than men are. However, is not always possible to replicate this result. The same controversial results emerge in experiments. In some cases, women are more compliant (see, among others, Hasseldine, 1999; Lewis et al., 2009; Spicer and Becker, 1980), while in others no significant difference emerges (see, among others, Chung and Trivedi, 2003; Kirchler and Maciejovsky, 2001). Overall, women tend to be more honest as they are usually more likely to be prosocial (Grosch and Rau, 2017).

*Field of study*: The literature on tax morale analyses the effect of education on tax morale and what emerges is, again, controversial evidence. In some studies, education and tax morale are positively correlated while in others the relation is the opposite. This result is obvious. Well-educated people are supposed to understand the benefits of public services better and are more likely to identify cases where the State wastes public resources. However, they are more likely to understand opportunities for evasion. In our experiment, we prefer to avoid any generic control for the level of education since we run an experiment with highly educated participants (university students and graduates). We decided, instead, to control for the field of study and include in the econometric analysis a dummy for economics since students of that subject are supposed to be taught to behave selfishly.

*Risk aversion*: The literature on tax compliance shows that there is a positive correlation between risk aversion and tax morale. This relationship is intuitive: the higher the level of risk aversion, the higher the probability of compliance due to fear of being detected and sanctioned.

*Belief about the fact that the other participants behave honestly*: Generally, taxpayers tend to be conditional co-operators. Thus, their level of compliance depends on peers' virtuous behavior.

*Employed*: We ask subjects if they have a job. We think it is a relevant point since people with a job are supposed to have more confidence in the fiscal system.

*Past participation in an experiment*: Subjects have to declare whether they previously participated in a lab experiment. This information allows checking if people proficient in lab experiments behave differently. We do not have any specific hypothesis on this. The effect may be erratic and depend on both their previous experience (whether they had participated in an experiment where the other participants were cooperative or not) and the ability they develop to make choices that may increase her/his final income.

## Funding

The research leading to these results received funding from the European Research Council under the European Union's Seventh Framework Programme (FP7/2007–2013)/ERC Grant Agreement n. [295675]. The funders had no role in study design, data collection and analysis, decision to publish, or preparation of the manuscript.

## References

Alm, J., McClelland, G.H., Schulze, W.D., 1992. Why do people pay taxes? J. Public Econ. 48, 21–38.

Andrighetto, G., Zhang, N., Ottone, S., Ponzano, F., D'Attoma, J., Steinmo, S., 2016. Are some countries more honest than others? Evidence from a tax compliance experiment in Sweden and Italy. Front. Psychol. 7, 472.

Baillet, D., Parks, C., Joireman, J., 2009. Social value orientation and cooperation in social dilemmas: a Meta analysis. Group Process. Intergroup Relat. 12 (4), 533–547.

Batson, D., 1987. Prosocial motivation: is it ever truly altruistic? Adv. Exp. Soc. Psychol. 20, 65–122.

Chung, J., Trivedi, V.U., 2003. The effect of friendly persuasion and gender on tax compliance behavior. J. Bus. Ethics 47 (2), 133–145.

Erat, S., Gneezy, U., 2012. White lies. Manag. Sci. 58 (4), 723–733.

Esping-Andersen, G., 1990. The Three Worlds of Welfare Capitalism. Polity Press, Cambridge.

Fischbacher, U., 2007. Z-tree: zurich toolbox for ready-made economic experiments. Exp. Econ. 10 (2), 171–178.

Greiner, B., 2004. The Online Recruitment System ORSEE—A Guide for the Organization of Experiments in Economics. Papers on Strategic Interactions. Max Planck Institute of Economics, Strategic Interactions Group.

Grosch, K., Rau, H.A., 2017. Gender differences in honesty: the role of social value orientation. J. Econ. Psychol. 62, 258–267.

Hasseldine, J., 1999. Gender differences in tax compliance. Asia-Pacific J. Tax. 3 (2), 73–89.

House, B.R., 2018. How do social norms influence prosocial development? Curr. Opin. Psychol. 20, 87–91.

Kirchler, E., Maciejovsky, B., 2001. Tax compliance within the context of gain and loss situations, expected and current asset position, and profession. J. Econ. Psychol. 22 (2), 173–194.

Lago-Peñas, I., Lago-Peñas, S., 2010. The determinants of tax morale in comparative perspective: evidence from European countries. European Journal of Political Economy 26 (4), 441–453.

Lewis, A., Carrera, S., Cullis, J., Jones, P., 2009. Individual, cognitive and cultural differences in tax compliance: UK and Italy compared. J. Econ. Psychol. 30, 431–445.

Murphy, R.O., Ackermann, K.A., Handgraaf, M.J., 2011. Measuring social value orientation. Judgm. Decis. Mak. 6 (8), 771–781.

Ottone, S., Ponzano, F., Andrighetto, G., 2018. Tax compliance under different institutional settings in Italy and Sweden: an experimental analysis. Economia Politica 35 (2), 367–402.

Pickhardt, M., Prinz, A., 2014. Behavioral dynamics of tax evasion—a survey. J. Econ. Psychol. 40, 1–19.

Poteete, A.R., Janssen, M.A., Ostrom, E., 2010. Working Together: Collective Action, the Commons, and Multiple Methods in Practice. Princeton University Press, Princeton, NJ.

Spicer, M., Becker, L.A., 1980. Fiscal inequity and tax evasion: an experimental approach. Natl. Tax J. 33 (2), 171–175.

Torgler, B., 2002. Speaking to theorists and searching for facts: tax morale and tax compliance in experiments. J. Econ. Surv. 16 (5), 657–683.

Trivedi, U.V., Shehata, M., Lynn, B., 2003. Impact of personal and situational factors on taxpayer compliance: an experimental analysis. J. Bus. Ethics 47, 3.

Van der Linden, S., 2011. Charitable intent: a moral or social construct? A revised theory of planned behavior model. Curr. Psychol. 30 (4), 355–374.

Chapter 4.4

# Can upfront declarations of honesty improve anonymous self-reports of sensitive information?

Andrea Isoni[1,2], Daniel Read[1], Julia Kolodko[1], Julián Arango-Ochoa[3], Jiarong Chua[4], Shristi Tiku[4], Alanda Kariza[4]

[1]*Business School, Coventry, United Kingdom,* [2]*University of Cagliari, Italy,* [3]*Universidad EAFIT, Medellín, Colombia,* [4]*University of Warwick*

## Chapter Outline



**JEL Classification:** C99, D91

## 1. Introduction

Researchers, businesses, or other private or public organizations often rely on information obtained through spontaneous self-reports made in surveys or questionnaires. It is often hard, if not impossible, to verify the accuracy of the information provided, but in many cases systematic misreporting can be expected. For instance, since higher income results in higher tax bills, income declarations for tax purposes are more likely to be biased downwards than upwards (e.g., Hurst et al., 2014); similarly, reports of miles driven for car insurance purposes result in lower insurance premiums if low than if high (e.g., Shu et al., 2012);

**Dishonesty in Behavioral Economics. https://doi.org/10.1016/B978-0-12-815857-9.00017-0**

own alcohol consumption is under-reported much more often than it is over-reported (e.g., Stockwell et al., 2004, 2014); and so on. Yet, the accuracy of the information provided is often crucial to the entity that collects it. The public finances can be administered better and more fairly when all income is declared and taxed; insurance companies can set more accurate premiums the more certain they are of each driver's risk; the provision of care for alcohol-related problems can be planned and delivered more effectively if the magnitude of those problems can be assessed with accuracy.

Systematic misreporting may be caused by a variety of factors. Individuals may not recall the information accurately, or it may be costly to provide accurate estimates. These influences may have asymmetric effects. It is probably easier to forget some drinks you actually had than to imagine drinks you did not have, or to forget some taxable income than to falsely remember income you did not receive. Such genuine mistakes can be avoided (at least in part) by redesigning the relevant questionnaires. In the case of alcohol consumption, this can be done by breaking down the types of beverages and considering different time frames (e.g., Stockwell et al., 2004), and in the case of income reporting formal recording systems can bypass human error.

But misreporting can also be deliberate, at least in the form of small deviations that individuals can justify to themselves as approximations or misremembering (e.g., Gino, 2015), or in the form of self-deception (e.g., Bodner and Prelec, 2003). The law can set out penalties in case of (fraudulently) inaccurate reports, and companies can often deny service to customers who deceive. But in other cases, such as the self-report of alcohol consumption to one's General Practitioner, it may be hard to use the prospect of some form of penalty to avoid deliberate misreporting.

In this chapter, we focus on *anonymous* self-reports about *sensitive* and *socially (un)desirable* information for which there are strong priors of systematic bias, and which is often impossible to verify independently. Because we deal with sensitive information about behaviors that are either socially desirable (e.g., eating healthily, exercising, …) or undesirable (e.g., smoking, littering, giving bribes, …), *social desirability bias* (e.g., Edwards, 1953; Miller et al., 2008) leads us to expect that the former type of behaviors will be over-reported and the latter under-reported. This bias can be somewhat mitigated by assurances of confidentiality or by making self-reports anonymous (e.g., Acquino and Lo Sciuto, 1990; Ong and Weiss, 2000). But anonymity per se will not eliminate misreporting in such circumstances (e.g., Lelkes et al., 2012).[a]

We investigate whether the systematic self-serving bias that characterizes self-reports can be mitigated by priming honesty before the declaration is

---

a. In Chapter 2.4, Cicognani (2019) show that 61% of students admit to have cheated in written university examinations when asked to fill in an anonymous survey. Given the socially undesirable nature of the behavior they study, this is likely to be a conservative estimate of the real figure.

made, when it is not possible, or possible in principle but extremely difficult, to associate the information with the identity of the declarer. As described in Section 2, we use an upfront declaration of honesty that is a modification of the one proposed by Shu et al. (2012). In Sections 3–5, we report the results of four studies, in which use this method in an attempt to reduce the predictable bias of self-reports in a variety of contexts: healthy lifestyles, littering, and petty corruption. We find that upfront declarations of honesty are ineffective at changing reports in the desired direction. In Section 5, we discuss the possible reasons for our findings and their broader implications.

## 2. Upfront declarations of honesty

In most cases, the person who makes a self-report is asked to declare that the information provided is true and accurate to the best of their knowledge. Most tax return forms include a clause to this effect, and so do many questionnaires or surveys. Typically, such declarations are made *after* the relevant self-report. Their primary objective is to ensure that the person takes responsibility for the declaration, but they also remind the declarer of the importance of providing accurate information, and often of the consequences of not doing so, including any associated penalties. They may also serve as moral reminders about the importance of being honest, which most people regard as an important part of their self-identity (e.g., Mazar et al., 2008). This is reinforced by the requirement, which often accompanies such clauses, that one's signature—also strongly linked to one's identity (e.g., Kettle and Häubl, 2011)—is apposed next to the declaration. In the reminder of this chapter, we will refer to these statements as *honesty clauses*, even if they do not make direct reference to honesty.

Shu et al. (2012) argue that the typical placement of honesty clauses is suboptimal. Even if people regard honesty as important, and even if reminding people about honesty is more likely to lead to honest behavior, a reminder *after* the declaration has been made comes too late (in spite of the legal implications being independent of which declaration comes first). They propose to use the honesty clause *before* the declaration is made. In a series of experiments, they demonstrate that this can systematically improve the quality of self-reports. Experimental participants declared lower earnings in an experimental task, and lower travel expenditures to the lab, when they signed the clause before the relevant declaration than when they signed it afterwards. The effect was stronger for people who had ethics-related thoughts in a word completion task carried out after the declaration, suggesting that the clause is likely to prompt persistent honesty-related moral thoughts. In a field study with a motor insurance company, they also found that the numbers of miles driven implied by odometer reports were on average 10% higher when the honesty clause was presented at the beginning of the form than when it was presented at the end. They suggested that relocating the honesty clause before the declaration is a very cheap intervention (the form has to be printed or otherwise set up anyway, and the location of the clause is unlikely to affect the cost significantly), which can be very effective at nudging individuals toward making more accurate self-reports.[b]

In interpreting their findings, Shu et al. emphasize that "it is important to make morality salient, right before it is needed most, so that it can remain active during the most tempting moments" (2012, p. 15198). This suggests that the nudge works because of *moral-reminding* properties of the honesty clause. This effect is likely to persist in the absence of an explicit signature by the declarer, like the cases we consider in this chapter (although it may be weaker). On the other hand, the signature may have other effects of its own, in particular allow for the identification of the declarer, which matters when there may be adverse consequences from misreporting. This suggests another mechanism through which the nudge may work: signing makes the declarer identifiable, and therefore liable for any penalties deriving from the provision of inaccurate information.[c] This factor is conceptually different from the desire to maintain an honest self-perception. Crucially, it is deactivated if the declaration is made anonymously. Therefore, in addition to the practical importance of establishing whether the upfront placement of the honesty clause works for anonymous self-reports, our study may shed some light on the mechanisms through which this nudge works.

Our application of a variant of Shu et al.'s nudge may be seen as a likely scenario in the everyday use of behavioral insights. A public or private entity has a particular objective—in our case, improving the quality of anonymous self-reports of certain kinds of information—and scans the behavioral science literature for potentially useful interventions. The placement of an honesty clause at the front of the form stands out in this search as an intervention that is very easy to implement, relatively inexpensive, and promising to tackle the problem in hand. Even though the intrinsic nature of the problem means it is impossible to determine what the true information would have been had the bias been absent, the effectiveness (or otherwise) of the nudge may be cheaply verified by randomly deploying it or not, as is done nowadays in many randomized controlled trials carried out by an increasing number of behavioral insights teams around the world (e.g., Halpern, 2015). The results of the exercise are informative irrespective of whether the underlying bias can be quantified. If self-reports differ between the two treatments, we have identified a straightforward intervention that works. If self-reports do not differ, it could be that anonymity has completely eliminated the bias, or that the nudge does *not* work. But for practical purposes, it means the nudge does not help in the situations that we study.

---

b. In Chapter 3.4, Hao and Hauser (2018) discuss a related method, consisting in making a preannouncement about one's possibly dishonest behavior, which could have similar effects. Other forms of honesty priming, such as recalling the ten commandments from the bible (e.g., Mazar et al., 2008), or completing word tasks involving concepts of honesty (e.g., Rasinski et al., 2005) have been found to work in experimental settings, but seem less attractive in applications because, unlike the upfront placement of the honesty clause, they do not feel a natural part of the self-report procedure.

c. An illustration can be found in Chapter 4.1, where Dai et al. (2018) show that people respond to the probability of being inspected and the severity of the punishment when deciding whether to pay the right fare in a laboratory transportation game.

## 3. Study 1: Healthy lifestyles

Our first study focuses on healthy lifestyles, in particular, behaviors such as healthy eating (a diet high in fruit and vegetables and low in junk food), exercising, smoking, and drinking. These behaviors are usually misreported in surveys. The amount of exercise is often overstated, especially among the obese population (e.g., Lichtman et al., 1992). Calorie intake (e.g., Subar et al., 2003), smoking, and alcohol consumption (e.g., Moore and Ames, 2002; Stockwell et al., 2004, 2014) are all grossly understated. In the case of drinking, the alcohol consumption reported in surveys is typically between 40% and 60% of the consumption inferred from sales data (e.g., Knibbe and BIoomfield, 2001). Devising survey methods that narrow this gap is a key priority in this area of the public health literature. We examine whether this can be achieved, at least partly, by placing an honesty clause at the beginning of the survey.

### 3.1 Study 1a: Student survey

#### 3.1.1 Methods

215 students from the University of Warwick were approached in the university campus during the interval of the first football match played by the England national team at the Euro 2016 tournament. The students, mostly male, were watching the game on the campus big-screen TV. Those who volunteered filled in an anonymous pen-and-paper "Healthy Lifestyle" survey comprising questions about their age and gender, and, for the previous 7 days, their total consumption of fruits and vegetables (in "servings"), and of sweet and salty snacks (in units), plus their average daily calorie intake, their exercise (in hours per week), the total number of cigarettes smoked in the week and alcoholic beverages consumed (in "standard drinks," which could be computed with the aid of a table printed after the relevant question). The survey was very short and took on average less than 5 min to complete. There was no reward for participation.

Participants were randomly allocated to one of four conditions: a *No Clause* condition without an honesty clause, a *Clause First* condition with the clause at the beginning, a *Clause plus Explanation* condition in which the honesty clause appeared at the beginning and was accompanied by an explanation of its purpose,[d] and a *Clause Last* condition, in which the honesty clause appeared after all the questions.[e]

---

d. In addition to testing whether the honesty nudge works in this setup, we intended to test whether disclosing its intent would alter its effectiveness. This aspect goes beyond the objective of this chapter. Answering this question requires the nudge to affect self-reports, but since this did not happen, we will not dwell on this any further. Because this condition was common to all the studies reported here, we will, nevertheless, show the corresponding results.

e. Since this condition only features in this study, we will omit it from the rest of our discussion. None of our conclusions is affected by its inclusion in the analysis.

The honesty clause, which in the Clause First condition appeared after the age and gender questions and before the lifestyle questions, read as follows:

*By ticking here, I declare that all the answers given in this survey will be as accurate as possible.*
*Please provide your initials:*

Although participants were not required to write their full signature, having to tick a box next to a sentence starting with "I declare" and then having to provide their initials could still be enough of an identity prompt for the mechanisms suggested by Shu et al. to be activated. So, there are reasons to believe that, if the clause works for its moral-reminding properties, it could also work in our setup.

### 3.1.2 Results

38 respondents were excluded for incomplete, irrelevant, or illegible responses. Out of the remaining 178 respondents (33% female, mean age 21), only one failed to tick the declaration box (in the Clause plus Explanation condition). The top panel of Table 1 reports mean, median, and standard deviation of the answers to the healthy lifestyle questions in the four treatments, plus the *p*-value in a Kruskal–Wallis test comparing the answers across treatments.[f]

The bottom panel of the table summarizes the responses to the questions about fruit and vegetable intake, exercise, smoking, and drinking into a single Healthy Lifestyle Index (HLI) computed as follows. For each item, the participant's response is divided by the recommended figure from the National Health Service (NHS) and World Health Organization (WHO) guidelines (35 units a week for fruit and vegetables combined, 2.5 h for exercise, 140 cigarettes a week and 14 standard drinks).[g] For behaviors with positive health consequences (fruit and vegetable eating, exercising), the resulting ratio is capped at 1. For behaviors with negative health consequences (smoking and drinking), after capping the ratio at 1, we subtract it from 1. So, in all four cases, the best behavior (hitting the recommended target for fruit and vegetable eating or exercising, not smoking nor drinking) results in a score of 1, and the worst behavior (not eating fruits nor vegetables, not exercising, smoking at least 20 cigarettes a day and having at least 14 standard drinks a week) results in a score of 0. These four scores are then added, so that the HLI ranges between 0 and 4, with 4 being the most desirable.[h]

f. We do not include the calorie intake question because most participants responded providing figures around the recommended 2000–2500 daily calories.

g. NHS (2015a) recommends five portions of fruit and vegetables daily. NHS (2015b) recommends 2.5 h of exercise per week. Heavy smokers are defined as those smoking at least 20 cigarettes a day (e.g., Qian et al., 2010). NHS (2015c) recommends not to exceed 14 standard drinks per week. We did not find analogous recommendations for sweet and salty snacks, so we did not include this information in the computation of the HLI.

h. For similar approaches see, e.g., Pronk (2012).

**TABLE 1** Results of Study 1a

| | No clause (*N* = 49) | Clause first (*N* = 39) | Clause plus explanation (*N* = 53) | Sig.[a] |
|---|---|---|---|---|
| *Servings of fruit* | | | | |
| Mean | 12.9 | 9.2 | 8.3 | **0.005** |
| Median | 10.0 | 5.0 | 7.0 | |
| Std. Dev. | 9.5 | 16.1 | 7.5 | |
| *Servings of vegetables* | | | | |
| Mean | 9.8 | 9.0 | 9.2 | 0.223 |
| Median | 7.0 | 6.0 | 7.0 | |
| Std. Dev. | 7.0 | 15.6 | 7.6 | |
| *Sweet/salty snacks* | | | | |
| Mean | 11.2 | 9.1 | 18.3 | 0.210 |
| Median | 10.0 | 6.0 | 6.0 | |
| Std. Dev. | 10.1 | 10.3 | 58.0 | |
| *Hours of exercise* | | | | |
| Mean | 6.4 | 5.6 | 6.2 | 0.649 |
| Median | 5.0 | 4.0 | 5.0 | |
| Std. Dev. | 6.9 | 7.0 | 6.1 | |
| *Cigarettes* | | | | |
| Mean | 8.4 | 19.8 | 7.5 | 0.498 |
| Median | 0.0 | 0.0 | 0.0 | |
| Std. Dev. | 20.8 | 45.8 | 20.9 | |
| *Standard drink units* | | | | |
| Mean | 12.7 | 24.3 | 21.7 | 0.267 |
| Median | 10.0 | 13.0 | 14.0 | |
| Std. Dev. | 11.1 | 36.4 | 24.5 | |
| *Healthy Lifestyle Index (HLI)* | | | | |
| Mean | 2.8 | 2.4 | 2.5 | **0.019** |
| Median | 2.8 | 2.4 | 2.6 | |
| Std. Dev. | 0.6 | 0.6 | 0.7 | |

Significant values in bold.
[a] *p-Value in a Kruskal–Wallis test comparing the three treatments.*

Given our prior that participants overstate good behaviors and understate bad ones, we expect over-reporting of fruit and vegetables intake and exercising, and under-reporting of snacks, cigarettes, and alcohol consumption. Therefore, if the nudge works as intended, we should see lower answers in the first two cases, and higher ones in the remaining three. The numbers and statistical tests in Table 1 show that, with the exception of the fruit question (and possibly the cigarette question in the Clause First condition), the data are inconsistent with this prediction. This is confirmed by pairwise comparisons between the No Clause and Clause First conditions for each question. The distribution of responses is only different for the fruit question ($p < 0.05$ in a two-tail Mann–Whitney test). For most questions, adding an honesty clause at the beginning of the survey has little effect on the answers of our participants.

By aggregating across behaviors, the HLI has the advantage of picking up any general tendency to misreport, as well as reducing the noisiness of the responses. Since higher values of HLI are more desirable, the effect of the nudge should be to reduce the HLI. The value of HLI is lower in the Clause First than in the No Clause condition, and this is significant in a pairwise Mann–Whitney test ($p < 0.05$). So, the nudge may have some effect, although small overall.[i]

## 3.2 Study 1b: Online sample

### 3.2.1 Methods

In Study 1a, the analysis based on the HLI suggests that the honesty nudge could have some potential to reduce misreporting of lifestyle behaviors. In Study 1b, we tried this out in a larger and more varied (although far from fully representative) sample of the UK population. This may be important because, especially with respect to some of the behaviors of interest, students may be atypical. For instance, there may be more drinking in the student population than overall, and drinking may be perceived as more socially desirable by students and young people than it is in the general population. In Study 1b, we used the online platform Prolific.ac (see Palan and Schitter, 2018), whose participants have a more varied demographic profile.[j]

We made a few changes to the survey. The first concerns the honesty clause. In order to make the clause more likely to prime honesty, we mentioned it explicitly. We also replaced the requirement to write one's initials with the requirement that the participant provided their unique Prolific ID, in an attempt to preserve the salience of the declaration.[k] Although this is a unique personal

i. This effect seems to be driven by the female participants, for whom the HLI is 2.97 ($n=21$) in the No Clause condition and 2.13 ($n=6$) in the Clause First condition (but note the small sample sizes). For males, the effect is much smaller, the corresponding values being 2.62 ($n=28$) and 2.40 ($n=32$). The effect is slightly stronger for participants aged more than 20 (the median age).

j. See https://www.prolific.ac/.

k. Evidence suggests that signatures in electronic forms do not feel the same as actual signatures (e.g., Chou, 2015). A similar effect may apply to apposing one's initials.

identifier, which allows researchers to contact individual participants or reward them for their performance, for our purposes anonymity is preserved, because researchers using the Prolific.ac platform cannot use these IDs to trace the identity of the participants, and participants are expected to know this. In Study 1b, we used the following honesty clause:

*By ticking here, I declare that all the answers given in this survey will be as honest and accurate as possible.*

*Please provide your Prolific ID to indicate that you agree with this declaration (You can find it in the URL at the top of this web page):*

We also changed the fruit and vegetable questions using examples from the NHS guidelines (NHS, 2015a) to help participants estimate the number of servings, by providing pictures analogous to the one we used for standard drinks. The question about exercising was split into two questions about moderate and vigorous exercise respectively, defined in accordance to the NHS (2015b) guidelines. We removed the Clause Last condition, because the study was computerized using the Qualtrics software and we did not allow participants to go back and change their answers—consequently, an honesty clause at the end could have no effect. When an honesty clause was present, it was not possible for participants to proceed with the lifestyle questions unless they had ticked the checkbox and inserted their Prolific ID.

### *3.2.2 Results*

A total of 596 (63% female,[l] mean age 34) participants completed the 5-min survey in exchange for a flat payment of £0.50. Five participants were excluded because they reported to be less than 18 years old at the time of the study, and two because they took less than 60 s to complete the study. The results are shown in Table 2, which is analogous to Table 1. The HLI is computed after combining moderate and vigorous exercise into a single variable.

For all the questions, except for the hours of vigorous exercise, the use of an upfront honesty clause does not change answers in the predicted direction. For vigorous exercise, there is a significant difference ($p < 0.05$ in a Kruskal–Wallis test), but in the wrong direction, with more exercise reported with the nudge than without. The same picture emerges if one looks at the HLI. The values for the three treatments are remarkably similar: 3.0, 3.0, and 3.1, and clearly not statistically significant.[m] When applied to a larger and more varied sample, the honesty nudge has no effect on the answers to our healthy lifestyle questions.

---

l. It is not uncommon for online samples and surveys conducted on nonrepresentative samples to include a majority of female participants.

m. This applies to both female and male participants, irrespective of their age.

**TABLE 2** Results of Study 1b

| | No clause (N = 195) | Clause first (N = 196) | Clause plus explanation (N = 198) | Sig.[a] |
|---|---|---|---|---|
| *Servings of fruit* | | | | |
| Mean | 11.8 | 11.6 | 12.6 | 0.856 |
| Median | 7.0 | 7.0 | 7.0 | |
| Std. Dev. | 26.1 | 15.8 | 32.5 | |
| *Servings of vegetables* | | | | |
| Mean | 17.9 | 13.7 | 15.7 | 0.549 |
| Median | 12.0 | 10.0 | 10.0 | |
| Std. Dev. | 39.6 | 15.4 | 29.9 | |
| *Sweet/salty snacks* | | | | |
| Mean | 8.1 | 8.8 | 8.9 | 0.302 |
| Median | 7.0 | 7.0 | 7.0 | |
| Std. Dev. | 6.5 | 6.3 | 6.7 | |
| *Hours of vigorous exercise* | | | | |
| Mean | 2.0 | 2.4 | 2.7 | **0.026** |
| Median | 1.0 | 1.0 | 2.0 | |
| Std. Dev. | 2.7 | 3.2 | 4.1 | |
| *Hours of moderate exercise* | | | | |
| Mean | 3.2 | 3.6 | 3.6 | 0.335 |
| Median | 2.0 | 2.0 | 2.0 | |
| Std. Dev. | 3.6 | 4.7 | 3.6 | |
| *Cigarettes* | | | | |
| Mean | 7.5 | 7.6 | 7.7 | 0.912 |
| Median | 0.0 | 0.0 | 0.0 | |
| Std. Dev. | 22.7 | 25.6 | 27.2 | |
| *Standard drink units* | | | | |
| Mean | 5.3 | 5.8 | 5.5 | 0.754 |
| Median | 2.0 | 1.0 | 2.0 | |
| Std. Dev. | 8.3 | 10.6 | 8.9 | |

**TABLE 2 Results of Study 1b—cont'd**

| | No clause (N=195) | Clause first (N=196) | Clause plus explanation (N=198) | Sig.[a] |
|---|---|---|---|---|
| *Healthy Lifestyle Index (HLI)* | | | | |
| Mean | 3.0 | 3.0 | 3.1 | 0.547 |
| Median | 3.1 | 3.1 | 3.1 | |
| Std. Dev. | 0.7 | 0.7 | 0.7 | |

Significant values in bold.
[a] *p-Value in a Kruskal–Wallis test comparing the three treatments.*

## 4. Study 2: On-campus littering

Our second study focuses on a different kind of behavior, littering, for which it is also difficult to obtain unbiased self-reports. Admitting to littering may be problematic because of social disapproval and the fact that in many countries littering is illegal and there may be penalties associated with it.[n] According to a report prepared for Keep American Beautiful (2009), only 15% of the interviewed sample admitted to littering. But accurate self-reports about littering behavior may be extremely useful in understanding littering behavior and devising interventions to curb the phenomenon. We explore whether upfront declarations of honesty may make people more prone to admit to littering.

### 4.1 Methods

We designed a survey about cigarette butts and chewing gum littering at the University of Warwick. The questions we are interested in were part of a larger study whose main objective was to identify the behavioral and environmental aspects that are responsible for this kind of behavior. Cigarette butts and chewing gums were identified by the University's ground management as two of the greatest littering issues on campus. Because the number of smokers in the student population is relatively small and decreasing, participants were first asked to indicate whether they were smokers—in which case they filled in a survey about cigarette butt littering—or not—in which case they went on to complete a survey about chewing gum littering if they reported consuming chewing gum. The survey was distributed via the University's Student Union and via the Decision Research at Warwick's SONA database. We will focus on the chewing gum survey, because very few participants completed the cigarette butt survey.

n. In the UK, where this study was conducted, littering is illegal according to the Environmental Protection Act 1990 and incurs a maximum penalty of £80. See https://www.gov.uk/guidance/fixed-penalty-notices-issuing-and-enforcement-by-councils.

In exchange for completing the survey, participants who provided their University email address were entered in a prize draw to win 1 of 20 prizes worth £30 each, either as an Amazon voucher or as a top-up to their student card, which entitles students to a 10% discount on purchases made in the majority of the University outlets. Although the university email address could in principle allow us to identify the participants, in the consent form presented in the first screen of the Qualtrics™ survey, they were told that their data would be kept confidential and used only for research purposes, with no personal information stored with the data. For those participants who entered their email address, the survey cannot be considered completely anonymous.

We randomly allocated the participants to the same three conditions as in Study 1b, *No Clause*, *Clause First,* and *Clause plus Explanation*. The nudge was the same as in that study, except that participants were asked to provide their initials, as in Study 1a. The disclosure statement was also the same. The honesty clause read as follows:

*By ticking here, I declare that all the answers given in this survey will be as honest and accurate as possible.*

*Please provide your initials:*

The questions about littering were all of the same form and always came immediately after the honesty clause, if there was one. Participants were asked:

*In the last month, how many times have you...*

**(a)** *... dropped a chewing gum on the ground?*
**(b)** *... dropped a chewing gum down a drain?*
**(c)** *... dropped a chewing gum in a bush?*
**(d)** *... dropped a chewing gum in a lake?*
**(e)** *... stuck a chewing gum under a bench?*
**(f)** *... stuck a chewing gum under a chair or table?*
**(g)** *... in any other way littered chewing gum?*

Questions (a)–(f) were presented in a sequence which was randomly determined for each participant. Question (g) was always last. For each of the seven questions, participants could pick an answer from the Likert scale "Never" (coded 1), "Once or twice a month" (2), "Once or twice a week" (3), "Several times a week" (4), and "Almost every day" (5).

## 4.2 Results

The chewing gum littering survey was completed by 128 participants (71% female, mean age 22.5). Table 3 reports, for each of the seven questions and each of the three conditions, the mean and standard deviation of the answer (min 1, max 5) as well as the percentage of participants who admitted to littering as specified by the question. The last row shows the percentage of participants

**TABLE 3 Results of Study 2**

| | No clause (*N*=38) | Clause first (*N*=53) | Clause plus explanation (*N*=37) | Sig.[a] |
|---|---|---|---|---|
| *Ground* | | | | |
| Mean | 1.16 | 1.19 | 1.16 | |
| Std. Dev. | 0.37 | 0.62 | 0.44 | |
| % Admits | 16% | 13% | 14% | 0.949 |
| *Drain* | | | | |
| Mean | 1.27 | 1.08 | 1.16 | |
| Std. Dev. | 0.73 | 0.27 | 0.44 | |
| % Admits | 21% | 8% | 14% | 0.163 |
| *Bush* | | | | |
| Mean | 1.11 | 1.04 | 1.27 | |
| Std. Dev. | 0.39 | 0.19 | 0.51 | |
| % Admits | 8% | 4% | 24% | **0.010** |
| *Lake* | | | | |
| Mean | 1.00 | 1.00 | 1.16 | |
| Std. Dev. | 0.00 | 0.00 | 0.69 | |
| % Admits | 0% | 0% | 5% | 0.190 |
| *Under bench* | | | | |
| Mean | 1.03 | 1.04 | 1.08 | |
| Std. Dev. | 0.16 | 0.19 | 0.49 | |
| % Admits | 5% | 4% | 3% | 1.000 |
| *Under chair or table* | | | | |
| Mean | 1.05 | 1.09 | 1.03 | |
| Std. Dev. | 0.23 | 0.35 | 0.16 | |
| % Admits | 5% | 8% | 3% | 0.802 |
| *Other* | | | | |
| Mean | 1.41 | 1.21 | 1.38 | |
| Std. Dev. | 1.07 | 0.45 | 0.76 | |

*(Continued)*

**TABLE 3** Results of Study 2—cont'd

| | No clause (*N*=38) | Clause first (*N*=53) | Clause plus explanation (*N*=37) | Sig.[a] |
|---|---|---|---|---|
| % Admits | 18% | 19% | 27% | 0.582 |
| | | | | |
| *% Admits any* | 42% | 36% | 43% | 0.743 |

Significant values in bold.
[a] *p-Value in a Fisher's exact test comparing the three treatments.*

in each treatment who admitted at least one type of littering behavior. The last column reports, for each question and the aggregate percentage, the significance level in Fisher's exact test comparing admissions across the three treatments.

The picture that emerges from Table 3 is very clear, and very much in line with the results of Studies 1a and 1b. Introducing an upfront honesty clause does not make it more likely that the surveyed participants admit to littering on campus. There is only one significant difference, for the question on littering by throwing chewing gum into a bush, but in all other cases the observed variability is well within what can be expected from pure chance. The nudge proves rather ineffective in this context.[o]

## 5. Study 3: Petty corruption

Our final application is to the case of petty corruption. Transparency International (2017a) defines petty corruption as "everyday abuse of entrusted power by low- and mid-level public officials in their interactions with ordinary citizens, who often are trying to access basic goods or services in places like hospitals, schools, police departments and other agencies." In the vast majority of cases, petty corruption represents illegal behavior which is, nevertheless, quite widespread, especially in developing countries, with detrimental effects on society and economic growth (e.g., Bardhan, 1997; Svensson, 2005).

Given its illegal nature, measuring corruption is intrinsically difficult (e.g., Sampford et al., 2006). Various indexes are used (e.g., the Control of Corruption Indicator, see Kaufmann et al., 2004; the Corruption Perception Index, CPI,

o. There is, however, an interesting difference between females and males. In the Clause First condition, fewer females than in the No Clause condition admit to littering, contrary to the expected effect of the nudge. For males, the nudge seems to be working in the predicted direction, even though the sample sizes involved are relatively small to reach firm conclusions. There are no differences based on whether the participants' age is above or below the median.

published by Transparency International, 2017b), which combine data from a variety of sources, including self-reports of daily experiences of corruption. Such self-reports are likely to be biased due to social desirability bias in the context of unethical behaviors (e.g., Krumpal, 2013; Randall and Fernandes, 1991). Quantifying the bias is difficult, but it may be considerable. For instance, in a study of 37 forms of unethical behavior, Zuber and Kaptein (2013) find that the ratio between the proportion of people reporting observations of those behaviors and the proportion of those who admit to having engaged in them ranges from a minimum of 1.46 (for "improperly gathering competitors' confidential information") to a maximum 6.7 (for "engaging in (sexual) harassment or creating a hostile work environment").

In this study, we focus on self-reports concerning a variety of behaviors that are typical of petty corruption and ask whether adding an honesty clause at the beginning of our survey makes participants more likely to admit to having engaged in such behaviors. Using a sample of Indonesian citizens, who come from a country in which petty corruption is a common phenomenon (Indonesia ranks 90th of 176 countries in terms of CPI), we focus on behaviors that they are likely to have experienced frequently, and ask them if they have ever engaged in such behaviors.

## 5.1 Methods

509 participants (66% female, mean age 28) were randomly allocated to the same three conditions as in Study 1b and Study 2: *No Clause*, *Clause First*, and *Clause plus Explanation*. In the honesty clause, we replaced the word "ticking" with the word "signing" to strengthen the perceived connection between the declarer and the declaration, even though no actual signature was requested. The clause read as follows:

> *By signing here, I declare that all the answers given in this survey will be as honest and accurate as possible.*
>
> *Please provide your initials:*

We asked each participant the following questions, which always appeared in the same order, based on our perception of the severity of the corresponding behaviors:

(Q1) *Have you ever used professional assets, equipment, or company property such as an office laptop or car for personal matters or purposes?*
(Q2) *Have you ever worked on tasks unrelated to your job while at work?*
(Q3) *Have you ever given money to a public servant to expedite the process of obtaining official documents* (e.g., *identity card, tax identification number, marriage certificate, etc.*)*?*
(Q4) *Have you ever given money to a police officer to expedite the process of obtaining a driving license?*

(Q5) *Have you ever given money to a police officer to obtain documents other than driving license* (e.g., *letter of good conduct, report of missing items, etc.*)?
(Q6) *Have you ever given money to a police officer to avoid being fined?*
(Q7) *Have you or your parents ever given money or gifts to your school's staff for you to pass or be admitted?*
(Q8) *Have you ever given money or gifts to secure a contract?*

The participant could answer each question by clicking on either "Yes" or "No."[p]

As a reward for completing the survey, participants residing in the UK at the time of the study (many of the participants were Indonesians studying in the UK) were offered the opportunity to be entered in a prize draw for 1 of 20 Amazon.co.uk vouchers worth £20 each. This required them to provide their email address, but this was not entered until the end of the survey, so the questions of interest were answered in complete anonymity. The survey could be completed either in English or in Indonesian (Bahasa Indonesia), as chosen by the participant on the first screen.

## 5.2 Results

The results of Study 3 are presented in Table 4. For each of the eight questions, the table reports the percentage of participants admitting to having engaged in the relevant behavior in each of the three conditions, as well as the *p*-value in a $\chi^2$ test comparing responses across conditions. The bottom panel summarizes the total number of behaviors admitted by each participant and compares these across conditions using a Kruskal–Wallis test.

The results clearly indicate that making an honesty declaration before a self-report about one's involvement in petty corruption practices does not make participants more likely to admit that they have engaged in those behaviors. For none of the eight behaviors do we find a significant effect of the nudge. Overall, the total number of behaviors admitted by our participants is very similar in the three conditions (3.53, 3.49, and 3.54 in the No Clause, Clause First, and Clause plus Explanation conditions respectively).[q] It is safe to conclude that the honesty declaration has no effect on people's willingness to disclose this kind of potentially unethical behaviors.[r]

---

p. After these eight questions, we asked participants to report their attitudes toward similar behaviors by stating how acceptable or otherwise they found specific instances of those behaviors. The answers were not affected by the nudge manipulations and will not be discussed any further.

q. The 318 participants who answered in English reported to have engaged in more of the listed behaviors (3.68 on average) than the 191 participants who answered in Indonesian (3.26 on average). This difference, which is statistically significant ($P < 0.01$ in a Mann–Whitney test), is in line with evidence suggesting that people tend to lie more in their native language than in a foreign language (e.g., Bereby-Meyer et al., 2017).

r. This conclusion applies to both female and male participants, irrespective of their age.

**TABLE 4** Results of Study 3

| | No clause (*N*=176) | Clause first (*N*=155) | Clause plus explanation (*N*=178) | Sig.[a] |
|---|---|---|---|---|
| *Q1 (Company asset misuse)* | 68% | 62% | 66% | 0.477 |
| *Q2 (Side job)* | 84% | 88% | 85% | 0.634 |
| *Q3 (Bribe public servant)* | 50% | 54% | 54% | 0.683 |
| *Q4 (Bribe police for driving license)* | 56% | 55% | 49% | 0.315 |
| *Q5 (Bribe police for other document)* | 30% | 32% | 39% | 0.202 |
| *Q6 (Bribe police to avoid fine)* | 52% | 46% | 52% | 0.515 |
| *Q7 (Bribe teacher or school to pass)* | 10% | 5% | 6% | 0.238 |
| *Q8 (Bribe to obtain contract)* | 3% | 6% | 3% | 0.264 |
| *Number admitted by participant*[b] | | | | |
| Mean | 3.53 | 3.49 | 3.54 | 0.956 |
| Std. Dev. | 1.60 | 1.58 | 1.58 | |

[a] *p-Value in a $\chi^2$ test comparing the three treatments.*
[b] *p-Value in a Kruskal–Wallis test comparing the three treatments.*

## 6. Discussion and conclusion

We investigated whether the strong and systematic biases that are often found in self-reports of socially (un)desirable behaviors are attenuated by the use of a declaration of honesty made before the self-report. If the honesty declaration had worked, it could have provided a simple way to improve the quality of anonymous self-reports in many contexts in which an independent verification is impossible or prohibitively expensive.

In four studies involving more than 1400 participants and covering behaviors ranging from healthy lifestyles to petty corruption, we found no evidence that this nudge can work when self-reports are made in the kinds of circumstances likely to be encountered by most data collectors, including survey firms or government agencies.

Although our design does not allow us to measure the extent of the underlying bias, it seems unlikely that the failure of the nudge to work as intended can be explained by the absence of a bias. That the situations that we study are notoriously prone to social desirability bias has been extensively documented. We do not believe we crafted our questions so cleverly as to eliminate any tendency to systematically misreport sensitive information. If we had, we would have made a remarkable discovery, of potentially great impact in many fields of social science.

The most plausible interpretation of our findings is that the situations we studied differ in important ways from those in which the effectiveness of the honesty nudge has been demonstrated. One clear difference between our setting and many others is that the responses we observe are evidently not verifiable—there is no way to follow up and compare the truth of the world with our respondents' claims. There are two closely related ways this matters. First, the respondent need have no concern that the falsity of their claims can be used against them. Second, in our setting admitting to bad behavior actually provides evidence that the bad behavior occurred that would not otherwise exist. To illustrate this, suppose you discovered a fool-proof way to stop the odometer of your car from registering miles driven. An honesty nudge may not remind you that someone might read your odometer, because even if they did they would not know that the reading is false, and giving higher mileage than your odometer says in an outbreak of honesty will give away that you have tampered with it.

Another important difference is that, in many experimental settings, the behavior to be detected is not socially undesirable in itself. Suppose, for instance, you signed an honesty pledge before stating how many questions you answered correctly in a test. Announcing a small or a large number would not by itself be dishonest, or wrong, or socially undesirable. This is unlike admitting to littering, or heavy drinking, or corruption, which are fundamentally undesirable behaviors (and worse the more you perpetrate them). To put it another way, honesty nudges might well prevent you from being bad (as in cheating on a test), but not lead you to admit to being bad (as in admitting that you cheated on a test). Honesty declarations may induce you to admit to being bad, however, if they remind you that bad behavior might be detected anyway (and could therefore be compounded by dishonesty).

Another, and again related, possibility is that the honesty declaration did not work in our studies because we do not ask participants to provide their signature or disclose their full identity. While we did ask for significant affirmations of identity, such as a unique Prolific identification number (Study 1b), or the participants' initials (other studies), perhaps the honesty declaration requires an even more powerful affirmation of identity for participants to connect it to their self-image, which is the main mechanism proposed by Shu et al. (2012). If a strong identity affirmation is the key to the effectiveness of an honesty declaration, however, it reduces the usefulness of the declaration since many settings do require anonymity. A survey of corrupt practices, as in our Study 3, would be almost impossible without an underlying assurance of anonymity, and if an honesty declaration cannot survive such assurance it cannot be used to get people to honestly state their degree of corruption or corruptibility.

Overall, while our use of the honesty declaration differs in some respects from the way it has been used before, we took some effort to make those differences small. We found the honesty declaration had no effect. This finding is important for behavioral scientists considering using honesty declarations, because it suggests when they are not likely to work. On the basis of our findings, we can speculate that both the nature of the behavior of interest—in particular, whether it is intrinsically *undesirable* or not—and the verifiability of the information provided—i.e., if false information is *detectable* or not—may determine whether the honesty nudge works or is needed in the first place. This is illustrated in Table 5.

For undetectable and not undesirable behaviors, the honesty nudge may not be needed, as there may be no reason to make a distorted report. Shu et al. have focused on detectable information about behaviors that are not intrinsically undesirable, and found the nudge to work. We have established that, for undetectable and undesirable behaviors, the nudge does not work. We speculate that it may work for undesirable behaviors when these are detectable but, as we explained above, finding an appropriate setting to put this to the test is particularly challenging, as in most cases anonymity is required.

More generally, since behavioral insights are often heralded as effective solutions to many social and behavioral problems, it is vital to know the circumstances in which nudges are ineffective as well as effective. We have shed some

**TABLE 5** Effectiveness of the Honesty Nudge

| | Verifiability | |
|---|---|---|
| **Nature of behavior** | **Detectable** | **Undetectable** |
| Undesirable | Honesty nudge works | Honesty nudge does not work |
| Not undesirable | Honesty nudge works | Honesty nudge not needed |

light on a particular nudge, but clearly more research is needed to identify when this and other nudges can or cannot be expected to exert their desired effects.

## Acknowledgments

Andrea Isoni and Daniel Read received financial support from the Economic and Social Research Council via the Network for Integrated Behavioural Science (award no. ES/P008976/1). Julián Arango-Ochoa was supported by a Chevening Scholarship, part of the UK government's global scholarship program, funded by the Foreign and Commonwealth Office (FCO) and partner organizations.

## References

Acquino, W.S., Lo Sciuto, L.A., 1990. Effects of interview mode on self-reported drag use. Public Opin. Q. 54 (3), 362–395.

Bardhan, P., 1997. Corruption and development: a review of issues. J. Econ. Lit. 35 (3), 1320–1346.

Bereby-Meyer, Y., Hayakawa, S., Shalvi, S., Corey, J., Costa, A., Keysar, B., 2017. Honesty Speaks a Second Language. Available at SSRN, https://ssrn.com/abstract=3048145, https://doi.org/10.1111/tops.12360.

Bodner, R., Prelec, D., 2003. Self-signaling and diagnostic utility in everyday decision making. In: Brocas, I., Carillo, J. (Eds.), The Psychology of Economic Decisions: Volume One: Rationality and Well-Being. Oxford University Press, pp. 105–125.

Chou, E.Y., 2015. What's in a name? The toll e-signatures take on individual honesty. J. Exp. Soc. Psychol. 61, 84–95.

Cicognani, S., 2019. Dishonesty among university students. In: Bucciol, A., Montinari, N. (Eds.), Dishonesty in Behavioral Economics. Academic Press.

Dai, Z., Galeotti, F., Villeval, M.C., 2018. Fare-dodging in the lab and the moral cost of dishonesty. In: Bucciol, A., Montinari, N. (Eds.), Dishonesty in Behavioral Economics. Elsevier.

Edwards, A., 1953. The relationship between the judged desirability of a trait and the probability that the trait will be endorsed. J. Appl. Psychol. 37, 90–93.

Gino, F., 2015. Understanding ordinary unethical behavior: why people who value morality act immorally. Curr. Opin. Behav. Sci. 3, 107–111.

Halpern, D., 2015. Inside the Nudge Unit: How Small Changes Can Make a Big Difference. Ebury Press, London.

Hao, L., Hauser, D., 2018. Cheating: perceptions and profit. In: Bucciol, A., Montinari, N. (Eds.), Dishonesty in Behavioral Economics. Elsevier.

Hurst, E., Li, G., Pugsely, B., 2014. Are household surveys like tax forms? Evidence from income underreporting of the self-employed. Rev. Econ. Stat. 96 (1), 19–33.

Kaufmann, D., Kraay, A., Mastruzzi, M., 2004. Governance matters III: governance indicators for 1996, 1998, 2000, and 2002. World Bank Econ. Rev. 18 (2), 253–287.

Keep American Beautiful, 2009. Littering Behavior in America: Results of a National Study. Available at: https://www.kab.org/sites/default/files/News%26Info_Research_LitteringBehaviorinAmerica_2009Report_Final.pdf.

Kettle, K.L., Häubl, G., 2011. The signature effect: signing influences consumption-related behavior by priming self-identity. J. Consum. Res. 38 (3), 474–489.

Knibbe, R.A., Bloomfield, K., 2001. Alcohol consumption estimates in surveys in Europe: comparability and sensitivity for gender differences. Subst. Abus. 22 (1), 23–38.

Krumpal, I., 2013. Determinants of social desirability bias in sensitive surveys: a literature review. Qual. Quant. 47, 2025–2047. https://doi.org/10.1007/s11135-011-9640-9.

Lelkes, Y., Krosnick, J.A., Marx, D.M., Judd, C.M., Park, B., 2012. Complete anonymity compromises the accuracy of self-reports. J. Exp. Soc. Psychol. 48 (6), 1291–1299.

Lichtman, S.W., Pisarska, K., Berman, E.R., Pestone, M., Dowling, H., Offenbacher, E., … Heymsfield, S.B., 1992. Discrepancy between self-reported and actual caloric intake and exercise in obese subjects. N. Engl. J. Med. 327 (27), 1893–1898.

Mazar, N., Amir, O., Ariely, D., 2008. The dishonesty of honest people: a theory of self-concept maintenance. J. Mark. Res. 45 (6), 633–644.

Miller, T.M., Abdel-Maksoud, M.F., Crane, L.A., Marcus, A.C., Byers, T.E., 2008. Effects of social approval bias on self-reported fruit and vegetable consumption: a randomized controlled trial. Nutr. J. 7, 18.

Moore, R.S., Ames, G.M., 2002. Survey confidentiality vs anonymity: young men's self-reported substance use. J. Alcohol Drug Educ. 47 (2), 32–41.

National Health Service, 2015a. 5 A Day Portion Sizes. Retrieved from, http://www.nhs.uk/Livewell/5ADAY/Pages/Portionsizes.aspx.

National Health Service, 2015b. Physical Activity Guidelines for Adults. Retrieved from, http://www.nhs.uk/Livewell/fitness/Pages/physical-activity-guidelines-for-adults.aspx.

National Health Service, 2015c. Alcohol Units. Retrieved from, http://www.nhs.uk/Livewell/alcohol/Pages/alcohol-units.aspx.

Ong, A.D., Weiss, D.J., 2000. The impact of anonymity on responses to sensitive questions1. J. Appl. Soc. Psychol. 30 (8), 1691–1708.

Palan, S., Schitter, C., 2018. Prolific.Ac—a subject pool for online experiments. J. Behav. Exp. Financ. 17, 22–27. https://doi.org/10.1016/j.jbef.2017.12.004.

Pronk, N., 2012. An optimal lifestyle metric: four simple behaviors that affect health, cost, and productivity. ACSMs Health Fit J 16 (3), 39–43.

Qian, J., Cai, M., Gao, J., Tang, S., Xu, L., Critchley, J.A., 2010. Trends in smoking and quitting in China from 1993 to 2003: National health service survey data. Bull. World Health Organ. 88, 769–776.

Randall, D.M., Fernandes, M.F., 1991. The social desirability response bias in ethics research. J. Bus. Ethics 10 (11), 805–817.

Rasinski, K.A., Visser, P.S., Zagatsky, M., Rickett, E.M., 2005. Using implicit goal priming to improve the quality of self-report data. J. Exp. Soc. Psychol. 41 (3), 321–327.

Sampford, C., Shacklock, A., Connors, C., Galtung, F. (Eds.), 2006. Measuring Corruption. Ashgate Publishing Limited, Hampshire.

Shu, L.L., Mazar, N., Gino, F., Ariely, D., Bazerman, M.H., 2012. Signing at the beginning makes ethics salient and decreases dishonest self-reports in comparison to signing at the end. Proc. Natl. Acad. Sci. U.S.A. 109 (38), 15197–15200.

Stockwell, T., Donath, S., Cooper-Stanbury, M., Chikritzhs, T., Catalano, P., Mateo, C., 2004. Under-reporting of alcohol consumption in household surveys: a comparison of quantity–frequency, graduated–frequency and recent recall. Addiction 99 (8), 1024–1033.

Stockwell, T., Zhao, J., Macdonald, S., 2014. Who under-reports their alcohol consumption in telephone surveys and by how much? An application of the 'yesterday method' in a national Canadian substance use survey. Addiction 109 (10), 1657–1666.

Subar, A.F., Kipnis, V., Troiano, R.P., Midthune, D., Schoeller, D.A., Bingham, S., Sharbaugh, C.O., Trabulsi, J., Runswick, S., Ballard-Barbash, R., Sunshine, J., Schatzkin, A., 2003. Using intake biomarkers to evaluate the extent of dietary misreporting in a large sample of adults: the OPEN study. Am. J. Epidemiol. 158, 1–13.

Svensson, J., 2005. Eight questions about corruption. J. Econ. Perspect. 19 (3), 19–42.

Transparency International, 2017a. How Do You Define Corruption? https://www.transparency.org/whoweare/organisation/faqs_on_corruption.

Transparency International, 2017b. Corruption Perception Index 2016. https://www.transparency.org/news/feature/corruption_perceptions_index_2016.

Zuber, F., Kaptein, M., 2013. Painting with the same brush? Surveying unethical behavior in the workplace using self-reports and observer-reports. J. Bus. Ethics 125 (3), 401–432.

# Index

Note: Page numbers followed by *f* indicate figures and *t* indicate tables.

Kolibri 360 GmbH
Ferdinand-Jühlke-Straße 7
99095 Erfurt, Deutschland
produktsicherheit@kolibri360.de